The Story of the
MEXICAN WAR

GENERAL JOHN E. WOOL AND HIS STAFF IN SALTILLO, MEXICO

From a daguerreotype believed to be one of the first war photographs ever made

AMERICAN CLASSICS

THE STORY
OF THE
MEXICAN WAR

ROBERT SELPH HENRY

FREDERICK UNGAR PUBLISHING CO.
NEW YORK

To

A DESCENDANT OF THE

TEXIANS

PREFACE

THE war between Mexico and the United States in 1846-1848 was the first war in history to be reported adequately and comprehensively in the daily press. Eight years before the London *Times* sent William Howard Russell to the Crimea, correspondents of New Orleans papers—Kendall of the *Picayune,* Freaner of the *Delta,* Thorpe of the *Tropic*—were giving organized coverage to America's first expeditionary forces.

Letters, journals, narratives and sketches by participants, many of them published almost contemporaneously with the war, and the columns of the American newspapers which sprang up in the wake of the armies in Mexico, add color and life to the reporting of the war.

Official documents, correspondence and reports, published under the authority or at the call of Congress almost as soon as events took place, provide background and detail.

Biographies of participants, many of whom became leading figures in the war of the sixties; special studies of particular operations or features of the war; and histories based upon the publications and documents of both sides, round out the materials from which this story is drawn. Most of these materials are identified in the notes found at the end of each chapter.

The story is told from the viewpoint of a "North American" who does not lack appreciation of the qualities shown by Mexican soldiers in defense of their country. General Grant wrote of them, after he had seen Shiloh and Vicksburg and the great battles of 1864 and 1865 in Virginia, "I have seen as brave stands made by some of these men as I have ever seen made by soldiers."

Prevailing impressions of the Mexican War have been derived, directly or indirectly, from the writings of those who seem to have regarded the westward push of American population north of the Missouri Compromise line as a mission to civilize a continent, while looking upon the like westward push of population south of 36 degrees 30 minutes of North latitude as due to the machinations of the "slave power." That the Mexican War was undertaken to conquer territory for slavery was the thesis of numerous speeches, pamphlets and books, such as William Jay's *Review of the Cause and Consequences of the Mexican War*, published in Boston just a century ago. The views of this school of writers were accepted as almost undisputed truisms for more than half a century.

Forty years ago, however, a more just and balanced view began to develop among students of the subject. Thirty years ago, in the preface to his monumental two-volume history of *The War with Mexico*, Professor Justin H. Smith of Dartmouth College expressed this newer view. He entered upon his study of the subject, he wrote, with substantially the view of the war "prevailing in New England" but after "full inquiry, an episode which has been regarded both in the United States and abroad as discreditable to us, appears now to wear quite a different complexion." It was Professor Smith's expressed hope that "new opinions, resting upon facts, will be acceptable now in place of opinions resting largely upon traditional prejudices and misinformation."

But opinions so based changed slowly at best, even under the impact of such a mass of facts as were marshalled and presented not only by Professor Smith but by other scholars—among them, J. S. Reeves, Eugene Irving McCormac, George Pierce Garrison, George Lockhart Rives, E. D. Adams and Eugene C. Barker—whose conclusions are quite different from those which are traditional. So this story of the Mexican War—not a history but a story—is written in the hope that it may help bring about a wider understanding of what scholars have learned of the causes, course and consequences of that war.

Illustrations on the jacket and in the text are from John Frost's *Pictorial History of the Mexican War*, published in 1848. The photograph of American soldiers at Saltillo, made in 1847 and in all probability the very first photograph of soldiers in wartime, is from the collection of Mr. H. Armour Smith of the Hudson River Museum, Yonkers, New York, to whom I am greatly obliged for permission to reproduce it here. It has previously appeared in the *Journal of the Illinois State Historical Society.*

I am also obliged to Mr. L. Falcone for drafting the sketch maps, and to Mrs. Robert R. Dickey, Mrs. Charles O. Morgret and Mrs. Charles G. Day for assistance in the preparation of the manuscript.

Alexandria, Virginia   ROBERT S. HENRY

TABLE OF CONTENTS

LIST OF MAPS

The Story of the
MEXICAN WAR

CHAPTER 1

War Unplanned and Unsought

ON the Fourth of July, 1845, and in the tenth year of its independence, the Republic of Texas voted to give up its separate nationality and become a state of the United States.

On the same day, and in anticipation of the event, steamboats unloaded a regiment of infantry at New Orleans—the first stage in the movement of the first unit of the tiny army with which the United States was to occupy the nation's newest frontier. The troops came from Fort Jesup, in western Louisiana, where for a year they had been stationed as part of an Army of Observation, under command of Brevet Brigadier General Zachary Taylor.

General Taylor's instructions were that "so soon as" the offer of annexation made to Texas by the Congress of the United States on March 1, 1845, should be accepted, "Texas will then be regarded . . . so far a part of the United States as to be entitled to defense and protection from foreign invasion and Indian incursion," and that he should be prepared when he learned of the event to move his troops to a point "on or near the Rio Grande."

Being well assured by the beginning of July that the special convention called by the Congress of Texas would accept annexation, General Taylor started his infantry down the Red River to New Orleans, there to await word of final and definite action. Upon receiving such word, he started his one regiment of dragoons on the long overland march from the Sabine frontier to the southwestern outpost of San Antonio de Bexar. The general himself followed the infantry, arriving in New Orleans on July 15.

In the hour before midnight of July 22, the advance regiment of infantry left its temporary quarters in the lower cotton press, marched with drum and fife through moonlit streets to the levee, and boarded

15

the steamship *Alabama*. General Taylor and his staff of four officers having come aboard, at three o'clock in the morning the *Alabama* backed out into the stream, dropped down the Mississippi, and by noon was through the Southwest Pass and into the Gulf, on its way to the lower coast of Texas.[1]

There was, or at least there was supposed to be, need of haste to interpose Taylor's protective force between the scattered settlements of southwestern Texas and the renewal of hostilities threatened by Mexico as a consequence of annexation by the United States of what was still regarded as a province in revolt.

Title to the ill-defined area of Texas had at various times and for a variety of reasons been claimed by France, by Spain, by Mexico and even by the United States, as well as by the Republic of Texas.

The first European settlement within the area, that of La Salle and his followers on the shores of Matagorda Bay in the years 1685-1689, became the basis of a vast and vague claim by the French, even though the settlement itself ended in tragic failure. Subsequently, Texas had been explored and to some extent settled by the Spanish working up from New Spain, partly with the idea of heading off any French advance westward from Louisiana. After 1763, however, when Louisiana also came under the Spanish crown, the viceroys of New Spain had less reason to push, or even to protect, the feeble settlements in Texas, which entered upon a half century of neglect and decay. Missions and settlements were abandoned and population declined, until by the time of Mexican independence there was but a handful of people in three inconsiderable settlements about Bexar (now San Antonio), La Bahía (now Goliad) and Nacogdoches.

It was not, indeed, until the very last year of the rule of Spain in Mexico that real and effective steps toward settlement were taken. In that year of 1821 the viceroy granted colonization rights to Moses Austin, Connecticut-born *empresario* from Missouri. Two years later, after the death of Austin and the end of Spanish rule, these rights were confirmed by the Government of Mexico to his son, Stephen F. Austin.

Under the leadership of Austin, and later of other colonizing *empresarios,* the settlement of Texas progressed during the next dozen years. Afterward, as part of the great propaganda struggle leading up to the abolition of slavery in the United States, it was repeatedly asserted and came to be widely believed that this settlement was a plan, or plot, of the "slave power" to extend its domain into new cotton-growing territory. It is much more likely that the existence of slavery retarded rather than hastened Southwestern settlement. The evidence is that the settlement of Texas was simply another step in the westward push which had carried settlement from the Atlantic Seaboard to and across the Mississippi, in the free Northwest as well as in the slave states. The lure in both cases was land, and the movement was that of individuals. The settlers of Texas were no more the emissaries of some potent "slave power" than the settlers north of Missouri were advance agents of organized abolition. Throughout the period of settlement and the subsequent republican period of Texas history there were few, if any, owners of numerous slaves or great plantations of the sort found in the older South. Texas was a frontier, settled on the familiar frontier pattern of individualism.[2]

In the first decade of Texan settlement, the territory had been part of the Mexican state of Coahuila y Tejas. By 1834, after the Mexican Constitution of 1824 had been subverted by successive revolutionary movements, some Texans sought to secure greater representation for their territory in the state government, while others sought separation from Coahuila to form an independent state in the Mexican nation. All such efforts were treated as revolutionary by General Santa Anna, who at the moment and at intervals over the next twelve years was dictator of Mexico. So treated, the movement became truly revolutionary when, on March 2, 1836, the Texan settlers declared their independence and, in Houston's overwhelming victory over Santa Anna on the banks of the San Jacinto on April 21, made good that declaration.

The existence of Texas as a nation was recognized in due time not only by the United States but by Britain, France and other European states. But in much the same way as Spain had for fifteen years refused to recognize that Mexico was independent, and had even feebly attempted its reconquest, so Mexico had refused to recognize the fact of Texas independence and, during nine years, had kept alive the threat of hostilities.[3]

In annexing Texas, the United States inherited this state of smoldering war. Indeed, according to announcements by the Mexican Government made while various propositions for annexation were under consideration, the mere fact of annexation was to be regarded by Mexico as a declaration of war, without other formality. Upon ascertaining that the United States had offered annexation to Texas, General J. N. Almonte, the minister at Washington, asked for his passports in a final note protesting the injustice of "despoiling a friendly nation of . . . her territory." The implication of renewed hostilities across the border called for prompt movement of the protective force of the United States to the new southwestern frontier.[4]

Just where this frontier might be was another point in dispute. In earlier times, following the Louisiana Purchase in 1803, and through the administrations of Presidents Jefferson, Madison and Monroe, the United States had claimed the Rio Grande as the boundary between Spanish territory and the lands acquired from France. In the treaty of 1819, by which the Floridas were acquired from Spain, this claim to the Rio Grande was relinquished, and the Sabine was accepted as the boundary between Louisiana and Texas.[5]

From 1819 to 1836 the Sabine was indisputably the boundary between the United States and first Spain, and then Mexico, although the treaty by which it was established was vigorously denounced in Congress by Henry Clay and others as having yielded to Spain "that part of Louisiana lying west of the Sabine."[6]

When the Republic of Texas came into existence, a new question arose—the boundary between Mexico and Texas. The new republic laid claim to the Rio Grande, likewise known as the Rio Bravo del Norte, as its southern and western boundary. The claim was first asserted by the Texans, in fact, even before the declaration of their independence and while the province of Texas was seeking to establish itself as a separate state in the Mexican Union. When the state troops under Edward Burleson surrounded the troops of the central government under General Martin Cos at San Antonio in October 1835, and compelled their surrender, the articles of capitulation stipulated that Cos would retire beyond the Rio Grande, with Burleson assisting by furnishing him provisions "to the Rio Grande." The same boundary was asserted in the Texan Declaration of Independence of 1836, and was accepted by Dictator Santa Anna, after his defeat and capture at San Jacinto, by General Vicente Filisola, who succeeded Santa Anna in command of the Mexican army in Texas, and by the commanders of its three brigades.

Santa Anna afterward asserted that this treaty of May 12, 1836, was made in "his own name only," and was one which the Mexican Government had the right to nullify. The Mexican Congress did, in

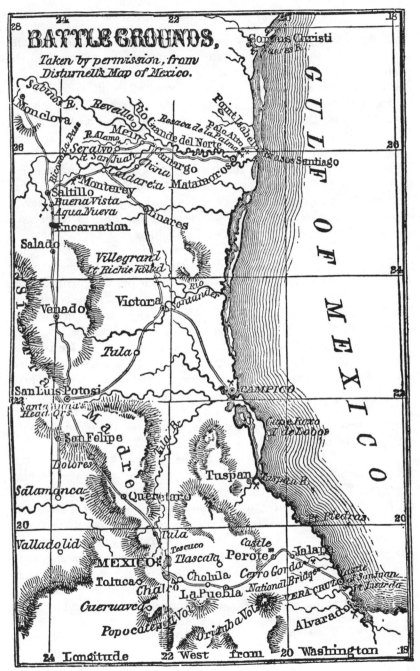

FROM *THE MEXICAN WAR* BY E. D. MANSFIELD (NEW YORK, 1848)

19

fact, reject the terms made by Santa Anna and his generals to secure the release of the captured dictator, and continued to maintain the claim of Mexican dominion over all of Texas, while the Texan Republic, through acts of its Congress, asserted its territorial rights and jurisdiction clear to the Rio Grande. So far as actual occupation was concerned, the Texan claim was tenuous indeed—but such as it was, and for whatever it was worth, it passed to the United States upon annexation.[7]

While continuing to deny the existence of Texas as an independent state and its power to annex itself to the United States, and in no way abating the Mexican claim to everything up to the Sabine, Mexico also asserted subsequently a lesser claim to the Nueces River as a boundary line between the states of Tamaulipas and Texas.[8]

Between the Nueces and the Rio Grande lay an almost unsettled wilderness. Toward this disputed and all but deserted frontier, General Taylor moved his protective force without precise instructions as to where it was to be placed, other than that it should be "on or near the Rio Grande," and that he should carefully "avoid any acts of aggression" toward Mexican troops reported to be on the east bank of that river "unless an actual state of war should exist." He reached the Texas coast on July 25 and, in the exercise of his discretion, landed on St. Joseph's Island, off Aransas Bay, on the twenty-sixth. Three days later he started moving south, stuck for two days on a sand bar, and finally on July 31 established his camp near the hamlet of Corpus Christi, then better known as Kinney's Ranch, and the most southerly settlement of the Texans.[9]

So doing, Taylor placed himself on the right, or south, bank of the Nueces, in accordance with the instructions then on the way to him from the War Department. The point was of no practical importance at the time. Subsequently, in the minds of those who believed that the United States forced war on Mexico as part of a preconceived plan of conquest, it became a prime point of indictment that United States forces had in time of peace encamped in and marched across the territory below the Nueces claimed by Mexico—though, for that matter, all Texas to the Sabine was so claimed, and Mexico had announced more than once that entry of Texas into the Union was in and of itself to be regarded as equivalent to a declaration of war.[10]

Neither the general nor the administration at Washington acted as if they expected war with Mexico, and certainly they made no particular effort to prepare for one. There were no substantial increases in military appropriations, no more than a nominal increase in the size of the army and no increase at all in the navy. The general at Corpus Christi did not ask for additional transportation, and the scale of preparations by the Quartermaster General's Department may be gauged by the fact that after shipping thirty four-horse wagons in August the Department ordered another twenty, with the admonition that "the making of the wagons should not be hurried," and another fifty in September, and that was the sole enlargement of the transportation of the army in advance of possible hostilities. The Quartermaster General's subsequent complaint that "no provident foresight has been exercised by anyone in command" was well founded.[11]

The War Department did, however, send troops to Taylor's Army of Occupation from its posts scattered along the Atlantic and Gulf coasts and the Canadian border as far west as Lake Superior, and from the chain of posts stretching along the western frontier from Fort Snelling in Minnesota to Fort Jesup in Louisiana. One battalion attracted attention by moving from Detroit to Corpus Christi, an estimated 2,500 miles, in only twenty-one days. The journey—seven days on the canal to Cincinnati, three days down the Ohio River to Cairo, five days on a larger Mississippi River steamer to New Orleans, two days at that post and three more on the Gulf—was marked by heat and mosquitoes on the canal, by "heat, stench and confusion" at Cairo, by the loss of tents in landing on the Texas coast, and by the birth of children to the wives of two soldiers who were accompanying their husbands to the new station. Nevertheless, one diarist wrote:

A movement of this kind brings into bold relief our grand system of internal navigation, which, in connection with our rivers, enables the government, in an incredibly short period, to send troops from one extremity of the Union to the other.[12]

Forces at Corpus Christi numbered, by the middle of October, 1845, nearly 4,000 men, half of all the Army of the United States. It was, in fact, the largest troop concentration seen in the country since the close of the War of 1812, thirty years before. Officers who had never drilled units larger than a company, or at most a battalion, were to have the chance to take part in drills by regiments and by brigades, though that was not to be until there had been much practice in the still unfamiliar battalion formations. In the meanwhile, according to the private memoirs of one of the field officers, there was but "one field officer on the ground who could change a single position of the troops according to any but a militia mode"—and he was that one.[13]

The routine of daily drills was relieved, after the army was assembled, by almost daily horse races, by the exhibitions of an American circus which somehow managed to set up in business, and by the performance of a "very clever company" of actors appearing in the army theater which opened its doors on January 8, 1846, under the general managership of courtly Captain John Bankhead Magruder—whose next duty in Texas was to be that of the major general commanding at Galveston for the Confederate States. Scenery for the theater, which seated 800, was painted by army men, and some of the plays were put on by army talent. One of the amateurs was Lieutenant U. S. Grant of the Fourth Infantry, who according to the later recollections of Lieutenant James Longstreet managed to achieve so little feminine appeal in the part of Desdemona that the lieutenant playing opposite him balked at going on as Othello.[14]

As the little army was built up in numbers and progressed in drill and discipline through the fall and winter months, it found the few inhabitants of the frontier friendly, trading unbroken or half-broken mustangs for goods which promptly went into Mexico without benefit of the Mexican customs service. The inhabitants introduced the newcomers from the north to "a Mexican preparation called temales, made of corn meal, chopped meat, and cayenne pepper, nicely wrapped in a piece of corn-husk, and boiled," which the newcomers found palatable. The fishing was superb, the game plentiful beyond belief, the summer sunshine tempered by breezes from the Gulf, and the autumnal climate, at least before the northers began to blow, delightful.[15]

The soldiers were quartered in camps stretching more than a mile along the shore, with tents pitched over platforms and supplies stored in sheds. Rations were simple but sufficient—bacon, pork or beef, bread, flour or cornmeal, as the basis, with allowances of coffee, beans or rice, sugar, vinegar, salt, candles and soap. To use the soap, laundresses were attached in the proportion of four to each company, receiving, in addition to food, fuel and soap, fifty cents a month from each soldier for whom they did washing.[16]

The near-by town of Corpus Christi, which had numbered fewer than twenty houses when the soldiers came, mushroomed as many a camp town has since. At the end of November its population was estimated at a thousand, and a month later at twice that number. They were housed in all manner of shelter from rude sheds to tolerably substantial frame houses. A majority of the floating population were described as gamblers and "grocery keepers," the word grocery apparently being a euphemism for grogshop, although it is hard to see how there was sufficient profit to sustain so many camp followers around a camp of only 4,000 men, most of whom received only seven dollars a month, presumably paid bimonthly, and not always paid then.[17]

But a dollar was a substantial unit of purchasing power in 1846, and the camp and its surroundings were fully the equal of what most of the soldiers had been accustomed to on the frontier. Except for a chronic scarcity of firewood and an alkaline touch to the water, a deal of sickness caused by the prevailing ignorance of camp sanitation, and the violent vicissitudes of winter weather in which a howling norther might coat the cotton walls of the tents with crackling ice on the morning after an evening like spring, there was not a great deal to complain of in the situation at Corpus Christi.[18] But even with the daily drills, the horse racing, the hunting, the theatrical amusements and the interest added to life by the assemblage in one place of so large a part of the army, as the months passed there was time and opportunity for grumbling in plenty among all ranks, and for some spectacular discords over questions of rank among the higher officers.

General Taylor's force—one regiment of dragoons, five regiments of infantry, four batteries of field artillery—seemed to him to be "fully adequate to meet any crisis which might arise," and he so reported.[19] But then neither the general, nor those under his command, nor for that matter the government at Washington, were expecting anything much in the way of a fight.

There was, it is true, no lack of war talk. As Taylor was moving toward Texas, the Mexican foreign minister was advising his representatives at Paris and London that Mexico had no choice but to fight.[20] That had been the official position in Mexico, indeed, ever since the beginning of negotiations for annexation of Texas to the United States and, before that, had been the Mexican attitude toward the revolted province. In the summer of 1844, when the treaty for the annexation of Texas as a United States territory was under consideration, the government of General Santa Anna had sought from the Mexican Congress extraordinary grants of money to carry on war with

Texas on that issue. The opposition to Santa Anna vehemently charged that the real purpose for which the money was sought was not war in the north but tightening the grip of the ruler at home. The special taxes were voted nevertheless and, in addition, the Mexican Congress was called upon for authority to float a loan of ten million dollars for the Texan war.[21]

Perhaps as part of this campaign for special war taxes and loans, the tone of Santa Anna's utterances toward Texas became more threatening in this summer of 1844. His commander on the de facto frontier of the Rio Grande, General Adrian Woll, notified the Texans on June 19 of the resumption of hostilities, and on the following day proclaimed that all persons found more than one league from the left bank of the Rio Grande—and hence suspected of intent to communicate with the Texans—were subject to be shot after summary trial, and that persons "rash enough to flee at sight of any force of the Supreme Government" were to be pursued, taken and summarily shot.

President Tyler was aroused to protest against threats of invasion directed against Texas because it was negotiating with the United States. His note was published by the Santa Anna government,[22] but not even this incitement to resentment against the northern neighbor was sufficient to carry the loan measure through the Mexican Congress, or to save Santa Anna from the effect of long accumulating resentments. Revolt spread from state to state and from garrison to garrison until, on December 6, 1844—after the annexation treaty had been rejected by the United States Senate— Santa Anna was again driven from power and subsequently, in June 1845, was once more banished from the country.[23]

As an almost accidental result of this Decembrista revolution of 1844, there came to the Presidency of Mexico General José Joaquín Herrera, president of the National Council, and a man of judgment and pacific intent but without skill in the pyrotechnics of politics.

The Herrera government was inclined to peace but the events of 1845, unhappily, lent themselves to political incendiarism. When the United States offered annexation to Texas in March, the Mexican minister Juan N. Almonte withdrew from Washington and diplomatic relations were broken. Later, in May, in an attempt to head off Texan acceptance of the United States offer, a proposition for Mexican recognition of Texas upon condition that there be no annexation to the United States was put before the Herrera government by Captain Charles Elliott, British Chargé d'Affaires in Texas. Grudgingly, and after much stormy debate, the Mexican Congress made such a belated and conditional offer of recognition to Texas, only to have it unanimously rejected in June by the Texan Congress.[24]

The fact, however, that the Herrera government had been willing to make a pacific offer to Texas furnished more ammunition to those whose political stock in trade was war in the north. The Herrera government, therefore, was compelled both by its sense of duty and by the state of Mexican opinion, to undertake to strengthen the forces on the northern frontier. Accordingly, General Mariano Paredes, commanding at San Luis Potosí, was ordered to dispatch reinforcements to the Rio Grande. But General Paredes had other plans. He had had much to do with bringing Santa Anna back to power in 1841, and driving him out again in 1844. He was believed to have designs of establishing European monarchy in Mexico, and certainly he was contemplating making himself the beneficiary of his next venture in president making. At any rate, he did not dispatch the heavy reinforcements ordered for the garrison along the Rio Grande, facing Taylor's force on the Nueces.[25]

Meanwhile, President Polk—who, succeeding Tyler on March 4, 1845, was to carry through to completion the annexation of Texas—continued on his course of seeking a settlement of differences with Mexico. President Herrera's government was sounded out, both through the aid of the British minister at Mexico and through an American resident there, on the question of whether or not a diplomatic representative from the United States would be received. On October 15, Señor Manuel de la Peña y Peña, Mexican Minister of Foreign Relations, privately advised that such a representative would be received, upon condition that the United States fleet then in the Gulf off Vera Cruz be withdrawn.[26]

Commodore David Conner, commanding the squadron, at once withdrew from the neighborhood of Vera Cruz without waiting for orders, passed on word of President Herrera's acceptance to Washington, and advised General Taylor that Mexico had "accepted the proposal to arrange existing troubles by negotiation."[27] There seemed to be sufficient justification for the feeling that a peaceful settlement of a chain of disputes going back fifteen years might be in prospect.

The United States acted promptly—too promptly, as events turned out, and too broadly for President Herrera. Word of Mexican willingness to receive a representative reached Washington on November

6. On the tenth, President Polk named as his representative in Mexico John Slidell. The new envoy, a native of New York and resident of Louisiana, was well connected in both North and South. August Belmont of New York was his nephew by marriage, and close friend. Commodore Matthew C. Perry of the United States Navy was a brother-in-law, while another brother-in-law was a young Louisiana soldier, Pierre Gustave Toutant Beauregard. Slidell was considered well equipped for his task. He spoke Spanish, for one thing, was a highly successful lawyer of large experience, had had political experience as congressman-at-large from Louisiana, and was destined to serve in the Senate of the United States. He is chiefly remembered today, however, by the fact that his removal by a United States warship from the deck of the British mail steamer *Trent,* while he was on a diplomatic mission for the Confederate States of America, precipitated a crisis between the United States and Great Britain which had in it distinct possibilities of war.

In his 1845 diplomatic venture to Mexico, Mr. Slidell's status, so far as the United States was concerned, was that of a minister plenipotentiary, empowered to deal with any and all questions in dispute between the country he represented and that to which he was accredited. In this capacity he landed at Vera Cruz on November 30, and proceeded up to Mexico to present his credentials.[28]

Slidell's arrival so promptly was something of a bombshell to the Herrera government. The government had agreed to receive a diplomatic representative, but the sort of representative it had in mind, it now developed, was not one with broad and general powers to deal with all matters in dispute but one limited to dealing with the single subject of Texas. No such limitation had been expressed during the negotiations, but with Slidell's unexpected and not altogether welcome, arrival it was held that the Mexican national honor would not permit the resumption of general and unlimited diplomatic intercourse with the nation which had annexed Texas. The National Council, therefore, decided to notify the Yankee representative that he could not be received in the character in which he had presented himself but only as a "commissioner" with whom the Texas question and no other might be discussed. Such notification from Señor de la Peña y Peña, was received by Slidell on December 21.[29]

To Slidell, under his instructions, there was nothing to discuss about the annexation of Texas. In the United States' view, Texas had been an independent nation, had maintained its independence for almost a decade, and had exercised its sovereign independence by joining the Union, for which it required no consent from Mexico either before or after the fact.

But there were numerous other questions for discussion between the nations. There were old questions of claims of American nationals against the Mexican Government. And there was the new question of just where the Texan boundary lay and the questions of the status of California and New Mexico.

Claims for damages sustained by American nationals, compensation for which could not be secured through the Mexican courts, had been the subject of dispute and negotiation with various Mexican administrations for fifteen years. In 1838, the United States had accepted the suggestion of Mexico that the claims be submitted to arbitration, and a convention to that effect was drawn. When Mexico failed to ratify the first convention, a second claims convention was agreed on in 1839. After further delay, the King of Prussia was accepted by both parties as the neutral member of the arbitration commission which was organized in 1840. In the following year the claims commission awarded $2,000,000 in damages to United States claimants. Mexico accepted the award but suggested that payment be made in twenty quarterly installments. The United States accepted the suggestion but after the third installment, payments lapsed.[30]

The new question of boundaries was in a way related to the old question of claims. Mexico concededly owed the claims and was without funds with which to pay them. What was more natural, in the mind of President Polk, than to have the United States Government assume and pay the debts due from the Government of Mexico to the United States claimants—as in an earlier day the United States had assumed payment of claims against Spain in connection with the acquisition of Florida—if Mexico in return should be willing to accept the boundary of the Rio Grande claimed by Texas?

A "better boundary," Polk proposed to his Cabinet on September 16, "would be the Del Norte from its mouth to the Passo, in latitude about 32 degrees north, and thence west to the Pacific Ocean, Mexico ceding to the United States all the country east and north of these lines." For such a boundary, the President said—and the Cabinet agreed—"the amount of pecuniary consideration to be paid would be of small consequence. He supposed it might be had for fifteen or twenty millions, but he was ready to pay forty millions for it, if it could not be had for less."[31]

Such a purchase would have included not only the disputed Texan areas but also the narrow strip of settlements along the upper Rio Grande in the immense and otherwise unsettled interior territory known as New Mexico, and Upper California. The Democratic platform upon which Polk was elected in 1844 declared for the annexation of Texas and for the maintenance of the American position in the boundary dispute with the British in the Oregon country. It said nothing, however, about California. That was Mr. Polk's personal platform—and the fact that California became a part of the United States just before the discovery of gold in the Sacramento Valley would have made it the prize of an international grab bag is due as much to the determination with which he pursued the idea as it is to any other one thing.

The importance to the United States of San Francisco Bay was pointed out to Slidell in instructions of November 10, 1845, from Secretary of State Buchanan, who noted that "the government of California is now but nominally dependent upon Mexico," advised that "it is to be seriously apprehended that both Great Britain and France have designs upon California," and warned that the United States would vigorously oppose its "becoming either a British or a French colony." The new envoy was therefore desired by the President to use his best efforts to obtain a cession of California but only to do so in the event that he could "discover a prospect of success" after sounding out the Mexican authorities. In that case, "the President would not hesitate to give, in addition to the assumption of the just claims of our citizens on Mexico, twenty-five millions of dollars for the cession." In fact, Mr. Slidell was told, "money would be no object, when compared with the value of the acquisition" of California.[32]

Acquisition of territory by purchase was not new to the United States. Louisiana had been acquired that way during the Presidency of Jefferson, and Florida while Monroe was President. After the United States relinquished the old French claim to Texas, in the treaty of 1819, President John Quincy Adams and his Secretary of State, Henry Clay—both of whom were to become leaders in opposition to the annexation of Texas—had sought without success in 1825-1827 to purchase from Mexico all or part of the Texan territory lying west of the Sabine. The effort was renewed, again without success, in 1829 while Andrew Jackson was President and Martin Van Buren Secretary of State. There is no discernible difference in principle between the two efforts at purchase, but subsequently Adams was to see Jackson's attempt to purchase Texas from Mexico as evidence of an effort to extend the territory and influence of slavery. Texan independence brought an end to efforts at purchase.[33]

Acquisition of California had been discussed, insofar as the San Francisco Bay area was concerned, as early as the time of President Jackson, and had been seriously considered by President Tyler and his Secretary of State, Daniel Webster, as a means of securing settlement of claims due from Mexico, even though the common opinion of the time about California was that it had but "two tracts of country capable of supporting a large population"—the San Francisco Bay area and the vicinity of Los Angeles.[34]

By 1845, when Polk became President, it was becoming more and more apparent that some change in the status of California was impending. In the same year in which the Texans made good their independence, the very different population of Mexican California also revolted against the centralist government, and set up a new state government. Two years later, in 1838, the new government was recognized by President Anastasio Bustamante. After five more years, Santa Anna, who had come back into power, dispatched troops to restore the national supremacy but by February 1845 these troops too had been driven out of California, and the native government with Pío Pico as governor and José Castro as *comandante general* had been recognized. The vast area of California, with a scattered population of not more than 15,000 whites and 24,000 Indians, of whom 4,000 were domesticated, was in truth an international vacuum.[35]

It was, moreover, a vacuum with dangerous possibilities. Quite obviously, Mexican national supremacy was not likely to be restored in any effective fashion, and there was always the possibility of occupation by one of the great colonizing powers of Europe. It is known now that the British had no design to take California, but all that Polk could have known then was that local British officers in California favored a British protectorate and that there was a British fleet on the coast with some sort of instructions on the subject.

In the circumstances, Polk not only authorized Slidell to sound out the Mexican Government on the purchase of its rights in the province but also, in October 1845, sent instructions to the United States consular agent at Monterey, and to the commander of the squadron in the Pacific, as to what should be their course in either of two possible turns of events. If any other power should attempt to occupy California, they should oppose the attempt. If native Californians should assert their independence, they should assist them.

The President's instructions to Consul Larkin and Commodore

Sloat were thus conditioned upon the contingencies of actual hostilities with Mexico, an attempt at occupation of California by a European power, or an assertion of independence by the native Californians. President Polk was seeking none of these things. He wanted
California but he wanted it by purchase. California was months away
from Washington, however, and in the touchy state of relations with
Mexico, the President was bound to take precautionary steps, leaving it
to distant agents to act on their own responsibility within the frame-
work of general instructions.[36]

Meanwhile, Polk's real reliance was upon the mission of Slidell,
who, as the United States understood the Mexican undertaking to
receive a representative, would have an opportunity to discuss the
purchase of California. The sending of the Slidell mission has been
imputed to Polk as in itself a Machiavellian move, designed to provoke a proud and sensitive Mexican nation to war. To neither Polk
nor Slidell did it appear at the time as anything other than a move for
a peaceful settlement of disputes which had led to a break in the
normal diplomatic relations between the two governments. As the
party which had broken relations, Mexico would ordinarily have had
to make the first move for their resumption. Polk, however, realizing
the difficulties in the way of restoring harmonious relations, had taken
an unofficial "feel" of the situation, and had what he believed to be
sufficient assurance that his proposed mission would be welcomed.
Sending Slidell to Mexico was in itself a bid for the preservation of
peace. His instructions to offer payment for the cession of territory,
intended to meet the chronic financial difficulties of the Mexican Government, were not to be put forward if they should endanger the
peaceful outcome of the mission. The Slidell mission was a mission of
peace, not one intended to provoke a war.

Refusal to receive Slidell except as a commissioner limited to Texan
questions was a concession to the war talk in Mexico, but even so it
did not save the tottering Herrera government. On December 14,
1845, General Mariano Paredes y Arrillaga, commanding the principal garrison of the north at San Luis Potosí, "pronounced" against
the government for having "admitted a commissioner with whom it
was endeavoring to arrange for the loss of the integrity of the republic," for having "allowed a plenipotentiary of the United States to set
foot in the country, and reside in the capital, with a view to bargain
for the independence and nationality of the country," and for sundry

other acts. On the last day of the year Herrera yielded to the mounting tide against him and left the capital city. On January 4, 1846, General Paredes took over the Presidency and, in doing so, ringingly reasserted Mexico's claim to all of Texas clear to the Sabine, and his intention of defending the national territory.[37]

Slidell, meanwhile, had notified President Polk of the refusal of the Herrera government to receive him, had asked for instructions, and had remained in Mexico to await them. His dispatch announcing his rejection was received in Washington on January 12, 1846. On the day following, orders were dispatched to General Taylor to advance his camp from Corpus Christi to the vicinity of the mouth of the Rio Grande—a movement which Taylor himself had suggested as early as October 4, 1845. With communications what they were in that time, however, Taylor did not receive his instructions until February 3, and did not actually advance until well into March.[38]

At the same time that military forces were being moved to the Rio Grande, President Polk sent forward instructions to Slidell to try again to present his credentials, on the off-chance that the new government of President Paredes might accept them. On March 1, 1846, Slidell once more sought to be received, was once more rejected on the twelfth, and on the twenty-first departed for the United States.[39]

The political necessities of the Paredes government were such, in truth, that no other course was possible. Herrera had been driven from the Presidency chiefly on the ground of his apparent willingness to treat with the United States, and there was no way for Paredes, even if he had wanted to do so, to reverse himself now.

Moreover, while the question was at issue, there had arisen the highly interesting possibility of war between the United States and Great Britain over the question of the Oregon country. President Polk's message to Congress on December 2, 1845, had reiterated the Democratic platform declaration claiming as United States territory all of the Oregon country—a term which then included what is now British Columbia, clear up to the Russian boundary of fifty-four degrees, forty minutes, north latitude, as well as the American states of Oregon, Washington, Idaho and part of Montana. The possibility of war was brought nearer, it seemed, when in February the United States rejected a British proposal for neutral arbitration of the dispute. Forces on both sides were working for reasonable adjustment, however, and the question was to be finally and peacefully disposed of with the signing of the boundary treaty of June 15, 1846. But as affairs seemed to stand in the winter and spring of 1845-1846, when President Paredes was called upon to act on the acceptance or final rejection of Slidell, there looked to be an excellent chance that the United States was about to be embroiled in war with Great Britain. To repel Slidell's proferred credentials, and to do it with rousing words designed to appeal to national pride and heighten national belligerency, seemed not only sure-fire as a political hit at home but safe enough as a military venture.

For a century, now, the general picture of the war between the United States and Mexico has been that of a mighty nation deliberately forcing predatory war upon a weaker neighbor. That was the picture painted at the time by Whig politicians opposed to what they called "Mr. Polk's war." It was the picture painted, in even darker colors, by the growing and highly expressive body of abolitionist writers and agitators who were opposed to any expansion of the United States to the southwestward as being in the interest of slavery. Such a picture is naturally and understandably gratifying to the pride of the nation which fought bravely against odds, only to be defeated. Such a picture, if accepted as true, is naturally and understandably one in which the winning nation could take no pride.

The people of the United States, for the most part, despite their regard for many of the soldiers and sailors who fought the war, have accepted the picture drawn by party politicians and extremist agitators, and so for a century have had toward the war with Mexico an apologetic, even a shamefaced, attitude which is not justified by the facts.

The issue which caused Mexico to break off diplomatic relations with the United States was not the conflict of claims to the empty strip of territory between the Nueces and the Rio Grande. It was the annexation of Texas. The United States held off from such annexation for nine years and during three Presidencies, until it was abundantly clear that Texas had made good her independence and there was no chance of reconquest by Mexico, and until there was substantial reason to believe that Texas, rebuffed by the United States, was on the point of allying herself with Great Britain. And this, it should be recalled, was at a time when the United States and Britain were not the sharers of more than a century of unbroken peace but were less than a generation away from the war of 1812-1815 and were actually embroiled in boundary disputes at both ends of the not-yet-settled line between the United States and British North America. In all the circumstances, the United States was amply justified in annexing Texas—an act which no one would undo today.

President Polk's frankly expressed desire to secure for the Union California and the territory intervening between California and Texas has been accepted as evidence of warlike intent toward Mexico. The argument runs that Polk desired California, that there was a war and that Polk got California, ergo Polk wanted war. The logic of the argument is patently faulty, and the facts are against the assumption. Polk wanted California—another territory which had slipped from the Mexican grasp and was about to become fair game for European colonization—but he did not want it badly enough to have a war for it. Slidell's instructions were that he was not to allow the suggestion of purchase to jeopardize his mission for peace. The President's desire to purchase was not, in fact, presented to Mexico and had no part in bringing on the war which, as events turned out, ended with California as part of the United States—another result which no one would today undo.

Polk's position on California was of a piece with his whole policy toward the extension of European "dominion or sovereignty" to any part of the North American continent and its adjacent islands, beyond where it was then established. Instructions to a diplomatic agent accredited to the government of the Hawaiian Islands, in September 1845, pointed out the possibility of British annexation of that "commanding commercial position" and laid out the independence of the islands as "the clear policy as well as the duty of the government of the United States." One month later, the instructions sent to Consul Larkin at Monterey made it even plainer that the United States would resist any extension of "the system of colonization by foreign monarchies on the North American continent" and would "vigorously interfere to prevent California from becoming a British or French colony." In the next month, November 1845, Secretary Buchanan's instructions to Slidell upon his departure for Mexico expressed the same idea, and the position was publicly and positively stated by President Polk himself in his first message to Congress, on December 2, 1845. ". . . Existing rights of every European nation should be respected," the President wrote, but ". . . it should be distinctly announced to the world as our settled policy that no future European colony or dominion shall, with our consent, be planted or established on any part of the North American continent."[40]

How firmly the President stood on this doctrine was shown in a revealing passage between him and James Buchanan, his Secretary of State, at a meeting of the Cabinet on the night of the declaration of war with Mexico. Mr. Buchanan, never one for the bold and decided course, insisted that the United States should give assurance to the European powers that it would not "acquire California or any other part of the Mexican territory" as a result of the war. Otherwise, he "thought it almost certain that both England and France would join with Mexico in the war. . . ." Mr. Polk replied that "neither as a citizen nor as President would I permit or tolerate any intermeddling of any European Powers on this continent," and that "sooner than give the pledge proposed," he would "meet the war which either England or France or all the powers of Christendom might wage . . . and would take the whole responsibility" for the consequences, "let them be what they might."[41]

Thus the Polk Doctrine—as it came to be called many years later—took its place beside the Monroe Doctrine as one of the foundations of American continental policy. It extended the Monroe Doctrine to cover *any* new establishment of European dominion or sovereignty, even with the consent or at the request of the peoples who might come under it, while at the same time it narrowed the application of the doctrine to North America. Such a declaration today might be regarded as rhetorical rather than substantial, but not so when the doctrine was promulgated by President Polk. The United States had not then become a truly continental power, let alone a world power. It had no assured foothold on the Pacific Coast, only a claim to the Oregon country which still was in dispute with Great Britain. California, governmentally speaking, was little better than a derelict awaiting salvage. Great Britain, which had been believed to have plans to annex Texas, was believed to have plans still in California and Yucatán. There was always the possibility that Cuba might pass from the failing hands of Spain to some strong and active maritime and commercial power. The French kingdom, soon to pass through the metamorphosis of the Second Republic to become the Second Empire, was increasingly active as a colonizing power. In Mexico itself there was a strong party favoring the resolution of governmental troubles by bringing in a European prince, and in Europe there could have been found, no doubt, princes of reigning houses who would be willing to undertake the task—as, indeed, a prince of the House of Hapsburg was to do nearly two decades later.

But, runs the criticism of Polk's policy, firmness toward European expansion in America was not applied toward mighty Great Britain in the case of Oregon as it was toward the weak neighbor, Mexico. The essential difference, however, lay not in the policy of President Polk but in the different attitudes of the British and the Mexican governments. There were questions at issue in both cases, with rights and claims and counterclaims to be adjusted. The British Government was both willing and able to negotiate; the Mexican Government may have been willing, but was politically unable to do so. Negotiation led, in one case, to a reasonable and satisfactory settlement. Refusal to negotiate, in the other case, resulted in war.

Considerations of policy, however, were not a major factor in the war talk in the United States in 1845 and 1846. Such talk, for the most part popular and not governmental, reflected the strains and tensions which had grown up, almost from the beginning of Mexican independence, between what were described in those days as the two largest republics in the world. To governmental differences there were added differences in language, customs, temperament, values and attitudes, things which can so easily be distorted and magnified. And there was a popular recollection of the then-recent war for Texas independence. The massacre of the men who surrendered at Goliad had not been forgotten. "Remember the Alamo!" was still a living phrase, and George W. Kendall's *Narrative of the Texan Santa Fé Expedition,* in which the vicissitudes and sufferings of the Texan prisoners at Mexican hands in 1841 and 1842 were movingly recounted, was a current best seller.

In Mexico, the same human impulses were working in reverse. Talk of war against the Texans had been part of the political stock in trade of a succession of leaders ever since before San Jacinto. With the annexation of Texas, the talk was transferred to the Yankee nation which most Mexicans believed had been behind the Texans all along. The government of Señor Herrera had tried to stem the talk and deal with the situation pacifically and from the standpoint of national interest rather than national resentments, but pacific intentions had been too heavy a political load for Herrera to carry. The Paredes government had come to power on a torrent of war talk.

It seems now that no sensible Mexican Government would have invited the chances of war with the United States when war could have been avoided. But at the time when President Paredes had to decide, there were factors which may well have encouraged him in a course to which he was impelled by inflamed opinion and the necessities of domestic politics. Strange as it seems now, there was at the time a belief in many quarters, European as well as Mexican, that in a war between the two nations there was more than an even chance of Mexican victory.

A factor now almost forgotten but one which must have been potent in the calculations of President Paredes was the belief, in the spring of 1846, that the Oregon boundary dispute might well lead to war between the United States and Great Britain. There was reliance, too, on the fact that despite differences in population Mexico could put in the field a much larger number of experienced soldiers than the United States. The Mexican cavalry, in particular, was rated by both Mexican and European observers as stronger in numbers and training, and any war between the two countries was likely to be fought in an area where cavalry would be important. It was recognized, of course, that the United States had by far the greater financial strength and productive capacity, but a century ago there was no such appreciation as there is today of the vital importance of these factors in war. The strength of the United States, moreover, was not organized for military purposes. For thirty years the country had been at peace except for frontier troubles with the Indians, while for almost as long a time military activities had been a major occupation for many Mexicans.

Added to the possibility of the United States being engaged in two wars at once, and reliance on the military ardor and experience of the Mexican forces, there was some degree of reliance in Mexico on the effectiveness of that considerable and very vocal body of opinion in the United States which looked on the annexation of Texas, and all things connected with or growing out of it, as part of an unholy conspiracy to extend the territory and enlarge the power of slavery. The last Mexican minister in Washington had reported in 1844, indeed, that annexation of Texas by the United States would certainly result in the secession of the New England states, and that if New York and Pennsylvania did not do likewise, they would at the least refuse to have any part of a war with Mexico. "The strongest assurances for this belief . . . ," he said, came "from members of Congress and Senators and from influential persons in the said states."[42]

This view of affairs on the part of the Mexican Government is the more understandable when it is recalled that no criticisms of United States policy were more scathing than some which originated in the

United States itself. These opinions had been duly compiled, translated and circulated south of the Rio Grande. They were to have small effect on the vigor of the prosecution of the war, and the Mexican Government was to be disappointed in whatever reliance it placed on them as a divisive and weakening force in the United States. Their effect was not immediate and on the course of the war, but was delayed and in the field of ideas and reputation. In that field these criticisms of United States policy, extreme and exaggerated as they were, were to help exacerbate the sectional differences which, fifteen years later, were to erupt into a greater war. And the same opinions, working through that curious craving for self-criticism, or even self-abasement, which is the other side of the shield of American national pride, have ever since colored feeling about the war with Mexico.

Into that war, in the spring of 1846, the two nations drifted through a fog of misunderstanding and a welter of war talk. It was a small war, in modern eyes, with never a time when a United States commander could put into action more than 10,000 men, and rarely a time when a Mexican commander could muster many more. But small as it was in scale, it was big with consequences. It remade the map of North America, rounding out the United States to continental proportions. It provided military experience to young men who, in a few years, were to become leaders on both sides in the war between the states of the South and of the North. It helped to lay the train of events which ended in that great struggle, out of which the United States emerged as a nation, rather than a federation.

It was, in short, an inescapable and a not inglorious step in the historical process by which the United States of America was brought to its present place in the world.

---

1 Ex. Doc. 60, H. R., 30th Cong., 1st sess., pp. 79-82, 801-803; Henry, Capt. W. S., *Campaign Sketches of the War with Mexico* (New York, 1847), pp. 8-13; Pub. Doc. 378, Sen., 29th Cong., 1st sess., pp. 21-22. Captain Henry's *Sketches* appeared serially over the signature "G. de L." in the New York *Spirit of the Times.*

2 Reeves, Jesse S., *American Diplomacy under Tyler and Polk* (Baltimore, 1907), p. 59; Smith, Justin H., *The Annexation of Texas* (New York, 1911. Corrected Edition, 1941), pp. 7-9; Rives, George Lockhart, *The United States and Mexico, 1821-1848* (New York, 1913), I, 118-154.

3 Reeves, *American Diplomacy,* p. 72. United States recognition of Texas, on March 3, 1837, was more than ten months after the victory at San Jacinto, and after, in the language of Daniel Webster, "independence was an apparent and an ascertained fact." France entered into a treaty of amity and commerce with Texas in 1839, Great Britain in 1840 (ratified in 1842). Smith, *Annexation of Texas,* pp. 57-63, 76-80.

4 ". . . the Mexican Government will consider equivalent to a declaration of war

against the Mexican Republic the passage of an act for the incorporation of Texas
with the territory of the United States; the certainty of the fact being sufficient for the
immediate proclamation of war." Bocanegra, Secretary of Relations, to Thompson,
U. S. Minister, August 23, 1843, Ex. Doc. 2, H. R., 28th Cong., 1st sess., p. 27. "The
Mexican Government is resolved to declare war as soon as it receives information of
such an act." Almonte, Mexican Minister, to Upshur, Secretary of State, November 3,
1843. Same, p. 38. Reeves, *American Diplomacy*, pp. 157, 188.

5 The treaty of February 22, 1819, which brought Florida into the United States
and ran a boundary with Spain between the Gulf of Mexico and the Pacific, was
negotiated by John Quincy Adams, Secretary of State under President Monroe.

6 The Sabine boundary is discussed in Rives, *U. S. and Mexico*, I, 20-26.

7 "The occupation of the country between the Nueces and the Rio Grande . . . is
a disputed question." A. J. Donelson, U. S. Charge d'Affaires in Texas, to Taylor,
June 28, 1845, Ex. Doc. 60, H. R., 30th Cong., 1st sess., pp. 804-806; Chase, Lucien
B., *History of the Polk Administration* (New York, 1850), pp. 84-86, 89-96; Call-
cott, Wilfrid Hardy, *Santa Anna: The Story of an Enigma Who Once Was Mexico*
(Norman, Oklahoma, 1936), pp. 140-141. Binkley, William C., *The Expansionist
Movement in Texas, 1836-1850* (Berkeley, 1925), pp. 128-131.

8 Ex. Doc. 60, H. R., 30th Cong., 1st sess., pp. 125-132. The boundary question is
discussed in Polk's message to Congress, December 8, 1846, Ex. Doc. 4, H. R., 29th
Cong., 2nd sess., pp. 9-16.

9 Henry, *Campaign Sketches*, p. 14; Croffut, W. A. (ed.), *Fifty Years in Camp
and Field, The Diary of Major General Ethan Allen Hitchcock, U. S. A.* (New York,
1909), pp. 193-194; Ex. Doc. 60, H. R., 30th Cong., 1st sess., pp. 82, 97-102; Pub.
Doc. 378, Sen., 29th Cong., 1st sess., pp. 21-22.

10 Ex. Doc. 60, H. R., 30th Cong., 1st sess., pp. 82, 83, 802-807; Chase, *Polk Administration*, pp. 122-129.

11 Same, pp. 566, 576-577, 579, 650.

12 Blackwood, Emma Jerome (ed.), *To Mexico with Scott, Letters of Captain
E. Kirby Smith to His Wife* (Cambridge, 1917), pp. 13-17; Henry, *Campaign
Sketches*, p. 38.

13 Pub. Doc. 1, Sen., 29th Cong., 1st sess., pp. 220 a, b and f; Ex. Doc. 60, H. R.,
30th Cong., 1st sess., pp. 94-111; Croffut (ed.), *Fifty Years*, pp. 198-199.

14 Henry, *Campaign Sketches*, pp. 44, 45, 47; Longstreet, James, *From Manassas
to Appomattox* (Philadelphia, 1896), p. 20; French, Samuel G., *Two Wars: An
Autobiography* (Nashville, 1901), p. 34; Meade, George, *Life and Letters of General Meade* (New York, 1913), I, 43-44.

15 Henry, *Campaign Sketches*, pp. 27, 31, 40-45; Ex. Doc. 60, H. R., 30th Cong.,
1st sess., p. 650.

16 Same, p. 112; Kirby Smith, *To Mexico*, pp. 17-19; *General Regulations for the
Army of the United States*, 1841 and 1847 (Washington).

17 Henry, *Campaign Sketches*, p. 44; Croffut (ed.), *Fifty Years*, p. 206.

18 Ex. Doc. 60, H. R., 30th Cong., 1st sess., p. 112; Henry, *Campaign Sketches*,
pp. 45-46. On December 1, the coldest day of the winter, the thermometer fell to
twenty-three degrees, and there was a half inch of ice on the Nueces. Duncan, Lt. Col.
Louis C., "A Medical History of General Zachary Taylor's Army . . . in Texas and
Mexico, 1845-1847," *The Military Surgeon*, Vol. XLVIII (1921), p. 79.

19 Ex. Doc. 60, H. R., 30th Cong., 1st sess., p. 103.

20 Rives, *U. S. and Mexico*, II, 93.

21 Rives, *U. S. and Mexico*, I, 657-659, 664-665.

22 Ex. Doc. 1, Sen., 28th Cong., 2nd sess., pp. 27, 29, 34; Ex. Doc. 341, Sen., 28th
Cong., 1st sess., p. 84; Smith, *Annexation of Texas*, pp. 362, 363; Rives, *U. S. and
Mexico*, I, 663-668.

23 Rives, *U. S. and Mexico*, I, 668-678.

24 The Mexican gesture toward conditional acknowledgment of the independence of Texas was made by the Mexican Congress on May 3, 1845, and rejected by the Texas Congress on June 18, 1845. Smith, *Annexation of Texas*, pp. 430, 456; Ramsey, Albert C. (ed.), *The Other Side: Or Notes for the History of the War Between Mexico and the United States* (written in Mexico, translated from Spanish, New York, 1850), pp. 27-28. The original of this work by Ramon Alcaraz and fourteen other Mexican writers was published at Mexico in 1848 under the title, *Apuntes para la historia de la guerra entra Mexico y los Estados-Unidos*.

25 Ramsey (ed.), *The Other Side*, pp. 33-41.

26 Ex. Doc. 60, H. R., 30th Cong., 1st sess., pp. 5, 12-17; Smith, Justin H., *The War with Mexico* (New York, 1919), pp. 88-93; McCormac, Eugene Irving, *James K. Polk: A Political Biography* (Berkeley, 1922), pp. 383-385; Quaife, Milo Milton (ed.), *The Diary of James K. Polk* (Chicago, 1910), I, 33-36, 91-93; Nevins, Allan (ed.), *Polk, The Diary of a President, 1845-1849* (New York, 1929), pp. 9-11, 25-26.

27 Ex. Doc. 60, H. R., 30th Cong., 1st sess., p. 112.

28 Same, pp. 23, 27-28; Quaife (ed.), *Polk's Diary*, I, 93-94; Sears, Louis Martin, *John Slidell* (Durham, 1925), Chapters I, II, III.

29 Ex. Doc. 60, H. R., 30th Cong., 1st sess., pp. 22-49; Ramsey (ed.), *The Other Side*, pp. 28-29; Smith, *War with Mexico*, I, 92-98; Reeves, *American Diplomacy*, pp. 281, 282, 288.

30 Same, I, 76-81, 427-432; Ex. Doc. 60, H. R., 30th Cong., 1st sess., pp. 40-41.

31 Quaife (ed.), *Polk's Diary*, I, 34-35; Nevins (ed.), *Polk*, p. 10.

32 Ex. Doc. 52, Sen., 30th Cong., 1st sess., pp. 71-80; Rives, *U. S. and Mexico*, II, 69.

33 Rives, *U. S. and Mexico*, I, 166-171, 239-241; Reeves, *American Diplomacy*, pp. 60-65.

34 Rives, *U. S. and Mexico*, II, 45-47; Frost, John, *Pictorial History . . . of the Mexican War* (Philadelphia, 1848), p. 390. One observer, however, Waddy Thompson, believed California to be more valuable than Texas. Reeves, *American Diplomacy*, pp. 100-101.

35 Smith, *War with Mexico*, I, 319; Rives, *U. S. and Mexico*, II, 30-34, 38-42. The population estimates are by John Parrott and Thomas O. Larkin, U. S. consuls at Mazatlán and Monterey. Ex. Doc. 70, H. R., 30th Cong., 1st sess., pp. 7-8.

36 Rives, *U. S. and Mexico*, II, 166-168; Smith, *War with Mexico*, I, 325-327; McCormac, *James K. Polk*, pp. 386-389; Moore, John Bassett (ed.), *The Works of James Buchanan* (Philadelphia and London, 1908-1911), VI, 275-278; Adams, Ephraim D., "English Interest in the Annexation of California," *American Historical Review*, Vol. XIV, July 1909; Barker, Eugene C., "California as the Cause of the Mexican War," *Texas Review*, Vol. II, No. 3, p. 217.

37 Ex. Doc. 60, H. R., 30th Cong., 1st sess., pp. 49-50; Chase, *Polk Administration*, pp. 117-118.

38 Ex. Doc. 60, H. R., 30th Cong., 1st sess., pp. 90-91, 107-109, 116, 120.

39 Same, pp. 53-78.

40 McCormac, *James K. Polk*, pp. 690-694; Quaife (ed.), *Polk's Diary*, I, 70-71; Nevins (ed.), *Polk*, pp. 18-19; Pub. Doc. 1, Sen., 29th Cong., 1st sess., pp. 14-15.

41 Quaife (ed.), *Polk's Diary*, I, 396-399; Nevins (ed.), *Polk*, pp. 91-92.

42 Almonte's dispatch of March 15, 1844, quoted in Rives, *U. S. and Mexico*, II, 243-244.

CHAPTER 2

"War Exists"

A T ten o'clock in the morning of March 8, 1846, the United States
forces started their advance to the Rio Grande. Colonel David
Twiggs's regiment of dragoons and Major Ringgold's battery
of "flying artillery" led the way, to be followed on successive days by
the three brigades of infantry, marching one day apart. Finally, on the
eleventh, General Taylor and his headquarters moved, and the camp
on the Nueces, after seven months of occupancy, was deserted.

Preparations for moving had been going on in a rather leisurely
way since February 3, when General Taylor received his orders to advance to the boundary claimed by Texas. During the three weeks
required to reconnoiter possible routes to the new base, and during
two more weeks of preparation, arrangements were made for the
movement of the sick, the heavy baggage and the surplus supplies
back to St. Joseph's Island for transshipment, under naval escort
furnished by Commodore Conner, to the new base down the coast.

The new base selected was Point Isabel, on the mainland opposite
the southern tip of long, narrow Padre Vallin Island which lies just
off the coast. The point was reached from the sea through an inlet
between Padre and Santiago islands, known as the Brazos Santiago,
which is to say the Arms of Saint James. "The Brazos," as the whole
port area came to be called, was so shallow that almost everything had
to be lightered in from ships standing outside the inlet. Even so, it
was more usable as a port than the mouth of the Rio Grande nine miles
to the southwest, which was obstructed by a bar of mud deposited by
the rolling river as it met the sea.

Part of the preparations for the march had consisted of sending
pacific messages to the Mexican authorities and inhabitants. These had
been sent informally through the mule traders from Matamoros, who

visited the camp at Corpus Christi, and through the reconnaissance parties sent forward and also more formally in General Taylor's Orders No. 30, issued to the United States troops as the march started. This order was translated into the Spanish tongue and copies were sent forward to Matamoros, Camargo and Mier, the principal towns along the south bank of the Rio Grande. Mexicans living on the north bank of the river were assured that they would be secure in their civil and religious rights, and that what the army needed would be purchased at fair prices.[1]

The march of Taylor's forces was westward from Corpus Christi some thirty miles, and then southwest toward the Rio Grande, or, as it was frequently called in those days, the Bravo. Some of the soldiers had been at Corpus Christi more than seven months, almost all of them as much as four months, and, as was—and is—the way of soldiers, they were ready to move on. They moved through a way which was brightened by "great abundance" of brilliant and gorgeous wild flowers, and enlivened by great flocks and flights of game, large and small, furred and feathered. The marching feet of the little army plodded through muck soils and clay soils, but mostly they plowed through a dry, powdery dust which aggravated a thirst which the scarce and scarcely potable surface waters along the way did little to slake. And regardless of the soils under foot, the sun, already at summer strength in that low latitude, blazed down on faces and necks too little protected by a uniform cap designed for service in a less actinic climate. "The sun," one soldier correspondent wrote, "streamed upon us like a living fire."

The prevalent sunburn is responsible for one of the best glimpses we have of the sort of appeal which General Taylor had for his soldiers, and subsequently for the people of the United States. Lieutenant Samuel G. French, who despite his New Jersey birth and rearing was to become a major general of the Army of the Confederate States, suffered from sunburn. To alleviate the situation he acquired and wore a huge sombrero of the country, for which violation of uniform regulations, he was assured by his comrades, he would surely suffer when "Old Zack" caught up with him. As the general, who had left Corpus Christi last, passed toward the head of the column, he overtook and camped with the brigade with which young French's battery was marching. The lieutenant under the big hat spied the old general "in front of his tent sitting on a camp stool eating breakfast. His table was the lid of the mess chest. His nose was white from the peeling of the skin, and his lips raw. As I came up he saluted me with: 'Good morning, lieutenant; sensible man to wear a hat.' "2

The general was not one to stickle on the niceties of uniform, being himself, from all accounts, a person most unmilitary in his outward appearance. But of non-uniform raiment he must have had an extraordinary wardrobe, judging from the variety of his nondescript garments described by various writers—a blue-checked gingham coat, a "dusty green coat," an "old brown coat," a linen roundabout, a linen waistcoat, linen trousers, attakapas pantaloons, a "common soldier's light blue overalls," blue trousers without any braid, even a "frightful pair of trousers," a "broad-brimmed straw hat," a "big Mexican straw hat," or an "old oil cloth cap." Only twice in all his long stay in the Texas and Mexican lowlands does anyone record his appearance in uniform. Once was at Corpus Christi upon the occasion of a formal review which had to be called off because of the feud over the relative rank of Colonel David E. Twiggs and Brevet Brigadier General William J. Worth. The other time was at the Brazos, when the general put on his regimentals to meet Commodore Conner, the naval commander who was reported to be a precisionist in such matters—while the commodore showed up in undress, in deference to the general's well-known distaste for military trappings!3

On March 19, eleven days and approximately 130 miles out from Corpus Christi, the advance cavalry and the first brigade of infantry encamped near the Arroyo Colorado. The crossing of this considerable salt lagoon, it was believed, might be opposed. Captain Joseph K. F. Mansfield of the Engineer Corps—the same who, as Major General Mansfield, United States Volunteers, was to yield his life on the bloody banks of a little Maryland creek, the Antietam—went forward to reconnoiter a crossing. On the banks of the lagoon he received word from a party of Mexican officers that they had been ordered to fire if the crossing were attempted. The message was reinforced by the sound of numerous bugles blowing the assembly at various points beyond the arroyo, and by a copy of the sonorous proclamation by General Francisco Mejía, commanding the Mexican forces at Matamoros. In the proclamation the United States was charged with dissimulation, fraud and the basest treachery. Recalling the repulse on the banks of the Panuco of the Spanish attempt at reconquest of Mexico, the address promised that in like fashion the banks of the Bravo would "witness the ignominy of the proud sons of the north, and its

deep waters serve as the sepulchre of those who dare to approach it."
The appeal of the proclamation may have been somewhat chilled in
the minds of those to whom it was addressed, however, by its closing
exhortation to "oppose our naked breasts to the rifles of the hunters of
the Mississippi."

To message and proclamation, General Taylor's laconic reply was
that he would immediately cross the stream, and would open fire if
opposed. His forces moved up to the arroyo; the engineers were set
to work to cut down the twenty-foot banks to facilitate crossing; batteries were posted to cover the advance. Four light companies were
told off to lead the way, under command of Captain Charles F. Smith
of the artillery. This Captain Smith, who was thus called to lead the
first advance against what was thought to be a hostile force, was to be
heard of more and more in the war which was fast coming on. And
in another war to come, as Major General Smith, U.S.V., he would
play a great, but little remembered, part in making possible the train
of events that led to Union victory. His self-denying willingness to
serve wholeheartedly under men who were his juniors in age, experience, reputation and regular rank, his alertness at Fort Donelson, his
skillful management of the movement up the Tennessee River to the
encampment on the field of Shiloh—all these were essential to the
early victories of U. S. Grant which carried him forward to the highest
command. But before the victories were won, C. F. Smith would die
from blood poisoning resulting from a shin skinned on the thwart of
a Tennessee River skiff.

With the eyes of the army upon them, Captain Smith's four companies followed General Worth and his staff on a dash down the bank,
splashed their way through the armpit depth of the lagoon and scrambled up the opposite bank, to find the small parties of Mexican cavalry
which had been cleverly disposed to suggest the presence of a larger
force well away on their retreat toward the main body at the Bravo.[4]

Crossing over, General Taylor waited for the rest of his force and
his baggage train of 300 wagons—about one wagon for each ten soldiers—to come up, before resuming the advance on the twenty-third.
"The character of the country entirely changed this side of the Colorado," Captain Henry reported in his diary, "the land is much richer
and the country more picturesque." Fresh-water ponds along the line
of march were covered with ducks and plover "so tame that you could
hardly drive them away," while the brush was alive with "hares, called
jackass rabbits," whose speed was "wonderful." The army had en-

tered the region which, more than half a century later, was to become the fabulously fertile garden spot known to Texans simply as "The Valley."

With forces closed up and marching in four parallel columns so disposed that they could go into action promptly if need be, Taylor made fifteen miles on the twenty-third. On the next morning he struck the road connecting Point Isabel and Matamoros, and divided his force. Worth, with the infantry brigades, turned right toward Matamoros, eighteen miles away. Taylor, with the cavalry and the wagon train, marched ten miles to the left, to Point Isabel.

Approaching the little port that was to be his new base, the general was served with a communication from the prefect of the northern district of Tamaulipas, protesting that occupation of territory which "never belonged to the insurgent province" of Texas but to the state of Tamaulipas meant that "hostilities have been openly commenced." At the same time, the little hamlet at Point Isabel, known to the Mexicans as the Fronton de Santa Isabela, was burned by order of the port captain, an act which Taylor regarded as "a decided evidence of hostility."

Informing the bearer of the prefect's dispatch that he "would answer it when opposite Matamoros," Taylor kept on his march to Point Isabel. Within three hours after his arrival, the supply ships reached the Brazos, under escort of two brigs-of-war and a revenue cutter, and the work of landing supplies and preparing and strengthening the base began.

Meanwhile, Worth advanced with the infantry to the plains about Palo Alto, some eight miles from Matamoros, and there awaited the arrival of the commanding general and of supplies. On the fourth day, Taylor came up and before noon of March 28, the United States forces stood upon the bank of the Rio Bravo, opposite Matamoros, with "colors flying and music playing."[5]

While the engineers were putting up a flagpole for raising the Stars and Stripes, General Taylor sent his second-in-command, Worth, across the river to interview the Mexican command. Worth was met by the courtly General de la Vega, the Mexican second-in-command, in an interview conducted under difficulties, with Worth's English translated into French by a United States officer, whose French in turn had to be translated into Spanish for de la Vega. Even without the language difficulty it would have been too much to expect any great results from an interview, and none were had in fact.

The attitude of the Mexicans, Worth reported, was "decidedly hostile," whereupon Taylor reported to Washington that since the militia of Texas were so far away "that we cannot depend upon their aid," recruits were needed to restore the strength of his regular regiments.

This strength, during the long months on the Nueces, had declined through sickness, detachments and expiration of enlistments, and now on the Rio Grande it was beginning to suffer from desertions. "Efforts are continually making to entice our men to desert," Taylor reported on April 6, "and, I regret to say, have met with considerable success." Four men had been drowned, up to that time, while attempting to swim the river and two had been shot by pickets, but despite such deterrents about thirty men made their way across into the Mexican lines, to form the nucleus of what was to become the San Patricio Battalion of United States deserters in the Mexican army. Many of those who thus left the United States forces were not natives or citizens of the country but were foreigners enlisted as soldiers in a time when the life of a soldier was hard and monotonous and army discipline harsh and rigid. Flogging was still permitted and such punishments as bucking and gagging were not uncommon.[6]

Some of the officers, moreover, were setting no very high standard of steadfastness. A brigade commander was relieved of his command and put in arrest for "neglect of duty and being 'tight,' " and General Worth departed for the United States in a huff with intent to resign because the President ruled that his rank of brevet brigadier general did not entitle him, in the absence of special assignment to duty in that rank, to command over David E. Twiggs, his senior as a colonel in the regular line of the army.[7] While high officers were thus embroiled over the meaning and effect of rank by brevet, the Mexicans were plying the soldiers of foreign birth, "English and Irish . . . French, Germans, Poles and individuals of other nations," with proclamations and inducements starting at 320 acres of land for a private, to come across the lines.[8] And it was not quite as if they were being asked to desert to the enemy in time of war, for as yet there was no recognized war and was not to be for yet another month.

During that month both sides continued their preparations, still at a leisurely pace, and at the same time continued their interested observation of each other. Work and drill were plainly visible across the separating river, while "when the sun was declining" the regimental bands of both sides would play their best airs. The "female population" of Matamoros, according to one young United States officer, would "assemble to see and to be seen, and listen to the music" on the northern bank "playing 'Yankee Doodle' because it made a loud noise, the 'Star Spangled Banner' because it waved over us, 'Hail Columbia' because it was inspiriting, and the sweetest airs from the operas for the beautiful senoritas with the rebozas." The United States officers and soldiers who lined the northern bank of the river to "enjoy the scene before them" found "delight in the exquisite music of the fine bands" on the Mexican side, "surpassing anything ever heard from a military band."[9]

But along with afternoon concerts and promenades, work went ahead on fortifications. On the day after Taylor appeared, the Mexicans began the construction of a sizable sandbag work, Fort Paredes, covering the main ferry of Las Anacuitas, with other smaller works above and below. Five days later, the United States engineers broke ground on their side of the river for a bastioned fieldwork, Fort Texas, large enough for several hundred men.

Even before work began on the fort, Taylor was notified by General Mejía that, without in any way conceding the right of United States troops to be anywhere in Texas, their further advance to the bank of the Bravo was regarded by Mexico as a "positive declaration of war" and the "opening of hostilities by invading troops."

A salute of twenty-one guns on the south bank announced, on April 11, the arrival of a new Mexican commander, General Pedro de Ampudia, a supporter of Paredes in his pronunciamento for the Presidency, who had come with some 2,000 additional troops to relieve Mejía. General Ampudia made his arrival known by serving upon Taylor peremptory notice to "break up your camp and retire to the other bank of the Nueces River" within twenty-four hours. Otherwise, he warned, "arms and arms alone must decide the question."

General Ampudia's notice, coming three days after Taylor had received word of the final rejection of the Slidell mission, both brought the possibility of open hostilities nearer and also, by its emphasis upon the Nueces line, narrowed the issue in a sense from the whole of Texas to the strip between the rivers Nueces and Bravo.

Taylor's immediate and inevitable reply to Ampudia's peremptory notice was that his instructions did not permit him to "retrograde" from his position, and that there he stayed. In view of the tenor of the Mexican note he went further and instituted a naval blockade of the mouth of the Rio Grande, which up to that time had been open to

Mexican navigation. Two ships bearing supplies for Matamoros were warned off by United States naval forces, leading to still another exchange of notes between the two commanders, more positive and pointed than before.

The day before Ampudia's arrival, the chief quartermaster of the United States forces, Colonel Trueman Cross, left camp by himself and did not return. A week later, Lieutenant Theodric Porter led out a party hoping to find some trace of him. On the nineteenth, soldiers began straggling in with stories of a surprise fight in a rain storm, in which the lieutenant and several of his men were killed. It was one of the ironies of the war which was fast approaching that Lieutenant Porter's father, as the first commander of the Navy of Mexico, had assisted in raising the Spanish blockade of the coast of the young republic, and that his brother, the future Admiral David Dixon Porter, had started his naval career as a Mexican midshipman.

On April 24, General Mariano Arista arrived to replace Ampudia in command. This third Mexican commander at Matamoros within a month was a tall, sandy-haired, red-whiskered, freckle-faced soldier who in his young manhood had lived for some years in Cincinnati and in later life was to become President of the Republic of Mexico. Upon the day of his arrival he set about to carry out the orders he brought with him from the Minister of War, dated April 4, to attack. To Taylor he sent a communication "conceived in courteous terms, but saying that he considered hostilities commenced, and should prosecute them," to which Taylor replied that he had "refrained from any act which could possibly be interpreted into hostility" and that if there should be hostilities, "the responsibility must rest with them who actually commence them."

On the same day that he dispatched his note, Arista sent a force of 1,600 cavalry under General Anastasio Torrejon—a native of Pensacola—to cross the river above Matamoros.

That evening, hearing reports of the crossing, Taylor sent out a reconnoitering party of sixty-three dragoons under Captain Seth Thornton. On the next day, the twenty-fifth, the party was led, or decoyed, into a corral at the Carricitos ranch, and there surrounded and attacked. Eleven were killed, others wounded and the remainder, with few exceptions, captured. Among the captives was the unfortunate Captain Thornton, who was to meet death in battle in the Valley of Mexico, and his second-in-command, Captain William J. Hardee, who survived the war to become the adapter from the French of the text on infantry tactics used by both armies in the great war of the sixties, in which he himself was to be distinguished as a lieutenant general, C.S.A., commanding a corps of the Army of Tennessee.

At reveille on April 26, the Mexican guide who had accompanied the Thornton party made his way into camp with news of its ambushing and destruction. Before noon the story was confirmed by a wounded dragoon sent in on a cart by General Torrejon, with a courteous note to the effect that he was without hospital facilities to care properly for the wounded but that the other officers and men were held as prisoners of war. The wounded man could give only a confused account of what had happened but it was clear that this was no affair of rancheros or irregulars, such as the ambush of Colonel Cross and of Lieutenant Porter's party.

On that day, April 26, 1846, General Taylor reported to Washington that "hostilities may now be considered as commenced." At the same time, acting under the authority extended to him when he first moved into Texas, he called directly upon the governor of that state for four regiments of volunteers, two of horse and two of foot, and upon the governor of Louisiana for four regiments of foot, a total "auxiliary force of nearly 5,000 men, which will be required to prosecute the war with energy, and carry it, as it should be, into the enemy's country."[10]

On May 9, not knowing of the events which had taken place on the border two weeks before, the Cabinet met in Washington. Around the table were James Buchanan of Pennsylvania, Secretary of State, who was disposed to approach public issues with one eye on how they affected his ambition of becoming President, to be realized ten years later; Robert J. Walker of Mississippi, Secretary of the Treasury, more skillful and successful in dealing with the nation's finances than with his own; William Learned Marcy, former governor of New York, Secretary of War, ponderous perhaps in his mental processes but clear in his thinking and a shrewd and solid citizen withal; George Bancroft, historian and Boston Brahmin, Secretary of the Navy and founder of the Naval Academy at Annapolis; John Y. Mason, college mate of the President at the University of North Carolina, Attorney General, in which post he had also served under President Tyler; and Cave Johnson of Tennessee, Postmaster General and staunch friend and sagacious political counselor of the President.

At the head of the Cabinet table sat President Polk, a man whom contemporary partisanship and posthumous parroting combined to write down as small, "mendacious," at the best "mediocre." And yet few administrations have achieved for the United States so much that no one would now undo. The long-vexed Oregon question was settled. An independent United States Treasury was soundly established. Annexation of Texas was consummated. California and the Southwest were brought into the Union. The Monroe Doctrine was significantly broadened into the "Polk Doctrine" that "no future European colony or dominion shall with our consent be planted or established on any part of the North American continent."

There is no single Presidential administration in United States history with a more impressive and complete record of accomplishment— and in all these accomplishments Polk himself played a major part. Indeed, as M. M. Quaife put it, the accomplishments would not have been possible had Polk "been lacking in the qualities of leadership essential to the occupant of the presidential chair." This "stern, rigid, precise, purposeful man in the White House," as Professor Andrew Cunningham McLaughlin described him, ". . . saw clearly along the line he intended to follow and took a hard, firm grasp of things that were near at hand." But he was not brilliant in the sense that the great triumvirate in the Senate were brilliant. He had not Webster's legal profundity or oratorical power, nor Clay's persuasive magnetism, nor Calhoun's almost mystical power to grip the imagination of his followers. He did not arouse enthusiasm but he did get things done, partly by his dogged and determined will, partly by his unremitting industry—he was away from the seat of government only twice during a four-year term—and partly by his solid sense and his knowledge of the processes and workings of government. This practical knowledge he had gained in a service of seven terms in the House of Representatives, in one of which he was chairman of the Ways and Means Committee and in two, Speaker of the House, and in his one term as governor of Tennessee. Contributing to Polk's extraordinary record of accomplishment may have been the fact that he was not a candidate for re-election or even renomination. He came to the White House while still under fifty, the youngest President up to that time, and might well have sought a more extended career, but in his letter accepting the nomination of the Baltimore convention, he made a one-term pledge to which he adhered as a "fixed and unalterable resolution," even when besought by party leaders to accept a renomination.[11]

When Polk was nominated by the Democrats in 1844 as the first convention dark horse, the fashion among the Whigs was to ask derisively, "Who is James K. Polk?" From that time on, political partisanship and abolitionist agitation combined to depict him as small and insignificant, cold and crafty, devious and mendacious. Even in his own party, Thomas H. Benton, whose *Thirty Years' View* afforded material which affected the views of two generations of writers, became bitterly antagonistic to Polk after the latter approved in part disciplinary action against Benton's son-in-law, Frémont. Polk, in no position to challenge actively this picture of himself during his Presidency and the pendency of the war, died less than four months after his term of office ended—and for two generations the history of his administration was written, in large measure, by its opponents; by those who followed, directly or indirectly, the acid-etched views of John Quincy Adams' *Memoirs;* or at best by those who were not fully informed of the thoughts, acts and purposes of "this silent President."

Polk left a diary, however, which is as complete a record as has ever been kept of four years in the White House. Unfortunately, it was not until 1910, more than sixty years after his death, that the diary was published. With its publication, shedding light into dark places and showing the other side of accepted pictures, there began a re-evaluation which has shown Polk in his truer stature. M. M. Quaife, who edited the diary, found that "whatever Polk lacked in brilliancy was fully compensated by solid staying qualities of another sort." Allan Nevins, editor of selections from the diary, described Polk as a "truthful, high-minded leader" whose record was "impressive." Eugene Irving McCormac found him to be "a constructive statesman and unusually able executive and a sound patriot." Justin H. Smith, for whom Polk's personality had no charm, termed him "Polk the Mediocre," and yet, he said, "he was mediocre only as compared with great standards."[12]

Such was the President who sat at the head of the Cabinet table at its meeting on May 9, 1846. To him, John Slidell had reported, on the day before, upon his return from the fruitless mission to Mexico. This report the President communicated to the Cabinet and, as he had done before, discussed with them the question of putting the whole situation before Congress in a comprehensive message, which would outline the status of unpaid awards for claims, the repeated and continued threats of hostilities over the annexation of Texas, the dispute over the boundary, and finally the rejection of the Slidell mission, sent, as was supposed, on an undertaking by the Mexican Government to receive a representative in an effort to clear up all such questions in controversy.

President Polk's feeling was that relations with Mexico "could not be permitted to remain" in this unsatisfactory condition. The United States was not yet entirely out of danger of war with Great Britain over the Oregon question, however, and neither the President nor his Cabinet was ready to advise war with Mexico. In their minds, the occupation of the Texas frontier was not an act of war but such an occupation of an area in dispute prior to and pending negotiation as, for example, John Quincy Adams had proposed for the southern portion of the Oregon country as lately as January 1846.[13] Measures of peaceful occupation of the strip south of the Nueces, such as naming Corpus Christi a United States port of entry, and making the territory around it an internal-revenue collection district, had been enacted by Congress with the acquiesence of both Whigs and Democrats. The Nueces, in fact, had not at that time attained to the importance which it afterward assumed as the boundary between justified defense and unjustified aggression.

So, on the afternoon of May 9, even as the bearer of Taylor's dispatch neared Washington, the Cabinet decided once more to delay decisive action on the Mexican question, at least until the following Tuesday.[14]

At six that evening—it was a Saturday—Taylor's dispatch of April 26 was delivered. By 7:30 the Cabinet had been reassembled. By ten it had recommended war measures and adjourned. That night, the President started on his war message. The next day, Sunday, he worked both before and after church, methodically marshaling his facts with their supporting documents and his recommendations, while the village capital seethed with excitement and the White House was thronged with Congressional callers, some of whom were already quite willing to recommend themselves for high command in the new army to be raised. As the President wrote and conferred with chairmen of Congressional committees and Cabinet members, confidential clerks were borrowed from the War and Navy departments to transcribe copies to go to the Capitol.[15]

At noon on Monday, May 11, tense, crowded Houses of Congress heard the message—"Mexico . . . has shed American blood upon the American soil. . . . War exists, and . . . exists by the act of Mexico herself."[16]

The House of Representatives acted promptly and decisively. Before the day closed, a bill had been passed 174 to 14, declaring that "by the act of the Republic of Mexico, a state of war exists between that government and the United States," authorizing the President to accept 50,000 volunteers, and appropriating $10,000,000 for war purposes.

The next morning the bill went across to the Senate. There it was opposed in debate by a few Whigs, Southern as well as Northern, and by John C. Calhoun, leader of Southern separatist sentiment. It was objected that the preamble declaring that war existed was not correct since "according to the sense of our Constitution" there could be no war without action by Congress. On final passage on the afternoon of the twelfth, however, only two senators voted against the war measure, preamble and all, with forty for it. That evening the House accepted inconsequential amendments which the Senate had made, and at one o'clock the next afternoon, May 13, the President signed the bill.[17]

But already, even before and quite regardless of Congressional action—as the next dispatches from the Rio Grande were to show—battle had been joined and war did indeed, and beyond all question, exist.

---

[1] Ex. Doc. 60, H. R., 30th Cong., 1st sess., pp. 116-119; Henry, *Campaign Sketches*, pp. 52, 53.

[2] Henry, *Campaign Sketches*, pp. 53-58; Kirby Smith, *To Mexico*, pp. 22-28; French, *Two Wars*, pp. 42, 43.

[3] *The American Flag* (Matamoros), Vol. L, No. 17, July 27, 1846; Rives, *U. S. and Mexico*, II, 147; Grant, U. S., *Personal Memoirs of U. S. Grant* (New York, 1885), I, 100-102; Parker, Capt. William Harwar, *Recollections of a Naval Officer* (New York, 1883), p. 53; Claiborne, J. F. H., *Life and Correspondence of John A. Quitman* (New York, 1860), I, 288; Engelmann, Otto B., "The Second Illinois in the Mexican War," *Journal of Illinois State Historical Society* (Springfield), XXVI (1933-1934), 438.

[4] Ex. Doc. 60, H. R., 30th Cong., 1st sess., pp. 123-128; Henry, *Campaign Sketches*, pp. 59-60.

[5] Ex. Doc. 60, H. R., 30th Cong., 1st sess., pp. 129-132; Henry, *Campaign Sketches*, pp. 61-67; Doubleday, Rhoda Van Bibber Tanner (ed.), *Journals of Major Philip Norbourne Barbour . . . And His Wife . . .* (New York, 1936), p. 17; Kirby Smith, *To Mexico*, pp. 33, 34.

[6] Ex. Doc. 60, H. R., 30th Cong., 1st sess., pp. 132-138, 302, 303; Croffut (ed.), *Fifty Years*, p. 221; Doubleday (ed.), *Journals*, pp. 28-32. Severity of army punishment was fully matched in the navy. Punishment returns for naval vessels show that on some of the larger ships floggings averaged almost one a day. Most of the floggings were "with the cat" or multiple lashes, or "with the colt," a knot in the single lash. The number of lashes inflicted varied, the usual number being a dozen or less, but as high as seventy-five were reported. Ex. Doc. 26, 31st Cong., 1st sess., pp. 1-80.

[7] Doubleday (ed.), *Journals*, pp. 31, 32, 36; Henry, *Campaign Sketches*, p. 71; Croffut (ed.), *Fifty Years*, pp. 204-206, 220, 221; Meade, *Life and Letters*, I, 87, 88; Quaife (ed.), *Polk's Diary*, I, 284, 285. General Worth's trip to the United States

caused him to miss the opening battles of the war. When he heard of them he withdrew his resignation and hastened to the front.

8 Ex. Doc. 60, H. R., 30th Cong., 1st sess., pp. 303-304; Henry, *Campaign Sketches*, pp. 72-73.

9 Doubleday (ed.), *Journals*, p. 26; French, *Two Wars*, p. 45; Kirby Smith, *To Mexico*, p. 34.

10 Ex. Doc. 60, H. R., 30th Cong., 1st sess., pp. 138-148, 290-292, 1203-1206; Henry, *Campaign Sketches*, pp. 73-83; Kirby Smith, *To Mexico*, pp. 38-40; Doubleday (ed.), *Journals*, pp. 45-46.

11 Quaife (ed.), *Polk's Diary*, I, xiv, xv, xxx; III, 318-321; Nevins (ed.), *Polk*, pp. 94, 298-299; McCormac, *James K. Polk*, p. 258.

12 McCormac, *James K. Polk*, p. 725; Nevins, Allan, *Ordeal of the Union* (New York, 1947), I, 228; Smith, *War with Mexico*, I, 129; Quaife (ed.), *Polk's Diary*, I, xiii, xxviii.

13 *Congressional Globe*, 29th Cong., 1st sess., pp. 127, 128 (January 2, 1846).

14 Quaife (ed.), *Polk's Diary*, I, 384-385; Nevins (ed.), *Polk*, pp. 81-82.

15 Quaife (ed.), *Polk's Diary*, I, 386-390; Nevins (ed.), *Polk*, pp. 82-86.

16 Ex. Doc. 60, H. R., 30th Cong., 1st sess., pp. 4-10.

17 Smith, *War with Mexico*, I, 181-183, 190.

Corpus Christi.

CHAPTER 3

Battles on the Rio Grande

"HOSTILITIES may now be considered as commenced," General Taylor reported on April 26, but during the first week they were not, on the United States side, very active hostilities. The general knew from the Thornton affair that a Mexican force was across the river above him, but, as he reported, he "was ignorant to a great degree of its movements" and in the "unfinished state" of his fortifications did not feel that he "could prudently attempt any enterprise against this force for several days." During those days, while Taylor "hastened operations on the field work," Torrejon's force passed clear around him, crossed the road to the base at Point Isabel and took up a position on the river ten or twelve miles below, to cover the crossing of the rest of the Mexican army.[1]

General Arista had come to Matamoros with personal instructions from President Paredes, in a letter of April 18, to take the initiative in hostilities.[2] The initiative which he had taken on the twenty-fourth, he was keeping. On April 30, the main Mexican force began crossing the Rio Grande at Longoreño, below Matamoros. On the afternoon of the next day, while Arista was struggling to finish his crossing with insufficient ferriage, word came to Taylor that communication with his base at Point Isabel was under threat. Orders were quickly issued, tents hastily struck, wagons packed, and at half past three in the afternoon, the United States forces started on a hurried night march through the chapparal toward the Point. Left behind in Fort Texas, under command of Major Jacob Brown, were the sick, the women attached to each unit in those days as laundresses and a small garrison—the Seventh Infantry, the foot artillery of Captain Allan Lowd, and the 6-pounder field battery of Lieutenant Braxton Bragg.

The army made a fatiguing forced march of eighteen miles that evening, followed by a chill and cheerless midnight bivouac without fires, and toward noon of the next day reached the base at Point Isabel.

General Arista, meanwhile, disappointed that the delay in crossing the river had kept him from cutting off the United States forces in what seemed to the Mexicans to have been a hasty and inglorious retreat, took position where he might certainly intercept Taylor on his return. And while waiting for Taylor to come back, or perhaps to hasten his return, he sent Ampudia, his second-in-command, to invest Fort Texas.

From Point Isabel, Taylor reported to Washington that he "proposed remaining here, if not necessarily called back to the river, until the arrival of some ordnance supplies and perhaps recruits from New Orleans." But within a few hours of the writing of the report, there came the dull boom of cannon from the direction of Matamoros, starting at five in the morning of May 3 and continuing at intervals throughout the day. Knowing that the little garrison left behind was under attack, "the camp was wild with excitement," and, according to Captain Henry, orders were issued for a return march to start at 1:00 P.M. If there were such orders, however, they were countermanded and the army was put to work with pick and shovel to strengthen the defenses at the base. Meanwhile, Captain Samuel H. Walker of the Texas Rangers was sent to open communication with the fort on the river. "Though not at all solicitous in regard to the safety of our fort," General Taylor wrote, "I was anxious to hear from Major Brown."[3]

Captain Walker, with four volunteer companions, made his perilous way into the fort on the night of the third, and out again the next night, bearing a dispatch from Brown that all was well with the garrison. In fact, in the long-range artillery bombardment to which the fort was subjected on the first two days only one man had been killed. On the morning of the fifth the investment of the fort was completed, with Mexican forces occupying Taylor's old camping grounds and firing into the earthwork at shorter range. On the sixth Major Brown received the wound from which he was to die three days later, to be remembered in the renaming of the position he had defended as Fort Brown, and later in the name of the Texas city of Brownsville.

That afternoon, the fort was served with a summons to surrender. Captain Edgar Hawkins, in command, did not read Spanish and the phrasing of the demand was rather beyond the range of his interpreter's scanty knowledge of the language. "The exact purport of

your despatch I cannot feel confident that I understand, as my interpreter is not skilled in your language," Captain Hawkins courteously
replied, "but if I have understood you correctly, my reply is that I
must respectfully decline to surrender." Whereupon the garrison continued its work of cutting up its tents to make sand bags, to be used in
repairing the damage done by the shell falling in the fort, and settled
down to the anxious business of standing siege.[4]

On the same day, May 6, the recruits from New Orleans reached
Point Isabel, and Commodore Conner's Home Squadron, which had
been lying off Vera Cruz, rounded to off the Brazos. On the next day
Commodore Conner sent ashore 500 bluejackets and marines, under
Captain Gregory of the frigate *Raritan*. The new arrivals, both the
recruits and the men of the fleet, were detailed to garrison the works
at the base, while Taylor, listening to the "occasional guns heard in
the direction of Matamoros which showed that everything was right
in that quarter," wrote to the War Department that he "would march
this day." And, he added characteristically, "if the enemy oppose my
march, in whatever force, I shall fight him."[5]
The march did not start until three in the afternoon, and the column
made but five or six miles that day, being burdened with a baggage
and supply train of more than 200 wagons which Taylor insisted on
bringing with him, rather than leaving them at the base to be sent for
after the battle which was anticipated. In this matter of logistics, as in
many another matter of strategy and tactics, some of Taylor's more
studious officers doubted his technical proficiency. But no man of the
2,200 who followed him out of Point Isabel doubted his dauntless will
or his grip on the loyalties of his troops. And as for the troops, they
trusted the plain, indomitable old general at their head, while everybody, of all ranks, was eager to have at the Mexicans, and to get it
done while the army was still wholly "regular" and neither diluted
with nor assisted by volunteers. The Mexicans, Captain Philip Barbour wrote his wife, "*must* be driven back across the Rio Bravo before
the arrival of volunteers, or the Army is *disgraced.*"[6]
The idea that there could possibly be any other result seems not to
have occurred to the general or his troops, when it was announced that
if the enemy was still in position on the road to Matamoros the general
would "give him battle," in which it was "enjoined upon the battalions of infantry that their main dependence must be in the bayonet."[7]

Twelve miles more the United States troops marched on the morning of May 8. Meanwhile, learning of their approach, Arista had called back to himself the force with which Ampudia was investing the fort. From the Tanques of Ramireño, where Arista had encamped to secure a sufficient supply of water, he advanced on the morning of the eighth to a position a little beyond the edge of the woods skirting the plain of Palo Alto—"Tall Timber."

Through shimmering noonday heat waves, the two bodies of troops sighted each other across the level plain, at a distance of two miles or so. Arista's men were in position, drawn up across the road that led southwestward to the river crossings at Matamoros. Taylor halted, waiting for his encumbering wagon train to close up, and then moved on for another mile or so, to within less than a mile of the Mexicans. There he halted once more for the purpose of watering horses and men. Arms were stacked, and "every man was made to go to the pond, half of each regiment at a time, and fill his canteen." Refreshed, the troops formed in battle order to the right and left of the road, and resumed the advance.

Meanwhile, General Arista rode across the front of his forces, exhorting them to battle and receiving from them the encouragement of tossing banners and shouted vivas. About the same time, two horsemen rode forward from the United States lines to within a hundred yards of the Mexicans, where they dismounted, calmly surveyed the lines to discover whether artillery might be hidden by the long prairie grass, mounted, and returned to report. The intrepid observers were Lieutenant Jacob Blake of the Topographical Engineers, whose distinguished service was to be noted in the next day's dispatches after he was dead of an accidental shot from his own pistol, and Lloyd Tilghman, who in 1862, as a brigadier general, C.S.A., was to have the painful duty of surrendering Fort Henry to another lieutenant then on the field of Palo Alto, U. S. Grant, and within the year after that was to meet death fighting in Mississippi against troops of the same commander.

At three o'clock in the afternoon, when the forces were no more than half a mile apart, the Mexican artillery opened. Taylor's advancing line halted, and his three batteries of artillery, placed in the intervals between infantry units, wheeled into action. On the right was the battery of Major Samuel Ringgold, on the left, that of Captain James Duncan—fine light field batteries, both. In the center were two heavy 18-pounders which had been dragged from Point Isabel by ten

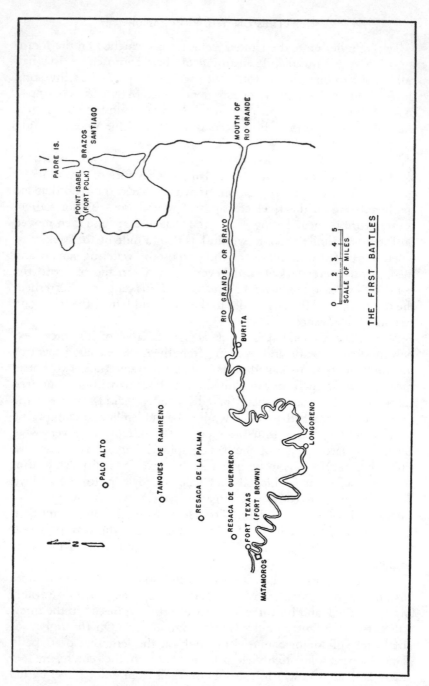

THE FIRST BATTLES

SCALE OF MILES
0 1 2 3 4 5

PADRE IS.
POINT ISABEL
(FORT POLK)
BRAZOS SANTIAGO
MOUTH OF RIO GRANDE
RIO GRANDE OR BRAVO
BURITA
LONGORENO
RESACA DE GUERRERO
FORT TEXAS
(FORT BROWN)
MATAMOROS
RESACA DE LA PALMA
TANQUES DE RAMIRENO
PALO ALTO

N

yoke of oxen to each gun. From all three units there burst a fire so rapid, so well directed and so destructive, that there was no need for the United States infantry to depend on the bayonet, and no opportunity for effective countermeasures on the part of the Mexicans.

The most ambitious effort at attack was on the Mexican left, where Torrejon and a thousand or so of his lancers, with two guns, were thrown around and against Taylor's right flank. The flank regiments, first the Fifth Infantry and then the Third, formed in squares and beat off the charge with the fire of their muskets, while Lieutenant Randolph Ridgeley, with a section of Ringgold's battery, swept into action on the run, unlimbered, and opened on the Mexican guns before they could fire a shot.

One interested observer, Lieutenant U. S. Grant of the Fourth, noted that most of "the infantry stood at order arms as spectators, watching the effect of our shots upon the enemy, and watching his shots so as to step out of their way," as the Mexican solid shot ricocheted and rolled through the tall grass.

And yet, though they could not advance, and though the charges of their lancers were thrown back by the steady infantry squares, even as the unexpected cannonade plowed great gaps in their ranks the Mexican troops stood firm with a "constancy," reported Taylor, which was "the theme of comment and admiration."

In the course of the first hour's firing, a wad from one of Duncan's guns set fire to the waist-high, dry grass which covered this part of the field. The breeze from the Gulf swept fire and smoke toward the Mexican line, until the cloud between the two armies was so dense that for an hour all but the most desultory firing was suspended. Under cover of this screen of smoke and flame, and during the lull in the firing, Taylor advanced his right, changing direction through some 35 degrees. Arista, too, changed direction of his line, withdrawing his left and throwing his right forward, so that the relative position of the lines was not greatly changed.

After the change of front, Duncan's battery swung out to the left, under cover of the smoke, and opened upon the right of the Mexican line with an enfilading fire, unexpected and destructive. The blow was too much but still there was no break or rout. The troops fell back as darkness was approaching, but in such good order that no one on the United States side could be quite sure that the field of Palo Alto had been surely won.

This, of course, was the time for the United States infantry to come in with the bayonet and turn the retreat into a rout or a roundup. But darkness was approaching, and there was that train of wagons which could not be exposed to the possibility of capture or cavalry raid. So as the Mexicans fell back to the edge of the woods, Taylor's forces went into bivouac and began to count losses, while the surgeons went at their bloody tasks. The losses of the victors were only nine killed and forty-four wounded, but there lay on the field, also, the Mexican dead and most of their wounded, not less than 250 in all. "The surgeon's saw was going the livelong night," as searching parties brought in the wounded of both sides, impartially.[8]

Of the United States officers killed, the most distinguished was Major Ringgold. He had done as much as anyone to bring the field-artillery arm to the degree of proficiency which converted the anticipated battle of bayonets into what Taylor was to call in his dispatch of the next day, quite properly, the "cannonade of yesterday."

To Major John Munroe and his garrison back at Point Isabel, twenty or more miles away, and to the officers and men just landed from the navy, the sound of the cannon battle came clearly. When the sound did not move on toward the river, apprehension began. When darkness fell, and no word came back, apprehension changed to anxiety. Toward midnight, a camp follower made his way into the camp with ghastly stories of a stricken field, from which he himself had barely escaped with his life. The young men of the naval detachment, hearing the story, were wild to march out, darkness and all, to go to the rescue of the army. Commodore Conner, however, took a more cautious and more practical view of the matter, and forbade a night march to the rescue by sailors who were acquainted neither with the terrain to be covered nor the tactics to be used. And so it was that the affair of the next day, May 9, was likewise strictly a regular army "show," with neither volunteer nor naval collaboration. "It is a glorious fact for the army," Captain Ephraim Kirby Smith exulted to his wife, "that there were no volunteers with us."[9]

This battle of May 9, known variously by the names of the Resaca de la Palma, across which the United States attack was launched, and the Resaca de Guerrero, behind which Arista's forces made their stand, was to be quite different from the cannonade of Palo Alto. It was not fought in an open plain, suitable for the use of the guns, but in an area of dense and thickety chapparal, broken with the resacas, or remnants of beds in which the river had formerly wound its way through the alluvial plain. These abandoned river beds formed either sunken lagoons or dry depressions, favorable to an occupying and defending force.

The actual withdrawal of the Mexicans from the field of Palo Alto did not get under way until sunup of the ninth, and even then there was much question on the United States side as to whether the retreat was genuine or feigned. The uncertainty of the situation was such that some of the senior officers requested a council of war to consider what ought to be done next. At the council, according to reports which leaked out, seven of the ten present favored either withdrawing to the Point or, at best, entrenching the camp at Palo Alto and awaiting reinforcements. But Taylor was of a different mind, and it was Taylor's will which counted. The order was forward.

Most of the morning was spent arranging for the protection of the embarrassing wagon train. Its position was entrenched, and heavy guns mounted. A regiment of dismounted artillerymen were detailed to guard it, reducing the striking force of the army to a bare 1,700 men. Only then, toward noon, did it become possible to go forward and find out what had become of the force which Arista had drawn back into the chapparal.

Captains George A. McCall and Charles F. Smith—both future major generals of the Union Army—were sent forward with infantry detachments. It was three o'clock in the afternoon when reports came back that the enemy had been found and his position developed. Arista had drawn up his force so as to take advantage of the protection afforded by the Resaca de Guerrero which curved across the road, with its concave side facing the United States forces. The curving wings of the position were protected by a virtually impenetrable growth of thorny brush. Only where the road to Matamoros crossed the depression, in the center, was there a slight clearing, offering some opportunity for approach and assault.

The battle was to be fought hand to hand, with regimental lines broken and platoons and small parties pushing ahead through the thorny brush. There was even the "singular spectacle" of Ringgold's battery of horse artillery, now under Lieutenant Ridgely, pushed forward along the road by hand, to draw the fire of the Mexican batteries and of their infantry unseen in the thickets, and answering it by firing at the smoke, all without the usual cover and support of infantry.

On both sides men fought with the utmost bravery but there was a difference. The United States forces believed in their commander, who coolly moved forward as the battle advanced, and were confident of victory. The Mexican troops, shaken by the terrible cannonading of the day before, were dismayed by rumors of treachery in the high command. General Arista knew nothing of the rumors, attributed by some Mexican authorities to jealous supporters of his rival and second-in-command, Ampudia. Indeed, he knew little of the fight, discounting reports that a battle was impending and insisting that the advance was a mere skirmish. Throughout the engagement he remained in his tent, immersed in paper work.

While the infantry hacked and fought their way through the brush, Captain Charles May was ordered to charge down the road with his company of dragoons and take a particularly troublesome Mexican battery on the far side of the Resaca. As he advanced May found that the Mexican guns were more strongly emplaced than had been realized. Halting, he rode back to where Taylor sat nonchalantly on Old Whitey, one leg hooked over the pommel of his saddle, and asked for further instructions.

"Charge, Captain! Charge, *nolens volens*" were his new orders.

May, with his long black beard streaming in the wind, dashed forward with his dragoons. As he reached the advanced position where the stubborn Ridgeley and his gunners were hanging on, Ridgeley hailed him.

"Hold on a minute, Charley, till I draw their fire!" he called.

May hesitated until the Mexican battery and its supporting troops had emptied their pieces at Ridgeley, and then dashed forward, to and across the Resaca—dry where the road crossed it—and into, over and beyond the Mexican guns. Before the hard-bitted dragoon horses could be stopped, turned round and brought back to the Mexican battery, the cannoneers had retaken their position. The squad or two left with May were handled roughly as they came back through the reoccupied battery, and the guns were left in Mexican hands.

"Take those guns, and by God keep them!" roared the old general, as he sent in the Eighth Infantry and part of the Fifth to do the job— which they did.

All this while, United States troops in platoons and small parties were working their way through the brush and around the horns of the crescent of the Resaca. In the center, Ridgeley's gunners followed the infantry to turn the captured Mexican cannon upon their retreating owners. The Mexican wings began to break, to crumble, and finally, late in the afternoon, gave way with a rush. General Arista himself barely escaped, leaving behind his "portfolios, writing desk, canopy, and other baggage," including "several pieces of massive plate," and the papers on which he had been so engrossed while the battle raged.

As the whole of the Mexicans broke for the river, three or four miles to the rear, the United States units which had not been engaged swung into hot pursuit, while the garrison at Fort Brown, which had sustained itself through 160 hours of siege and bombardment, took the routed army under a flanking fire as it streamed past. To losses on the battlefield, officially reported as 262 killed, 355 wounded and 185 missing, there were added losses by drowning, as the fleeing soldiers plunged into the rolling current of the Bravo. Taylor's loss of thirty-nine killed, eighty-two wounded, was heavier than on the day before but still was but a fraction—not more than one sixth—of the loss of the Mexicans.[10]

On that night—it was Saturday, May 9—two men were writing, 2,000 miles apart. In Washington, President Polk was starting his war message to Congress. In "Camp 3 miles from Matamoros, 10 P.M.," General Taylor was writing the terse narrative of the day. "The enemy has recrossed the river," he reported, "and I am sure will not again molest us on this bank."[11]

---

1 Ex. Doc. 60, H. R., 30th Cong., 1st sess., pp. 288-289.

2 Ex. Doc. 4, H. R., 29th Cong., 2nd sess., p. 16; Smith, *War with Mexico*, I, 155, 458.

3 Ex. Doc. 60, H. R., 30th Cong., 1st sess., pp. 289, 292-293; Pub. Doc. 388, Sen., 29th Cong., 2nd sess., pp. 31-37; Henry, *Campaign Sketches*, 86-89.

4 Henry, *Campaign Sketches*, pp. 89, 103-104; Kirby Smith, *To Mexico*, pp. 44-45; Ex. Doc. 60, H. R., 30th Cong., 1st sess., p. 299; Ex. Doc. 388, Sen., 29th Cong., 2nd sess., pp. 31-37.

5 Ex. Doc. 60, H. R., 30th Cong., 1st sess., p. 294; Conner, Philip Syng Physick, *The Home Squadron Under Commodore Conner in the War with Mexico* (privately printed, 1896), p. 8; Parker, *Recollections*, p. 50; Ex. Doc. 30, H. R., 30th Cong., 2nd sess., pp. 1161, 1162.

6 Doubleday (ed.), *Journals*, p. 47.

7 Ex. Doc. 60, H. R., 30th Cong., 1st sess., p. 487; Henry, *Campaign Sketches*, p. 89.

8 Taylor's report of the Battle of Palo Alto is published in Pub. Doc. 388, Sen., 29th Cong., 1st sess., pp. 2-6, 13-23. Other sources include Ex. Doc. 60, H. R., 30th Cong., 1st sess., pp. 295-296, 1102-1106; Meade, *Life and Letters* (New York, 1913), I, 79, 80; Henry *Campaign Sketches*, pp. 90-92, 95; French, *Two Wars*, pp. 49-50; Kirby Smith, *To Mexico*, pp. 45-49; Grant, *Memoirs*, I, 93-96; Doubleday (ed.), *Journals*, pp. 53-57; Ramsey (ed.), *The Other Side*, pp. 39-49; Ripley, R. S., *The War with Mexico* (New York, 1849), I, 116-123; Wilcox, Cadmus M., *History of the Mexican War* (Washington, 1892), pp. 48-58; Rives, *U. S. and Mexico*, II, 144-151; Smith, *War with Mexico*, I, 162-169.

9 Parker, *Recollections*, pp. 51-52; Kirby Smith, *To Mexico*, p. 53.

10 The story of the battle at the Resaca is developed in Taylor's report, Pub. Doc. 388, Sen., 29th Cong., 1st sess., pp. 6-37, and Ex. Doc. 60, H. R., 30th Cong., 1st sess., pp. 295-296, 301, 1104-1106; and in Ramsey (ed.), *The Other Side*, pp. 50-56;

Kirby Smith, *To Mexico*, pp. 49-53; French, *Two Wars*, 51-54; Henry, *Campaign Sketches*, pp. 94-100; Doubleday (ed.), *Journals*, pp. 57-61; Grant, *Memoirs*, pp. 96-99; Wilcox, *Mexican War*, pp. 58-67; Ripley, *War with Mexico*, I, 123-129; Stevens, Isaac, *Campaigns of the Rio Grande and of Mexico* (New York, 1851), p. 20; Rives, *U. S. and Mexico*, II, 152-156; Smith, *War with Mexico*, I, 169-175. One of Lieutenant Meade's letters to his wife was written on a sheet of General Arista's personal stationery, captured with his papers. Meade, *Life and Letters*, I, 102.

[11] Ex. Doc. 60, H. R., 30th Cong., 1st sess., pp. 295-296; Quaife (ed.), *Polk's Diary*, I, 387; Nevins (ed.), *Polk*, p. 84.

Soldiers Drinking.

CHAPTER 4

"Paying for Time!"

THE victories of Palo Alto and Resaca de la Palma, as one soldier diarist noted with pride, had been won solely by the "army proper."[1] And, he might have added, they were the work of the peacetime army, with peacetime allowances of transportation, supplies, equipment of all sorts. For it was not until after war started and battles had been fought that the government at Washington, or for that matter the command on the Rio Grande, undertook any real and definite preparation for hostilities.

General Taylor had asked on April 26 for additions to his force "to carry the war, as it should be, into the enemy's country."[2] But he had not suggested just where or how that was to be done, and Washington was much in the dark both as to the geography of the region into which the war was to be carried, and as to the general's requirements of equipment, supplies and especially transportation, with which the carrying was to be done.

All that was really known in faraway Washington in those early and anxious days was that Taylor with about 3,000 United States regulars was encamped opposite Matamoros, with his base at a region vaguely known as the Brazos, and that he was supposedly in grave danger of attack by overwhelming numbers. Preparations were driven forward, therefore, with something of the sense of urgency of organizing a rescue party, as well as an invading army.

Congress voted $10,000,000 promptly, on May 13, and authorized 50,000 volunteers, of whom 20,000 were to be raised at once. With the exception of regiments from Georgia and Texas and one battalion from Maryland and the District of Columbia combined, all the first calls for troops were to be made on states in the Mississippi Valley. Volunteers were to be enlisted "to serve for the period of twelve months or to the end of the war"—the latter date being, in the minds

65

of most, the earlier. The regular regiments were to be filled to authorized strength by bringing their companies up from a theoretical sixty-
four—the actual number was below fifty—to 100 men. A new regiment of mounted rifles, originally proposed for the protection of the
growing body of emigrants crossing the plains to the Oregon country, was to be added to the army, and a special company of sappers,
miners and pontoniers was to be organized.

Within a day or two after the enactment of the war bill, messages
were on the way to Commodore David Conner, commanding the
Home Squadron, to blockade the Gulf Coast ports of Mexico, and to
Commodore John D. Sloat, commanding the squadron in the Pacific,
to blockade the ports on that coast, to take and hold possession of San
Francisco Bay, to "conciliate the confidence of the people in California . . . towards the government of the United States," and to "encourage [them] to neutrality, self-government, and friendship."[3]

At the same time, orders went forward to Colonel Stephen W.
Kearny, commanding the post at Fort Leavenworth on the far Missouri River frontier, to call on the governor of Missouri for troops to
reinforce his regiment of dragoons, and with the combined forces to
march across the plains and mountains to Santa Fe—orders which,
before the end of the month of May, were to be so extended as to
send the expedition on to California as soon as New Mexico was se-
curely occupied.[4]

Running through all this rush of preparation there was the question
of command. The administration was Democratic. The general in
chief of the army, Winfield Scott, was a Whig. He was not only a
Whig, which in itself was sufficiently objectionable in that day of
narrow and intense partisanship, but in 1840 and again in 1844 he
had been an active aspirant for the nomination of that party for the
Presidency of the United States. His first wide military reputation,
like that of Presidents Jackson and Harrison, had been made in the
time of the second war against Great Britain, in which he rose to the
rank of brigadier general by the time he was twenty-eight. He had
served in the army ever since, with distinction. He was brilliant and
versatile, probably the army's most extensive student of military affairs and, with his six feet four inches of well-turned figure, almost
certainly its most magnificent presence. He was devoted to duty, in-
dustrious, capable—but he was an active and politically ambitious
Whig.

There was small choice, however, for President Polk. The next in rank of the army was the aging and flighty Major General Edmund Pendleton Gaines, whose quarrels with his superiors and his brother officers had enlivened army circles for a generation, and to whom no one would have thought of entrusting the command. And the third in rank, Brigadier General John E. Wool, a sound and qualified soldier—he had been Inspector General of the Army for twenty-five years—was quite as definitely, though not so actively, a Whig as Scott himself.

Of course, there was also Taylor, who up to this time was still only a colonel with his one-star general's rank only by brevet. Taylor was in no way disqualified by his politics because, so far as anyone knew, he had none. His years of service, starting before the War of 1812, had been spent almost entirely on the Western frontier, except for a term in Florida during the protracted war with the Seminoles—a war in which there was no glory and small credit to be won. There was a good deal of doubt as to his capacity for the command of the expedition into Mexico and, in fact, at the beginning he seems not to have been seriously considered, even by himself.

In all the circumstances, the President saw nothing for it but to name Scott as commander of the new army. Accordingly, on the afternoon of May 13, when he signed the war bill, he requested Secretary of War Marcy to call at the White House with General Scott, for a "conference in relation to the execution of the act declaring war against Mexico." General Scott presented a *projet,* as he was fond of terming such documents, for the number and disposition of the troops required. The President asked for a more complete plan, to be reported later in the day, and then offered Scott the command of the force to go into Mexico. The President confided to his diary that he "did not consider him in all respects suited," regarding him as "rather scientific and visionary in his views," but felt that "his position as commander-in-chief of the army entitled him to it if he desired." The general did desire it, and at once accepted.

On the following evening, from eight until midnight, the President, the Secretary of War and the general toiled over war plans—to which apparently neither the President, the head of the War Department nor the professional general in chief of the army had devoted any real thought during all the long months in which war had been threatening. It was agreed that "the first movement should be to march a competent force into the northern provinces and seize and hold them until peace was made." The President did not believe that as many as 20,000 men would be required, in addition to the regular army, but he kept the opinion to himself in deference to Scott's "experience in his profession," being unwilling "to take the responsibility of any failure of the campaign by refusing to grant to General Scott all he asked."[5]

On the day following, General Scott issued a memorandum to the staff departments of the army, announcing that "twenty odd thousand troops" were to be raised immediately, and that "subsistence, arms, accoutrements, ammunition and camp equipage must be thrown in advance upon the several rendezvous or points of departure." These points, tentatively listed, were river ports on the Ohio, Cumberland, Mississippi and Red rivers. The needs for transportation by water and land, and whether pack mules or wagons, or both, were required, were to be ascertained as rapidly as possible, and boats for use on the Rio Grande were to be "early provided."[6]

The general threw himself into these preparations with his usual whole-souled application, putting in fourteen hours a day at his desk. The President worked with the same concentrated attention and for similar long hours. But they did not work well together. Both were intensely anxious to get on with the job, but the general had the better conception of the immense amount of belated preparations which had to be made before any real movement forward could be undertaken. He purposed, therefore, to spend the early months of the summer pushing things forward at home, and not to go to the frontier until toward the end of the summer, to be ready for an advance in September.

On May 19, Polk received word of this plan through Secretary Marcy, and received it very coldly. His idea of the place of the commander of an expeditionary force was with the force, not in Washington. "I remarked to the Secretary of War," he wrote, "that any such delay was not to be permitted, and that General Scott must proceed very soon to his post, or that I would supersede him in the command."[7] The Secretary communicated to the general the fact of the President's dissatisfaction over delay, though not his remark about removal. About the same time, Scott learned that Marcy had recommended to the Military Committee of the Senate a provision authorizing the appointment of two new major generals and four brigadiers. "I smelt the rat," Scott wrote later, "and immediately told the Secretary that I saw the double trick, first, to supersede me, and, at the *end* of the war, say in six or eight or twelve months, disband every general who would not place Democracy above God's country."[8]

He did more. He wrote the Secretary one of the long, argumentative letters at which he fancied himself so adept, and at which in fact he was so astonishingly inept. This letter, written on May 21 and delivered to the Secretary the same day, after outlining in detail his "multitudinous and indispensable occupations," referred to the fact that he had "learned from you that much impatience is already felt, perhaps in high quarters, that I have not already put myself in route for the Rio Grande. . . ." The letter continued with the observation, "I am too old a soldier . . . not to feel the infinite importance of securing myself against danger . . . in my rear, before advancing upon the public enemy." After pages more in like vein, he concluded with a statement of his "explicit meaning—that I do not desire to place myself in the most perilous of all positions:—*a fire upon my rear, from Washington, and the fire, in front, from the Mexicans.*"[9]

"After night" of the twenty-first, Secretary Marcy sent this truly extraordinary epistle to the President. During that day, as it happened, the President had been shown an earlier letter of the general's of an almost equal indiscretion, in which he had declared that the new rifle regiment proposed for the protection of the Oregon wagon trains was "intended by western men to give commissions or rather pay, to western democrats, not an eastern man, not a graduate of the Military Academy, and certainly not a Whig, would obtain a place." That night the President noted in his diary that General Scott's "bitter hostility toward the administration is such that I could not trust him" in the command of the army in the war, "and will not do so. . . ."

In this opinion he was strengthened when he was told on the next day that Scott, Wool and Adjutant General Roger Jones—they being the three general officers then present in Washington—were working with members of Congress against the passage of the bill authorizing the appointment of additional generals. "Such conduct," the President noted, "is highly censurable. These officers are all Whigs and violent partisans, and not having the success of my administration at heart seem disposed to throw every obstacle in the way of my prosecuting the Mexican War successfully. An end must be speedily put to this state of things."[10]

Thus within less than ten days after the declaration of war there began that almost paranoiac bitterness between President and army chiefs which was to spread, in time, to the relations among the several generals themselves. The rancorous controversies which ensued did not paralyze action, but they absorbed thought, attention and energy which might far better have been reserved for the business of fighting the war.

Scott's letter to Marcy was read to the Cabinet at its meeting of May 23, resulting in the opinion that he ought not to be entrusted with the command. That evening the Southern mail brought the great news of Taylor's victories at Palo Alto and Resaca de la Palma, which was confirmed by official dispatches arriving on the twenty-fifth. On that day the Cabinet considered and approved Secretary Marcy's reply to Scott which concluded with the statement that, in all the circumstances, "the President would be wanting in his duty to the country if he were to persist in his determination of imposing upon you the command of the army in the war against Mexico," and directed the general to remain in Washington and devote his "efforts to making arrangements and preparations for the early and vigorous prosecution of hostilities against Mexico."

The Secretary's letter, most unexpectedly taking Scott at his word, was delivered to the general about 6:00 P.M. It took him so aback that he at once answered in another epistolary indiscretion, starting with the announcement that he had received the letter as he "sat down to take a hasty plate of soup" and continuing with disclaimers of intent to impute to the President—"I spoke not of the *highest quarter*"—his earlier intimation of a "fire upon my rear." The disclaimers were not effective with the President, while the "hasty plate of soup" brought upon Scott's head a perfect flood of popular ridicule. Certainly there was nothing reprehensible about being so devoted to duty as to have time for no more than such a meal, but the tone of the general's reference to it touched off the risibilities of the populace toward "Marshal Tureen."[11]

News of victories on the Rio Grande, however, brought a new possibility into the list of commanders—Taylor. On the very day the news reached Washington, "a number of leading Whigs," described as in a panic about General Scott's "hasty plate of soup," called upon the general in chief to ask "whether Taylor was a Whig or not, and whether he might not advantageously be Scott's substitute as their next Presidential candidate?" Scott gave his "backsliding Whig friends" an estimate of Taylor, "omitting (it is believed)" the opinion afterward expressed in his autobiography that the old frontier soldier was "quite ignorant, for his rank, and quite bigoted in his ignorance" and that "few men ever had a more comfortable, labor-saving contempt for learning of every kind." On the other hand, Scott believed him possessed of a "good store of common sense," even if "slow of thought," and with the "true basis of a great character: pure, uncorrupted morals, combined with indomitable courage." Then and there, Scott ruefully wrote, Taylor was "fixed as the next Whig candidate for the Presidency."[12]

Whether or not he had any intimation of such a prospective candidacy, President Polk was virtually constrained to leave the victor of Palo Alto and the Resaca in command on the Rio Grande. On the twenty-sixth, therefore, three days after the news of those battles reached Washington, after consultation with the Cabinet, the President sent to the Senate the nomination of Zachary Taylor as a major general by brevet, with assignment to duty in that rank.[13]

General Taylor, meanwhile, found himself standing on the north bank of the Rio Grande, unable to cross for lack of boats. The "salvation" of the Mexican army, according to one of its historians, "was owing to General Taylor not having made use of his victory," while the general himself wrote the War Department that "a ponton train, the necessity of which I exhibited to the department last year, would have enabled the army to cross on the evening of the battle, take this city, with all the artillery and stores of the enemy, and a great number of prisoners; in short, to destroy entirely the Mexican army."[14]

Without doubt a ponton train would have helped, but the crossing was actually made without one, although not until the ninth day after the victory at the Resaca de la Palma. The first of those days, May 10, was occupied in burying the dead of both armies, for "already," as one soldier wrote his wife, "the vultures were at their widespread feast, the wolves howling and fighting over their dreadful meal."[15]

On the eleventh there was an exchange of prisoners, with the return to the United States lines of Captains Thornton and Hardee and their men who, Taylor reported, had been "treated with great kindness by the Mexican officers." On the twelfth Taylor was at the main depot at Point Isabel on a "hasty visit" to see Commodore Conner about naval co-operation in "investing Matamoros and opening the navigation of the river," leaving Colonel Twiggs in charge of the main body of the army, under orders to attempt no aggressive move. On the fifteenth, the day after the general's return, Lieutenant Richard Graham—soon to die in the taking of Monterey—and an intrepid party of soldiers swam the river, cut out some boats from the Mexican bank, and brought them across to the north side. Two more days were spent in examining the river above Matamoros to select a point for crossing.[16]

Commodore Conner found it too risky during the next several days to put the navy's boats through the breakers crashing on the bar at the mouth of the river. On the seventeenth, however, Lieutenant Colonel Henry Wilson marched his newly arrived battalion of the First Infantry, reinforced by companies of volunteers from Mobile and New Orleans, along the sandy length of low-lying Santiago Island, waded the shallow channel of Boca Chica at its southern end, marched eight miles on the mainland to the river, found means of crossing the Rio Grande, and occupied the hamlet of Burita, lying on a slight rise of ground on the right bank of the river eight miles above its mouth. The commodore co-operated in the movement by sending in Captain Aulick with 200 men from the *Potomac* and the *Cumberland,* to arrive on the eighteenth.[17]

On the same day, as Taylor was preparing to march upstream from Fort Brown to the place selected for his crossing, General Tomas Requeña came over from Matamoros under flag of truce with proposals from Arista for an armistice. Refusing this, Taylor countered with the proposition that while he was determined to take and occupy Matamoros, "General Arista might withdraw his forces, leaving the public property of every description." Arista's answer was to have been given by midafternoon but it did not come. Instead, Arista withdrew from Matamoros at 5:00 P.M. Taylor, meanwhile, had marched four miles up the river to the point selected for crossing where at sunset word was received of the evacuation.

Early on the morning of the eighteenth the crossing started, the men using boats which had been brought back from the Mexican bank by the party of swimming soldiers. When only a few units had crossed a civil deputation appeared to surrender the city, the regular Matamoros ferries were brought into use, and by nightfall the United States Army stood on the south bank of the Rio Grande. On the following day, the nineteenth, the veteran Colonel John Garland with all the cavalry, regular and irregular, put forth in what proved to be an ineffectual pursuit of the Mexican forces in retreat.[18]

The greatest curiosity prevailed among the United States soldiers about the town at which for nearly two months they had gazed from across the river. One correspondent, who had served in the Florida war, noted that it was "much like St. Augustine, only with larger, wider streets and finer public buildings." Patrols sent through the city found that Arista had left behind some 400 of his wounded, many of them lying untended on the floors of the buildings used as hospitals. Colonel Twiggs, the military governor of the occupied city, left the civil authorities in the exercise of their ordinary functions, but carried on a vigorous search for public property left behind by the retreating army. This search turned up, among other things, a dozen wagonloads of segars belonging to the government tobacco monopoly, and therefore public property subject to seizure. Distributed among the troops, these gave every man "enough to keep him smoking two months."

The strangers from the north found much of interest and attraction in this first Mexican city they had seen. Bushrod Johnson, later to command a division of the Confederate States Army, and Philip Barbour, soon to be killed at Monterey, were struck by the lemon and citrus trees "hanging full of fruit." There was a "delicious evening climate," with fandangos for those who were interested, which was just about all whom Colonel Twiggs would permit to come in from the camps outside the town. The strolling soldier had a good chance, too, to observe through the latticed and unglazed windows of the houses flush with the streets a "great deal of beauty—some most strikingly beautiful faces." And in the afternoons, it was possible to watch the "fair ones bathing unadorned in the Rio Grande; no offense is taken by looking at them enjoying their aquatic amusements."[19]

As Taylor's forces were settling down in and around Matamoros, during the latter days of May, Arista's defeated forces were struggling through a wasteland in which food and water were lacking. The draft oxen were killed, the guns drawn by hand, and dismounted dragoons struggled along on foot carrying their precious saddles and horse furniture. Only on the twenty-eighth, after a trying march of ten days, did the remnants of Arista's army come to rest at Linares, from which point they could move either to Victoria, the capital city of the state of Tamaulipas, or to Monterey, capital of Nuevo León, as the course of the war might determine.[20]

During the same last days in May the volunteers from the United States started coming in. The three-months volunteers whom Taylor had called for from Louisiana began to arrive by sea on May 22, led by Colonel Persifor F. Smith, a judge turned into a capable soldier. On June 10, after a cross-country march, the three-months men from

Texas came in, under command of the first governor of the state, James Pinkney Henderson.

And this was but the start, for General Gaines, commanding the Western geographical division of the army, in a high flush of enthusiasm and without communicating with either Taylor or the War Department, had called on the governors of states in the Mississippi Valley for an indefinite number of thousands of volunteers for the period of six months. The governors and the volunteers responded to the call, with all the fervor of organizing a rescue party to go to the relief of the embattled Americans on the Rio Grande—but there was no warrant in law for the call or for the manner in which the troops were organized. Many of the six-months men were sent to the Rio Grande, but since few would volunteer for a longer term of service, "Gaines's Army" was sent home before serious work started—and its name became in the familiar speech of the Mississipi Valley for a generation, an accepted symbol of futility.[21]

Unaware of the flood of man power which was to descend on him, without adequate equipment, supplies and transportation, Taylor asked the War Department on May 21 for instructions. In the same dispatch he wrote that "future movements must depend in great degree on the extent to which the Rio Grande is navigable for steamboats."

A river steamboat, the *Neva*, made its way up to Matamoros on the twenty-fourth, arriving a day after requisition had been made on Colonel Hunt, the army quartermaster at New Orleans, for another boat. On the twenty-eighth, Taylor's able adjutant general, Captain W. W. S. Bliss, instructed Captain John Sanders of the Engineers to return to the United States and procure four steamboats of light draft, which could be run on the always tortuous and usually shallow Rio Grande.

From New Orleans Captain Sanders reported to the Secretary of War on June 5 that General Taylor, "with his usual close and strict economy in all public expenditures, had limited the number (of boats) to the fewest which under the most favorable circumstances, could answer his purposes. Colonel Hunt . . . thinks with me that the number should be doubled; that is, increased to eight." Without waiting for the Secretary's authorization, Captain Sanders and Colonel Hunt started on the difficult task of rounding up craft which could first stand the sea voyage from the mouth of the Mississippi to the mouth of the Rio Grande and then navigate the latter stream with its bends and shoals. By June 11, Hunt reported that he had two, and by the nineteenth, seven, purchased and chartered. Sanders had two more by the twenty-fifth, when he set out up the Mississippi and Ohio as far as Pittsburgh, boat hunting, with authorization from the War Department to buy as many as he and Lieutenant Colonel Joseph Taylor of the Quartermaster Department, and a brother of Zachary, might think necessary.

During all this while General Taylor was fuming at Matamoros. His June third field return showed that he had there and at the Brazos nearly 8,000 men, and he was, he reported, "embarrassed" by numbers. A week later he reported that he had too many volunteers—the three-months men whom he had asked for and the six-months men whom General Gaines had bestowed on him—and not enough of anything else, especially steamboats. Until they arrived, he wrote, he was "completely paralyzed" for lack of transportation, and additional numbers of volunteers were but an added embarrassment.

One source of misunderstanding and friction between the field commanders and the government at Washington throughout the war was the inescapable time lag in the transmission of reports, dispatches and information, and the return of reports of action taken. No more striking example of such chronic irritation is to be found than Taylor's correspondence at this period. He had not asked for transportation until late in May, and then had asked for it on a most modest scale. But his requisitions had far to go, and no action on them could have been prompt enough to relieve his mind of the anxiety and strain imposed on him by his isolation and his uncertainties. So it was that on June 17, less than a month after his first request for a steamboat and at a time when, had he but known it, seven were on the way to him, he complained bitterly to the War Department that he had no steamboats and no information as to the government's plan and expectations, that he was "altogether in the dark," and could account for the "extraordinary delay" in dealing with his requests only by thinking that "orders have been given by superior authority to suspend the forwarding of means of transportation from New Orleans."

Taylor's impatience, especially against the office of his old friend, Quartermaster General Thomas S. Jesup, was to grow into a festering grievance. This was particularly true after repeated suggestions that he would make a good Whig nominee for the Presidency had taken root in his mind and persuaded him to the extraordinary idea that the

President and the Secretary of War, and later the general commanding the army—"Polk, Marcy [and later Scott] and Company"—were sacrificing him and his army for reasons of political jealousy. But much of the difficulty seems to have stemmed originally from the general's reticence in reporting in season, and in advance of definitely foreseeable need, what the reasonable requirements of action in this quarter might be.

General Taylor's repeated and insistent complaint that he had not been furnished with sufficient steamboats was met by the Quartermaster General, for example, with the reasonable statement that Taylor had not asked for steamboats until after the middle of May, and then only for one boat. Subsequently, late in May, the requisition was increased to four boats. "I limited my action in the matter," Jesup reported, "to doubling the number called for by General Taylor, and authorizing a further increase, if considered necessary, by his brother and one of his agents. The number required by the General was, I believe, nearly quadrupled, ultimately, by the officers of the Quartermaster's department."[22]

But even if the general in the field had been seasonable in reporting his needs, and there had been no laxity anywhere along the line in supplying them, the operations of the force on the Rio Grande would have suffered from the almost total lack of preparation for war in the War Department. Partly this was due to lack of forethought and planning, particularly in the all-important matters of logistics. Partly it was due to the parsimony with which the army had been treated in the years leading up to the war. Thus, Taylor asked in September 1845 for a ponton train. The Quartermaster General's office referred the requisition to the engineer department, charged by the regulations with the planning and construction of military bridges. The officer in charge of the engineering department thought that since this was to be a portable bridge it might be charged against the appropriation for transportation of the army—but it turned out that there was no appropriation there, either. So it was not until the new war appropriations were made that the "Indian rubber company at Boston" was put to work making a ponton train of thirty-one rubber-covered boats, which did not reach Mexico until October, long after all need for it was past, only to become the subject of a published study on *Military Bridges with India-rubber Pontoons* by a studious young captain of Engineers, George W. Cullum.[23]

Much the same sort of thing happened with the army's wagon

trains. "An army of several thousand men," Colonel Trueman Cross, chief quartermaster with Taylor's forces, reported from Corpus Christi, "has hastened hither . . . and landed upon a desert coast, for active operations, without bringing with them, for the most part, any means of field transportation whatever." The colonel was far in advance of his time in his ideas of military field transportation, looking toward trains of wagons of "an established pattern" with interchangeable parts "so that one complete wagon might be readily made out of two or three crippled ones," manned by enlisted drivers instead of the unsatisfactory hired teamsters then used in the army. General Taylor, however, he reported as late as February 16, 1846, had not given him "a line of instructions or any order whatever" about transportation or other preparations.

It was not until after the declaration of war and the authorization of enlarged expenditures that anyone seems to have become really concerned with wagon transportation. Then the Quartermaster's Department, which had ordered a total of only 100 wagons in the fall of 1845, went to work with a rush. On May 15, 200 were ordered to be built at Philadelphia, to be followed in a matter of days by orders for 300 more at Cincinnati, 200 at Pittsburgh, 600 at Troy, New York, others at Buffalo, at Savannah and Columbus, Georgia, and still others wherever it could be learned that there was someone willing to build wagons for the government. Between Washington, Philadelphia and New York, indeed, the newly installed telegraph line was used to speed up the orders, while everywhere General Jesup was spurring on his agents to "do the best you can, and in the shortest possible time." The wagons were, in the vivid phrase used earlier by Colonel Cross, "almost taken from the stump after the troops were in the field." They "must be ready," General Jesup wrote, "cost what they may . . . send every kind of wagon that you think can be made useful with the army of occupation. It is of the utmost importance that we get as many as possible to the scene of operations in the shortest practicable time." The rush continued until, in September, the Quartermaster General was able to report that "we now have a greater number of wagons than the service requires"—though that was not the same thing as having enough when and where they were needed.[24]

The same sort of expensive improvisation in transportation was necessary at the Brazos. Ships drawing more than eight feet of water could not enter the inlet, and even those which could had to anchor close to Santiago Island, to be unloaded into lighters for transshipment of their cargoes to Point Isabel, four miles away on the mainland. From Point Isabel, or Fort Polk as the base had been designated, stores for Taylor's army had to be moved to the Rio Grande, nine miles away, either by wagon—a haul which included fording the channel of Boca Chica—or by transshipment in light-draft steamers or schooners which went outside the Brazos and around into the mouth of the Rio Grande, where there was usually five feet of water or less on the bar. Cargoes were again unloaded on the bank, a short distance inside the bar, to be reloaded on river steamers. To lessen this immense amount of handling and rehandling, General Jesup proposed in the fall of 1845 that a short railroad be built from the Brazos to the banks of the Rio Grande. Such a work, which would in all probability have been the world's first military railroad, and which according to the general's subsequent estimate would have saved the government half a million dollars, was not built, because neither the Quartermaster General nor the corps of Topographical Engineers had an appropriation which could be used for such a purpose.[25]

A government which had held its military expenditures down to a minimum found itself where, as General Jesup wrote, it must "pay for *time!*"[26]

[1] Henry, *Campaign Sketches*, p. 112.

[2] Ex. Doc. 60, H. R., 30th Cong., 1st sess., p. 288.

[3] Same, pp. 233-236, 774.

[4] Same, pp. 153-155; Ex. Doc. 4, H. R., 29th Cong., 2nd sess., p. 49.

[5] Quaife (ed.), *Polk's Diary*, I, 395-396, 400-401; Nevins (ed.), *Polk*, p. 96.

[6] Ex. Doc. 60, H. R., 30th Cong., 1st sess., p. 546.

[7] Quaife (ed.), *Polk's Diary*, I, 407-408; Nevins (ed.), *Polk*, p. 96.

[8] Elliott, Charles Winslow, *Winfield Scott, The Soldier and the Man* (New York, 1937), p. 425.

[9] Pub. Doc. 378, Sen., 29th Cong., 1st sess., pp. 5-6.

[10] Quaife (ed.), *Polk's Diary*, I, 413-418; Nevins (ed.), *Polk*, pp. 99-100.

[11] Pub. Doc. 378, Sen., 29th Cong., 1st sess., pp. 7-9, 12-13.

[12] Scott, Lt. Gen. LL. D., *Memoirs, Written By Himself* (New York, 1864), II, 381-383, 389-391.

[13] Quaife (ed.), *Polk's Diary*, I, 428-429; Nevins (ed.), *Polk*, p. 105.

[14] Ramsey (ed.), *The Other Side*, p. 56; Ex. Doc. 60, H. R., 30th Cong., 1st sess., pp. 297-298. General Taylor had suggested the possible need of "a moderate supply of pontons and ponton wagons" on Aug. 26, 1845, Doc. 60, p. 103; Pub. Doc. 1, Sen., 29th Cong., 1st sess., p. 284.

[15] Kirby Smith, *To Mexico*, p. 53.

[16] Ex. Doc. 60, H. R., 30th Cong., 1st sess., p. 297; Henry, *Campaign Sketches*, pp. 104-105; Tanner (ed.), *Journals*, pp. 61-62.

[17] Ex. Doc. 60, H. R., 30th Cong., 1st sess., p. 522; Ex. Doc. 1, H. R., 30th Cong., 2nd sess., pp. 1163, 1164; Henry, *Campaign Sketches*, p. 132. The statement is made, however, in Conner, *Home Squadron*, p. 8, that Captain Aulick's naval force from the Potomac occupied Burita before Colonel Wilson, and was "thus the first to invade Mex-

ico and there unfurl our flag." But Parker, who was a midshipman in the naval party, expresses disappointment at finding the army there upon arrival. Parker, *Recollections*, p. 56.

18 Ex. Doc. 60, H. R., 30th Cong., 1st sess., pp. 298, 300, 301; Henry, *Campaign Sketches*, pp. 106-109, 113.

19 Henry, *Campaign Sketches*, pp. 110-111, 118-119; Kirby Smith, *To Mexico*, p. 54; Tanner (ed.), *Journals*, pp. 66-70.

20 Ramsey (ed.), *The Other Side*, pp. 57-61.

21 Ex. Doc. 60, H. R., 30th Cong., 1st sess., pp. 301, 307-309; Henry, *Campaign Sketches*, p. 118; Wilcox, *Mexican War*, p. 77; Pub. Doc. 378, Sen., 29th Cong., 1st sess., pp. 19-31.

22 Ex. Doc. 60, H. R., 30th Cong., 1st sess., pp. 305, 547-561, 578, 581, 585, 586, 588-594, 609, 612, 617, 631, 636, 653, 655-658, 751-753, 763-764.

23 Ex. Doc. 60, H. R., 30th Cong., 1st sess., pp. 638-640; *The American Flag* (Matamoros, Oct. 4, 1846)—"Steamer *Neptune* is off the bar at the Brazos with the ponton train"; Gardner, Charles K., *A Dictionary of All Officers . . . in the Army of the United States . . .* (New York, 1853), p. 134, entry "Cullum."

24 Ex. Doc. 60, H. R., 30th Cong., 1st sess., pp. 576, 577, 579, 583-585, 587, 593, 595-611, 613-630, 632-637.

25 Same, pp. 571-573, 697.

26 Same, p. 605.

Drilling raw Recruits.

CHAPTER 5

Delays, Disturbances and Disorders

THE nation not only had to "pay for time," in the phrase of General Jesup, but was to find that even the most expensive improvisations could not make up for lack of planning and preparation.

The Powers of Europe were advised by diplomatic circular on May 14—the day after the war bill was enacted—that the purpose of the United States was "conquering an honorable and permanent peace"[1] but in truth there had been little thought of the steps necessary to that end, and no consideration as to where, and how, the main military effort should be made. So, while expeditions were set on foot across the plains to New Mexico and California, and naval activities were undertaken on both coasts, it was apparently accepted at first that the proper point of departure for "conquering a peace" was the Rio Grande frontier where hostilities had begun.

As early as June 8, 1846, however, Secretary of War Marcy had begun to doubt the practicability of reaching the heart of Mexico from the Rio Grande. Writing General Taylor on that day to advise him of his brevet commission as major general and his assignment in that rank to command the forces in Mexico, the Secretary raised the question whether Taylor's campaign should be "conducted with the view of striking at the city of Mexico or confined . . . to the northern provinces." If it should be determined "to penetrate far into the interior of Mexico," the Secretary asked, "how are supplies to be obtained?" And if supplies should have to be brought from the United States, he asked further, "what are the facilities and difficulties of transportation?"

In asking the views of the commander on the ground as to these fundamental questions, the civilian Secretary showed a better grasp of military realities than General Scott, the military chief of the army, who wrote Taylor on June 12 that the force under his command would soon be augmented to a total of about 23,000 men, with whom he was called on, whenever he should deem it safe to do so, to "take up lines of march beyond the Rio Grande, and press your operations toward the heart of the enemy's country. . . . The high road to the capital of Mexico will, of course, be one of those lines."

To General Scott's somewhat rhetorical instructions and Secretary Marcy's more practical inquiries, Taylor replied on July 2 with a letter to the Adjutant General, outlining the difficulties of moving inland, even up the river to Camargo, and the transportation conditions which would limit to about 6,000 men any column advancing beyond. Expressing doubt whether even so limited a force could be subsisted beyond Saltillo, the general continued:

From Camargo to the city of Mexico is a line little if any short of 1,000 miles in length. The resources of the country are, to say the best, not superabundant, and over long spaces of the route are known to be deficient. . . . I consider it impracticable to keep open so long a line of communication. It is, therefore, my opinion that our operations from this frontier should not look to the city of Mexico, but should be confined to cutting off the northern provinces—an undertaking of comparative facility and assurance of success.

Even before these views reached Washington, Secretary Marcy wrote to Taylor on July 9 that if

it should appear that the difficulties and obstacles to conducting a campaign from the Rio Grande . . . for any considerable distance into the interior of Mexico will be very great, the department will consider whether the main invasion should not ultimately take place from some other point on the coast—say Tampico . . . or Vera Cruz. . . . The distance from Vera Cruz to the city of Mexico is not more than one-third of that from the Rio Grande. . . .

On August 1, being himself still at Matamoros although the movement of his troops upriver was well along, General Taylor gave his views, as requested, on the point raised in the Secretary's letter. The question whether a "simple occupation of the frontier departments" without an expedition against the capital would be sufficient to cause the enemy to desire an end of the war, he wrote, was one for the government to determine. The question of "whether a large force can be subsisted beyond Monterey," he wrote, "must be determined by actual experiment." If there was to be another expedition, as suggested, he thought that one from Tampico was "out of the question," and as to the practicability of the Vera Cruz route, he had no opinion.[2] The general was uncommunicative, if not downright unco-operative, for to the usual distrust of the "old field soldier" for authorities at head-quarters desks, he had begun to add the darkling suspicion of an "intention . . . to break me down," and a morbid conviction that his force was to be sacrificed, "for all of which I shall be made the scape goat."[3]

But regardless of well-grounded doubts as to the practicability of an advance from the lower Rio Grande as the major effort of the war, momentum carried the movement forward—momentum, impatience and the lack of any other plan which gave more promise of conquering a peace.

The movement upriver began on June 6, with the occupation of Reynosa, sixty miles inland from Matamoros by road and twice as far by river, by a battalion of regular infantry under Lieutenant Colonel Wilson and a section of Captain Braxton Bragg's battery of artillery, commanded by a steady reliable young Virginian, Lieutenant George H. Thomas,[4] whose sturdy stand in the closing hours of the great battle of Chickamauga was to deprive his old battery commander, become General Bragg, C.S.A., of the fruits of victory. The movement to the advanced base at Camargo, however, did not really get under way for another month, and by the time the designated forces had been assembled there, ready for the advance from the river into the interior, it was nearing the end of August.

Long before this time, there were men in embarrassing plenty, but the army on the Rio Grande was learning the profound truth of the saying that it had no more of anything than it could haul. General Taylor wanted steamboats, and he wanted wagons and horses and pack mules, and harness and horseshoes and horseshoe nails, and blacksmith tools and all manner of supplies for his regulars and his short-term volunteers scattered along the lower reaches of the river and about the primitive port at the Brazos. The general wanted them more acutely than ever because, when his movement up the river should have got well under way, the Rio Grande was flowing full with a June rise which would have made it possible to push steamboats, if the army had had them, all the way up the river to Camargo—300 miles by the meanderings of a river which one soldier described as easily "out crooking the crookedest."[5]

Lack of transportation, however, was but one of the paralyzing lacks of Taylor's "torrent of volunteers." There was lack of training and lack of time in which to train. In its war act of May 13, Congress had established an enlistment period of twelve months for volunteers—a term which, as events proved, was mistakenly short—but the thousands of volunteers who first flooded Taylor's camps were enlisted in most instances for three months, and in no case for more than six, the time being counted from reporting to the several rendezvous for troops back in the states. One six-months command, however—the Texas regiment of foot which Taylor was particularly anxious to retain because they were "inured to frontier service . . . hardy, and can subsist on little"—was forwarded to Camargo. There, calling on "Old Zack" himself in the free and easy fashion of that army, a deputation of discontented soldiers found the commanding general in the act of shaving. As they started to state their grievance, he half turned and answered them, bluntly, "I suppose you want to go home. Well, I don't want anybody about me who don't want to stay. I wouldn't give one willing man for a dozen that wanted to go home," and turned back to his shaving.

The commander of the regiment was Albert Sidney Johnston, graduate of West Point, former commander of the Texas army, and a vigorous and inspiring leader. But his men did want to go home, and so voted at a regimental meeting. Colonel Johnston—who was to become the second ranking officer of the Confederate Army and was so to inspire his men at Shiloh as to lead to the widespread belief that it was only his death on that field which robbed them of victory—addressed his homesick regiment in a moving appeal, but only one man changed his vote. Johnston was "disgusted and mortified and did not scruple to tell his men so to their teeth," but nevertheless the regiment was disbanded and all except enough to make up one company, who volunteered to stay on, were sent home. Colonel Johnston himself remained to serve without rank and without pay as a staff assistant to General Taylor. "The government, therefore," Captain Henry acidly observed, "lost the services of six hundred men, for whom they have incurred the expense of clothing, subsistence, and transportation, and have not received one iota of service in return; within one hundred and fifty miles of the enemy, where the great majority of the army expected battle, they took their discharge."[6]

But before the three-months and the six-months soldiers went home, their places were being taken by the twelve-months volunteers called out under the Act of Congress of May 13, 1846. The outpouring of volunteers under this act was extraordinary. Quotas assigned to the states from which the early regiments were to be drawn were overfilled right from the start. Ohio had three regiments in camp near Cincinnati within three weeks after the requisitions reached the state, and was turning away companies which still were coming in. Lew Wallace, a young lawyer in Indianapolis, who in time was to command a division in the Union Army and still later was to win a wider fame as the author of *Ben-Hur,* recruited in three days the company of which he became second lieutenant. Three regiments of infantry were called for from Illinois and fourteen regiments volunteered. The three regiments asked for in Kentucky—one of cavalry and two of infantry—were filled so quickly, and so many more were anxious to enlist, that the governor had to stop volunteering by proclamation. One company of the Baltimore Battalion was raised, and on the train on its way to Washington, in thirty-six hours.[7]

The most extraordinary outburst of volunteering, however, came in Tennessee, the state of which Sam Houston had been governor and where Davy Crockett of the Alamo had been a congressman. The state was called on for one regiment of cavalry and two of infantry, a total of 2,800 men. More than 30,000 came forward, and none would withdraw. The companies "filled up so fast that it soon become difficult even to *purchase* a place in the ranks," while selection of the companies to be accepted into service had to be accomplished by lot. The requisition for troops was received on May 26. Organization of the First Tennessee Infantry, with William B. Campbell, who had served in the Florida fighting, as colonel, was completed by June 3. On that day the regiment's twelve companies of 1,050 men marched from camp into the city of Nashville to receive from the young ladies of the Female Academy its "Eagle Banner Blue." On the next day the regiment was on steamboats on the way to New Orleans, and a week later was presenting arms to General Gaines, standing on the porch of the St. Charles Hotel to receive the salute. During the next week the regiment was quartered in a warehouse on the riverbank. Guards were posted to keep the men in their quarters but by evasion, artifice and finesse, including the unauthorized use of officers' extra uniforms to enjoy the "free ingress, egress and regress" which went with their rank, a fair proportion of the soldiers managed to sip the juleps and cobblers of the St. Charles and the Verandah. On June 17, the command was crammed aboard three small sailing vessels for an agonizingly seasick voyage of a week to the Brazos.

On June 23, less than one month after the governor of the state had received the requisition for troops, transports bearing the regiment came to anchor some two miles off the bar. Unloading did not start until the next day, however, and was soon interrupted by a howling windstorm and torrential rain, which threatened to pile up the ships among the wrecks that already lined the shores of the islands on either side of the inlet. It was thus not until the thirtieth that the job of lightering the men and their supplies to the camps on Santiago Island was completed. Even so, a regiment had been raised, organized, to some extent equipped and transported by river steamer and ocean vessel from interior towns in Tennessee to the Mexican shore, all in the space of one month and four days from the time the requisition for troops was received by the governor of the state.[8]

Just as the War between the States was the first railroad war, the War with Mexico was the first steamboat war. The United States Navy was still largely a navy of sail, and many sailing ships were used along with steamers in transport service between New Orleans and other United States ports and the meager harbor and landing facilities at the Brazos and the mouth of the Rio Grande. Nevertheless, it was the river steamboats which brought major parts of the United States forces to their place of embarkation for the country's first major military effort across the sea, and it was these same river steamboats that made possible the line of communications up the Rio Grande to the foothills of the Sierra Madre.

The same storm that delayed the unloading of the twelve-months volunteers likewise battered and delayed the advance units of the flotilla of steamboats on their way across the Gulf from New Orleans to the Rio Grande. In the first days of July, however, they began to arrive. There were a dozen of them in the river by July 23 and half again as many more a month later. Somehow the force at Camargo grew, despite the laments of the quartermasters at the transportation task involved in "putting more than 10,000 men, with more than 4,000 animals, more than 400 miles up river."[9]

The steamboats which were the main dependence for this task were assembled almost wholly from the Western waters of the United States—the Mississippi and its tributaries, the Alabama, the Chattahoochee and the Apalachicola. Nothing that drew more than five feet of water could cross the bar at the mouth of the river, and some of the boats drew as little as eighteen inches light and no more than three and a half feet fully loaded. Most of them were underpowered for the stiff work of bucking the swift current of the river, and especially of working their way around its abrupt twists and turns. To see such a boat struggle for an hour to get around a hairpin bend, only to be swept sideways into the bank, was no uncommon sight. Nevertheless, when there was a fair boating tide in the river, as there was during the greater part of the summer of 1846, the running time from the mouth to Camargo was commonly less than a week. The deck crews and firemen of the boats were usually Mexicans, attracted by the high pay and the novelty of the work; the captains, mates and engineers were United States steamboat men. Wood, frequently green mesquite of low steaming capacity, was purchased from the inhabitants.[10]

In their camps on the lower reaches of the river, the newly arrived twelve-months volunteers had all the troubles of new soldiers in camp in an environment of strange flora and fauna—especially insects. The men "soon began to be annoyed by flies, the usual concomitant of camps, swarming in such countless numbers that it was difficult to eat without partaking of them." The mosquitoes—"night fowls" the men called them—were of such extraordinary size and ferocity that one of the Tennessee volunteers, doubtless a devotee of cockfighting, proposed that they be "crossed with game cocks to give the latter good bill hold." The breezes blowing in from the sea tempered the heat of the days, and the nights were pleasant enough as far as temperature went. Sleep, however, was murdered by mosquitoes which some of the men claimed could bite through boots! Drifting sand in the sea-island camps where the arriving troops had their first experience of Mexican camp life was so all-pervading that one volunteer complained to the regimental doctor that he had swallowed it until he "had a sandbar in my innards, upon which everything grounds, and I can't get a thing up or down."[11]

Discipline was slack in most of the commands, training was sketchy, and there was more than enough time for sheer tedium to do its work as the volunteers clamored to move upriver. They had enlisted in this war to fight, and they didn't see why the regulars should have any monopoly of that occupation. In fact, if they weren't to be allowed to fight Mexicans, they would just as lief fight regulars. Or lacking regulars, they would fight volunteers from other states, or even those from other outfits from their own states. And even if there was no fighting to be done, there were guns to shoot off, just to see if they would fire or perhaps just to hear them shoot, until one disgusted young lieutenant of the Topographical Engineers—his name was George G.

Meade and he was to be heard from seventeen years later at a place in Pennsylvania called Gettysburg—wrote that a day in his tent was more dangerous than a day in battle.

Disputed ownership of a catfish caught on the bank of the Rio Grande brought on what promised for a time to be a full-scale regimental fight between the First Ohio and the Baltimore-Washington Battalion. Men and officers of both outfits turned out with guns in hand, ball cartridges were issued, and both sides rushed to the riverbank to support the embattled claimants to the catfish. By the time the colonel of the Ohio regiment had broken his sword on some of the Baltimoreans, and the men of the two commands were in virtual line of battle, cooler heads among the officers reduced the impending battle to muttering frustration.[12]

This exuberant enthusiasm for fighting somebody, or anybody, came to its climax during the movement upriver of the First Regiment of Georgia Volunteers on the steamer *Corvette*. While loading at Burita, a member of the Kennesaw Rangers of Cobb County had called a fellow Georgian of the Irish Jasper Greens of Savannah a "d——d Irish son of a B——h," according to the Matamoros newspaper. Fighting between the two companies was the result. Peace was restored during the day but after dark, with the boat tied up at the bank and the two companies crowded on the boiler deck with only a rope stretched between them, fighting started again. Lieutenant Colonel Redd formed the other Georgia companies "and was proceeding to enforce order, when Colonel [E. D.] Baker of the [Fourth] Illinois Volunteers marched his men to the boat and demanded its surrender into his charge." Whereupon intrastate brawls were promptly forgotten for an interstate scrap. "The row, which had been momentarily checked, started anew," the newspaper reported, "and shots became more numerous than before." The affair in the dark lasted but a few minutes but at least one Georgian was killed and several were wounded on either side, including the Illinois colonel, shot in the neck. He survived his wound on the Rio Grande to die on the Potomac, in 1861, from the fire of Southern arms at the little battle of Ball's Bluff.[13]

General Taylor reported, on August 1, that his efforts to conciliate the people of the country were suffering from the volunteer troops. Indeed, as early as May 17, and while still on the north bank of the Rio Grande, he had been "pained to find himself under the necessity of issuing orders on the subject of plundering private property."

From that time forward, the general's orders displayed his "determination that the army shall not be disgraced by . . . plunder," although the repetition of the orders, especially after the arrival of more and more volunteers, is in itself evidence of lack of success in enforcing this determination. "With every exertion," the general reported, "it is impossible to control these troops [the volunteers], unaccustomed as they are to the discipline of camps, and losing in bodies the restraining sense of individual responsibility." That there were occasions, however, in which the disposition to plunder was controlled is indicated by the fact that when the Tennessee volunteers, on their way up to Camargo, "foraged a cotton field for melons" at one of the landings, they were required by their officers to pay for the melons taken.[14]

During all these weeks the regulars, the volunteers and the followers of the army were making of the lower Rio Grande something of a little America. As early as July ice was to be had at the Brazos, "sold from a Boston vessel at one dollar per pound." Wood was so scarce that cooking was done with coal brought from Ohio or Pennsylvania. Water, still brought to the sandy island from the Rio Grande, was neither "very fresh or palatable after standing in barrels"—which was partially responsible for the fact that "all kinds of liquor," to be had from the sutlers whose wares were displayed under awnings, "were at a premium."[15]

Close behind the army, and even ahead of much of it, there came business enterprises of various sorts. On June 1, less than two weeks after the occupation of Matamoros, a newspaper made its appearance there—*The Republic of the Rio Grande and Friend of the People,* printed in both English and Spanish. The editor was Hugh McLeod, West Point graduate who had resigned from the army to serve in the Texas revolution, had become adjutant general of that republic and military commander of its ill-fated expedition to Santa Fe in 1841. McLeod had as his editorial mission persuading the people of the states of Tamaulipas, Nuevo León, Coahuila and Chihuahua to an appreciation of the merits of a separate Northern Mexican federation. By July 4, however, the paper was in the hands of new owners, Fleeson, Peoples & Co., who announced in their Independence Day issue—"single copy, one bit"—that they did not "feel themselves altogether qualified to work out a republic on the Rio Grande" and so had "pulled down the colors . . . and hoisted THE AMERICAN FLAG," the name by which the paper was thereafter known during the two years of its publication.

By the time of this change, another paper had been established under the intriguing title of *The Reveille*,[16] and other lines of United States business had begun to bloom out in Matamoros. While the army still had but one steamboat in the river, a Mississippi River captain put the *Frontier* steamboat in commercial service with deck passage between Matamoros and Point Isabel at $3.00, and passage in the cabin, $10. Before midsummer merchants from the states were advertising their goods, both dry and wet, even including ice. A New Orleans daguerreotypist had opened a studio, and a watchmaker, a shop. The American Eating House, the Matamoros Lunch House, the United States Hotel and the French Restaurant were in competition with the Italian Fonda, already in existence. In the building known as Arista's headquarters Mrs. Phyllis Hamblen was operating the American Hotel. Next door "Old Dan Murphy" ran a bar and bowling alley.

The veteran Murphy's amusement enterprise was but one of several. "Grand Dress and Fandango Balls," admission $1.00, were given three nights a week at the Washington Ball Room, with its adjunct bar. The Olympic Arena was offering a "theatrical extravaganza" which included tightrope performances and Spanish dances. And early in July there landed from the steamer *Virginia* the *corps dramatique* of Mr. and Mrs. Hart, which included in its roster of actors eighteen-year-old Joseph Jefferson, the same whose *Rip Van Winkle* was afterward to delight whole generations of theatergoers.

During the summer weeks the company presented, with the help of an orchestra made up mostly of soldiers from the band of the Second Dragoons, a series of plays now long forgotten. Indeed, to judge from the account of one evening at the theater given by a Maryland volunteer, John R. Kenly, not a great deal of attention was paid to the plays at the time. "Such an audience!" wrote Kenly. "The Texas Rangers were there, pistols and knives in their belts . . . while drunken volunteers from nearly every southern State of the Union were mingled with regulars of the horse, foot, and artillery arms of the service, in a medley of wild, riotous dissipation and confusion. I do not believe that anybody ever did know what was being played that night in that theatre." Jefferson himself, writing near the close of a long career, described it as "the most motley group that ever filled a theatre."

As the summer wore on, the heat became oppressive and the Matamoros Theatre shifted its attractions to vaudeville—though not so denominated—and then, after the manager absconded with the pay roll, abandoned the losing struggle to keep open. Joe Jefferson and another member of the company, it was announced, having "given up comedy for the present, turned their attention to the sale of Cigars, Tobacco, etc." in a "very neat little store in one end of Bill Foyle's Lunch House." Mr. Jefferson's line of goods, he subsequently recalled, included pies and cakes, on which it was hard for the hungry customers to tell "which were the currants and which the flies." Mr. Foyle's establishment, as Jefferson recalled it forty-five years later, bore the name of "The Grand Spanish Saloon," and featured games of chance as well as spirituous refreshments. Contemporary announcements show that it disputed with the Resaca House the honor of having originated the "Rough and Ready," a concoction of wines and cordials offered customers after the effective date of General Taylor's order prohibiting the sale of spirits.[17]

By the time of this order Matamoros had become, according to the letters of Lieutenant George G. Meade to his wife, "a mass of grog-shops and gambling houses," with the army guardhouses "filled daily with drunken officers and men, who go to the town, get drunk and commit outrages upon the citizens"—conduct attributed solely to volunteers. The Mexican inhabitants, wrote Lieutenant Meade, appreciated the good conduct of the *"troops de ligna,"* as they called the regulars, and dreaded the *"volantarios."*

Regardless of just which elements among the invading forces were responsible, the situation was such that on August 2 the general issued his order that no more spirituous liquors were to be permitted to "enter the river or the city of Matamoros," and that none should be sold after August 15, 1846. The order applied not only to the merchants at Matamoros but also to the army sutlers, who were the 1846 version of the post exchanges of today, and to captains of steamboats, as well. It was greeted with some jibes—including a published call for a meeting of the "Friends of Temperance" to be held at "early candlelight at the house of Mr. Wm. Foyle" on the day the order became effective—and some of the American saloons had to be closed for varying seasons for its violation, but the *American Flag* editorially credited it with some decrease in the "tumult and fighting among the American inhabitants."[18]

During this period Matamoros was crowded with the short-term volunteers passing down the river on their way to home and discharge, some of whom rioted in the plaza until they were dispersed by the bayonets of the guard. Altercations and fights, some fatal, were distressingly common among the soldiers, many of whom, according to the newspaper, were to be "found lying in the street drunk all over the city," in which state they were sometimes murdered and the bodies stripped of clothing and belongings. Assaults and indignities by United States soldiers upon the Mexican population were also noted and reprehended, although the editor of the *Flag* newspaper objected vigorously to the sight of United States offenders cleaning the streets under military guard, even though an epidemic was feared in a city described as "little better than a sink hole . . . every street blocked up with filth."

But there were other and more pleasant tones in the picture. The Flying Artillery Battery which had been Ringgold's and was now Ridgeley's delighted all with its exhibition drill in the plaza. There was added to the American places of resort the novelty of a "Soda Fountain," serving drinks made of "soda water with syrups." The "swarms of dark-eyed brunettes" to be seen in front of the cathedral of a Sabbath morning drew rapt attention and rapturous remark, and the "elegance and ease with which a pretty señorita will handle and puff the delicate cigaritto" brought at least one United States observer around to approval of smoking for ladies. An impressionable *Yanqui* published a poem inscribed "to Doña Señorita María Innocenta, the Daughter of Don Rafael López de Aropoza," while another paid his sentimental respects in a column of verse "to Señorita Doña Carmelita."

There was preaching "by request" and 4,000 Testaments were received from the American Bible Society. It became "no longer a novelty to see an American lady" in Matamoros, and there was even a wedding, that of Mr. John M. Garnier of New Orleans to Miss Caroline Pruyne of St. Augustine. "Taking all things together," the editor of the *Flag* opined in true booster fashion, "Matamoros (barring the fleas) is no bad place to live in."

But while devoting its major attention to Matamoros happenings, including the movement of troops, past, present and planned, the *American Flag* was also prompt with its news of political developments, both at home and in Mexico.

As early as July 4, only a little more than two weeks after Thurlow Weed, the Whig Warwick, came out for Taylor for President, the Matamoros newspaper reported that "a large meeting has been held in Trenton, N. J., which nominated Gen. Z. Taylor as a candidate for the next Presidency, and one has been called in New York for the same object," to which item of news the paper added a note of prophecy, "The Hero of Resaca de la Palma would be hard to beat."[19]

By the end of July most of the regulars were at Camargo, and the movement of the twelve-months volunteers was under way—the Baltimore and Washington Battalion, the brigade from Ohio, two regiments each from Tennessee and Kentucky, and regiments from Georgia, Alabama and Mississippi, with other regiments left behind to garrison the base at the Brazos and the camps about Matamoros and Burita. On August 4, with his troops and his transportation in such readiness as could be achieved with the means at hand, the commanding general boarded the steamer *Whiteville* for Camargo, the first stop on a road which was not to carry him to "the heart of the enemy's country," and was not to achieve the United States' aim of "conquering a peace"—but which was to lead him to the walls of Monterey, the pass at Buena Vista and the White House in Washington.[20]

---

[1] Moore, John Bassett (ed.), *The Works of James Buchanan*, VI, 484.

[2] The correspondence of Marcy, Scott and Taylor appears in Ex. Doc. 60, H. R., 30th Cong., 1st sess., pp. 324-326, 329-331, 335, 337. Subsequently, in his *Memoirs*, General Scott stated that both he and General Taylor doubted that the Rio Grande was the right basis for offensive operations against Mexico, and that Taylor moved "against his own judgment" as a result of "extraordinary importunities from Washington, one object being to decry Scott's plea for adequate preparation, and his doubts as to the line of operations." Scott, *Memoirs*, pp. 384, 391-392. The statement is not sustained by the published correspondence.

[3] Samson, William H. (ed.), *Letters of Zachary Taylor from the Battlefields of the Mexican War*, from the collection of William K. Bixby (Rochester, 1908), letters of June 21 and June 30 to Dr. R. C. Wood, pp. 13, 19.

[4] Henry, *Campaign Sketches*, p. 117; Ex. Doc. 60, H. R., 30th Cong., 1st sess., pp. 323, 398-399.

[5] Henry, *Campaign Sketches*, p. 120; (Robinson, J. B.), *Reminiscences of a Campaign in Mexico; by a Member of "The Bloody First"* (Nashville, 1849), p. 85. The book shows no author on the title page but the preface is signed as above.

[6] Ex. Doc. 60, H. R., 30th Cong., 1st sess., pp. 321-323, 524-525; Johnston, William Preston, *The Life of Gen. Albert Sidney Johnston* (New York, 1879), pp. 135-136; Henry, *Campaign Sketches*, p. 152; Doubleday (ed.), *Journals*, p. 101.

[7] Pub. Doc. 1, Sen., 29th Cong., 2nd sess., p. 47; Smith, *War with Mexico*, I, 195, 475; "An Officer of Ohio Volunteers" (J. L. Giddings), *Sketches of the Campaign in Northern Mexico* (New York, 1853), pp. 19, 20; Kenly, John R., *Memoirs of a Maryland Volunteer* (Philadelphia, 1873), p. 19. The movement of the Baltimore Battalion from that city to Washington, on June 4, 1846, is one of the earliest, if not the earliest, movement of a body of troops in wartime on a railroad.

[8] Robinson, *Reminiscences*, pp. 59-78.

[9] Ex. Doc. 60, H. R. 30th Cong., 1st sess., pp. 612, 671-673, 677, 690-692, 694-

696, 699, 732-734; Tanner (ed.), *Journals*, p. 93. The growth of the flotilla was hindered by the loss of the *Neva*, sunk, the *Enterprise*, blown up in a boiler explosion, and the *Colonel Harney*, lost on the bar at the Brazos.

10 Ex. Doc. 60, H. R., 30th Cong., 1st sess., p. 733; Tanner (ed.), *Journals*, pp. 91-93.

11 Robinson, *Reminiscences*, p. 89; Henry, *Campaign Sketches*, p. 159; Kenly, *Memoirs*, p. 43; Siousatt, St. George L. (ed.), "Mexican War Letters of Col. William Bowen Campbell of Tennessee . . . ," *Tennessee Historical Magazine*, June 1915, pp. 137-139.

12 Meade, *Life and Letters*, I, 91; Kenly, *Memoirs*, pp. 47-51; Giddings, "An Ohio Officer," *Sketches*, p. 38.

13 *The American Flag* (Matamoros), Vol. I, No. 30; Kurtz, Wilbur G., Jr., "The First Regiment of Georgia Volunteers in the Mexican War," *Georgia Historical Quarterly*, Vol. XXVII, No. 4, pp. 14-17. Colonel Baker was a close friend of Abraham Lincoln, who named a son that died in infancy for him. He was a member of Congress when war began, and was one of those whom Polk mentioned as having called on him with a "desire to be appointed to high commands in the Army of Volunteers which their bill proposed to raise." Quaife (ed.), *Polk's Diary*, I, 388-389. He was Lincoln's predecessor in the House of Representatives. Baker removed from Illinois to California, and subsequently to Oregon. He was representing that state in the Senate in 1861 when he raised a regiment of former residents of California.

14 Ex. Doc. 60, H. R., 30th Cong., 1st sess., pp. 336, 489-490; Claiborne, J. F. H., *Life and Correspondence of John A. Quitman* (New York, 1860), I, 239-240.

15 Giddings, "An Ohio Officer," *Sketches*, pp. 30-33; Sioussat (ed.), *Campbell Letters*, p. 136.

16 Spell, Lota M., "The Anglo-Saxon Press in Mexico, 1846-1848," *American Historical Review*, Vol. XXXVIII, No. 1 (October, 1932). *The Reveille* was published by a Bostonian, Samual Bangs, who previously had published the *Gazette* at Corpus Christi while the army was encamped there.

In addition to printers and reporters who published American newspapers with the armies in Mexico, special correspondents were sent out to cover the campaigns. The best known and most successful of these correspondents were from the New Orleans papers, among them George Wilkins Kendall of the *Picayune*, James L. Freaner of the *Delta*, and Thomas B. Thorpe of the *Tropic*. They (especially Kendall) established services for handling news which were both faster and more reliable than the government's own means of communication. From New Orleans, which was the news center of the war, express riders on relays of horses, railroad trains where available, and the newly developed telegraph were used to spread the news over the United States. Among the newspapers which had special arrangements with New Orleans sources were the Baltimore *Sun*, the Philadelphia *Public Ledger*, and the New York *Herald*. Other newspapers, however, in the free and easy fashion of the time, helped themselves liberally to the fruits of this pioneer journalistic enterprise. See Bullard, F. Lauriston, *Famous War Correspondents* (Boston, 1914) and Copeland, Fayette, *Kendall of the Picayune* (Norman, 1943).

17 Kenly, *Memoirs*, pp. 43-44, 53; *The American Flag* (Matamoros), Vol. I, various dates; Jefferson, Joseph, *The Autobiography of Joseph Jefferson* (New York, 1890), pp. 67, 68, 70.

18 Ex. Doc. 60, H. R., 30th Cong., 1st sess., p. 497; *The American Flag* (Matamoros), Vol. I, various dates; Meade, *Life and Letters*, I, 91, 109-110. Liquor found in violation of the order was to be confiscated and sent to New Orleans for sale—one half of the proceeds to go to the informers and one half to the benefit of the hospital department.

19 *The American Flag* (Matamoros), July 4, 1846.

[20] Ex. Doc. 60, H. R. 30th Cong., 1st sess., pp. 496-497. Among the officers of the volunteer regiments sent forward to Camargo in July and August were men destined to play a larger part in the war of the sixties: Samuel R. Curtis, Ohio colonel, who as major general, U. S. V., was to win at Pea Ridge, or Elkhorn Tavern, the victory which held Missouri for the Union; George W. Morgan, of Ohio, who as major general, U. S. V., would defend Cumberland Gap; William B. Campbell of Tennessee, who was to become a brigadier general, U. S. V. Campbell's lieutenant colonel, Samuel R. Anderson, was to attain like rank in the Confederate Army. Benjamin F. Cheatham, a captain in the same regiment, was to become a Confederate major general, commanding a corps of the Army of Tennessee. Even the surgeon of this regiment, Dr. James W. Starnes, turned cavalryman in 1861, commanded one of Nathan Bedford Forrest's cavalry brigades, at the head of which he met death near Tullahoma, Tennessee, in 1863. Of all the officers commanding this first group of twelve-months volunteer regiments to move into the interior of Mexico, however, the one who was to achieve widest fame was Colonel Jefferson Davis of Mississippi.

The City of Matamoras.

CHAPTER 6

ENTER: Santa Anna

PUBLIC attention was fixed in the summer of 1846 on the army on the Rio Grande which had fought and won battles against seemingly insuperable odds, and which was presumed to have set its feet on the highroad to the "halls of the Montezumas"—a phrase which seems to have had the greatest appeal to the romantic taste of the times. But while this was, and was for some months to continue to be, the main military effort of the nation, it was by no means the only one.

While Taylor was accumulating the sea-borne troops and his river and land transportation for the advance from Matamoros, other troops were marching overland to rendezvous at San Antonio de Bexar for an advance across the Rio Grande at Chihuahua; an expedition was marching from the frontier post of Fort Leavenworth, directed immediately at Santa Fe and destined ultimately to reach both Chihuahua and California; naval forces in the Pacific were occupying the coastal towns of California and even penetrating as far inland as the Pueblo de Los Angeles; and other naval forces were not only covering the crossings of the Gulf by Taylor's troops and supplies but were also blockading Mexican ports from Tampico to the borders of Yucatán, which at that time was in a state of chronic rebellion from, and virtual independence of, the central government of Mexico.

The blockading duty on the Gulf Coast was arduous. With the single exception of Vera Cruz, as was noted by Lieutenant Raphael Semmes, United States Navy—better known to a later generation as "Semmes of the *Alabama*"—"there was no town on the whole Gulf Coast of Mexico, within effective cannon range of which, a sloop-of-war could approach. The maritime towns of the enemy were more effectually defended by reefs, sand-bars and shallows, than were his

95

inland towns by redoubts and intrenchments."[1] The first repulses suffered, indeed, and the first loss of a United States ship were due to these forces rather than to enemy action.

On August 6, Commodore Conner organized a gunboat expedition for the capture of Alvarado, a port some thirty miles southeast of Vera Cruz. To reach the town, the expedition had to cross the shallow bar at the mouth of the Alvarado River and go up against the rolling current. The heavier ships anchored well off the mouth of the river, while the gunboats, sailing vessels all, stood in and engaged the forts. A boat expedition was organized to go in the next morning, using sail and oars, no steamers being available. By nine o'clock, however, with the weather threatening, the commodore recalled the expedition and ordered its return to the anchorage off Vera Cruz. The bitter disappointment of the eager youngsters on the ships was not assuaged by the fact that the British frigate *Endymion,* one of the four which had captured Stephen Decatur's *President* in 1814, not only witnessed the lack of success of the United States Navy on this first of its several attempts at Alvarado, but also outsailed some of the fleet as it beat up the coast on the return to the anchorage at Anton Lizardo.[2]

This anchorage, formed by a group of low-lying islands, reefs and sunken rocks twelve miles southeast of Vera Cruz, early became the headquarters of the United States blockading squadron, but the squadron's real base was the Navy Yard at Pensacola, 900 miles distant. Not until October, however, was there any system of supply ships in operation, even for such essential items as coal for the few steamers in the squadron, or for fresh water. Throughout the summer, vessels stayed on the station until they absolutely required refitting and reprovisioning, when they sailed for Pensacola. Even there, long delays were encountered because of the inadequacy of facilities for the burden suddenly thrust upon them.

Day after day the heavier units of the squadron lay at anchor within the shelter of the reefs, while the active units on blockade patrolled their beats before the ports. Upon those stationed at Anton Lizardo, the great masonry fortress of San Juan de Ulúa, lying off Vera Cruz, exerted an almost irresistible fascination. Many, if not most, of the junior officers and the eager young midshipmen were all for showing the world that the United States Navy could take the massive pile which had for so long been the symbol of Spanish power. Back in the states were two other officers who had seen the Mexican fortress and who believed it could be taken by the navy—Commander David

Glasgow Farragut, the same who was afterward to demonstrate what could be done by ships, even of wood, against land fortifications, and who was to become the first to hold the rank of admiral in the United States Navy; and a Lieutenant David Dixon Porter, who was to work so ably with Farragut, and to succeed him as admiral. The equally bold Raphael Semmes, however, who was on blockade duty with the Home Fleet, agreed with the views of Commodore Conner and other senior officers, that while it would have been possible to take San Juan de Ulúa from the sea, its taking would not have justified the almost certain price in the loss of ships and men. Whatever practical results its taking might have produced, in the absence of an invading army to hold the position and gather the fruits of its capture, were being achieved, from day to day, by the slow and unspectacular but comparatively riskless method of blockade.[3]

Such considerations, however, did not deter Lieutenant James Parker of the brig *Somers* and a party of midshipmen and sailors from planning to cut out and capture the schooner *Creole,* lying at anchor under the guns of the fortress—in emulation, perhaps, of the Lieutenant Richard Somers for whom their ship was named, who gave his life in an effort to cut out a ship from the harbor of Tripoli in the Barbary Wars. As part of their plan, the party paid a late afternoon visit to one of the British ships of war lying under Sacrificios Island, an anchorage some three miles from San Juan de Ulúa. After dark, instead of returning to their own ship in the usual way, the daring party pulled straight in for the *Creole,* boarded her and secured the unwary crew. Hearing something of the scuffle, the sentries on the castle walls called to know the trouble. Parker, in fluent Spanish, answered that his crew were drunk and that he was having to put them in irons, and went ahead with his plans. It was discovered, however, that the wind was such that it would not carry the schooner away from its anchorage, whereupon it was fired and burned, while Parker and his party pulled safely away.

This gallant, and unauthorized, exploit delighted the fleet but embarrassed Commodore Conner, for, unknown to the cutting-out party, the comings and goings of the burned vessel were the means by which the commodore was kept in communication with secret agents on the shore—a circumstance which could not even be hinted at in the midst of the praises showered on the party for their deed in the tradition of the namesake of their ship and of Stephen Decatur himself.[4]

The first loss of a ship by the United States Navy in the war came on August 15, 1846, when the twelve-gun brig *Truxtun* went aground on a reef off the mouth of the Tuxpan River, 120 miles north of Vera Cruz, as Captain Carpender ran her in too boldly and too close. The brig soon settled on the reef and the captain and crew were surrendered, except for a party under Lieutenants Bushrod Hunter and Otway Berryman, who not only escaped in one of the brig's small boats but on the second day out captured a Mexican coasting vessel in which they completed their voyage to Anton Lizardo. Some of the guns from the sinking *Truxtun* were salvaged by the Mexicans and mounted in the forts covering the mouth of the Tuxpan River. Captain Carpender and his crew were, in time, exchanged for General de la Vega and other prisoners taken at Resaca de la Palma.[5]

Mostly, however, the blockade during the summer months of 1846 was uneventful. Time was allowed for notice of the blockade to reach the commercial nations, and be transmitted to their ships. During that time vessels arriving off the Mexican ports were merely turned back, without question of capture as blockade-runners. Their ships' stores, in fact, constituted one of the sources of supply for the United States fleet, which was able to purchase surplus items from shipmasters who had been disappointed of their plans to enter Mexican ports. The monthly British mail steamers continued to operate, also, to and from Vera Cruz and Tampico.[6]

To this general and strict blockade there was a significant individual exception. On the very day on which the blockade was ordered, May 13, there went from George Bancroft, Secretary of the Navy, to Commodore Conner, a "private and confidential" note—"If Santa Anna endeavors to enter the Mexican ports, you will allow him to pass freely."[7]

Back of this laconic instruction for a leak in the blockade was the desire of President Polk to see the government of General Paredes, which was so irreversibly committed to war with the United States, replaced with a government which might be more amenable to bringing the war to an end by diplomatic measures rather than fighting it out. This idea had been planted in the mind of the President as early as February 1846, while Taylor was still at Corpus Christi, when Colonel A. J. Atocha, Spanish-born naturalized citizen of the United States, who had been in the banking business in Mexico and was a friend of Santa Anna, called on President Polk to offer suggestions for the restoration of peaceful relations between the two countries.

"He said that Santa Anna was in favor of a treaty with the United States," the President noted in his diary on February 13, "and that in adjusting a boundary between the two countries the Del Norte should be the western Texas line, and the Colorado of the West down through the Bay of San Francisco should be the Mexican line on the north, and that Mexico should cede all east and north of these natural boundaries to the United States for a pecuniary consideration, and mentioned thirty millions of dollars as the sum." The colonel gave it, however, as Santa Anna's opinion "that the United States would never be able to treat with Mexico, without the presence of an imposing force by land and sea." Three days later, Atocha was again closeted with the President, repeating the suggestion of the earlier meeting for a cession of the country east of the Del Norte and north of a Colorado of the West—which as a matter of fact did not exist as supposed—for which $30,000,000 would be satisfactory. "I then remarked," the President noted, "that Mexico must satisfy the claims of American citizens and that if the government of Mexico had any proposition to make . . . it would be considered when made; to which Col. Atocha said no government or administration in Mexico dared make such a proposition, for if they did there would be another revolution by which they would be overthrown. He said they must appear to be forced to agree to such a proposition. . . . He said the last words which General Santa Anna said to him when he was leaving Havana a month ago was 'when you see the President, tell him to take strong measures, and such a treaty can be made and I will sustain it.' . . ."

Although Polk confided to his diary that "Col. Atocha is a person to whom I would not give my confidence. . . . I therefore heard all he said but communicated nothing to him," the seed sown by him did suggest a way in which peace might possibly be brought about. Whether as a result of that seed, or for some other reason, the President decided, as soon as war became an actuality, to open the way for Santa Anna to return to Mexico, insofar as the United States blockade was concerned.[8]

A month later, in mid-June, President Polk entrusted Commander Alexander Slidell Mackenzie, United States Navy, with a mission to Santa Anna. Mackenzie—he was a younger brother of John Slidell and had taken the additional surname "Mackenzie" at the instance of an uncle—sailed for Havana, where the exile who had sought asylum from Mexico was combining outward absorption in the heeling and handling of his gamecocks with very real and astute political planning and plotting. Mackenzie's instructions were oral but, exceeding his authority, he committed them to writing and, when he interviewed Santa Anna on July 7, delivered him a copy as a message from the President.

The substance of this message, as subsequently reported by Mackenzie to Secretary of State Buchanan, was that Polk was willing to see Santa Anna return to power and had given orders to the blockading squadron to permit his passage, and that the United States would be willing to negotiate a treaty with the government which Santa Anna might set up, if such a treaty would settle all claims and disputes as to boundaries. For transfer of territory to the United States, "ample consideration in ready money" was proposed. As a result of his interview, Mackenzie was completely convinced of the sincerity of Santa Anna in his "offers to respond with such a peace as has been described." The Mexican exile, in fact, went farther and suggested and advised naval and military moves by the United States which, in his opinion, would conduce to carrying out such a plan.[9]

Before Mackenzie's report on his interview reached Washington, the President and his Cabinet considered and acted on still another plan by which they hoped the war might be brought to an end by diplomacy rather than fighting. Waiving any question of diplomatic protocol which might arise from the fact that it was the Mexican Government which had broken off diplomatic relations in the spring of 1845, it was determined that Secretary of State Buchanan should send to the Mexican Minister of Foreign Relations a proposal that the United States would send an envoy to Mexico, or would treat with a Mexican envoy in Washington, for the purpose of making a "peace just and honorable for both parties." Such a proposal was sent on July 27, 1846, through Commodore Conner, commanding the United States squadron off Vera Cruz.[10]

Before President Polk's proposal for negotiation could reach Mexico, however, there had been another change in the government there. From January 1846, when he came into power, until June, General Paredes had ruled without benefit of Congress. On June 6, after the disaster of Resaca de la Palma and the loss of Matamoros, the Congress reconvened. Six days later General Paredes was formally elected to the Presidency which he had been holding, in actuality, for six months—and was to hold for only three weeks longer.

It was not until July 1 that Congress went through the formality of declaring war upon the United States, and granted the President its formal leave to depart from the seat of government and take personal command of the new forces which were soon to march to the north to repel invasion.

Before the expedition could march, however, there was the matter of money. The national treasury was empty, and the United States naval blockade was keeping it that way by cutting off both imports— and with them import duties—and the export of precious metals on which Mexican finances so largely depended. The government turned, therefore, to the one other possible source of revenue, and secured from the Church a loan of a million dollars.

Still the President, armed with his formal election and his official authorization to go to the armies, did not march. Indeed, confronted by a rising storm of pronunciamentos such as those he himself had inspired and directed against Herrera only a little more than half a year earlier, denounced for his suspected monarchist intentions, undermined by factional intrigues, beset by military disasters and unable to achieve any degree of domestic unity even under the cohesive pressure of a foreign war, Paredes was virtually at the end of his effort to rule Mexico.

A few troops were started north, however, and it was given out— untruthfully—that the President had gone to take command in person, leaving Vice-President Nicolás Bravo in charge as acting chief executive. On August 3, in an effort to mollify somewhat the mounting opposition, Bravo proclaimed the restoration of the Organic Bases of government as they had existed under President Herrera. It was also his intention, though not publicly announced, to bring the war to an end—a step which it was thought could be taken with the better grace by Bravo, who was not so publicly committed to a war to the bitter end.

On the same day, however, on which the return to the Organic Bases was proclaimed, word reached the capital that the garrison at Vera Cruz had pronounced for the exile in Havana. On the next night, August 4, General Mariano Salas, commanding the citadel in the capital, likewise pronounced for the old favorite of the army. Paredes, who had set out with intent to bring back the troops which had started for the north and use them to suppress the gathering storm of revolt, was himself taken prisoner by a revolting regiment and was returned to his capital, even as the half-armed supporters of Acting President Bravo were overwhelmed by the forces of General Salas.

By August 6—as General Taylor was steaming up the Rio Grande to join the forces accumulating at Camargo—the "Most Excellent Señor Mariano Salas, General-in-Chief of the Liberating Republican Army, exercising the Supreme Power" was in full command in the capital. General Salas knew, however, and everyone else knew, that he was but the forerunner of one on whom, as a Mexican writer put it, the fickle capital had "shut her gates with execrations" less than two years before. The stage was set for the return of the consummate actor whose entrances and exits had for nearly twenty years so largely determined the outer form, if not the deeper substance, of Mexican history.[11]

In the thirty-five years of his public life, Antonio López de Santa Anna had been an officer of royalist Spain and a rebel against that power; an imperialist under Iturbide and the instigator of the revolt which drove the Emperor Agustín I from the country; a successful rebel against the republican government which he had helped to set up, and the popular hero of the defeat at Tampico of the Spanish expedition of reconquest; again in revolt and then, before he was forty, President of the republic. Elected as a federalist, within little more than a year he had become, in effect, the dictator of a centralist government. Within little more than another year he had led his army into Texas, had won a siege at the Alamo, had lost a small battle and a great province at San Jacinto, and had become a prisoner of war of the Texans. On parole, he had journeyed across the United States to Washington, whence he had been returned on a United States vessel to Vera Cruz, to find himself out of power and apparently forever through with a career, either civil or military.

Two years of retirement, and once more opportunity came to him as it had at Tampico—this time from the French at Vera Cruz in the affair which came to be called the War of the Pastries. Volunteering for service, Santa Anna had the fortune to receive a wound from the cannon of a retiring landing party which resulted in the amputation of a leg. The "Hero of Tampico" was a hero once more, and within a matter of weeks was once more President *ad interim*. By 1841 he was again President in good earnest, again talking war against Texas, and soon again dictator. It was in this period of power that his amputated leg was brought from Vera Cruz and, with vast pomp and ceremony, reinterred at the capital in a magnificent mausoleum, specially constructed to receive it. After four years of rule signalized by such self-glorification and by wide and general oppressions, in December 1845 he was once more driven out of the capital. Even his amputated leg was torn from its mausoleum and dragged through the streets by the mob, while its owner was permitted to leave the country, as it was thought, forever.

Knowing that his time had come to take the stage once more, and secure in the knowledge that the blockading fleet would permit his passage, the fifty-two-year-old Santa Anna, his seventeen-year-old second wife, and their suite boarded the British steamer *Arab* in Havana harbor on the night of August 8, 1846. Toward noon of the sixteenth, the *Arab* steamed into the harbor at Vera Cruz and the ex-dictator, soon to be restored to that state, came ashore to be greeted in a carefully staged military welcome in which, however, it was noted that "not one *viva* was heard." The principal spontaneous activity, in fact, was that of a crowd of boys joyously shooting firecrackers supplied at the expense of the city.[12]

Santa Anna himself, sanguine though he was, was not certain of the reception which awaited him. His first act, therefore, was to issue from "heroic Vera Cruz," a resounding proclamation of ten long printed pages, in which he extolled his patriotism, denounced the perfidy of Herrera in proposing to deal with the United States, and that of Paredes in looking to the establishment of a monarchy under a foreign prince, and called for the holding of a national assembly to which the provisional executive should be in entire submission, with the constitution of the year 1824 to govern until the new constitutional code would be completed.

He concluded:

The slave of public opinion myself, I shall act in accordance with it . . . subjecting myself, afterward, entirely to the decisions of the constituent assembly, the organ of the sovereign will of the nation.

Mexicans! There was once a day, and my heart dilates with the remembrance, when . . . you saluted me with the enviable title of soldier of the people. Allow me again to take it, never more to be given up, and to devote myself, until death, to the defense of the liberty and independence of the republic.[13]

Having put forth this resounding appeal, the "slave of public opinion" retired to his estates, extending for miles along the National Highway between Vera Cruz and Jalapa, while those in alliance with him—Almonte, Rejón, Alvarez, Gómez Farías and his son, among others—completed the manipulation of events and public opinion necessary for his triumphal return to the capital and to power.

Among the preparations for his return, Rejón, Minister of Foreign

Relations in the provisional cabinet of Acting President Salas, dispatched on August 31 a ringing denunciation of Polk's July 27 proposal for peace negotiations, because it did not include an acknowledgment of the guilt of the United States as an aggressor, with a stern refusal to consider propositions of negotiation until the convening, on December 6, 1846, of the new Mexican Congress.[14]

This refusal, in effect, to treat for peace was received in Washington on September 15. Meanwhile, even before the reply to the July 27 peace note was started on its way from Mexico, Polk was making still another effort to pave the way for peace by negotiation. On August 4, 1846—the same day on which Paredes was ousted from office, and while Santa Anna was still in Havana—the President sent a confidential message to the Senate, asking its approval of an appropriation of $2,000,000 to be used as an advance payment for any territory acquired by treaty, following the precedent set in the case of President Jefferson and the purchase of Louisiana. Acquisition of Mexican territory, Polk believed, would be "the best mode of securing perpetual peace and good neighborhood between the two Republics." Two days later the Senate adopted by overwhelming majorities resolutions agreeing with this view and approving the appropriations asked for. Fortified with this confidential and preliminary approval by the Senate, the President presented the project to the House of Representatives, where appropriation bills must originate.

There a bill was introduced making the appropriation "for the purpose of defraying any extraordinary expenses which may be incurred in the intercourse between the United States and foreign nations," to be spent under the direction of the President. With the outstanding exception of Representative John Quincy Adams, who agreed with Polk's position, many Whig and abolitionist members of the House joined in violent and vituperative objection to the measure, imputing to the President such designs as extending the domain of slaveholding by bribery of Mexican officials.

To meet such imputations, David Wilmot, antislavery Democrat from Pennsylvania and a supporter of the measure, offered as an amendment the requirement which was to become famous as the "Wilmot Proviso," that there should never be slavery in any territory secured from Mexico. The proviso offered by Wilmot was adopted— Polk confided to his diary that he regarded it as "mischievous & foolish"—and the bill as amended passed the House on Saturday, August 8, by a vote of eighty-seven to sixty-four.

Coming up in the Senate on Monday the tenth, the last morning of the session, the bill was filibustered to death by Senator John Davis of Massachusetts—and thus ended whatever chance there might have been then to treat with any government in Mexico in an effort to restore peace without fighting out the war to its end.

Polk, bitterly criticized, was in no position to make full public defense but to his diary he confided his reasons for asking for the appropriation for what might have been called a peace offensive:

Mexico is indebted to the U. S. in a large sum, which she is unable to pay. There is also a disputed question of boundary. The two countries are now engaged in War. When peace is made the only indemnity which the U. S. can have will be a cession of territory. . . . For a suitable cession of territory we are willing to assume the debts to our own citizens & to pay an additional consideration. My information induces the belief that Mexico would be willing to settle the difficulty in this manner. No Government, however, it is believed, is strong enough to make a treaty ceding territory and long maintain power unless they could receive, at the time of making the treaty, money enough to support the army. . . . Having no doubt that I could effect an adjustment of the pending war if I had the command of $2,000,000, I felt it to be my duty to ask such an appropriation. . . .

Regardless of the validity of his reasons, however, President Polk found himself estopped from carrying out his plans by a parliamentary device in Congress, while Santa Anna, whatever his original intentions may have been, was quite as effectively blocked by well-founded fear of stirring up a popular storm which he could not possibly have weathered.[15]

While stern refusals to treat with the United States issued from the Foreign Office of the Mexican republic, the lines were being laid and the wires pulled for the return of Santa Anna to actual, though not nominal, power. On September 5 he left his estate of Encero for an entry into the pleasant little capital of the state of Vera Cruz, Jalapa. Eleven days later, on September 15, Acting President Salas rode out from the city of Mexico to meet the returning hero. A parade of tableaux escorted him as he and Gómez Farías, the old liberal leader who had accepted the ex-dictator on his profession of conversion to faith in a federal rather than a centralized government, rode together in an open carriage, passing beneath triumphal arches thrown across the streets. The man who had had to flee the city in

January of 1845 was greeted in September of 1846 as "The well-deserving of his country: the immortal savior of the Republic: the hero of Tamaulipas."

Santa Anna was too wise to seek the semblance of political power at once, or perhaps he preferred the active leadership of the campaign in the north. At any rate, he wrote Almonte, Minister of War, that he would not assume "the chief magistracy when duty calls me to the field, to fight against the enemies of the republic. I should disgrace myself, if, when called to the point of danger, I should spring to that of power."[16]

The substance, however, if not the seeming, of power was Santa Anna's. Salas was recognized for what he was, a mere *locum tenens* holding the stage until the chief actor was ready to make his entrance. Meanwhile, with the daemonic, even if spasmodic, energy which endeared Santa Anna to so many of his countrymen, he plunged into the raising of forces, the raising of money, and the organizing of an expedition to support the army in the north.

---

[1] Semmes, Lieutenant Raphael, U. S. N., *Service Afloat and Ashore During the Mexican War* (Cincinnati, 1851), p. 78.

[2] Ex. Doc. 4, H. R., 29th Cong., 2nd sess., p. 630; Conner, *Home Squadron*, pp. 25, 54, 55; Parker, *Recollections*, pp. 65-67; Semmes, *Service*, pp. 82-83.

[3] Mahan, Captain A. T., U. S. N., *Admiral Farragut* (New York, 1916), p. 95; West, Richard S., Jr., *The Second Admiral: A Life of David Dixon Porter* (New York, 1937), pp. 43-44; Parker, *Recollections*, pp. 80-81; Semmes, *Service*, pp. 76-77.

[4] Parker, *Recollections*, pp. 59-60; Conner, *Home Squadron*, p. 7.

[5] Semmes, *Service*, pp. 82-83; Conner, *Home Squadron*, p. 27; Parker, *Recollections*, p. 78.

[6] Ex. Doc. 60, H. R., 30th Cong., 1st sess., pp. 233-234, 774-775; Parker, *Recollections*, p. 58.

[7] Ex. Doc. 60, H. R., 30th Cong., 1st sess., p. 774.

[8] Quaife (ed.), *Polk's Diary*, I, 222-230; Nevins (ed.), *Polk*, pp. 50-53; Ex. Doc. 4, H. R., 29th Cong., 2nd sess., pp. 19-21.

[9] Reeves, Jesse S., *American Diplomacy Under Tyler and Polk* (Baltimore, 1907), pp. 299-307; Callcott, *Santa Anna*, pp. 228-234; Semmes, *Service*, pp. 117-118; Rives, *U. S. and Mexico*, pp. 232-236; Sears, *John Slidell*, p. 20.

[10] Pub. Doc. 107, Sen., 29th Cong., 2nd sess., pp. 2-3; Nevins (ed.), *Polk*, p. 131; Quaife (ed.), *Polk's Diary*, II, 50-51.

[11] Smith, *War with Mexico*, pp. 212-219; Ramsey (ed.), *The Other Side*, pp. 81-82.

[12] Callcott, *Santa Anna*, pp. 237-238.

[13] Ex. Doc. 60, H. R., 30th Cong., 1st sess., pp. 776-785.

[14] Ex. Doc. 4, H. R., 29th Cong., 2nd sess., p. 43; Callcott, *Santa Anna*, pp. 240-241; Rives, *U. S. and Mexico*, II, 244-246.

[15] Pub. Doc. 107, Sen., 29th Cong., 2nd sess., pp. 1-8; Quaife (ed.), *Polk's Diary*, II, 50, 51, 70-78; Nevins (ed.), *Polk*, pp. 131-132, 135-138; Rives, *U. S. and Mexico*, II, 236-240; McCormac, *James K. Polk*, pp. 441-444.

[16] Smith, *War with Mexico*, I, 222-224; Callcott, *Santa Anna*, pp. 241-243.

CHAPTER 7

The Navy Conquers California

NEITHER concentration of attention on the army on the Rio Grande, nor efforts to achieve a settlement by diplomatic negotiation, nor vain hopes for a Mexican Government more disposed to put an end to hostilities, prevented the administration in Washington from pressing to the limit of its ability active military measures against the far northern provinces of Mexico.

Most remote of these provinces from both Mexico and the United States was Alta California—a vast domain stretching for nearly a thousand almost empty miles along the coast and running back to the ranges of the Rocky Mountains. Today, it is the home of more than 10,000,000 persons but then was inhabited by only a few thousand Indians, still fewer thousands of Californians of Spanish descent, and a handful—not more than a thousand or so—of foreign merchants and venturesome settlers from other lands.

To reach California from the Mexican capital required an overland journey of weeks; from Washington, a journey of months whether overland or by sea. Recognizing this fact, and in the light of the break in diplomatic relations between the United States and Mexico in the spring of 1845, seasonable instructions had been sent to Commodore John D. Sloat, commanding the United States naval forces in the Pacific. In a letter of June 24, 1845, Secretary Bancroft had informed the faraway commander of "the earnest desire of the President . . . to avoid any act which could be construed as aggression" but instructed him that if he "should ascertain beyond a doubt that the Mexican government has declared war against us" he should "at once . . . blockade San Francisco, and blockade or occupy such other ports" as his force would permit.[1]

Sloat's instructions were renewed, and at the same time Thomas O.

Larkin, United States consul at Monterey in California, was instructed as to his course, in messages dispatched by Secretary of State Buchanan in October 1845. The messages were entrusted to Lieutenant Archibald Gillespie of the United States Marine Corps. Having memorized their contents to prevent loss or capture, the lieutenant made his way across Mexico during the time in which Paredes was overturning the Herrera government. At Mazatlán on the Pacific Coast, he saw Commodore Sloat, delivered his message orally and took passage to the Sandwich Islands. There he took ship back to California, where he arrived on April 17, 1846, six months to the day from Washington, but still three months ahead of the written orders which were making their leisurely way around the Horn and up the West coast.

At Monterey Lieutenant Gillespie completed the delivery of his memorized instructions to the officers to whom they were directed. There was, however, another officer of the United States on the Pacific Coast—Brevet Captain John Charles Frémont of the United States Topographical Engineers. Frémont had left the settlements on the Missouri River in May 1845 to continue the explorations of the Oregon country and the routes thither which, together with his vivid personality and his reportorial skill, were to bring to him popular designation as "The Pathfinder." He was accompanied by sixty-two men, armed as was necessary for any expedition that was to pass the 2,000 miles of savage wilderness between the Missouri River and the Pacific, but not enlisted as soldiers. Early in December 1845 he and his companions arrived at the station of Captain Johann August Sutter, a Swiss adventurer who had acquired from the California Government title to more than 200 square miles of land on which he had located his combined ranch and fort of "Nueva Helvetia."

Frémont was received kindly by the hospitable Sutter, as he had been when he first came across the Sierra Nevada the year before, and was furnished with animals and supplies to replace those worn out and used up in the long march. With his new supplies Frémont moved on southward into the valley of the San Joaquin, where he did some exploring and a little fighting with Indians whom he described as the "Horsethief tribes." Leaving his men in the interior, he went himself to Monterey, where he arrived toward the end of January 1846. There, permission was sought and secured from José Castro, *comandante general* of the province, for the party to winter in the unsettled interior. Stretching this permission, Frémont moved his party into the settlements near the coast, seeking, as he wrote afterward, a suitable site for a seaside home for his mother. The middle of February found the party encamped between San José and Monterey; early March found them in the Salinas Valley, only twenty-five miles from Monterey itself. There, on March 3, the Americans were served with peremptory orders from Castro to withdraw from the province.

Frémont defied the order and promptly threw himself into a posture of defense on the summit of the Pico Gavilan—"Hawk Hill"—where he built breastworks, raised the American flag, and proclaimed his intent to fight, if attacked, or to perish. To Consul Larkin at Monterey he wrote, in an exalted strain, that he and his men, if attacked, would "fight to extremity and refuse quarter, trusting to our country to avenge us." Later in the day, however, Frémont came to the conclusion that his "sense of duty did not permit him to fight," and that night—March 9—he "retired slowly and growlingly," as he wrote his wife, before a force which he estimated at "three or four hundred men and three pieces of artillery." Whereupon, with great elation at Frémont's withdrawal, Castro proclaimed to the world the great feat of driving out the freebooting invaders. Frémont made his way north to Sutter's Fort, which was reached on March 21, and thence, by slow marches and with long halts, out of California.

It was in the month after this affair of proclamations and counter-proclamations that Lieutenant Gillespie arrived at Monterey, bearing an official letter of introduction to Captain Frémont from Secretary of State Buchanan and personal letters to him from United States Senator Thomas Hart Benton of Missouri, whose daughter Jessie was Frémont's wife. After delivering his memorized instructions to Consul Larkin, Gillespie started north after Frémont, whom he overtook in Oregon on the borders of the Klamath Lake on May 9—the very day, as it chanced, of Resaca de la Palma.

Along with his letters, Gillespie delivered to Frémont some sort of instructions, the nature of which was to become a matter of controversy. Frémont himself wrote afterward that they "had for their principal object to ascertain the disposition of the California people, to conciliate their feelings in favor of the United States; and to find out, with a view to counteracting, the designs of the British Government upon that country." Such purposes were not essentially different from the injunctions laid upon Sloat and Larkin, or from the written instructions which were received later. But that night, after the rest of the party were wrapped in their blankets and asleep around

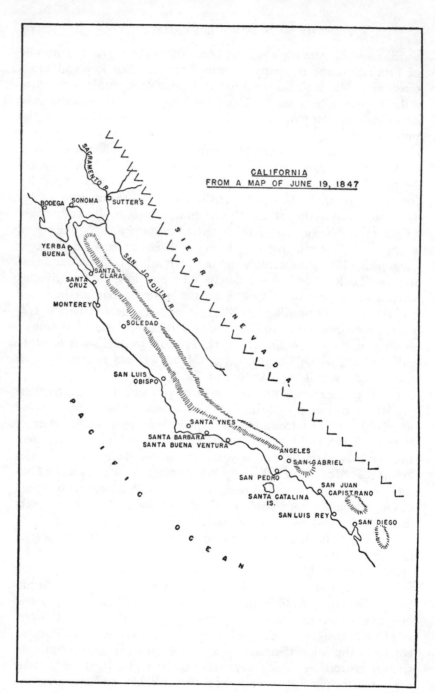

CALIFORNIA
FROM A MAP OF JUNE 19, 1847

SACRAMENTO R.

BODEGA SONOMA SUTTER'S

S'ERRA

YERBA
BUENA

SANTA
CLARA

SANTA
CRUZ

SAN JOAQUIN R.

NEVADA

MONTEREY

SOLEDAD

SAN LUIS
OBISPO

PACIFIC

SANTA YNES

SANTA BARBARA
SANTA BUENA VENTURA

ANGELES

SAN-GABRIEL

SAN PEDRO

SAN JUAN
CAPISTRANO

SANTA CATALINA
IS.

SAN LUIS REY

SAN DIEGO

OCEAN

110

the campfires, the leader sat late by the flickering firelight, reading and re-reading the letter which Gillespie had brought from Senator Benton. It was, Frémont testified, "apparently of mere friendship and family details" but it "contained passages enigmatical and obscure," the meaning of which he "studied out." As he read, and remembered "conversations and discussions . . . at Washington," it came to Frémont that under the President's "confidential instructions," as he afterward wrote, "I had my warrant" for "taking possession of California."

That night, after Frémont, resolved to return forthwith to the Sacramento, had finally fallen asleep, the Klamath Indians attacked the encampment, killed three and wounded others. The return was delayed for a few days of action and retaliation along the shores of the lake, but before the end of May Frémont, with Gillespie accompanying him, was back at Sutter's Fort.

By this time, the native Californians were in something of a state of turmoil. The revolution in Mexico which had turned Herrera out of office and brought Paredes in, back in December, had its delayed repercussions in far-off California in the late spring. Castro, the military commander, with headquarters at Monterey, came out for Paredes in April, and began to move against Governor Pío Pico, whose capital was at Los Angeles. Pico's countermove was to call a general convention of the people to meet in Santa Barbara on June 15, with the idea of proclaiming the independence of California and asking the protection of a foreign power. To await the outcome of this convention, Sir George Seymour, commanding British naval forces on that coast, sailed north from San Blas on June 14. But whatever may have been his intentions and those of Governor Pico about the Santa Barbara convention, they came to nought—for the convention itself was not held when Comandante Castro refused to permit those from the northern part of the province to attend.[2]

Meanwhile, the aging, ailing and anxious Commodore Sloat had started for California from Mazatlán, where he had been lying at anchor since November, awaiting news of the relations between his government and that of Mexico. Commodore Sloat was beset with uncertainty about a seeming difference in the two orders which had come to him. His instructions of June 1845—the only written instructions which he had received—were that he should act if and when he learned "beyond a doubt that the Mexican government has declared war against us." His instructions of October 1845, received orally through Lieutenant Gillespie as he passed through Mazatlán late in February 1846, were that he should act "in the event of actual hostilities between the Mexican government and our own." The difference in language began to assume importance in his mind as fragmentary reports came to his remote station on the west coast of Mexico.

Word of the ambush and attack upon the party of Captain Thornton—the "shedding of American blood on American soil"—came to him on May 17, a little more than three weeks after the event. Sloat's first intention was to go ahead with the execution of the orders received through Gillespie, but upon reflection he doubted if this was the same thing as the declaration of war mentioned in his formal instructions of the previous June. Two weeks later he heard reports of the battles of Palo Alto and Resaca de la Palma but the news was not confirmed. So for another week Commodore Sloat continued to hesitate, possibly because of uncertainty whether the fighting on the Rio Grande could be considered as a declaration of war. On June 7, however, he learned that the United States fleet on the Gulf side of Mexico was blockading Vera Cruz, and on the next day he sailed north to execute his orders to blockade San Francisco and such other ports as his force permitted.[3]

In June of 1846, then, American and British naval forces were converging on the California coast, Frémont's party was poised on the Sacramento, and Governor Pico and Comandante Castro were busy raising forces for a civil war over the location of the provincial capital at Monterey or Los Angeles, the custody of the customhouse and the division of the revenue. Of them all, only Sloat knew that there had been an outbreak of hostilities between the United States and Mexico, and even he was not quite sure that this constituted the "declaration of war" which was the contingency on which he was to act under his formal instructions of the year before.

There was still another force converging upon California whose commander not only knew that there had been a formal declaration of the existence of war by the United States but had been instructed not merely to blockade the California coast and perhaps occupy its ports, but to take and possess the whole of the province. This was Colonel Stephen Watts Kearny, of the First Dragoons, stationed at Fort Leavenworth on the west bank of the Missouri River in the unsettled country which was becoming known as Kansas. Colonel Kearny was ordered, on the very day war was declared, to take his own regiment and a force of Missouri volunteers, to be organized, across the plains and mountains to occupy Santa Fe, the village capital of the province of New Mexico, whose name and famed caravan trade exerted a powerful spell on the Western imagination. Before the expedition was completely organized, further, and very secret, orders went forward to Kearny, on June 3, to be prepared to march on after making secure the occupation of Santa Fe and take possession of California, where he was told he might expect to find the navy holding the seaports.[4]

First to act positively in this welter of explosive possibilities was Captain Frémont. Just why he acted, and what his intentions were, became clouded in controversy. There were those who believed that Polk was so determined to have a war for California that he constituted Frémont his agent to bring on one. Frémont himself ascribed his course to his own interpretation of certain "passages and suggestions" in the family letter from his father-in-law brought to him by Lieutenant Gillespie. But Senator Benton, strongly hostile to President Polk at the time of writing, negatived the idea of special and secret instructions, both in a Senate speech and in his *Thirty Years' View*. "Frémont had no orders from his government to commence hostilities," the Senator wrote, and—he added proudly—"acted entirely on his own responsibility."

It is difficult to believe that the President sent to a Captain of Topographical Engineers on survey and exploring duty a set of instructions which not only differed from those sent to the naval commander in the Pacific and to the government's confidential diplomatic agent in California, but which were well calculated to upset and defeat the very results which those instructions sought. A more likely cause for his course is that Frémont, a young man of impulsive imagination with a thirst for personal distinction, acted on his own responsibility and to the embarrassment of President Polk—much as the same Frémont, then become a major general of United States Volunteers, was subsequently to embarrass another President, Lincoln, by his premature and unauthorized proclamation of emancipation.

Frémont's interpretation of Senator Benton's letter was that "the time had come" to "act; discreetly but positively"—and act he did in a manner more positive than discreet. The first action was taken on June 10, when Ezekiel Merritt, described by Frémont as his "field-lieutenant among the settlers," and a dozen men from Frémont's camp seized 170 horses being driven from Sonoma toward the camp of the comandante Castro, and took them to Frémont's camp. The horses, it was believed, were to have been used by Castro to mount troops with which to raid and harry the places of the American settlers in the valley north of the Sacramento, and the seizure was to prevent such a use of them. But regardless of its motive, the act looked to the native Californians, already suspicious of the purposes of the settlers from the States who had begun to crowd into the northern valleys, uncommonly like large-scale horse stealing. One of Frémont's own men questioned the expediency of his action but a night of solitary confinement in what Frémont called a "rather dungeon-like room" infested with fleas of "indiscriminate ferocity" brought him to see the wisdom of his commander's course.

As his next "prompt precautionary measure," Frémont, still officially keeping in the background, "sent Merritt into Sonoma instructed to surprise the garrison of that place." On June 14, as Sunday dawned over Sonoma—the last and most northerly of the Mexican settlements in California, established to check the Russian advance from the north—Merritt and his party of thirty-four men seized the post, took possession of its cattle and small military supplies, and carried off as prisoners eighteen of its citizens. Among the prisoners were Mariano Vallejo, founder of the post and former *comandante general* of California, his brother Salvador, one of the pioneers of large-scale wine making in the province, and Jacob Leese, who was one of Consul Larkin's aides in the business of conciliating the Californians and who would have none of such highhanded business as the seizure of Sonoma.

While Merritt and ten of the settlers took the prisoners to Frémont at Sutter's, William B. Ide and most of the party remained at Sonoma. There, fortified by Vallejo's excellent California brandy, they raised a new flag, designed and executed by William Todd, a nephew of the Mary Todd who married a frontier lawyer named Abraham Lincoln. The flag bore the words "California Republic" and the device of a grizzly bear, which gave its name of the Bear Flag Republic to the new government that day proclaimed. The "object and desire" of proclaiming California a republic, according to Ide's letter to the nearest United States naval officer, was "to embrace the first opportunity to unite our adopted and rescued country, to the country of our early home." The navy, therefore, was asked for powder and supplies.

Commander John B. Montgomery, commanding the United States

sloop-of-war *Portsmouth,* then lying at Sausalito on the north shore of San Francisco Bay, was prompt with his expression of sympathy but firm in his refusal "to furnish munitions of war, or in any manner to take sides with any political party, or even indirectly to identify myself, or official name, with any popular movement (whether of foreign or native residents) of the country." Frémont, however, while he had not formally authorized the proclamation of the Bear Flag Republic, was in nowise averse to giving it his active concurrence and encouragement during the three weeks of its life.

Through that period, however, Frémont's course was contradictory. On June 16, the day after the raising of the Bear Flag, he wrote Commander Montgomery asking for supplies and money needed for his long homeward journey across mountains and plains. Montgomery furnished the supplies and money requested, entrusted Frémont with letters for officials in Washington, and wished him a pleasant journey. But Frémont did not leave for the States. Instead—waiting, no doubt, for word of the war between the United States and Mexico which he was convinced had occurred, or soon would occur—he moved west to Sonoma, where, by the end of June, he was in active command, and was busy devising plans for the conquest of California under the banner of the Bear.

So far as it went, this enterprise consisted of a skirmish at San Rafael, the capture and execution of two or three prisoners by each side, Frémont's exploit of crossing San Francisco Bay just inside the Golden Gate (so named by Frémont himself on that occasion) and spiking the ancient cannon of the abandoned Mexican post at the Presidio, and a big Fourth of July celebration at Sonoma, followed by a meeting of the settlers at which Frémont "was selected to take the chief direction of affairs" for the newly proclaimed Republic.

Frémont's course had its romantic and popular appeal leading to his election as the first United States senator from the State of California and to his nomination as the first Republican candidate for the Presidency. His course had an effect, as will appear, in inducing the hesitant Commodore Sloat to take decisive action. But it gave the pro-British Governor Pico an excellent excuse, and even a good reason, for asking British intervention at the first opportunity, and that was the one thing which would have been most disastrous to the interests of Frémont's government, especially with the Oregon question just coming to a settlement.[5]

But the opportunity, if Governor Pico was seeking one, did not appear. Instead, on July 2, Commodore Sloat's flagship *Savannah* sailed into the bay at Monterey, where the commodore found the United States sloops *Cyane* and *Levant* and learned that the *Portsmouth* was at San Francisco.

Sloat, however, still was not quite decided as to the course which he should pursue. His hesitance is the more understandable in the light of what had happened to another United States commodore, Thomas Ap Catesby Jones, who in October 1842 had assumed from news reaching him that the United States and Mexico were at war and had occupied the town of Monterey, to forestall what he had thought to be an imminent occupation by the British. Commodore Jones had found his mistake, had promptly withdrawn with proper salutes to the flag of Mexico, and had sailed to Los Angeles to present his explanations to Governor Micheltorena, but all this had not saved him from being recalled from his command.

With the example of what had happened to Jones fresh in mind, Commodore Sloat paid the usual courtesy call on the Mexican port authorities, and went into conference with Consul Larkin before taking any action. Larkin, who was not convinced that war had begun, urged delay until the Californians should be ready to seek United States intervention. Nothing had been said to Sloat about occupying the interior beyond the ports, but word came to him that another United States officer, Frémont, was in fact conducting some sort of military operation in the interior. And, besides, there was the haunting dread of British naval intervention.

The combination of circumstances drove Sloat to act and, when he did, to act more broadly than was contemplated in his original instructions. So doing, however, he unwittingly followed in July the course which had been enjoined upon him by orders dispatched from Washington on May 13, the day of the passage of the war bill by Congress, but which were not to reach him until the end of August.

Captain William Mervine was sent ashore on the morning of July 7 with a demand for surrender of the town, its munitions and public property, to avoid "sacrifice of human life and the horrors of war." By half past nine o'clock Comandante Mariano Silva had advised the "Señor Commodore" that he had neither munitions nor public property and that he was "withdrawing and leaving the town peaceful and without a soldier." Whereupon, at ten o'clock, Captain Mervine took ashore a party of 250 sailors and marines who, with "three hearty cheers" and amid the roar of a 21-gun salute from all the naval vessels in Monterey Bay, ran up the United States flag above the old Customs House.

The hoisting of the flag was accompanied by the reading of a proclamation to the inhabitants of California, prepared the day before by Sloat and Larkin. The proclamation went beyond a mere occupation of the port and took possession of the province for the United States, with promises of freedom from governmental vexations, reduction in burdensome customs duties, protection of personal rights and, in a remarkable bit of prophetic understatement, of "a great increase in the value of real estate and the products of California."

Along with the proclamation to the people went a general order to the United States forces that it was "of the first importance to cultivate the good opinion of the inhabitants," that the navy would be "eternally disgraced . . . by indignity offered to a single female," and that "plunder of every sort is strictly forbidden," under severe penalties.

Orders were dispatched at once to Commander John B. Montgomery of the United States sloop-of-war *Portsmouth* in San Francisco Bay to take possession of Yerba Buena, which was done early on the morning of July 9 with the hoisting of the United States flag, the firing of a 21-gun salute, and the posting of the commodore's proclamation in both languages—an event memorialized in Portsmouth Square in San Francisco. During the day, the Presidio and the half-ruined fort at the mouth of the Bay were occupied, and the defense of the town, whether against Mexican attack or anticipated British naval interference, was entrusted to a newly organized body of "Volunteer Guards of Yerba Buena." On the same day, in the plaza at Sonoma, Lieutenant James W. Revere of the *Portsmouth* hauled down the Bear Flag and ran up the flag of the United States, and dispatched parties to conduct like ceremonies at Sutter's Fort on the Sacramento and at the old Russian post of Bodega.

From Monterey Commodore Sloat sent couriers to Comandante Castro and Governor Pico, seeking their co-operation in the new order of things. The Bear Flag episode, however, had so alarmed and angered many of the native Californians that both Pico and Castro rejected the overtures. Castro replied with angry complaint of a "band of adventurers, headed by Mr. J. C. Fremont," whose action in "forcibly taking possession of the post of Sonoma, hoisting an unknown flag, making prisoners . . . committing assassinations and every kind of injury" he quite naturally associated with the United States of

America. Instead of yielding to the conciliatory persuasions of Sloat, Castro and his rival Pico laid aside their feud, united their strength and with a force of some 800 men and ten guns took position at Los Angeles, prepared to uphold the sovereignty of Mexico.

Frémont, no longer the acting commander of the military force of an independent government, marched for Monterey with a force of 160 horsemen, partly his own exploring followers, partly venturesome American settlers from the valley of the Sacramento. Arriving on July 19, he put himself and his force at the disposal of the United States naval commander.[6]

Meanwhile, on the sixteenth, Sir George Seymour had arrived in Monterey Bay with the British line-of-battle ship *Collingwood,* to find the United States forces in possession. About the same time there arrived in Monterey, also, the United States frigate *Congress,* commanded by Robert F. Stockton, who brought with him the original of the October 1845 orders which Sloat had received orally from Lieutenant Gillespie. Passed Midshipman Edward Fitzgerald Beale, on board the *Congress,* later testified that the approach of the British ship of the line, its intentions being unknown, caused the American frigate to clear for action and send its men to quarters. The precaution proved to be unnecessary, and, on the twenty-third of July, the British weighed anchor and sailed away. On the same day the ailing Commodore Sloat turned over his orders, his situation and his squadron to the newly arrived Stockton and, a few days later, hoisted his broad pennant on the *Levant* and sailed for home and retirement.

The new naval commander and the commander of the men from the Sacramento found much in common. Both were men of action who acted with a flourish. Both were eager for distinction and even, it might be said, avid of glory. Neither saw much opportunity for action or chance of glory in the situation inherited from Sloat, with the United States flag peaceably flying at all points of consequence in northern California and United States rule accepted by most of the Californians of that section. Neither seemed anxious that Consul Larkin, a pacific man, should succeed in his continued efforts to reach an accommodation with the Californians.

On the contrary, Stockton's first act in assuming command was to issue, on July 23, a proclamation roundly abusing Castro for his "boasting and abusive" attitude and his lack of hospitality toward Frémont, and denouncing him as a "usurper" who had kept California in a "constant state of revolt and misery." His own object, Stockton said, was to protect life and property from the "lawless depredations" of Castro's men. As soon as Castro was defeated and his following dispersed and responsible government restored, he said, United States forces would be withdrawn—this being while there still was doubt in the faraway Pacific of the fact of war between the United States and Mexico.[7]

Disregarding this element of doubt, Stockton proceeded to organize for further operations. On July 24, the California Battalion of Mounted Riflemen was formed, with Frémont as major and Gillespie, now become a true horse marine, as captain and second-in-command. Moving promptly, on the next day Frémont's battalion went aboard the sloop *Cyane,* Commander Samuel F. Du Pont, and sailed away south for San Diego. Sea voyages were novelties to most of the command and after a few hours at sea, their commander wrote, "we were all very low in our minds."

A few days later the commodore himself followed in the *Congress,* paused at Santa Barbara to raise the flag there, and proceeded on to San Pedro, where on August 7 he landed his "sailor army" of 360 men for the "trying and hazardous" march to Los Angeles—"a longer march, perhaps," Stockton wrote, "than has ever been made in the interior of a country by sailors, after an enemy."

On the way from San Pedro to Los Angeles, Stockton was met by a deputation seeking suspension of hostilities for negotiation. His reply was that he would stop to negotiate only after Castro had hoisted the American flag, and marched on. On the march, he and his sailor soldiers were joined by Frémont and eighty of his horsemen, coming up from San Diego. Castro, however, had retired to Sonora on the tenth, and his military force had evaporated. Consul Larkin entered the village capital of the province peaceably on August 12, but the official occupation was not until the next day when, as Stockton reported to the Secretary of the Navy, the combined force of sailors and riflemen "entered this famous 'City of the Angels,' the capital of the Californias, and took unmolested possession of the government house."

Another proclamation followed on August 17, by which time positive news had been received of an incontrovertibly official war between the United States and Mexico. In this proclamation, therefore, Stockton announced the annexation of California to the United States, imposed military law until civil government could be organized, promised protection to the Californians who peaceably accepted the new government, and offered liberty to the leaders upon their paroles, but established a 10:00 P.M. curfew for everybody.

By the twenty-second of August, Stockton reported to the Navy Department, "the flag of the United States was flying at every commanding position, and California was in undisputed military possession of the United States." The commodore turned, therefore, to the business of governing the newly acquired territory. A code of laws was drafted and dispatched to Washington for approval; regular postal facilities were established for the first time in California; the first newspaper was started, and the first schoolhouse put in service. Elections were called on September 15, to choose alcaldes and other municipal officers, who were to govern under the terms of the prevailing local usages. Commodore Stockton himself served as governor of the province, with Captain Gillespie as military commandant in the south and Major Frémont in the north.

Stockton reported to Secretary Bancroft:

Thus, in less than a month after I assumed the command of the United States force in California, we have chased the Mexican army more than three hundred miles along the coast; pursued them thirty miles in the interior of their own country; routed and dispersed them, and secured the Territory to the United States; ended the war; restored peace and harmony among the people; and put a civil government into successful operation.[8]

So peaceful did all seem that Stockton sent off part of his ships to blockade Mexican ports south of San Diego, and planned himself to leave soon, leaving Frémont in charge as governor. His plan was "to sail for the southern part of Mexico, capture Acapulco, and . . . advance toward the city of Mexico"—a march which was not destined to be made, for the seeming peace of affairs in California, as the event proved, was deceptive.[9]

---

[1] Ex. Doc. 60, H. R., 30th Cong., 1st sess., p. 231; Ex. Doc. 4, H. R., 29th Cong., 2nd sess., p. 378.

[2] Ex. Doc. 4, H. R., 29th Cong., 2nd sess., pp. 50, 51; Ex. Doc. 33, Sen., 30th Cong., 1st sess., pp. 373-376; Frémont, John Charles, Memoirs of My Life (Chicago and New York, 1887), I, 441, 454, 458-461, 463, 487-489, 508; Rives, U. S. and Mexico, II, 169-180; Smith, War with Mexico, I, 325-333; Frost, Pictorial History, pp. 440-446.

[3] Ex. Doc. 4, H. R., 29th Cong., 2nd sess., pp. 378, 640; Ex. Doc. 1, H. R., 30th

Cong., 2nd sess., p. 1006; Frémont, *Memoirs*, I, 536, 537; Rives, *U. S. and Mexico*, II, 190, 191; Smith, *War with Mexico*, I, 333, 334.

4 Ex. Doc. 60, H. R., 30th Cong., 1st sess., pp. 153-155.

5 Ex. Doc. 4, H. R., 29th Cong., 2nd sess., pp. 51, 52; Ex. Doc. 33, Sen., 30th Cong., 1st sess., pp. 178, 179; Benton, Thomas Hart, *Thirty Years' View . . . By a Senator of Thirty Years* (New York, 1856), II, 688-692; Frost, *Pictorial History*, pp. 447, 448; Rives, *U. S. and Mexico*, II, 184-189; Stockton, Robert F., *A Sketch of the Life of Commodore Robert F. Stockton* (New York, 1856), p. 112; Frémont, *Memoirs*, I, 518-526, 545; Nevins, Allan, *Frémont, Pathmarker of the West* (New York, 1939), Chapters XVII and XVIII.

6 Ex. Doc. 4, H. R., 29th Cong., 2nd sess., pp. 52, 378, 379, 640-649; Ex. Doc. 60, H. R., 30th Cong., 1st sess., pp. 258-265; Frémont, *Memoirs*, I, 534, 536, 537; Rives, *U. S. and Mexico*, II, 191-194; Wilcox, *Mexican War*, pp. 131-135; Frost, *Pictorial History*, pp. 436-440; Ex. Doc. 1, H. R., 30th Cong., 2nd sess., pp. 1006-1034.

7 Ex. Doc. 33, Sen., 30th Cong., 1st sess., p. 269; Ex. Doc. 1, H. R., 30th Cong., 2nd sess., pp. 1035-1037, 1043-1044; Stockton, *Life*, pp. 116-118; Nevins, *Frémont, Pathmarker*, pp. 290-292. Commodore Stockton was a grandson of Richard Stockton, signer of the Declaration of Independence, and was himself to become, after the war, a United States senator from New Jersey.

8 Ex. Doc. 4, H. R., 29th Cong., 2nd sess., pp. 379, 668-675; Ex. Doc. 60, H. R., 30th Cong., 1st sess., pp. 265-268; Ex. Doc. 70, H. R., 30th Cong., 1st sess., pp. 38-42; Frémont. *Memoirs*, pp. 544, 563. The first newspaper was the *Californian*, published by Walter Colton, chaplain of the *Congress*, at Monterey on August 15, 1846, with the aid of Robert Semple, a Kentucky printer, who was one of the "Bear Flag men." The second, the *California Star*, was published at Yerba Buena, beginning in the same year. Spell, "Anglo-Saxon Press in Mexico," *American Historical Review*, Vol. XXXVIII, No. 1.

9 Ex. Doc. 33, Sen., 30th Cong., 1st sess., p. 182; Stockton, *Life*, pp. 125-127.

Capture of Monterey.

CHAPTER 8

The Army of the West

NOT in two decades since Colonel Henry Leavenworth had founded the fort on which he bestowed his own name, had this westernmost post of the United States Army seen such goings and comings as in the month of June 1846, when the "Army of the West" was forming there, to march to and occupy Santa Fe.

Twelve-months volunteers were called for to reinforce the regulars of the First Dragoons, stationed at Fort Leavenworth, and the scenes of eager recruiting in the states east of the Mississippi were duplicated in the frontier state of Missouri. For Missourians there was a special interest, indeed a positive fascination, about an expedition to Santa Fe. During the quarter of a century in which the caravan trade to that ancient northern outpost of Mexico had grown to a volume of well above a million dollars a year, St. Louis had been the headquarters of the trade, and Independence, a steamboat landing near the great bend where the Missouri River turns from flowing south to flow east, was the recognized point for the rendezvous of the traders, whence their wagon trains struck out into the Southwestern wilderness.

So prompt was the response of the Missourians to the call to march to the distant and alluring City of the Holy Faith that three companies of mounted volunteers were at Fort Leavenworth as early as June 6, only two weeks after the call reached the governor. By the eighteenth, with seven of the eight companies present, the First Regiment of Missouri Mounted Volunteers was organized, and field officers were chosen by popular election. After speeches in which the several candidates expounded the reasons why they should receive the suffrages of the soldiers assembled on the parade ground, the men lined up behind the candidates of their choice. To command the regiment there was chosen a frontier lawyer of Kentucky birth and

Virginia antecedents, who had served as brigadier general of the Missouri militia in the 1838 "campaign" against the Mormons but was at the moment a private in the company from Clay County. The new colonel, Alexander W. Doniphan, was to lead the regiment on a march as extraordinary as any in American military annals.

Throughout the month of June steamboats were arriving at Fort Leavenworth "almost daily," and the little quadrangle of wooden buildings, flanked with blockhouses at the corners, became the center of a growing camp of men, horses, oxen, wagons and guns. Before the end of the month there had been added to the 300 or so regulars of the First Dragoons and the 860 Missouri Mounted Volunteers, a St. Louis company of mounted volunteers bearing the name of the Laclede Rangers; a small battalion of two companies of infantry, who had tried to enlist as cavalry but could not get in under the quota and who insisted on going along on foot; and two companies of volunteer light artillery from St. Louis, one "German" and one "American." The artillery was commanded in the beginning by Captain Waldemar Fischer, whose name is commemorated in Fischer's Peak overlooking the present-day city of Trinidad, Colorado, until a West Point graduate, Major Meriwether Lewis Clark, son of William Clark and namesake of his co-explorer of the Northwest, joined the column on the march. Two additional companies of the First Dragoons, which had been stationed at Fort Atkinson and Fort Crawford, on the far Upper Mississippi, were on their way to rejoin the main body of their regiment. The total force of the "Army of the West" was less than 1,700 men, mostly mounted, with sixteen small guns. To complete the expedition, there were fifty Delaware and Shawnee Indian scouts, a party of United States Topographical Engineers headed by Lieutenant William H. Emory—he was to do distinguished service as a major general of the Union Army—and an interpreter, Antoine Robidou, brother of the founder of the city of St. Joseph, Missouri.[1]

In command of the somewhat grandiloquently styled army was Colonel Stephen Watts Kearny, veteran of the War of 1812. His record of twenty-five years service in the West included an extended march only the year before which had taken him and his dragoons to the South Pass on the Oregon Trail, thence to Bent's Fort, and back to the States down the Arkansas River. He had a reputation for vigor in action and strictness in discipline—so much so, that when word of his command reached the lower Rio Grande, the Matamoros *American Flag* printed, in its issue of July 27, an old army anecdote that when a subordinate addressed a military unit as "gentlemen," Kearny had rebuked him. "There are colonels, captains, lieutenants, and soldiers in this command," he was reported to have said, "but no such persons as 'gentlemen.' "

Making all haste, Kearny started his advance trains of provisions and supplies down the Santa Fe Trail even while his troops were coming in to Fort Leavenworth, and by the middle of June had as many as 100 loaded wagons and 800 cattle, accompanied by parties of experienced hunters, moving ahead of his army.

The army itself started its movement in detachments. First to leave, on June 5, were two companies of dragoons under Captain Benjamin D. Moore, sent out in great haste when news came in that a wagon train which had left Independence early in the spring was carrying powder and munitions of war to Governor Armijo at Santa Fe. Captain Moore's orders were, if possible, to overtake and halt the train. This he failed to do, but, acting on orders, he detained other trading caravans until the army came up, when they were to follow in its rear.

The trains halted by Captain Moore totaled 414 wagons, but even so at least a dozen traders passed on into Santa Fe ahead of the army that summer. When they started, of course, war had not begun, but it was everywhere known that relations between the United States and Mexico were under the most intense strain. Relations between the remote federal cities of Mexico and Washington, however, were of less immediate consequence to the Santa Fe traders than relations with Don Manuel Armijo, who combined in his own person the offices and authority of governor and *comandante general* at Santa Fe, ruling in his own way, and with a minimum of interference from the central government, the remote province of New Mexico.

Don Manuel's exactions on the trade to Santa Fe, and through Santa Fe to Chihuahua and the other interior northern provinces of Mexico, were heavy, amounting in some instances to as much as $500 for a loaded wagon. But his customhouse permit was enough to allow goods to be sold anywhere in Mexico, and it was anticipated that in the state of strain between the two nations the goods the traders carried would be scarce and the price—and profits—high. Consequently, the freighted wagons of the merchant adventurers to Santa Fe had begun to roll out of Independence even before orders had left Washington for Kearny's march, and long before he was ready to move.[2]

Before the expedition was ready to move, instructions from the War Department had gone forward to Kearny, under date of June 3, to extend his movement from Santa Fe to California. To enable him to make this further advance, the War Department called on the governor of Missouri for an additional 1,000 mounted soldiers who were to follow Kearny's trail and take over his occupation of New Mexico when he went on to the Pacific.

In addition, Kearny was authorized to enlist a battalion from the Mormon emigrants who had been driven from Nauvoo, Illinois, the year before and were then encamped at Council Bluffs, Iowa, while their leaders sought ways and means to take them to a new home in California. It was correctly assumed that many of them would be willing to volunteer on condition of receiving their discharges in the new promised land. A battalion was quickly formed, to follow Kearny on his way "to take the earliest possession of Upper California" where—as in New Mexico—he was to "establish temporary civil government" and to conciliate the inhabitants and render them friendly to the United States.[3]

With his supply trains and advance companies already on the trail, Kearny got the main body of the Army of the West under way late in June. Doniphan's Missouri mounted men started in detachments, between June 26 and 29. On the latter day the Laclede Rangers and the two infantry companies marched, to be followed on the last day of the month by the artillery battalion and by Colonel Kearny and his staff. After their departure, the two companies of dragoons came in from the Upper Mississippi country, under command of Captain E. V. Sumner—the same who was to become commander of a corps of the Army of the Potomac—and, on July 6, took up the march. The Army of the West was in full motion.

The march angled southwestward from Fort Leavenworth, to cross the Kansas River at the mouth of the Wakarusa, on the ferry operated there by the Shawnees, and to strike the main Santa Fe Trail at the Narrows, sixty-five miles west of Independence. Some of the units lost time turning off, by mistake, on the Oregon Trail, at the point where it and the Santa Fe Trail forked. Once straightened away, however, they had as guides the well-rutted "road" made by the annual passage of the traders' wagons.

There was no halt to celebrate the Fourth of July—"the hottest day that ever shone." The infantry detachment, which "had no spirits and could not observe the day in the usual manner," celebrated by march-ing thirty-two miles—twenty of them without water and "under a burning sun." The regular dragoons had a sutler, however, from whom the men "were permitted to buy liquor to celebrate as best they might the national anniversary." Among the mounted Missourians, likewise supplied, the march was punctuated "ever and anon" with "the enthusiastic shout, the loud huzza, and the animating Yankee Doodle," while that evening "the greatest good humor prevailed in camp." Another soldier diarist observed, however, that "it seems we have as much of the spirit of '76 as the spirit of John Barleycorn, for marching across these plains is not what it is cracked up to be."

The march was through a country which Lieutenant Emory de-scribed as having the appearance of "vast rolling fields enclosed with colossal hedges" where trees lined the banks of streams. From the headwaters of the Osage, tributary to the Missouri, the route led across to the headwaters of the Neosho, tributary to the Arkansas, and on by the Council Grove. This famous spot, the site of the first of the Indian treaties by which the Santa Fe Trail had been opened twenty years earlier, was the last place from which a man could turn back to make his way to "the States" alone, and was even more noteworthy as the last place where good timber could be had for wagon repairs.

Buffalo began to be seen, and prairie-dog villages, before the march reached the Arkansas, which was struck at a distance of nearly 300 miles from Fort Leavenworth and at an elevation, as indicated by the expedition's barometers, of 1,658 feet above sea level. From that time on, as they marched across the treeless plains, the troops fre-quently had to depend on dried buffalo chips, the *bois de vache,* to cook their morning and evening meals. The lack of wood impressed the men from the forested country to the east, but one of them noted that about "these wide solitary domains of the prairies" there was a certain interest and charm, "although," he added, "they can never be occupied by civilized man."

On July 14 the advance was held up by the rushing waters of a flood in the Pawnee Fork, a tributary falling into the Arkansas from the north at the 99th meridian west from Greenwich. While rafts were being built for the crossing, Doniphan's Missourians came up and behind them, Sumner's dragoons, the artillery and the two companies of infantry, who "kept pace with the mounted men," al-though "their feet were blistered by their long and almost incredible marches." One of the provision trains sent out in advance was also overtaken at the Pawnee Fork, and mail—"the first and only intelligence received from the States"—was brought up by the sutler of the First Dragoons, who was postmaster of the expedition.

From the Pawnee Fork crossing, the march of the combined forces continued into "that portion of the prairie that well deserves to be considered part of the great desert," as it seemed to eyes accustomed to the different vegetation of the East, but a "desert" nevertheless which in a state of nature supported such herds of grazing animals that it was "thick with buffaloes, extending as far back as the eye could reach or until the sight of them was lost behind some rising ground." Buffalo hunts offered an "exciting and animating" chase, in which "no one was satisfied with killing a number sufficient to supply all his wants." As a result of such hunting, "the whole country" after the crossing of the Little Arkansas, was found to be "like a slaughter pen, covered with bones, skulls and carcasses of animals in every state of decay."

At the place where the more generally used Cimmaron Cut-off crossed the Arkansas, Kearny's army diverged from that route and took the longer and steeper, but better-watered and safer, route up the Arkansas. As the way climbed steadily up the great tilt of the continent toward the Rockies, many horses failed and had to be abandoned, partly as a result of the overeagerness of their riders in chasing buffalo and other game with grass-fed mounts.

By this time men, too, were failing from short rations, scant and strongly alkaline water, insect bites, and most of all, from the prevailing ignorance of camp sanitation. Kearny himself was one of the many who fell ill, with severe vomiting, and not less than 100 of Doniphan's men alone fell sick and had to be carried along in the freight wagons "without springs and roughly built, like common Santa Fe trade wagons" which were all the expedition had for an ambulance—"a miserable arrangement," as one soldier described them.[4]

On July 22 the advance party of dragoons crossed the Arkansas and went into camp below and on the opposite bank from Bent's Fort. Six days later, the two companies of infantry—"the long-legged infantry," one of the cavalrymen called them—came in, having covered nearly 600 miles in twenty-nine days and outmarched the mounted men who had left ahead of them. Within the next three days the remainder of the army arrived, the last units being the two companies of dragoons which had not left Leavenworth until July 6. "With admirable order and precision," as it seemed to Lieutenant

Emory, and "with the most scrupulous regard to military exactness," as it seemed to Private Hughes of Doniphan's regiment, the entire command was for the first time concentrated in a grassy meadow on the south bank of the Arkansas, at an elevation, according to Emory's barometer, of 3,942 feet. Near by was the camp of the consolidated trains of the merchants—414 wagons altogether.

Upstream, near the site of the present town of Las Animas, Colorado, was the famous trading post built fifteen years earlier by the three Bent brothers—grandsons of Captain Silas Bent, reputedly of the Boston Tea Party—and the two St. Vrains. With its adobe walls fifteen feet high and four feet thick, and with a "huge United States flag flowing to the breeze from an ash pole over the center of the gate," the fort was the only permanently occupied place between the Missouri and the New Mexican settlements. It was a crossroads of wilderness trails and not only a center of trade but a focus of news and rumor.

During the days of his brief pause at Bent's, Colonel Kearny took further steps to carry out his instructions to occupy New Mexico with as little fighting as might be. Three Mexicans captured by the advance of the army, and believed to have been spies sent by Governor Armijo, were conducted through the camp, shown everything the army had, and permitted to depart and report to Santa Fe what they had seen. On July 31 the colonel issued a proclamation to "the citizens of New Mexico," advising that he was entering that territory "with a large military force for the purpose of seeking union with and ameliorating the conditions of its inhabitants," promising protection to those who were well disposed and treatment as enemies to those who resisted. Eugene Leitensdorfer, a Santa Fe trader with acquaintance and influence among the Indians of the pueblos, was sent forward toward Taos, under escort.

Finally, on August 1, Kearny sent a letter to Governor Armijo, advising that he came "as a friend & with the disposition and intention to consider all Mexicans & others as friends who will remain quietly & peaceably at their homes & attend to their own affairs"; pledging "Such persons shall not be disturbed by any one in my command either in their Persons, their Property or their Religion"; but warning that he came "with a strong Military force & a yet stronger one now following as a reinforcement" and was determined to take possession of that country east of the Rio Grande which through the annexation of Texas had become part of the United States.

This message, half conciliatory, half minatory, was sent forward by

the hand of Captain Philip St. George Cooke of the dragoons—an officer who had been on the Santa Fe Trail as early as 1829, and who,
adhering to the Union rather than his native state of Virginia, was
to attain to the rank of major general of the Union Army but to be
chiefly remembered, ironically enough, because his daughter married
another Virginia cavalryman, James Ewell Brown Stuart, major general, C.S.A. With twelve of his dragoons, Captain Cooke set out for
Santa Fe on August 1.

Accompanying him was a man who was to have more influence on
the course of events than the letter Cooke bore—James W. Magoffin, a
Kentuckian who had made a comfortable fortune in twenty years of
the Santa Fe trade, who had lived in Chihuahua where he had married
into a Mexican family, but who was now a resident of Independence
in Missouri, and so a constituent of Senator Thomas H. Benton.
Magoffin had reached Bent's Fort only the day before, in a buggy in
which he had driven from Independence in sixteen days. Less than a
month before that he had been in Washington, where he was called
by Senator Benton to give President Polk and Secretary of War Marcy
the benefit of his knowledge of northern Mexico, and of Governor
Armijo. From Washington he bore letters to Kearny, who, perceiv-
ing the value of his special knowledge and abilities, hastened to send
him on to Santa Fe.

While Colonel Kearny was busy with his diplomatic measures, the
brief rest at Bent's Fort was used to recruit the strength of men and
horses, and to perfect the organization of the combined columns.
Lieutenant Emory noted the "excellent understanding . . . kindly
offices . . . and cordiality" prevailing "between regulars and volunteers," but the volunteer diarist Hughes was inclined to resent what
he considered Kearny's effort to impose "regular" ways upon the
free-and-easy volunteers. From the soldiers' standpoint, the most
memorable event of those days was the time when "the whole *caballada* took a general *estampeda*," that being the way in which one soldier used his newly acquired knowledge of Spanish to describe the
panic-stricken flight of a thousand or more horses, turned out to
graze, in "wildest and most terrible confusion." Most of the animals
were recovered, some as much as fifty miles from camp, but sixty-five
were irretrievably lost.[5]

The march of the combined army from Bent's Fort into what was
described as "the great American desert," a wind-swept waste of
"dreary, sultry, desolate, boundless solitude . . . heat, thirst, and

driven sand" was fully under way by August 2. The route lay up the Arkansas to the mouth of the Timpas, and up that stream toward the mountains to the southwest. On the second day out, Pike's Peak was glimpsed far to the right at sunset, with the Spanish Peaks rising ahead to the southwest. Still another day—the command was to shudder when it remembered those days on the Timpas, where what water there was in the stream was tinged with Epsom salts—and the route carried into the valley of the Purgatoire, a clear, palatable mountain stream. Just ahead was the stiff climb to the summit of the Raton—"the Mouse"—as the Mexicans called the mountain spur which separated the waters of the Arkansas from those of its Canadian fork. By the time the foot of the pass was reached, the men were on half rations—later to be cut to one third—and the horses were about given out, with wolves and buzzards following the column to feast on those who failed on the trail. Ammunition, much of which had been wasted in wanton shooting of buffalo and other game not needed for food, was down to fifteen rounds.

Two days were spent passing through the Raton Pass, where the barometer showed an elevation of 7,754 feet, a height from which the marching men gazed at the great panoramic scenes unfolded before them before dropping down on the New Mexico side of the pass. After another week of grueling marching the command reached the first settlement in New Mexico, and the first—other than the Bents' trading post—which they had seen in 775 miles. "The first object I saw," one officer reported, "was a pretty Mexican woman, with clean white stockings, who very cordially shook hands with us and asked for tobacco." Word was received that Armijo, breathing fire and resistance, was assembling his forces.[6]

The hard-driving Kearny drove his men even harder. On the following day a lieutenant and party of lancers appeared on the trail bearing a response from Armijo to the conciliatory note which Kearny had sent forward by Captain Cooke, phrased "so ambiguously . . . that it was impossible to know whether it was the Governor's intention to meet Gen. K. in council, or in conflict."

That night Kearny camped in sight of the town of Las Vegas, the first considerable place to be reached in New Mexico, while pounding along behind him came a party of three officers—Major Swords of the Quartermaster Corps, Captain Weightman, who commanded one of the batteries and had been left sick at Bent's, and Lieutenant Jeremy

Gilmer, who was to be chief engineer of Kearny's army—who had heard the rumor of impending battle and rode sixty miles in a night so as not to miss it.

But there was no battle at Las Vegas on August 15. Instead, there was a peaceful public ceremony and a proclamation. General Kearny—the three hard-riding officers who came in that morning had brought his commission as a brigadier general—marched into the town at seven in the morning, and at eight o'clock met the alcalde and the assembled people in the public plaza, proclaimed New Mexico to be part of the United States, assumed to absolve the people of allegiance to Mexico, promised them protection of property, and especially protection from the raids of the dreaded Navajos and Apaches, assured them freedom of religion, and concluded his address by administering to them en masse the oath of allegiance to the United States—altogether a proceeding which was to bring upon the general some criticism for his short-cut methods of conferring, or imposing, United States citizenship, but one which seemed to suit the people addressed.

The matter of national allegiance and citizenship having been thus summarily disposed of, Kearny descended the same rickety ladder by which he had climbed up, mounted his troops, had the guidons and colors unfurled for the first time on the march and moved toward a near-by gorge where it was reported that a Mexican force was waiting. As they neared the gorge, they passed from the walk to the trot, and then to the full gallop, and went through the gorge with a rush, without seeing a person.

"One by one," wrote Lieutenant Emory, "the guidons were unfurled . . . and a few minutes found us dragging our slow lengths along with the usual indifference in regard to every subject except that of overcoming space."

At Tecolote, later on the same day, the same sort of ceremony as at Las Vegas was repeated, and again on the next day, at San Miguel on the Pecos. There scouts came in with reports of strong Mexican forces at "the Cañon"—the pass through the mountain range between the waters of the Pecos and those of the Rio Grande del Norte which the road to Santa Fe followed, and through which the line of the Atchison, Topeka and Santa Fe Railway now runs. There was more truth to these reports than to earlier rumors of resistance, for on this day the Apache Canyon was occupied by New Mexican militia under Colonel Manuel Piño, and Governor Armijo was moving toward it with a few hundred regular soldiers and six guns.

On the seventeenth Kearny's men passed the ruins of the ancient Pecos village where, according to a tradition to which the newcomers gave credence, the remnants of the "Montezuma race" had for centuries kept alight a sacred fire of deliverance which had been extinguished with the removal of the tribe only a few years before. A number of Kearny's men explored the ruins, Lieutenant Emory and others carefully described them, and at least one 1846-model Kilroy "dared to ascend the Altar & stood in the very spot where the Vestal fire had blazed for ages & wrote my name upon the white-washed wall near & in rear of the sacred altar."

As Kearny neared the Pecos ruins, some five miles from the mouth of the supposedly defended canyon, "a large, fat fellow, mounted on a mule," the alcalde of a settlement some two miles up the river, came riding toward him "at full speed, and extending his hand to the general, congratulated him and . . . said, with a roar of laughter, 'Armijo and his troops have gone to hell and the Cañon is all clear.'" The statement as to the departure of the troops, no matter what their destination, was correct, and the canyon which could have been made nearly impregnable was indeed clear.

Armijo, perhaps as a result of the diplomatic endeavors of James Magoffin, had "a real disinclination to actual resistance." What determination to resist there was among the New Mexicans centered in Colonel Diego Archuleta, who is represented by Captain Cooke as having been persuaded out of his belligerence by Magoffin with the suggestion that since Kearny would take New Mexico only up to the boundary claimed by Texas, there would be opportunity in the western part of the province, beyond the Rio Grande, for a young man of his qualifications to lead a movement which might be a step toward annexation to the United States on terms favorable to the leader. If this was the case, Archuleta was to be disappointed because Kearny, unknown to Magoffin, was taking the whole of New Mexico, and not merely the old Texas claim. But whatever the moving considerations may have been, the divisions and dissension among the Mexican commanders, and the lack of support from the central government, preoccupied with revolution in the capital, were such that the force at the canyon had simply dispersed. Armijo and a handful of men had fled southward to Chihuahua, the cannon had been concealed in the woods, and the narrow gate of the pass had been left open and undefended.[7]

Two hours before day on the morning of August 18, in a drizzling rain, Kearny's force set forth to cover the last twenty-nine miles of the long way into Santa Fe, with "everything braced for a forced march," not because the distance was so great but because the road was bad and "the horses on their last legs." The march was so hard that when the head of the little column came in sight of Santa Fe in midafternoon, troops and wagons were strung out for three hours behind. It was not until six in the evening that the rear of the column was in, while some of the wagons did not arrive until the next day.

Lieutenant Governor Juan Bautista Vigil y Aland received General Kearny and his staff in the council room of the long, low adobe Palace of the Governors which occupied one side of the public plaza of Santa Fe, and ceremoniously served wine and brandy from the Passo del Norte. Rain and clouds had marked the day, but "as the sun was setting" the clouds broke, and "the United States flag was hoisted over the palace, and a salute of thirteen guns was fired with the artillery planted on an eminence overlooking the town"—the first powder burned in the campaign except in hunting. To the people gathered in the plaza to watch the ceremony, Kearny talked through his interpreter Robidou plainly and positively, much as he had at Las Vegas, before retiring to the home of a Mexican gentleman to partake of supper served "after the manner of a French dinner, one dish succeeding another," with "a bottle of good wine from the Passo del Norte and a loaf of bread placed at each plate." Most of the United States soldiers did not fare so well, however. Many of the wagons did not come in that night; the riding horses, which "had started the morning hungry, were staked on the barren sand without a spire of grass"; there were no cooked provisions for the men, and no wood with which to cook them; and at a sandy, gravelly campsite, not even water for men or beasts.[8]

On the next day, August 19, the people were more formally assembled in the plaza to hear the general on their future relations with the United States, while for days thereafter delegations were "coming in" from the surrounding country, to see what manner of men these were and to profess allegiance to the changed government.

On August 22—the same day, as it happened, that Commodore Stockton was setting up his government for newly occupied California—General Kearny issued a proclamation "claiming the whole of New Mexico, with its then boundaries," including the areas on both sides of the Rio Grande, "as a territory of the United States of America," absolving the people of their allegiance to Mexico, and even going to the length of characterizing as "traitors" those who did not accept the new order of things.

"The people of the territory are now perfectly tranquil," Kearny reported to the Adjutant General, "and can be kept so." Consequently, he wrote, he would send his surplus troops to Chihuahua to join the expedition of General Wool, supposed to have marched from San Antonio to occupy that point, and with the remainder he would be going on to California in about a month. He had had no word as yet of the Missouri reinforcements who were expected to take over the occupation duty in New Mexico, nor of the Mormon battalion which was to accompany him to California.

The Second Missouri regiment, as a matter of fact, was completing its organization at Fort Leavenworth, under command of Colonel Sterling Price, a Missouri Democrat who, in time, was to command the Missouri State troops in the troublous times of 1861, and finally to serve as a major general with the western armies of the Confederacy. The Mormon battalion was on its way, also, starting under command of Captain Allen and, after his death, of Lieutenant Andrew J. Smith, of the regular army, who as one of Sherman's major generals was to administer to Nathan Bedford Forrest one of the few reverses which that Confederate commander suffered.

Without waiting for the arrival of the new troops, Kearny went ahead with the formation of his new government and the preparations for the march to California. Private Willard Hall of the Missouri volunteers, a brilliant young lawyer who was to be elected to Congress while absent in the army, was put to work with Colonel Doniphan drafting a new constitution for the government of New Mexico. Without waiting for this organic charter, however, immediate changes were made in the arrangements under which the people of the territory lived. The customs exactions which had helped to keep the prices of the merchandise brought across the plains fantastically high were abolished, now that New Mexico had been declared a part of the United States. A new scale of license charges for local activities was imposed to provide what public revenue was needed—$2.00 a month to run a dry-goods store, $4.00 a month for a grocery, $5.00 a month for a tavern, $3.00 a month for each public billiard table, $1.50 per night for each monte table or game of chance, and $2.00 for each ball where money was charged for attending.[9]

Balls, or fandangos as they were more commonly called, were one of the features of Santa Fe life which fascinated the newcomers from across the prairies. "All descriptions of persons are allowed to come," one observer wrote, "free of charge, and without invitations." The festivities would start about nine in the evening, when the church bells would be used to call the ladies to attend. There was, to Anglo-Saxon eyes, "little order and still less attention to the rules of etiquette," the principal dance being "a kind of swinging, gallopade waltz" which required "such familiarity of positions as would be repugnant to the refined rules of polite society in our country."

The newcomers found much else that was strange and interesting in the ancient village capital. There was chili, "the first mouthful of which brought tears trickling down my cheeks, very much to the amusement of the spectators with their leather-lined throats." There were vendors of vegetables, bread, milk, cheese, fruits and chickens, who were like to have "drained most of the specie from the purses of the American soldiers," for, as the soldier diarist proudly noted, "we took nothing, not even a melon, or an ear of corn, a chicken, a goat or a sheep, from these poor people, for which we did not pay the money." The Americans—"here, all persons from the United States are called Americans, and the name is extended to no other race on the continent"—made the acquaintance of *uvas, huevos, cebolla, sandía* and *punche* for the familiar grapes, eggs, onions, watermelons and tobacco, and they also met *hojas,* corn husks neatly tied up in bundles for making the cigarritos to which the New Mexicans promptly introduced them.

There began, indeed, a closer acquaintance of habits on both sides, so much so that when a party of American officers newly arrived at the New Mexican settlements were proferred aguardiente and declined, the astonished comment was *"No quiere a! Ciertamente no es Americano."*

But with all the attraction of novelty Santa Fe still was distinctly disappointing to most of the Americans who had built up in their imaginations a picture of the magnet which drew the wagons of the traders across hundreds of miles of empty plains. It was ancient, old when even the oldest of the English settlements were made in America. For almost three centuries it had been the seat of government for an area of a hundred thousand square miles. But after all these years it was but a village, which the irreverent Americans, unmindful of antiquity or history, promptly dubbed "Mudtown" because of the prevailing adobe construction of the thick-walled houses, although it was conceded that they were cool in summer and warm in winter.[10]

To maintain even so small a force as that of Kearny, and the reinforcements which were following him, at such a distance from any center and source of supplies presented in those days of animal transport no small problem in logistics. Supplies were brought up to Independence or Fort Leavenworth by light-draft steamboats, not without difficulty, but the real difficulties began with the long overland haul. To transport the men under Kearny's command, and their matériel, and to keep them supplied, required first and last, the Quartermaster General reported, the use of 1,556 wagons, and the services of 459 horses, 3,658 draft mules, 516 pack mules and 14,904 oxen.[11] In the bloodless conquest of Santa Fe, the real obstacle to be overcome was not the enemy but distance and terrain.

---

[1] Organization and composition of the Army of the West are treated in Hughes, John T., *Doniphan's Expedition, Containing An Account of the Conquest of New Mexico, Etc.* (Cincinnati, 1848), pp. 24-27; Ex. Doc. 41, H. R., 30th Cong., 1st sess. (Emory, Lt. Col. W. H., *Notes of a Military Reconnaissance From Fort Leavenworth, in Missouri, to San Diego, in California*), pp. 7-8; Bieber, Ralph P. (ed.), *Southwest Historical Series III* (Glendale, California, 1935), pp. 22-24, 29-31, 36-40, 119-120, 125-126 (Journal of George Rutledge Gibson).

[2] Bieber (ed.), *Southwest Historical Series III*, pp. 40-43; Hughes, *Doniphan's Expedition*, pp. 29-30; Connelley, William Elsey, *Doniphan's Expedition* (Hughes's Reprint, annotated, and Hughes's Diary), (Topeka, Kansas, 1907), pp. 139-140; Pub. Doc. 1, Sen., 29th Cong., 1st sess., p. 211.

[3] Ex. Doc. 60, H. R., 30th Cong., 1st sess., pp. 153-155, 242-245.

[4] The course and incidents of the march up to Bent's Fort are treated in Ex. Doc. 41, H. R., 30th Cong., 1st sess. (Emory's *Notes*, pp. 10-14, 160-162, Lt. J. W. Abert's Notes, pp. 386-405); Hughes, *Doniphan's Expedition*, pp. 30-57 and Connelley (ed.), pp. 140-177; Bieber (ed.), *Southwest Historical Series III*, pp. 44-50, 126-165; Bieber (ed.), *Southwest Historical Series IV* (Glendale, California, 1936), pp. 73-90 (Journal of Abraham Robinson Johnston), pp. 115-138 (Journal of Marcellus Ball Edwards). The grassy and treeless prairies which supported such vast herds of buffalo and other game but which seemed to the men marching across them incapable of being "occupied by civilized man," are interestingly discussed in Malin, James C., *The Grassland of North America: Prolegomena to Its History* (Lawrence, Kansas, 1947).

[5] Events at Bent's Fort are treated in Ex. Doc. 60, H. R., 30th Cong., 1st sess., p. 168; Ex. Doc. 41, H. R., 30th Cong., 1st sess., Emory's *Notes*, pp. 14, 162; Hughes, *Doniphan's Expedition*, pp. 58-60, and Connelley (ed.), pp. 178-182; Bieber (ed.), *Southwest Historical Series III*, pp. 50-71, 165-178; Bieber (ed.), *Southwest Historical Series IV*, pp. 90-92, 139-143; Benton, Thomas Hart, *Thirty Years' View*, II, 682-684.

[6] The march from Bent's Fort to the outlying Mexican settlements is treated by Emory in Ex. Doc. 41, H. R., 30th Cong., 1st sess., pp. 15-25, 162-163; Hughes, *Doniphan's Expedition*, pp. 61-70, and Connelley (ed.), pp. 181-189; Bieber (ed.), *Southwest Historical Series III*, pp. 57-60, 173-191 (Gibson's Journal); Bieber (ed.), *Southwest Historical Series IV*, pp. 92-98 (Johnston's Journal), pp. 143-151 (Edwards' Journal).

[7] The occupation of the outlying settlements is treated in Hughes, *Doniphan's Ex-

pedition, pp. 70-75, and Connelley (ed.), pp. 60-61, 189-196; Ex. Doc. 41, H. R., 30th Cong., 1st sess., Emory's *Notes*, pp. 25-30; Bieber (ed.), *Southwest Historical Series III*, pp. 60-79, 191-202; Bieber (ed.), *Southwest Historical Series IV*, pp. 98-103, 151-158. The negotiations of Magoffin and Cooke are outlined in Drumm, Stella M. (ed.), *Down the Santa Fe Trail and into Mexico; The Diary of Susan Shelby Magoffin, 1846-1847* (New Haven, 1926), pp. xiii-xviii, 264, 265; Benton, *Thirty Years*, II, 682-684.

8 The march to and occupation of Santa Fe are treated in Ex. Doc. 41, H. R., 30th Cong., 1st sess., Emory's *Notes*, pp. 30-32; Hughes, *Doniphan's Expedition*, pp. 78-79, and Connelley (ed.), pp. 198-201; Bieber (ed.), *Southwest Historical Series III*, pp. 79-82, 202-206; Bieber (ed.), *Southwest Historical Series IV*, pp. 103-104, 158-159.

9 Ex. Doc. 60, H. R., 30th Cong., 1st sess., pp. 169-174, 177-220, 551.

10 Ex. Doc. 41, H. R., 30th Cong., 1st sess., pp. 32-36, 40, 443, 448; Hughes, *Doniphan's Expedition*, pp. 76, 81-83, 91-94, and Connelley (ed.), pp. 194, 195, 203-206, 214-217; Smith, *War with Mexico*, I, 296.

11 Ex. Doc. 1, Sen., 30th Cong., 1st sess., p. 545.

CHAPTER 9

The Siege and Surrender of Monterey

DURING the month of August 1846, in which Stockton and Kearny were setting up new governments in California and at Santa Fe, General Taylor was struggling with the double task of bringing the rear units of his army up the Rio Grande to Camargo, and getting the leading units under way on the march inland from that river depot.

The general and his staff landed at Camargo on August 8. Two days later, Captain Ben McCulloch of the Texas Rangers—the same who, become a major general of the Confederate service, was to lose his life in the battle which determined that Missouri should remain a Union state—was sent forward to reconnoiter roads toward Monterey. The general hoped "to move on Monterey by the 1st Sept," his chief of staff wrote, but Monterey, in his plans, was little more than a stopping place on the way to Saltillo, which place "the general anticipated no serious difficulty in reaching and occupying by the 1st of Oct."[1]

The general was advancing in a strangely divided state of mind. He had supreme confidence in his men—a confidence so great that he was to send them against fortified places with little more than the bayonet—but he had little confidence in the movement on which he was embarked.

Writing the War Department in July, in response to questions from the Secretary, he had expressed doubts both as to the practicability of subsisting more than 6,000 men at any distance beyond Saltillo, and also as to the value of anything which might be achieved by such an advance. As early as June, in fact, he had conceived the idea, and had written to his son-in-law, Dr. R. C. Wood, that there was an "intention to break me down," and before leaving Matamoros had confided that he "greatly feared" the failure of his movement forward. While waiting at Camargo for the arrival of his last reinforcements before advancing into the interior, he wrote that "be the consequences what they may, I must attempt something," and that the "country . . . shall not be disappointed; even if it should turn out to be a disaster."[2]

Indeed, the state of affairs at Camargo might well have daunted even so stout a heart as that of Zachary Taylor. With the knowledge of sanitation which the medical world then possessed and the state of discipline which prevailed, it is likely that almost any other place would have had somewhat the same record, but it was at Camargo that nearly 15,000 United States soldiers, regular and volunteer, were assembled in July and August, and it was at Camargo that an appalling percentage of them—as many as one third in some commands—sickened, and no small percentage died. It was Camargo, then, which came to be looked upon as a "Yawning Grave Yard."

The town is on the San Juan, just above its confluence with the Rio Grande, too far from the Gulf to get the effect of the cooling sea breeze at night, and too near sea level to enjoy the tempering effects of altitude. The place of encampment was rimmed with rocks which reflected the heat of the sun and put the thermometer above the hundred mark. The valley had been flooded by the great freshet in June, and the falling waters had left the town and its environs covered with a deposit of mud which dried into a fine blowing dust. The camps were strung out along the stream, which supplied water not only for man and beast but for bathing, washing and every other camp purpose as well. Dysentery, measles and malignant fevers attributed to "noxious gases and deadly miasmas" struck down men by the hundreds. The dead march "was ever wailing in our ears," one writer noted, while another declared that it became a sound so familiar that even the birds learned it. Funeral escorts "to that vast and common cemetery, the Chapparal," and the crashing of the three volleys fired over the grave of some soldier, "shroudless, coffinless, palled only in a blanket," almost ceased to attract attention. The Tennessee regiment which as yet had seen no armed enemy, was reduced by the end of August to less than half the strength of 1,040 men who had left Nashville only three months before. One hundred were dead, 300 had been discharged by reason of illness, the others were sick in camp.[3]

The Surgeon General estimated—though it was no more than an estimate—"the extent of sickness among the volunteers on the Rio Grande" as "fourfold that among the soldiers of the regular army." But whether regular or volunteer, the man who was wounded or fell ill in the War with Mexico needed strength and fortitude to survive both his disability and its treatment. The army had a medical department, with a surgeon general, and the foundations had been laid for the admirable service of later years, but hospital equipment was almost unknown and hospital organization depended largely on the use of detailed soldiers or walking patients as nurses and attendants. Sickness or a broken leg "were not anticipated," according to one diarist, such a thing as an ambulance being "not known in the army." Anesthesia had been discovered just before the beginning of the war but was still under suspicion as being dangerous and perhaps deleterious. Asepsis and antisepsis were a generation in the future. Surgery was crude—many of the surgeons had done no dissecting and had vague ideas as to the details of anatomy—while the principal reliances in medicine were the letting of blood, blistering, strong emetics and purgatives, and, as a sort of sovereign remedy of remedies, plenty of calomel.[4]

But with all the difficulties not only in camp sanitation but also in steamboat transportation and overland marching, the concentration was accomplished and the column which was to advance to the mountains was made ready. All available regular troops were to be taken but "the limited means of transportation, and the uncertainty in regard to the supplies that may be drawn from the theater of operations," as General Taylor explained in his orders, imposed "the necessity of taking into the field, in the first instance, only a moderate portion of the volunteer force." The organization of the column for the advance consisted of two divisions of regulars, the First under Brigadier General Twiggs and the Second under Brigadier General Worth, a "Field Division" of volunteers, under Major General William O. Butler, and the division of Texas volunteer horse, under Major General Pinckney Henderson. The four field artillery batteries were divided between the two regular divisions. The total strength of the marching army was 6,000, of whom about half were regulars.[5]

There was great demand for the privilege of being part of the column, and some grumbling from those to be left behind. There was, likewise, the usual criticism, especially from those at a distance, over the seeming slowness with which the army was organized and got under way. And conversely, there was the usual criticism among the army for the seeming neglect by "the government" to provide supplies and transportation. There was, indeed, the usual round of blame placing—with a certain amount of justification in nearly all of it. "The government" had been slow in providing for the needs of the army, the army had been slow in assessing its needs and making them known, the newspaper editors and the public had realized too little of the difficulties of advance into a country of great distances, sparse supplies and almost nonexistent transportation. Thousands of men in uniform, and therefore presumably soldiers, were pouring into the Rio Grande area, but what was not realized was that soldiers, as Lieutenant Meade put it, "are not all we want. We must have pork and beans to feed them, and means of carrying the pork and beans and baggage."

With the flotilla of steamboats on the Rio Grande bringing up supplies to Camargo, the next step was to get them forward as the column marched. Major H. L. Kinney—he whose ranch at Corpus Christi had been the scene of the first United States encampment— was called into service to contract for pack mules and their *arrieros,* the contract price being fifty-five cents per mule per day. Camargo soon was "alive with pack mules," 1,900 of them, to which were added 180 four-horse or mule wagons, brought up the river. With the cavalry and artillery horses, a total of 5,000 animals were required to carry and supply the forward column of 6,000 men.[6]

The regular troops were paraded on August 17, ten days after the arrival of General Taylor at Camargo, in a "grand review" which, to volunteer and regular observers alike, seemed "one of the most magnificent military displays since the last war"—that being the War of 1812. Taylor, "clad in plain undress, was conspicuous in the glittering group" of generals and their staffs who rode the line from right to left—a fact which was duly and approvingly noted by some of the volunteer observers.[7]

The advance began on the day after the grand review, when one brigade of Worth's division crossed the San Juan and marched by way of Mier toward Cerralvo, some sixty miles away, where an advance party of Texas Rangers and regular artillery and engineers had already established an outpost. It was not until a week later that the other brigade of Worth's division marched, and almost another week after that before, on August 31, Twiggs's division of regulars took to the road. It was still another week before Butler's division of volunteers took up the march, following the same road up the left, or north-western, bank of the San Juan. The two regiments of Texas cavalry—those of Colonel George Wood from eastern or interior Texas, and of Colonel Jack Hays from the western frontier of the state—marched by another road, via China and Cadareyta, on the opposite side of the valley.[8]

This dispersal of force may have been due to transportation difficulties, or it may have been adopted for greater convenience in marching, or perhaps it was just another evidence of the commanding general's disdain of the opposition, or lack of it, which he anticipated. Indeed, since the capture of Matamoros and the retreat of Arista to Linares, late in May, there had been little evidence of either the will or the means to make serious resistance to the advance of the United States troops. Arista had been removed from command for his failure, and had been succeeded by Mejía, who himself soon fell ill and turned over to General Tomas Requeña the task of marching the remnant of the Mexican army to Monterey. It was not until late in July that this principal city of northeastern Mexico was occupied in force, and its fortification undertaken in earnest.

Early in August, as a result of the change of government in the faraway city of Mexico, Ampudia once more became general in chief of the armies in the north of the republic. He brought with him to Monterey reinforcements from San Luis Potosí, raising the force to some 5,000 men and thirty-two guns. The month of August was spent on the defenses of the city, with soldiers "working like simple laborers." As the United States forces moved slowly forward from Camargo, bold plans for falling upon the Americans en route were debated, adopted and then, after juntas or councils of war were held, abandoned. Doubt, indecision and divided counsel prevailed—but even so, effective defenses were planned and to a considerable extent constructed.[9]

Meanwhile, the detachments of Taylor's army were closing up on Cerralvo. The first days of the march, through a region where water was to be had only at the night halts, were hard, but as the men entered the highlands of Nuevo León they found a region of clear running streams, with "air so pure it is a luxury to breathe it," and with ever-varying scenery as they drew nearer to the great wall of the Sierra Madre.

Cerralvo itself—"the prettiest site for a town I have ever seen"—

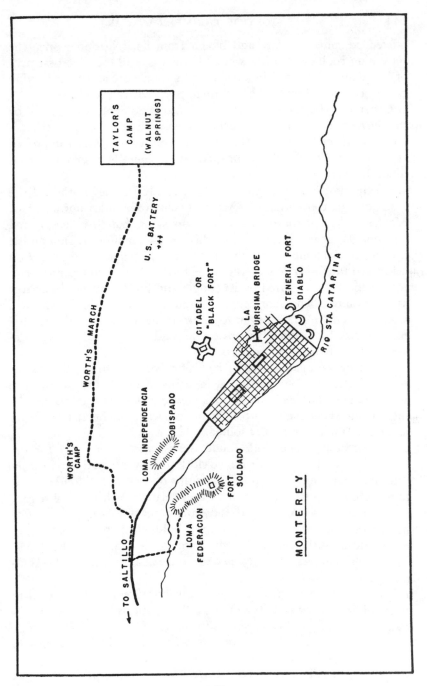

MONTEREY

TAYLOR'S CAMP (WALNUT SPRINGS)

U. S. BATTERY +++

WORTH'S MARCH

WORTH'S CAMP

TO SALTILLO

CITADEL OR "BLACK FORT"

LOMA INDEPENDENCIA

OBISPADO

LOMA FEDERACION

FORT SOLDADO

LA PURISIMA BRIDGE

TENERIA FORT

DIABLO

RIO STA CATARINA

143

offered perennial verdure and bloom from its irrigation works, the refreshing coolness of thick-walled buildings, and the divertissement of "fandangoes, monte, limonada, and a dash now and then of vino de Parras," which made the halt there pass swiftly enough.[10]

General Taylor himself arrived at Cerralvo on September 9, and by the thirteenth all troops advancing by that route were concentrated. "The health of the army," the general reported, "is much improved since approaching the mountains, and it is generally in excellent condition for service."[11]

On the morning of September 13, the advance began toward the next point of concentration—Marin, twenty-four miles northwest of Monterey. Again the march was by divisions, but this time spaced only one day apart. Marin was reached by the leading division on the evening of September 15—the night on which the Mexican nation celebrated the Grito de Dolores as the birthday of its independence— to find the town deserted by its people and plundered by the evacuating soldiery. "The poor people," wrote Lieutenant Meade who was with the advance party, began to return to the town after the United States forces took peaceable possession, and "were loud in their denunciations of their own soldiers."

The army was again closed up by September 17. On the next morning, with the divisions moving at intervals of one hour, the advance was resumed. The day's march was eleven miles, with camp for the night made at the hacienda San Francisco, where General Henderson and his 1,100 Texas cavalry joined.[12]

Sunrise of the nineteenth found the advance under way for the final march to Monterey. By nine o'clock the advance had come within three miles of the city when the Mexicans opened fire. Monterey was to be defended, after all, rather than evacuated. When firing began, the advance was halted, and the troops put into camp in a fine hundred-acre grove shading a group of bold, clear springs, known to the Mexicans as the Bosque de San Domingo but called by the Americans—perhaps because the trees were live oak and pecans—the Walnut Springs.

While Major Mansfield and his engineer officers went forward to reconnoiter the city and its defenses, the irrepressible Texas cavalry rode out to see how close they could venture to, and beyond, the edge of danger from the Mexican cannon. The foot soldiers, curious to watch the exhibition of daredevil equestrianism and, among the volunteers, equally curious to get their first glimpse of "that as yet unseen biped, a Mexican soldier," ventured out into cannon range and possible reach of the Mexican lancers, just to see. The practice became so general that orders had to be issued from army headquarters restraining these individual and unauthorized reconnaissances into the plain between camp and city.[13]

Mountain-girt Monterey—the present day spelling of "Monterrey" came later—capital of the state of Nuevo León and a city of some 10,000 inhabitants, was built in the Mexican style with stone-walled houses in regular squares surrounding a principal plaza and two or three smaller ones. The city lay on the left, or northern, bank of a tributary of the San Juan, issuing from a pass in the high sierra to the westward, known locally as the Rio San Juan de Monterey or the Santa Catarina. Northward from the city proper, at a distance of about a thousand yards, stood an unfinished cathedral, surrounded by the bastioned walls of the Citadel, or as the Americans sometimes called it, the Black Fort, extending some 200 yards on a side and mounting a dozen guns. The Citadel covered the junction of the roads leading into Monterey from the north and east. Between the Citadel and the solidly built part of the city there were houses and gardens, with walls and hedges, crossed by a small stream which, running through the northern edge of the town, turned east and south to fall into the river. The road from Marin to Monterey crossed this stream at the fortified bridge La Purísima. Lying just outside the northeastern corner of the city was a four-gun redoubt, La Tenería, taking its name from the tanyard near by. Running south and west across the eastern and southeastern faces of the city was a chain of small fortifications, the one nearest to the Tenería being the Rincón Diablo, or Devil's Corner.

Westward from the city, the road to Saltillo followed the stream, passing between two precipitous hills—the Loma Independencia to the north, the Loma Federación to the south. The Independence Hill, some 800 feet high, was crowned at its western end with a two-gun work, while halfway down the slope facing toward the city stood the fortified pile of the abandoned and semiruinous Obispado, the palace of a former bishop. On the Federation Hill, about half as high as the Independence, stood two small works, a one-gun redoubt at the western end, the Fort Soldado at the eastern.

Within the city proper the houses were loopholed for musketry, the *azoteas* or flat, parapeted rooftops offered admirable defense positions, and the streets were easy to barricade. The cathedral, in the

Plaza Mayor, was amply stocked with ammunition. The garrison, by this time, consisted of some 7,000 troops, with more than forty guns. All in all, Monterey was not "the perfect Gibraltar" which Captain Henry called it, but it was a sufficiently formidable obstacle for an army of 6,000 with no proper siege train.[15]

To take Monterey General Taylor divided his small force into what were virtually two separate armies—one, under his own direct command to operate from the east; the other, commanded by Worth, to circle to the northward around the town and the two fortified hills beyond, and to come in from the west. About two o'clock in the afternoon of September 20, therefore, General Worth led his division of regulars and Colonel Hays's regiment of Texas cavalry—about 2,000 men altogether—out of the camp at the Walnut Springs, and started on his long circuit.

As Worth marched, the divisions remaining under Taylor's direct command moved forward to demonstrate against the eastern approaches of the city. The demonstration consisted principally of standing to arms in the open country between the camp and the city until after ten o'clock at night, when the troops returned to camp. The artillery, however, stayed on to emplace in the bottom of an old quarry what turned out to be an almost wholly ineffectual battery of two 24-pound howitzers and one mortar—the nearest approach the United States forces had to a siege train with which to batter the Mexican defenses.

Worth's circuit proved more difficult than had been anticipated, and only a little more than five miles was made in the first four hours. With the coming of darkness, he went into bivouac near the foot of a spur of the mountains to the northwest of the city. The separation of the United States forces was observed by the defenders, and to a resolute and enterprising commander might have offered opportunity. The possibility of such counteraction, however, seems not to have been within the calculations of either Taylor or Worth—and, as the event showed, they were right in disregarding the possibility.[16]

The first real clash of the Monterey operation took place early in the morning of September 21 when the Texas cavalry, moving in advance of Worth's column, was set upon by a body of Mexican lancers. The charge of the lancers, gallantly made and momentarily successful, brought them under the flanking fire of Worth's infantry and his field batteries. Lieutenant Colonel Juan Najera, leading the charge, was killed, the attack was broken up and the Mexican soldiers were scattered and pursued. Worth's men marched on, coming for a time under a plunging and ineffectual fire from the guns on the summit of Independence Hill. Before noon the column had passed beyond the hill, the artillery had been brought up, and Worth was in position on the Monterey-Saltillo road, ready to turn upon the western defenses of the city.

The first attack, upon the redoubt at the western end of the summit of Federation Hill, was entrusted to the ever-reliable Captain Charles F. Smith, with a command of Texas cavalry and his own artillerymen, both turned infantrymen for the assault. Crossing the waist-deep Santa Catarina amid a shower of shot which churned its surface but miraculously struck no one, Smith's men started working their way up the rock-strewed slopes of the hill. As they did so, Captain Miles came up with reinforcements from the Seventh Infantry, while the Fifth Infantry, under Colonel Persifor F. Smith, was sent to attack the Soldado Fort on the eastern end of the hill nearer the city.

The work on the western end was captured and its gun turned on the Soldado, as the several parties were working their way up the flanks of the hill to the second position with a rush. The guns of both positions of Federation Hill were turned upon the fortifications on Independence, a third of a mile distant across the gorge through which road and river ran. One half of the job of taking the western outer defenses of Monterey had been accomplished with a loss of fewer than twenty men when, with coming of night and a violent storm, Worth's men, who had been thirty-six hours without food, made a fireless bivouac where they stood.[17]

On the east of the city no such success attended United States operations on that September 21. Before the middle of the morning the two divisions—Twiggs's regulars and Butler's volunteers—were drawn out of camp and lined up once more, while Major Mansfield and his staff of engineer officers reconnoitered the northern and eastern faces of the city, or as much as could be observed through the embowered environs, with the hope that what was to be primarily a diversion in favor of Worth's operations might result in securing a lodgment in the enemy's defenses.

Toward ten o'clock the message came from the engineers—borne by Lieutenant John Pope, who was afterward to command the Union Army at Second Bull Run with such conspicuous lack of success—to come forward.[18]

In response to the call from Major Mansfield, the Third and First Regular Infantry regiments and the Baltimore-Washington battalion of volunteers—Twiggs's division less the Fourth Infantry left behind as guard for the ineffectual battery in the quarry—moved forward. The division was commanded for the day by Lieutenant Colonel John Garland, General Twiggs being temporarily incapacitated for early-morning fighting by reason of medicine taken the night before.[19]

Garland's men went gallantly forward but their ill-chosen line of advance brought and kept them under fire from the Mexican Citadel, on the right flank and rear, at the same time that it exposed them to fire in front from the Tenería and other outlying batteries. Before reaching the defenses, moreover, the line was deflected to the right, exposing the left flank to direct fire from the Tenería. As the advance struck the streets of the town, it was broken, and once more the bulk of the force deflected to the right under severe musketry fire from the loopholed houses and roof parapets.

Uncertain where to advance, and unable to advance anywhere, the infantry was standing under punishment when Captain Braxton Bragg's field battery pushed ahead into the streets of the town. There it found itself unable to accomplish anything and unable to get out of the pocket, except with the aid of the infantrymen in lifting and turning the carriages by hand. And all the while, the huddled troops, "cooped in a shambles," were pelted with lead until they were ordered out—all but one small party, composed of fragments of several companies which had come under the command of Captain Electus Backus of the First Infantry. Having turned left instead of right as the troops struck the suburbs, Captain Backus' party was overlooked in the withdrawal, and was left behind in a building to the rear of the Tenería, whence it was able to bring musket fire to bear upon the defenders of that work through the open gorge—a position which was to be of real assistance in subsequent assaults.[20]

These assaults were not long in coming. The next attack was by the Fourth Infantry which, at the time of the first attack, had been left behind to guard the siege battery. Stopped by a stream which it could not cross, with "every street blockaded, every house a fortification," the second attack like the first was a bloody failure.

Almost at the same time as the advance of the Fourth regulars, the Ohio regiment of volunteers came forward against a point farther to the right, or west. This charge, too, was halted by fire from the fortified Purísima bridge and the loopholed houses near by, and the withdrawal of the Ohio regiment from what seemed a futile attack was ordered.

Before the Ohioans had left the field, however, word came that the Tenería fort had fallen. The capture was made by the volunteer brigade of Brigadier General John A. Quitman—Campbell's First Tennessee and Jefferson Davis' Mississippi Rifles. Quitman's men had come forward by a route to the east of that followed earlier by Garland, and consequently less exposed to the heavy flanking fires from the Citadel. Its attack had been aided, also, by the sharpshooting of Captain Backus' men but even so the loss, especially in the Tennessee regiment, had been severe—more than one fourth of all the casualties of the entire army. In the inter-service controversies which were to come later, it became a prime point with the volunteers that in this, their first battle with the Mexicans, they had taken the work which had repulsed the regulars. To this the reply of the regulars was that the volunteers were aided by the demoralizing effect upon the defenders of the fire of Backus' regulars from their position in the rear of the fort. There ensued, too, a lively controversy as to whether it was the Mississippi riflemen or the Tennesseans who first rushed the fort. At the moment of capture, however, there was a deal more interest in securing shelter from the spiteful fires from the Diablo and the Citadel than there was in future controversies about "who won the war."[21]

Receiving word that the Tenería had been taken, the Ohio regiment returned to the attack, passed between the Purísima bridge and the Tenería, crossed through the eastern suburbs of the city, and brought up against the Fort Diablo. There the regiment was exposed to flanking fire from the fortified bridgehead which it had left to its rear, while its muskets availed little against the fort firing into its ranks from the front. The division commander, Major General Butler, was wounded, as was Colonel Mitchell, commander of the regiment, before the futile attack was abandoned and the regiment ordered back.

For the most part the Mexicans had stood on the defensive during the day's operations, but as the day closed there was a counterattack, under the direction of General Mejía, against the retiring troops. There was, also, a sweep by the Mexican lancers across the plain between the city and the camp in which, according to a Mexican account, "more than 50 men of various partisan enemies" were lanced.[22]

The day's loss in the ill-planned and almost accidental piecemeal attacks of September 21 against the lower end of Monterey had been almost 400 men, killed and wounded, with nothing to show for it, on the east, except the possession of one small fort. With the coming of darkness the men who had taken the Tenería were withdrawn and sent back to the camp, to be replaced for the night by the Kentucky regiment which had guarded the mortar battery during the day, and by some of the regular troops who had been repulsed in the morning fight. The night was one of chill, pelting rain, through which the wagons went, picking up the wounded who dotted the plain.[23]

Operations of September 22 began, on the west of the city, at 3:00 A.M., when picked parties of Worth's force, commanded by Lieutenant Colonel Childs, began a silent approach against the western end of Independence Hill which was to be carried, if possible, by surprise. In the rain and mist, men of the Eighth Infantry, Texas Rangers, and artillerymen, all fighting on foot, made their way upward from ledge to ledge until, just at break of dawn, they were discovered and the battle began. At the same instant a noisy demonstrating party was sent toward the Obispado, to create the impression that the fortified Bishop's Palace also was to be the object of immediate attack. The ruse succeeded in holding the defenders in the Obispado, while the attackers worked their way up against the smaller fortification on the crest of the hill.

On the opposite side of the city the party occupying Fort Tenería had lain through the long night of rain "flat down in the mud to cover themselves from the fire of Fort Diablo." From this position, "just at the gray dawn of day," they observed the storming of the height which commanded the Bishop's Palace. Wrote Captain Henry:

The first intimation we had of it was the discharge of musketry near the top of the hill. Each flash looked like an electric spark. The flashes and the white smoke ascended the hillside steadily, as if worked by machinery. The dark space between the apex of the height and the curling smoke of the musketry became less and less, until the whole became enveloped in smoke, and we knew it was gallantly carried. It was a glorious sight, and quite warmed our chilled bodies.[24]

There remained to be carried, of the western outer fortifications, the larger and presumably stronger position of the Obispado, a quarter of a mile down the hill toward the city. In preparation for the attack, a 12-pound howitzer was dismounted, dismantled and manhandled up the steep western slope of the hill, to be there reassembled, remounted and turned upon the Obispado. Meanwhile, infantry columns advanced along both flanks of the hill to invest the palace under a close and harassing rifle fire. This, with the shelling from the height, brought on a Mexican sortie, in midafternoon, presumably for the purpose of recapturing the heights. The United States forces allowed the sortie to advance some way up the ridge before a concentrated and effective fire was opened from front and both flanks. The Mexicans faltered, broke and withdrew, to be followed so closely that besieged and besiegers together poured over the walls of the Obispado, from which the garrison fled. The western approaches to Monterey were thus, by late afternoon of September 22, firmly held by General Worth's detachment.[25]

On the eastern side, there was neither attack nor sortie on the twenty-second, and no change in the situation except that about noon the regulars and the Kentucky regiment who had guarded the captured Tenería during the night were relieved by the troops of Quitman's brigade.

Toward midnight, however, there was a change in the Mexican position, when Ampudia ordered the abandonment of all the outer fortifications to the east and north of the town, except the Black Fort, and the concentration of their garrisons in the closely built squares of houses around the Great Plaza and the Cathedral. The order was executed, according to Mexican accounts, only after "noisy confusion" resulting from objection and grumbling on the part of the troops, who had so well held their own in the fighting of the twenty-first.

It was not until morning, however, that the United States force holding the Tenería discovered that Diablo and the other works had been abandoned. The advance to occupy the abandoned works and to enter the streets of the city was made with due caution, but by eleven o'clock Taylor had, as one Mexican writer put it, "invested with firmness" the eastern side of the city.[26]

Hearing the firing to the east in midmorning, and supposing that it betokened an attack in which his forces were to have had a concerted part, but that the orders for his co-operation had gone astray, Worth vigorously pressed his attack from the west. And so, through midday of September 23—the third day of battle and the fourth day since the arrival of the Americans before Monterey—fighting went on in the streets and houses of the town itself.

The Mexicans "had erected across the streets solid masonry walls, with embrasures for guns to fire grape, sweeping the street; then all the houses in the neighborhood were occupied by their infantry, loopholes being made to enable them to fire in any direction." But instead of attempting to advance through fire-swept streets, as had been done on the first day, the attackers were more cautious and more practical. Their artillery—Duncan's and Mackall's batteries on the west, Bragg's and Ridgeley's on the east—was used to fire through the streets, while the infantry and the dismounted Texans began to burrow their way through the interior walls of the blocks of houses—thus providing for themselves, with pick and crowbar, covered ways toward the Plaza.

During the fighting on the eastern side of the town, General Taylor and his staff walked about the streets on foot, "perfectly regardless of danger." When an officer remonstrated with him about his imprudent exposure, his reply was to direct him to "take that ax and knock in that door." Before the order could be obeyed, the door was unlocked from the inside and the general and his followers were invited in to what seems to have been a principal drugstore of the city, where they were offered "delicious, ripe limes and cool water."

By midafternoon the men on the eastern side of the town had dug and fought their way to within two squares of the central plaza when, for reasons which are not clear, General Taylor ordered their withdrawal from the positions which they had gained.

On the other side of the town, however, General Worth not only maintained the similar position which his men had gained by the day's fighting, but brought up the one and only mortar of the United States forces, which had been sent around to him, and during the night methodically shelled the Plaza into which the Mexican forces had been driven back.[27]

With affairs in this state there arrived from General Ampudia at three o'clock in the morning of September 24, a note written at nine the night before, proposing that he surrender the city and withdraw, taking with him all personnel and matériel of war. To this proposition General Taylor replied at seven in the morning, demanding surrender of the garrison as well as the town, on terms that the garrison be allowed, "after laying down its arms, to retire to the interior, on condition of not serving again during the war, or until regularly exchanged." An answer was required by noon.

Hostilities were suspended while negotiations went on. The two commanding generals met at one o'clock and agreed to name commissioners to discuss the terms of capitulation—Generals Ortega and

Requeña and Don Manuel Llano, governor of Nuevo León, for Mexico; Generals Worth and Henderson and Colonel Jefferson Davis, for the United States.[28]

Long negotiations punctuated with threats to break off resulted finally in terms which Taylor described, in his dispatch to the government, as "less rigorous than those first imposed," the reasons given for the more lenient requirements being "the gallant defence of the town, and the fact of a recent change of government in Mexico, believed to be favorable to the interests of peace."

The terms, agreed on late on the night of September 24, provided for the surrender of the place and its munitions and public property, with the Mexican forces to retain their arms and accouterments, and the artillery to keep one field battery, not to exceed six guns, and for the retirement of the Mexicans within seven days beyond a line through the pass of Rinconada, forty miles beyond Monterey, beyond which line the United States forces should not advance for eight weeks, "or until the orders or instructions of the respective governments can be received."[29]

The capitulation was carried out toward noon of September 25— a day of bright and glorious sun—when the Mexican flag came down, to an eight-gun salute from its own battery; the United States flag went up, to a salute of twenty-eight guns—one for each state in the Union; the Mexican troops marched out, carrying their arms; and the United States troops came marching in to the tune of "Yankee Doodle."[30]

[1] Ex. Doc. 60, H. R., 30th Cong., 1st sess., pp. 408, 411.

[2] Samson, William H. (ed.), Taylor, Zachary, Letters from the Battle-Fields of the Mexican War. Reprinted from the originals in the collection of William K. Bixby. (Rochester, New York, 1908), pp. 13, 16-18, 51.

[3] Robinson, J. B., Reminiscences of the Campaign in Mexico by a Member of the "Bloody First" (Nashville, 1849), pp. 109-111; Giddings, J. L., Sketches of the Campaign in Northern Mexico. By an Officer of the First Regiment of Ohio Volunteers (New York, 1853), p. 83.

[4] Henry, Campaign Sketches, pp. 170-171; Ashburn, P. M., A History of the Medical Department of the United States Army (Boston, 1929), pp. 56-61; Pub. Doc. 1, Sen., 29th Cong., 2nd sess., p. 197; Duncan, "Medical History," The Military Surgeon (1921), pp. 82, 95.

[5] Ex. Doc. 60, H. R., 30th Cong., 1st sess., pp. 417-419, 498-500.

[6] Same, pp. 678-681; Henry, Campaign Sketches, pp. 154, 164; Meade, Life and Letters, I, 103.

[7] Ex. Doc. 60, H. R., 30th Cong., 1st sess., p. 411; Henry, Campaign Sketches, p. 155; Giddings, Sketches, pp. 79-80.

[8] Ex. Doc. 60, H. R., 30th Cong., 1st sess., pp. 411, 418, 421, 498, 500-503.

[9] Ramsey (ed.), The Other Side, pp. 63-68.

[10] Henry, *Campaign Sketches*, pp. 173, 175-176; Robinson, *Reminiscences*, p. 122; Kenly, *Maryland Volunteer*, pp. 82-95. On the march to Camargo the United States soldiers had their usual difficulties with language. Captain Henry tells of one neighborhood dancing affair at which the men from the north sought to instruct the "bonita señoritas" in an "Americanized fandango." The effort failed, so far as dancing was concerned, but the affair ended in a "gale of spirits." The same diarist tells of a soldier searching in the chapparal for a lost horse, who accosted a Mexican with the question whether he "had seen anything of a damned *caballo* with a *cabrista* on his neck?" To the Mexican's polite answer of *"No entiende, señor,"* the soldier explosively replied, "Don't understand! Why the damned fool don't know his own language!"

[11] Ex. Doc. 60, H. R., 30th Cong., 1st sess., p. 421.

[12] Same, p. 442; Meade, *Life and Letters*, I, 130; Henry, *Campaign Sketches*, pp. 189-190.

[13] Ex. Doc. 60, H. R., 30th Cong., 1st sess., p. 507; Giddings, *Sketches*, pp. 142-144; Henry, *Campaign Sketches*, p. 191.

[14] Monterey (the present-day spelling of the name with two *r*'s had not been adopted in 1846) takes its name from the Count of Monterey, the ninth viceroy of New Spain, in whose administration it became a city in 1596.

[15] Henry, *Campaign Sketches*, p. 219; description of the city, surrounding terrain, and several works of fortifications is drawn from the official reports published in Ex. Doc. 4, H. R., 29th Cong., 2nd sess., pp. 76-107, and from the several volumes of reminiscences and sketches.

[16] Ex. Doc. 4, H. R., 29th Cong., 2nd sess., p. 83; Kenly, *Maryland Volunteer*, p. 100; Henry, *Campaign Sketches*, p. 193; Ripley, R. S., *The War with Mexico*, I, 204-205.

[17] Ex. Doc. 4, H. R., 29th Cong., 2nd sess., p. 103; Ripley, *The War with Mexico*, I, 216-223; Meade, *Life and Letters*, I, 133-134; Webb, Walter P., *The Texas Rangers* (Boston, 1935), pp. 105-107.

[18] Ex. Doc. 4, H. R., 29th Cong., 2nd sess., p. 84; Henry, *Campaign Sketches*, p. 194; Ripley, *The War with Mexico*, I, 206-207.

[19] Kenly, *Maryland Volunteer*, p. 119. This was done, General Twiggs explained to Captain Kenly, in accordance with his usual custom in anticipation of battle, in order to "loosen the bowels, for a bullet striking the belly when the bowels were loose might pass through the intestines without cutting them."

[20] Ripley, *The War with Mexico*, I, 207-209; Henry, *Campaign Sketches*, pp. 194-196; Kenly, *Maryland Volunteer*, pp. 107-111, 119-120; French, *Two Wars*, pp. 61-64. In these personal reminiscences, several items stand out as of particular interest in the light of the subsequent careers of some of the men mentioned. Thus, Captain Kenly (whose commanding officer, Lieutenant Colonel William H. Watson was killed) in speaking of the efforts to "reorganize the broken troops" declares that his "attention was particularly attracted to one officer by reason of his *voice;* it was so clear, so distinct, so encouraging, and commanding, that when I first heard it I looked toward him and inquired who it was, and was told that he was Colonel Albert Sidney Johnston, of Texas, serving on the staff of Major General Butler. I was sorry when my command was taken from him, as he was the first officer that had succeeded in bringing some degree of order out of the confusion which prevailed." Thus wrote one who became a major general of the Union Army about an outstanding characteristic of the Confederate general whose personal leadership was to end in death at Shiloh.

Another instance in battle at Monterey of traits of character which were to be noted in a greater war fifteen years later is the account in Lieutenant French's memoir of the withdrawal of a section of the battery of Captain Bragg. In command of the section was Lieutenant John F. Reynolds, who as Major General Reynolds, U. S. A., was to be killed at Gettysburg. Second-in-command was Lieutenant French, who was to become a major general, C. S. A. In the withdrawal two wheel horses of a caisson were killed. Reynolds, French and their men cut the horses out and pushed them out of the way into the ditches on either side. "Having gotten out," French wrote, "Bragg ordered me back alone to the ditch in the edge of the town to save the harness that was on the horses." General Taylor, meeting the lieutenant on his way to carry out the order, countermanded it as "nonsense," and sent him back. "I write down these little things," commented French on this and another order of his captain evincing a like regard for public property, "for they give instances of the observance of details, characteristic of this officer."

21 Ex. Doc. 4, H. R., 29th Cong., 2nd sess., pp. 85, 91; Henry, *Campaign Sketches,* pp. 195-198; Meade, *Life and Letters,* pp. 163-164; Robinson, *Reminiscences,* pp. 138-140, 162, 167-174; Claiborne, J. F. H., *Life and Correspondence of John A. Quitman* (New York, 1860), pp. 247-249; Sioussat (ed.), *Campbell's Letters,* p. 144.

22 Ramsey (ed.), *The Other Side,* p. 74; Giddings, *Sketches,* pp. 170-182. The chronicler of the Ohio regiment declares that the Mexican cavalry lanced the United States wounded who lay in their path, and broke ranks to "murder indiscriminately all the wounded Americans in that part of the field" (p. 180). The same report is found in contemporary letters of surgeons attending the wounded quoted in Duncan, Louis C., "A Medical History," *The Military Surgeon,* 1921, pp. 91-93. A "few discharges" from Bragg's battery "effectually dispersed them," according to Ripley, *The War with Mexico,* I, 214.

23 Robinson, *Reminiscences,* p. 146.

24 Ex. Doc. 4, H. R., 29th Cong., 2nd sess., p. 105; Henry, *Campaign Sketches,* pp. 203-204.

25 Meade, *Life and Letters,* I, 135-136; Ripley, *The War with Mexico,* I, 226-228; Henry, *Campaign Sketches,* pp. 205-206; Ex. Doc. 4, H. R., 29th Cong., 2nd sess., pp. 104-105.

26 Ex. Doc. 4, H. R., 29th Cong., 2nd sess., p. 86; Ramsey (ed.), *The Other Side,* p. 76.

27 Ex. Doc. 4, H. R., 29th Cong., 2nd sess., p. 87; Meade, *Life and Letters,* I, 136; Henry, *Campaign Sketches,* pp. 206-209. Captain Henry's explanation for withdrawal was that Taylor had ordered it "upon the supposition that General Worth would commence throwing shells into the city in the afternoon." Ripley (I, 232) attributes the withdrawal to the fact that Quitman's brigade, the major portion of the force engaged, had been on duty the previous night, and also to a realization of "the lack of concert with Worth." General Taylor's own explanation was that "General Quitman's brigade had been on duty the previous night. . . ."

28 Ex. Doc. 4, H. R., 29th Cong., 2nd sess., pp. 79-82.

29 Ex. Doc. 60, H. R., 30th Cong., 1st sess., pp. 344-350.

30 Henry, *Campaign Sketches,* pp. 214-215.

CHAPTER 10

A New Campaign and a New Commander

O N September 15, President Polk and his Cabinet met, heard the Secretary of War read dispatches from the army in Mexico, and, as they had done so often during that summer of 1846, discussed "the manner of prosecuting the war."[1]

The situation, so far as it was known in Washington at that time, was that the naval blockade of the coast of Mexico was in effect; that Taylor had completed his movement to Camargo and was about ready to advance on Monterey; that Wool's Army of the Center, which, under Taylor's general command, was intended for the occupation of Chihuahua, was still forming at its remote interior base of San Antonio de Bexar; and that Kearny's Army of the West was somewhere out along the Santa Fe Trail, under instructions to occupy New Mexico and, if it could be done before the setting in of winter, to press on to faraway California.

It was not known in Washington that Kearny had occupied Santa Fe nearly a month before, but word had been received by the President, on August 31, of the occupation of posts in California by the navy early in July. Six weeks before he received this word the ship *Lexington* had sailed from New York to round Cape Horn, carrying ordnance supplies and Captain C. Q. Tompkins' company of the Third Artillery, under orders to "act in conjunction with the United States naval forces in the Pacific." General Scott's instructions were "to cooperate in perfect harmony" with naval officers of all ranks but not to come "under the orders, strictly speaking, of any naval officer, no matter how high in rank." During the long voyage—it was, as things turned out, to last more than six months—the condition of the army men was to be "that of *passengers*, not *marines*," but in the event of action they were expected to show themselves "at least as efficient as any equal number of marines whatsoever." Three of the company of whom this high expectation was held were Lieutenant William Tecumseh Sherman, later to come to command of the Army of the United States; Lieutenant Henry Wager Halleck, to become President Lincoln's wartime Chief of Staff; and Lieutenant Edward O. C. Ord, to earn distinction as a major general of the Union Army. Their long voyage, however, added nothing of military luster to their names, for it brought them to the Pacific too late for action in either the occupation or the pacification of California.[2]

The information of that occupation which came to Washington at the very end of August was "deemed to be reliable, though not official"—it had come through British diplomatic channels by way of Mexico[3]—and so formed part of the basis for instructions sent on September 11 to Colonel J. D. Stevenson, commanding a New York volunteer regiment which was also to take the route around the Horn. The regiment, enlisted for the war with the proviso that its members were to be discharged in California at the end of their service, was to come under the command of General Kearny whenever he should reach that distant shore. In the meanwhile it was to form an independent command "except when engaged in joint operations with the naval force" on the coast.[4]

Besides ordering reinforcements to California by sea, the War Department had, on September 2, directed the attention of its principal commander in Mexico to the possibility of occupying the State of Tamaulipas and its port of Tampico, and had asked his views as to whether such a step should be undertaken, and if so, with what force. In this dispatch Secretary Marcy observed to General Taylor that "the possession of the northern provinces of Mexico . . . is undoubtedly an important object with reference to bringing the war to a successful termination."[5]

There was a growing realization in Washington, however, that even if all the expeditions against remote northern provinces of Mexico stretching from Tampico to San Francisco Bay should be completely successful in themselves, they still would not be sufficient to dispose Mexico to make peace. To do that, there must be either a changed disposition on the part of that government or such a direct thrust at the seats of national population and power as would bring about a willingness to treat.

As to the first of these possibilities, there had been some hope of a changed attitude when Secretary Buchanan made his peace overture of July 27, but on September 19 the President was notified that the new Mexican Government, dominated by the returned exile Santa Anna, was to be no more pacific in disposition than the Paredes government which it had overturned and succeeded.

This disappointing news was brought to the President by Nicholas P. Trist, chief clerk of the State Department, who translated and read the note of Señor Manuel Crescencio Rejón, Minister of Relations. The substance of the note—along with a deal of denunciatory discussion of the causes of the war—was that there could be no final decision on the proposal for peace until the first meeting of the new Mexican Congress, scheduled for December 6.[6]

Despite disappointment at what was tantamount to refusal to discuss terms of peace, the United States Secretary of State replied to Señor Rejón, one week after receipt of his note, that "the President will now await with patience and with hope the final decision of the Mexican government." That no unnecessary obstacles might be placed in the way of peace, Polk instructed Secretary Buchanan to delete from the note a proposed reference to indemnity for the expense of the war. "It would be time enough," the President said, "to insist upon it after negotiations were opened, and we came to the terms of a treaty." In the meanwhile he was content with a simple suggestion that delay in opening negotiations "would render a satisfactory adjustment more difficult because of the increased expense of the war."[7] The phrase "unconditional surrender" was not to be given currency until sixteen years later when U. S. Grant was to win his first fame by insisting on such terms at Fort Donelson—but insofar as Mr. Polk was concerned there was to be no insistence on its 1846 equivalent. The door to negotiation was to be kept open.

There were strong reasons other than those of economy and humanity why the administration should be anxious to see the war brought to a speedy close. The campaign for seats in Congress was evidencing a waning of the spirit with which the war had been undertaken in the spring. The opposition—even though most of them had voted for the war bill of May 13—was denouncing the struggle as "Mr. Polk's War," brought on by him unnecessarily and unconstitutionally. Antislavery men were labeling the war a struggle to extend the hated institution. Even the Democrats were showing less enthusiasm for a war which seemed to have in it more of delay and disease than of dash and glory. The noise of the political campaign, duly echoed south of the border, where the essentially partisan motivation of much of it was not understood, doubtless helped to heighten Mexican resistance and to prolong the struggle.

At any rate by late September there was no escaping the fact that the struggle was going to have to be fought out. In considering plans of campaign, however, the administration at Washington was greatly embarrassed by what the President called "want of reliable information." General Taylor, the President confided to his diary, "gives but little information. . . . He seems to act like a regular soldier, whose only duty is to obey orders" and "seems disposed to avoid all responsibility of making any suggestions or giving any opinions." As to General Scott, the President noted that he was "no aid to the department."[8]

But regardless of what were conceived to be the deficiencies of the military high command, there had to be a decision as to broadening the campaign. On September 22, therefore—three days after receipt of the Mexican dispatch declining negotiations, and after two more Cabinet meetings on the subject—directions were started to General Taylor to occupy the Department of Tamaulipas.

The directions, however, were to a considerable extent discretionary. "It is not proposed to withdraw any [of the force] now with you in your advance to the interior," Secretary Marcy wrote, "nor to divert any of the reinforcements that you may need to carry on your operations in that quarter," nor to "weaken the force on that line [the lower Rio Grande] any further than it can, in your opinion, be safely done." In view of General Taylor's repeated complaints about too many men having been sent him, the Secretary might well have felt that he had enough to spare a column for Tamaulipas, but the final decision as to whether such a column should be sent was left to the general on the spot.

The Secretary also proposed for the higher posts of command in the Tamaulipas expedition three of the new generals from civil life, all active Democrats and all destined to serve in the war of the sixties as general officers in the Union or Confederate armies. Major General Robert Patterson, Irish-born veteran of the War of 1812 and a leader in militia affairs and Democratic politics in his State of Pennsylvania, was to command. He was to be accompanied by Brigadier General James Shields, likewise Irish-born, who before the war had been a state official in Illinois and commissioner of the General Land Office, and who in a unique career after the war was to serve as United States senator from three states—

Illinois, Minnesota and Missouri; and by Brigadier General Gideon J. Pillow of Tennessee, a former law partner of President Polk and one of the managers of his candidacy in the Baltimore convention which had nominated him for President.

Secretary Marcy wrote that these assignments to command were to be made only if they did not "interfere with previous arrangements in regard to these officers," but for the stated purpose of avoiding delay, the Secretary wrote directly to General Patterson to make preparations for the movement, though he was not to put his orders into execution until he "learned from General Taylor that a sufficient force for the enterprise can be spared, and received his directions in regard to it." The Secretary of the Navy wrote also to Commodore Conner, directing naval co-operation in taking Tampico.[9]

On September 25, three days after these dispatches were sent, General Taylor forwarded his dispatch to the Adjutant General of the army announcing the capitulation of Monterey and its terms, including the eight-weeks armistice entered into subject to the approval of the governments at Mexico and Washington.[10]

So through the last days of September and the first days of October these two sets of dispatches traveled south and north, crossing on the way.

On Saturday October 10 the Cabinet met again in regular session, and once more "the manner of prosecuting the Mexican war was the chief subject considered." The principal topic of the day was the revived suggestion for an expedition to Vera Cruz. Information had recently been received, the President noted, that an army might "land near Sacraficias, within three or four miles of Vera Cruz, and invest the town of Vera Cruz in the rear. This was information not heretofore known, & fearing that it might not be correct," the Secretary of State was asked to bring to Washington for consultation "the late United States consul at Vera Cruz (Mr. Dimond), now in Rhode Island," from whom "reliable information" might be obtained.

The President's diary entry evidences something approaching excitement at the possibility of landing "an army of a few thousand men" to besiege the city from the rear, while "by keeping up a strict blockade by sea, the city and fortress of San Juan de Ulloa must in the course of a very few days surrender. If this be practicable, it is of the greatest importance that it be done."[11]

On the same day on which this step in the unfolding plan of campaign was considered by the Cabinet, Lieutenant Lewis A. Armistead reported at the headquarters of General Taylor in Monterey, bearing the War Department dispatches of September 22 which directed the expedition to Tamaulipas.

On October 12, the second day after receipt of this dispatch, General Taylor briefly acknowledged it and pointed out that "even were there no other obstacles" he could not immediately comply with instructions because of his obligation under the terms of the Monterey armistice to make no advance south of the line Linares-San Fernando.[12]

Three days later the general placed his "impressions and convictions very fully before the government." It was done with military restraint, but there is no mistaking the intensity of the resentment which prompted the letter—a resentment which might have been less intense had the general ever received the earlier dispatch of September 2 in which his recommendations as to the proposed Tamaulipas expedition were asked. That dispatch, however, had fallen into the hands of the enemy and, being "in the clear"—one of the many lacks of the War Department of the time was a system of codes and ciphers—had served to inform the enemy of the possibility of a descent upon Tampico before either General Taylor or General Patterson knew of it.

General Taylor's views took no account of the qualified and conditional nature of the dispatches to both Patterson and himself. The point, as he saw it, was that since he was "justly held responsible . . . for the conduct of operations" he "must claim the right to organizing all detachments and regulating the time and manner of their service"; and that the War Department by "corresponding directly with subordinates" had violated "the integrity of the chief command in the field."

There was merit in the point, though there was also reason for the way in which the War Department, remote from the scene and not knowing just how far apart Taylor and Patterson were, had sought by communicating with them simultaneously to expedite preparations. It was such a situation as reasonable men face to face could have cleared up but in correspondence at arm's length, with letters taking three weeks or more in passage, the incident drove one more wedge into the widening rift between the commander in the field and the administration at home.

In the same lengthy dispatch General Taylor also expressed himself more fully than he had so far done on the proper development of the campaign. To the suggestion of an advance both inland upon San Luis Potosí and toward the seacoast at Tampico, his reply was that he did not have more than half enough troops to advance upon San Luis alone, that he was still more deficient in stores and means for their transport, and that consequently it was "quite impossible" to make both advances simultaneously. Even if he had the necessary troops, he added, it would be impossible to hold San Luis Potosí from his present bases at the mouth of the Rio Grande. A shorter line of communication could be established from Tampico but, because of the prevalence of yellow fever, he felt that Tampico could not be occupied before the last of November.

The best course which could be adopted in northern Mexico, in the general's opinion, was to stand on a defensive line, either the line of the Rio Grande which might hereafter be insisted on as the boundary between the republics, or the line of the Sierra Madre which "could be held with a force greatly less than would be required for an active campaign." But if the government should "determine to strike a decisive blow at Mexico," he gave it as his opinion that "the force should land near Vera Cruz or Alvarado; and, after establishing a secure depot, march thence on the capital." To do this would require, he estimated, not less than 25,000 troops, of whom at least 10,000 should be regulars.[13]

On October 11—the day after Lieutenant Armistead delivered the War Department's dispatches to General Taylor at Monterey—Captain Joseph H. Eaton delivered to the War Department General Taylor's dispatches telling of the struggle for Monterey, the capitulation of the city and the eight-weeks armistice. President Polk and Secretary Marcy were quite as much perturbed by what they read as was General Taylor over the dispatches about the Tamaulipas expedition. The President wrote in his diary:

In agreeing to this armistice, General Taylor violated his express orders and I regret I cannot approve his course. He had the enemy in his power and should have taken them prisoners, deprived them of their arms, discharged them on their parole of honor, and preserved the advantage which he had gained by pushing on without delay farther into the country, if the force at his command justified it.[14]

On the next day the matter was laid before the Cabinet, which unanimously agreed with the President that the eight-weeks armistice should be brought to an end, but that orders for its termination should be sent to General Taylor "in terms neither to approve nor condemn his conduct in granting the capitulation and the armistice."[15]

On the following day, therefore, Secretary Marcy drafted a carefully and considerately worded dispatch to the commander in the field. He commended the "skill, courage and gallant conduct" of the troops at Monterey, expressed "gratitude and praise" for their accomplishments, regretted that the general had not "deemed it advisable to insist upon the terms [for surrender] first proposed," but expressed confidence that circumstances of which the President was not informed had justified the change, and was equally confident that if the general had received the dispatch of September 22, advising of the rejection of peace overtures by the Mexican Government, he "would not have acceded to the suspension of hostilities for even the limited period specified in the articles of capitulation" at Monterey.

With these propitiatory introductory remarks, the Secretary instructed that the required notice of the termination of the armistice be given at once. As to the future conduct of operations General Taylor's views were solicited. Was it advisable to advance beyond Monterey? Or beyond Saltillo? Would it be possible to carry out the occupation of Tamaulipas, as "suggested in the communication of September 22 . . . without at all interfering with the contemplated operation of the forces under your immediate command?" And if the Vera Cruz expedition which was under consideration should be undertaken, could Taylor "spare a detachment of two thousand regular troops for that purpose?" In all this, it was repeated, there was no desire or intention "to weaken the force with you at Monterey, or to embarrass you by diverting troops which you may deem necessary as reinforcements to the execution of your own contemplated operations."[16]

On the morning of October 14 Major James Graham left Washington bearing this dispatch to General Taylor and another to General Patterson, putting him on notice of the proposed expedition into southern Tamaulipas which, however, was not to be launched without orders from Taylor.[17] Eighteen days later, on the evening of November 2, the major delivered his dispatch to Taylor at Monterey.

Receipt of the dispatch was briefly and formally acknowledged on the next morning. Three days later, on the sixth, Major Graham was sent forward to give notice to the Mexican commanding general that the armistice was to be terminated on November 13, the date on which it was anticipated that the notice would reach San Luis Potosí, to which point the Mexican forces had retired.[18]

It was not until November 8, however, that General Taylor completed and dispatched his hurt and indignant reply to Secretary Marcy's letter. As to the implied criticism of allowing the Mexicans "to retire with their arms," he declared that there was not, and with his limited force could not have been, a complete investment of Monterey; that insistence upon more rigorous terms would have resulted in "the escape of the body of the Mexican force, with the destruction of its artillery and magazines"; that there would have been no advantage in this other than "the capture of a few prisoners of war, at the expense of valuable lives and much damage to the city"; and that these doubtful advantages were outweighed in his mind by "considerations of humanity."

The eight-weeks armistice was justified on military grounds, as evidenced by "the fact that we are not at this moment (within eleven days of the termination of the period fixed by the convention) prepared to move forward in force," and the further assertion that the armistice had "paralyzed the enemy during a period when, from the want of necessary means, we could not possibly move." Enlarging vehemently upon his shortage of transportation and stores, the general did not fail, in passing, to comment once more on the course of the War Department in corresponding directly with his subordinate and "directing an important detachment from my command without consulting me."

Beside justification on military grounds, the general ascribed his consent to the armistice to "other considerations" as well. He knew, he said, that the government had made propositions to the Government of Mexico to negotiate, and he "deemed that the change of government" in Mexico fully warranted him in "entertaining considerations of policy." General Ampudia, he said, had "distinctly told" him that he had invited cessation of hostilities "to spare the further effusion of blood and because General Santa Anna had declared himself favorable to peace." As to that the general declared that "it is not unknown to the government that I had the very best reason for believing the statement of General Ampudia to be true"—a polite dig at the disappointed hopes of the administration when it permitted the passage of Santa Anna through the blockade.[19]

The disapproval of the Monterey armistice and the resentment of

General Taylor at what he considered a rebuke touched off vehement, even violent, debate, both in the army and in the States. "The Army," wrote a Maryland volunteer officer, "was very much divided in opinion; those opposed to its terms as being too lenient increased in numbers with the number of days elapsing from the surrender of the town. . . . It is worthy of note that I met with no one who had been in the assaults of the first day on the eastern defenses that found fault with the terms. . . ." But one of the Tennessee volunteers, who was in the storming of the Tenería Fort where the regiment suffered the heaviest losses of the siege, took just the opposite view. The terms "met with a burst of universal indignation and disapprobation from the army," he wrote, and even after time and subsequent events had "tended partially to allay these feelings" the capitulation still was the subject of "animadversions and regrets." Such views, on the other hand, were attributed by an Ohio soldier-writer to "mustang heroes and militia generals," and Colonel Jefferson Davis of the Mississippi Rifles, one of the commissioners to negotiate the surrender, was so incensed at what he referred to as "speculation" and "misrepresentation about the capitulation of Monterey" that he wrote for the newspapers an elaborate account of the negotiations and justification of the terms granted. His letter was in dissent from one of General Henderson of Texas, also one of the commissioners who negotiated the surrender but who did not like the terms granted. Colonel Davis wrote that he did not believe the United States forces could have compelled a surrender at discretion, and he felt that an effort to do so would have caused the enemy to retreat, "bearing his light arms." Concluding that it was not in Taylor's power to overtake and capture the retreating enemy in that event, he submitted that "the moral effect of retiring under the capitulation was certainly greater than if the enemy had retreated without our consent."[20]

While carrying on correspondence with Washington as to the justification for the Monterey armistice, General Taylor also took the necessary steps to resume hostilities, as instructed. On November 8, the same day on which he made his reply to Secretary Marcy, orders were issued for General Worth and his division to march on the twelfth to occupy Saltillo, capital of the state of Coahuila, situated some seventy miles southwest of Monterey.[21]

Having expressed himself to the Secretary of War and having made his arrangements for further advance into the territory of the enemy as soon as the armistice terms would permit, on the next day General Taylor unbosomed himself to his old friend, Major General Edmund Pendleton Gaines, in a long and intimate letter, in which he repeated in more detail and even more vigorous language his reasons for agreeing to the armistice; renewed and reviewed at length his series of criticisms and complaints as to the treatment of himself and his army; outlined in some detail the composition and situation of his forces and his plans for future operations; and developed his own recommendation for bringing the war to an end.

If we are (in the language of Mr. Polk and General Scott) under the necessity of "conquering a peace" . . . we must go to Vera Cruz, take that place, and then march on to the city of Mexico. To do so in any other direction I consider out of the question. But, admitting that we conquer a peace by doing so . . . will the amount of blood and treasure which must be expended in doing so be compensated by the same? I think not. . . .

His own plan was not to carry his operations beyond Saltillo but "to take possession at once of the line we would accept by negotiation, extending from the Gulf of Mexico to the Pacific, and occupy the same . . . and say to Mexico, 'Drive us from the country'—throwing on her the responsibility and expense of carrying on offensive war." General Taylor's thought was that "a course of this kind, if persevered in for a short time, would soon bring her to her proper senses, and compel her to sue for peace, provided there is a government in the country sufficiently stable for us to treat with, which I fear will hardly be the case for many years to come."[22] Such a plan, had it been adopted, would have produced a state of affairs which, to judge from the decade of experience between Mexico and Texas, would have been neither peace nor yet war.

General Taylor's letter of November 9 appeared in January 1847 in the *New York Express,* without the name of the recipient but with General Gaines's permission, and was promptly and widely reprinted, especially by those journals which felt that Taylor had been badly treated by the disapproval of the Monterey armistice. Some of the President's friends doubted the genuineness of so indiscreet a letter but the President himself had no doubts, and General Gaines cleared up the question on January 25 by revealing himself as the person addressed.

Two days later the Secretary of War wrote General Taylor that the letter "will in a short time be in possession of our enemy; and coming, as it does, from the general to whom the conduct of the war on our part is confided, it will convey most valuable information to the Mexican commander. . . ." Moreover, the Secretary pointed out, "the disclosure of your views as to the future operations of our forces, accompanied, as it is, with your opinion that the fruits of the war, if completely successful, will be of little worth to us, will, it is greatly to be feared, not only embarrass our subsequent movements, but disincline the enemy to enter into negotiations for peace." In view of the harmful effect of the letter, both at home and abroad, the Secretary not only "deeply regretted" its publication but republished the paragraph of the General Regulations for the Army prohibiting officers from writing for publication "private letters or reports relative to military marches and operations" or of "placing such writing beyond his control, so that it finds its way to the press, within one month after the termination of the campaign to which it relates," under penalty of dismissal from the service.

To President Polk General Taylor's letter was "highly exceptionable" and its publication "unmilitary and a violation of duty," especially since it "gave publicity to the world of the plans of campaign contemplated by the government, which it had been desired . . . to keep concealed from the enemy until they were consummated."[23]

The letter and its publication were the more unfortunate in that on October 20 a joint army-navy expedition against Vera Cruz had been decided on, and orders to that effect had been dispatched on the twenty-second by the hand of Robert McLane, who before leaving Washington had received instructions from the Secretary of War and the President. Three weeks later, and three days after General Taylor had written his controversial letter to General Gaines, Mr. McLane reached Monterey and presented his dispatches.

Taylor was advised first, that the Cabinet was unanimously of the opinion that he should not advance beyond Monterey, there being "no object to be attained by advancing further in that direction towards the attainment of peace," and further, that an expedition against Vera Cruz and the fortress of San Juan de Ulúa had been determined on. It was thought that 4,000 men, with the assistance of the navy in the Gulf, would be sufficient for the purpose "if the expedition could go forth without the object being known to the enemy." The general's attention was drawn to the possibility of abandoning the expedition to Chihuahua and drawing to himself the troops under General Wool, the decision being left to Taylor. If this were done, the Secretary suggested the further possibility that he might be able to spare men for the expedition to Vera Cruz, though it was made plain that this was not to be done if it would so weaken Taylor's force as to put it in danger. As to this, Taylor was to be the judge, but if it could be done, he was instructed to make ready 4,000 men, of whom something like half should be regulars, for embarkation for Vera Cruz. "Secrecy is of the utmost importance," Secretary Marcy added—in a war in which nothing was secret—and "the belief should be encouraged that Tampico is the destination of the expedition."[24]

General Taylor promptly agreed that there was no necessity and small value in occupying Chihuahua, and advised that General Wool had found no practicable route there, except that by way of Parras. This would bring Wool into the southern part of Coahuila, and in reach of Saltillo, to which point Taylor thought it highly desirable that his own command should advance. He did not believe that the descent upon Vera Cruz should be made with fewer than 10,000 men, which was more than he could spare from the line of the Sierra Madre. However, he believed that after moving on Tampico—which would not delay movements beyond—he could hold 4,000 troops, of whom 3,000 would be regulars, "ready to embark at some point on the coast."[25]

And so, both at Washington and with the army in Mexico, the Vera Cruz expedition—still limited in concept, however, to doing no more than taking the city and its island fortress—came gradually to take the dominant place in the planning of the campaign.

The question of command of the proposed expedition to Vera Cruz continued to agitate the inner councils at Washington through the early weeks of the autumn. On September 12, from the "Headquarters of the Army, West Point, New York," General Scott had written the Secretary of War asking him "to remind the President" of his standing request to "be sent to take the immediate command of the principal army against Mexico"—a step which he "had reason to believe" would be "neither unexpected nor undesired by that gallant and distinguished commander," General Taylor. But President Polk was not yet ready to accept General Scott in the capacity of principal field commander, nor had he changed his mind forty days later.

General Scott continued his study of the subject, however, and on

October 27, handed to Secretary Marcy a memorandum on "Vera Cruz and its castle," in which he came to the conclusion that mere capture of the town and fortress would not be worth the lives it would cost unless "the capture should be promptly followed by a march thence with a competent force, upon the capital"—which would require some 20,000 men.[26]

In the Congressional elections the administration suffered such heavy losses that the new House of Representatives—which, under the then provisions of the Constitution, was not scheduled to meet until December 1847—had a slight Whig majority. On the Saturday after the elections, November 7, Thomas H. Benton, Senator from Missouri, called at the White House with news from his son-in-law, Frémont, in California. That evening he returned for a long discussion of the progress of affairs in Mexico, in the course of which he urged the capture of Vera Cruz and the march to Mexico City. On the following Tuesday Senator Benton called again, to repeat his recommendation that the Vera Cruz expedition be carried on to the capital of Mexico as the one means of securing peace. The subject of command of such an expedition came up. The senator concurred in the view that Taylor was not the man, and volunteered that he had no confidence in Scott. His view, in fact, was that there should be a lieutenant general, ranking both Scott and Taylor, who should be "a man of talents and resources as well as a military man," and that "if such an office was created by Congress, he would be willing to accept the command himself." The President's reply was that "he would be glad to see him at the head of the army in such an expedition."

On November 11 Senator Benton again called at the White House for further conversation about the war in Mexico and command of the army. The President "did not think it probable that Congress would create the office of Lieutenant-General" but did think that if additional forces were called out, he might create an additional major-generalship, to which Senator Benton might be appointed. Since such an officer would be junior in rank to Scott and Taylor, however, the senator "would not desire" the military appointment, but might be willing to accompany the expedition to Mexico City as a commissioner for the negotiation of peace.

On November 12—the same day, as it happened, on which Mr. McLane was delivering to Taylor in Monterey the dispatches of October 22—the Secretary of War handed to the President another memorandum by General Scott on the Vera Cruz-Mexico City expedition. To capture Vera Cruz, the general wrote, would require a minimum of 10,000 men, who should be put afloat, at the latest, by the first of January; and an additional 20,000 men should be available for the movement inland not later than the season of the *vómito*, or yellow fever, on the coast, which was not to be feared before May.[27]

On November 13, while the President still was considering the proposals of General Scott, Taylor started his movement forward from Monterey, through the pass of the Rinconada up to the 5,000-foot elevation of the central plateau. Saltillo was occupied on the sixteenth, without opposition other than a formal protest from the governor of the state of Coahuila and reconnaissance was made twenty-five miles farther to the front.[28]

On the same day, in faraway Washington, General Scott submitted to Secretary Marcy a third memorandum on the Vera Cruz-Mexico City expedition, based on the decision of the President two days earlier to call into service nine additional volunteer regiments for the term of the war.[29] Taking into account the new forces anticipated, the general in chief calculated somewhat optimistically the numbers available on both fronts, outlined requirements as to boats, landing barges, ships and ponton train, and urged haste in securing them.

The Cabinet met again on the following day, when "the Mexican war occupied exclusive attention." Scott's latest memorandum was submitted, as were the views of Senator Benton. "Much conversation took place. . . . Great difficulty existed in selecting the commander of the expedition." There was a lack of confidence in Taylor's capacity, and objection to his partisan position. Patterson, who had been named to command the Tampico expedition, lacked experience. Scott was "hostile to the administration," but four of the six members of the Cabinet, nevertheless, favored him for the command. One was without decided opinion, one was opposed. The President's own feeling was that after Scott's "very exceptionable letter in May nothing but stern necessity and a sense of public duty could induce" him to make the appointment. But after a night's reflection these considerations prevailed—even though the President still would have preferred Benton if Congress could be induced to create the office of lieutenant general—and on November 18, with the concurrence of the Secretaries of War and the Navy, the President came to conclusion that he was "compelled to take General Scott."

Early on the following morning General Scott was invited to the White House where the President—as noted in the day's diary entry—

discussed with him the mutual confidence which must exist between the government at home and the general in the field and received assurances that the general "had the utmost confidence" in the administration and would cordially co-operate. Upon being told that Polk was "willing that bygones should be bygones and that he should take the command," General Scott appeared to be "so grateful and so much affected that he almost shed tears."[30]

The general's recollection of the event—set down, however, after he had learned that the President persisted in his desire to have the office of lieutenant general created and filled by Senator Benton—was quite different. The anxiety and gratitude, as he saw it, were on the part of President Polk. "Again and again," the general wrote, he was "assured that the country would be bankrupted and dishonored unless the war could be made plainly to march toward a successful conclusion, and that I only could give to it the necessary impetus and direction." The general felt that "not to have been deceived by such protestations would have been, in my judgment, unmanly suspicion and a crime."[31]

There can be little doubt that the general read into his conversation with the President something of his own expansive enthusiasm—but however the conversation between the two men may have run, the President had accepted the one commander, in all probability, who could have carried through the Vera Cruz-Mexico City expedition, and the general had received the command for which he so ardently longed.

---

1 Quaife (ed.), *Polk's Diary*, II, 139; Nevins (ed.), *Polk*, p. 148.

2 The *Lexington*, in fact, sailed from New York one week after the occupation of Monterey, in California. Pub. Doc. 1, Sen., 29th Cong., 2nd sess., p. 65. Ex. Doc. 60, H. R., 30th Cong., 1st sess., pp. 245-247; Howe, M. A. DeWolfe (ed.), *Home Letters of General Sherman* (New York, 1909), Chapter II; Sherman, General William T., *Memoirs* (New York, 1875), I, 12-18. Lieutenant Halleck took the opportunity on the long voyage of translating Baron Jomini's *Life of Napoleon*. His translation was published in four volumes in 1864, after Halleck had become chief of staff.

3 Quaife (ed.), *Polk's Diary*, II, 107-108; Nevins (ed.), *Polk*, p. 142.

4 The New York regiment sailed on September 25. Pub. Doc. 1, Sen., 29th Cong., 2nd sess., p. 65; Ex. Doc. 60, H. R., 30th Cong., 1st sess., pp. 159-162.

5 Same, p. 340.

6 Quaife (ed.), *Polk's Diary*, II, 144-145; Nevins (ed.), *Polk*, pp. 148-149; McCormac, *James K. Polk*, pp. 444-445; Ex. Doc. 4, H. R., 29th Cong., 2nd sess., pp. 43-44.

7 Same, pp. 44-45; Quaife (ed.), *Polk's Diary*, II, 156-157; Nevins (ed.), *Polk*, p. 152.

8 Quaife (ed.), *Polk's Diary*, II, 139-140, 151; Nevins (ed.), *Polk*, pp. 148-150.

9 Same, p. 150; Quaife (ed.), *Polk's Diary,* II, 150; Ex. Doc. 60, H. R., 30th Cong., 1st sess., pp. 341-345.

10 Same, pp. 345-347.

11 Quaife (ed.), *Polk's Diary,* II, 179-180; Nevins (ed.), *Polk,* pp. 154-155.

12 Ex. Doc. 60, H. R., 30th Cong., 1st sess., p. 350.

13 Same, pp. 351-354.

14 Quaife (ed.), *Polk's Diary,* II, 181; Nevins (ed.), *Polk,* p. 155.

15 Same, p. 156; Quaife (ed.), *Polk's Diary,* II, 183-185.

16 Ex. Doc. 60, H. R., 30th Cong., 1st sess., pp. 355-357, 370.

17 Same, p. 358.

18 Same, p. 361.

19 Same, pp. 358-360.

20 Kenly, *Maryland Volunteer,* pp. 144-145; Robinson, *Reminiscences,* p. 157; Giddings, *Sketches,* p. 208; Claiborne, *Quitman,* I, 262-270.

21 Ex. Doc. 60, H. R., 30th Cong., 1st sess., p. 362.

22 Claiborne, *Quitman,* I, 256-261.

23 Quaife (ed.), *Polk's Diary,* II, 353-357; Nevins (ed.), *Polk,* pp. 191-193; Ex. Doc. 60, H. R., 30th Cong., 1st sess., pp. 391-392.

24 Quaife (ed.), *Polk's Diary,* II, 198-200; Nevins (ed.), *Polk,* p. 159; Ex. Doc. 60, H. R., 30th Cong., 1st sess., pp. 362-367.

25 Same, pp. 374-376.

26 Same, pp. 372-373, 1268-1270.

27 Quaife (ed.), *Polk's Diary,* II, 219-231; Nevins (ed.), *Polk,* pp. 161-166; Ex. Doc. 60, H. R., 30th Cong., 1st sess., pp. 1270-1273.

28 Same, pp. 362, 377-378, 436, 511.

29 Same, pp. 1273-1274; Nevins (ed.), *Polk,* pp. 166-167; Quaife (ed.), *Polk's Diary,* II, 234-236.

30 Nevins (ed.), *Polk,* pp. 170-171; Quaife (ed.), *Polk's Diary,* II, 239-245.

31 Scott, *Memoirs,* II, 397-399.

Contest in the Streets, Monterey.

CHAPTER 11

Armistice without Peace

"THE task of fighting and beating the enemy," General Taylor reported from Monterey, "is among the least difficult that we encounter: the great question of supplies seemingly controls all operations in a country like this."[1] But the difficulties of maintaining a supply line of more than 400 miles from the Brazos with the available resources of steamboat and animal transport were hardly more exasperating than those of maintaining order and discipline.

General Worth's troops made up the garrison of the city of Monterey itself. The remainder of the army stayed in the camps at the Walnut Springs. There, in an open space in front of General Taylor's tent, Mexicans from the surrounding country "quietly established a market for the sale of their products" in a place where "they felt they were safe"—and, added Captain Kenly, "about the only safe place for them within a circuit of twenty miles." Within a few days after the surrender, he wrote, "a series of wanton outrages perpetrated upon the inoffensive inhabitants caused the liveliest sense of indignation among our best troops, and provoked bloody retaliation from the Mexicans." An example of what was declared to be not an uncommon situation was the wounding of a sergeant by a "gang of Mexican desperadoes, followed in a few days by a wholesale slaughter of Mexicans, but not by our men."[2]

The qualification, "not by our men," is typical of much of the comment on what Captain Henry referred to as the "many riots and murders" in the occupied areas, which seem usually to have been the work of men from some outfit other than that of the writer commenting. Thus, a writer from the First Ohio records that "while several of its number were treacherously murdered" by the Mexicans—the victims including Father Rey, attached to the regiment as an unofficial

173

chaplain, and a soldier detailed as his lay assistant—the regiment "never sought for blood save upon the battle-field."[3]

Writers from among the regulars, however—and most of the surviving memoirs were written by regular officers—were not so lenient in their discussion of the conduct of the volunteers. "The people are very polite to the regulars," Second Lieutenant George B. McClellan of the Engineers wrote, "but they hate the volunteers as they do old scratch himself. . . . You never hear of a Mexican being murdered by a regular or a regular by a Mexican. The volunteers . . . think nothing of robbing or killing the Mexicans."[4]

Lieutenant Meade, another future commander of the Army of the Potomac, wrote three weeks after the occupation of Monterey that "the volunteers have made themselves so terrible by their previous outrages as to have inspired the Mexicans with a perfect horror of them," and, a month later, that the "disturbances" created by the volunteers had "at last aroused the old General. . . ."[5]

When the mounted brigade of Texas Rangers came to the end of their enlistment and "expressed a desire to go home," they were mustered out with the thanks of the commanding general for their efficient service and his wishes for a happy return to their families and homes. To the Adjutant General of the Army, General Taylor reported that with the departure of the mounted Texans, "we may look for a restoration of quiet and order in Monterey, for I regret to report that some shameful atrocities have been perpetrated by them since the capitulation of the town."[6]

In this hope the general was to be disappointed, despite a "rigid system of police" and strict regulations limiting entrance into the city by members of commands other than the city garrison itself. "Officers of all grades" were called on "to give their aid in carrying out measures so essential to the due preservation of order and the restoration of confidence among the citizens of Monterey."[7]

In spite of every effort, however, there seems to have been a continuation of disorders. A month after the occupation of Monterey—by which time a sharp controversy had begun between regulars and volunteers as to their respective parts in the capture of the city—Lieutenant Meade wrote again of the volunteers:[8]

They are sufficiently well-drilled for practical purposes, and are, I believe, brave, and will fight as gallantly as any men, but they are a set of Goths and Vandals, without discipline, laying waste the country wherever we go, making us a terror to innocent people, and if there is any spirit or energy in the Mexicans, will finally rouse the people against us, who now are perfectly neutral. . . . They cannot take care of themselves; the hospitals are crowded with them, they die like sheep; they waste their provisions, requiring twice as much to supply them as regulars do. They plunder the poor inhabitants of everything they can lay their hands on, and shoot them when they remonstrate, and if one of their number happens to get into a drunken brawl and is killed, they run over the country, killing all the poor innocent people they find in their way, to avenge, as they say, the murder of their brother. . . . The cause is the utter incapacity of their officers to control them or command respect. The officers . . . know they are in service for only twelve months; at the end of that time they will return to their homes, when these men will be their equals and their companions, as they have been before, and in consequence they dare not attempt to exercise any control over them. Then, for the most part, they are as ignorant of their duties as the men, and conscious of their ignorance, they feel they cannot have the command over their people that the regular officers do over their soldiers.

The occasion of Lieutenant Meade's discussion was a series of events in late November, in which "a party of volunteers, to what regiment attached unknown, went into a house in the suburbs of the town, and after forcibly driving out the husband, committed outrages upon his wife." A Kentucky volunteer was found a day or so after with his throat cut, presumably in retaliation. Two Mexicans were shot, probably by Kentucky volunteers in revenge. Another Kentuckian was found with his throat cut; more Mexicans were shot. Renewed orders were issued to stop such outrages.

"The many outrages that have been recently committed in the city of Monterey, and elsewhere, upon the persons and property of Mexican citizens," one order ran, "render it necessary to restrict the extensive use of riding animals among the rank and file of the army." It was ordered that "all horses, mules, or donkeys, in possession of noncommissioned officers, musicians, privates, or laundresses" be sold before December 1, "after which date none will be tolerated in their possession." All animals found in violation of the order were to be "disposed of for the benefit of the hospitals."[9]

Despite efforts to restrict men with arms in their hands to the limits of the camp, the aroused Kentuckians—it was supposed—continued to seek revenge. A Mexican was killed, and a twelve-year-old boy was shot in the leg. When the child was brought and laid before the general's tent, he ordered the First Kentucky, the accused regiment, to march to the rear in disgrace. Upon promises of punishment for the guilty and better conduct in the future, the general relented in his order, "but the well-wishers of our cause," wrote Lieutenant Meade, "would have been glad to see him disband the whole regiment and send them home as a disgrace to the army and their state."[10]

The disorders, according to one volunteer writer, resulted from the "disobedience and dissipation" of a "few turbulent spirits," often "provoked by similar conduct on the part of the Mexicans." The *lex talionis*, it was conceded, was "too often" resorted to, and "the innocent probably suffered equally with the guilty."[11] Such conditions, with the innocent and inoffensive suffering at the hands of the lawless and violent, were probably not unknown before the occupation by United States forces. In fact, one lieutenant of regulars, who in time was to command the United States Army, wrote that "under the humane policy of our commander, I question whether the great majority of the Mexican people did not regret our departure as much as they had regretted our coming. Property and person were thoroughly protected, and a market was afforded for all the products of the country such as the people had never enjoyed before."[12] These comments of General Grant were written long years after but it might be that he was no further from a true perspective in one direction than were the anxious writers of the moment in the other.

The sufficiently difficult task of keeping order among the soldiers, whether the regulars or those whom General Scott called "the wild volunteers," was made immeasurably more difficult by the fact that there was nothing in the military laws of the time providing for trial and punishment of soldiers for offenses other than those specified in the Articles of War. When committed in the United States, offenses other than military were triable by the ordinary civil courts. Since no United States Army had operated for any length of time beyond the national boundaries before the War with Mexico, the competence of military tribunals in such cases was deemed questionable. The War Department, therefore, had asked Congress, at the session beginning in December 1845, to extend the jurisdiction of courts-martial when forces were serving in foreign countries, but Congress had failed to act. The Secretary of War informed General Taylor, on November 25, that another effort was to be made to secure Congressional authority for punishment of civil offenses committed by United States soldiers in foreign lands, but in the meanwhile there seemed to be no clear warrant for any punishment, even in most flagrant cases, except to send the culprit away from the army—which was eminently satisfactory to most of the culprits.[13]

Despite such legalistic handicaps in the maintenance of order, amounting almost to open invitation to disorder, the effects of occupation were not all bad. "The filthy conditions of the streets," Captain Henry wrote, "soon gave place to cleanliness; the stores were opened . . . and wherever we go, we pay for what we get at two or three times the usual price of the country, and both their civil and religious rights are protected." On the very day on which the Mexican troops began their departure from Monterey, the marketmen and women were in the Plaza, with delicious grapes and other fruit for sale.[14] The same thing was true of the camps at the Walnut Springs. "Scarcely had the sound of battle ceased," a Tennessee volunteer wrote, "ere our camp became a perfect market, where, from dawn to dark, hundreds of Mexicans of both sexes were vending all the fruits and productions of their highly favored clime. . . . Though for more than two months these hucksters continued in increased numbers to throng our camps, yet to the honor of our soldiery, but few instances occurred of any attempts to defraud or wrong them." To government rations were added bread, eggs, oranges, lemons, pomegranates, grapes and bananas brought daily into camp, with "now and then a cow, and then a goat . . . to be milked at the tent door, to the great gratification of our men." So extensive were the purchases and use of fruits from the Mexicans that Lieutenant Meade attributed the fact that nearly one third of the army suffered from chills and fever to injudicious indulgence in oranges, pomegranates and other fruits of the country.[15]

The city—as was to be expected, particularly after access to it was restricted—became a great magnet for the soldiers when they could get a day off and the necessary pass, limited to two per day per company. The palatial residence of General Arista, who had commanded the Mexican forces at Palo Alto and Resaca de la Palma, was a particular point of interest. Its cool, high-ceilinged, marble-floored rooms had been converted into a hospital, and the fine fruits in its rich gardens were reserved for use by the wounded and protected by sentries.[16]

Even more appealing to the sight-seeing soldier, perhaps, were the Great Plaza and the market plaza, in the center of the city. On the eastern side of the Great Plaza was the Cathedral, which during the battle had been used as a magazine for the storage of ammunition. Facing it, on the west, was the City Jail, in front of which thirty-four captured guns were lined up. In the rear of the Carcel Ciudad was the smaller market plaza, with its display of fruits and vegetables, and its men and women smoking paper-wrapped cigaritos. Nearly all the shops had reopened, some with "assortments of rare and valuable goods, particularly of Chinese fabrics." In time, however, the Mexican merchants packed up their goods and left for Saltillo, "it being impossible to compete with our merchants and sutlers, who, with true American energy, are pushing our goods forward."[17]

An "astonishing number of non-combatants sprang up, as if by magic, around the army of occupation. Where they came from so suddenly after the surrender, nobody could tell, but the place was filled with them. American stores, American goods, American drinks, and American faro have driven out Mexican shopkeepers and gamblers." There was, of course, an American newspaper—the *Monterey Gazette* published by Durant Da Ponte, son of the librettist of Mozart's operas. Mr. Hamblin's American circus gave its performances in the Mexican cockpit. "We Americans are a great nation!" Captain Henry wrote. "Whip the Mexicans one day, and offer them the amusements of a circus the next."

Despite the attractions of the town in the shape of "billiard saloons, restaurants and drinking saloons," solid work was done by the army in the way of drill and training. The camps in the Bosque de San Domingo—or the Walnut Springs as the Americans called it—were made "more permanent and orderly," and for weeks "the parade ground was daily beaten to dust under the feet of the men" in squad drills at all hours, company drills twice a day, and finally, battalion drills and drills of the regiments. There were guard mounts, dress parades, five daily roll calls, tattoo and taps, for daily routine. It was observed that "whatever may be said of those [officers] who received their commissions before entering the field, the men generally made judicious selections in filling the vacancies that afterward occurred. Many of the newly elected lieutenants were exceedingly active and trustworthy. . . ."[18]

Sickness was ever present, and sick call was responded to, at times, by almost as many men as reported for drill. The few overworked medical officers were "literally fatigued to death," serving not only their own soldiers but also many of the neighboring Mexicans who "were occasionally to be seen hanging around the outskirts" of the party assembled each morning at sick call. Though there was no such rate of mortality as at Camargo, there was "scarcely a day that the muffled drums of some regiment did not announce the departure of one or more poor fellows to the chaparral."[19]

One death—that of Captain Randolph Ridgeley, who had succeeded to the command of Ringgold's Battery after that officer was killed at Palo Alto—attracted the attention of the whole army. Captain Ridgeley's record as a bold and skillful artillerist was outstanding. He had braved danger in every battle, without a scratch, and was regarded as the best horseman in the army. He and a companion had gone into the city to sup with Lieutenant William W. Mackall, who had commanded one of Worth's batteries on the west side of Monterey, and who in later years was to serve as the chief of staff of the Confederate Army of Tennessee. Picking its way along a street whose paving stones had been torn up to make barricades and had not been replaced, Captain Ridgeley's horse stumbled on a loose stone and threw its rider against another, fracturing his skull. The death of many men by disease and even in battle passed all but unnoted; the death of this man by simple accident touched the heart of the army. With his death, Braxton Bragg succeeded to the command of the old Ringgold Battery, and Captain T. W. Sherman, later to become a major general of the Union Army and to be almost invariably confused with W. T. Sherman, took command of the Bragg Battery.[20]

Amid life—and death—in Monterey, and back along the line of communications through Camargo and Matamoros all the way to Brazos, officers and soldiers never ceased to speculate on where they would go next, and when, and what they would do. Some idea of the correspondence between the general and the War Department got around in the army and there were some information and a plethora of rumors about Mexican whereabouts and intentions. There was hardly an active man, therefore, who did not have and express ideas about what ought to be done, and how.

The last of the Mexican force marched out of Monterey on September 28, the same day on which General Santa Anna left the distant capital of Mexico to go to the aid of the forces in the north. It was known that the Mexican army had paused at Saltillo long enough for General Ampudia to communicate with the capital and to issue a proclamation of explanation and exculpation for his defeat, and that by mid-October it had fallen back another 250 miles to San Luis

Potosí, where Santa Anna himself waited to take direct command.[21]

It was at San Luis, on November 10, that Santa Anna received Taylor's notice of the resumption of hostilities on the thirteenth, to which he replied, "You may commence hostilities when you please, and I shall duly correspond to them." To this he added the warning that Taylor "ought to discard every idea of peace while a single North American treads in arms the territory of this republic, or while hostile squadrons remain in front of her ports."

This message was received by Taylor on November 14, as he was on his way to occupy Saltillo. "Peaceable possession" of the capital of Coahuila was taken on the sixteenth; Worth's force of some 1,200 regulars was left to garrison it and the surrounding country; and a week later Taylor was back at his camp near Monterey, working on his plans and combinations for occupying a line of posts extending from Parras, ninety miles west of Saltillo, through that point and Monterey, to Victoria and Tampico—a total distance, as the roads ran, of some 600 miles.[22]

The extreme right of this long line was to be held by the force of General John E. Wool. A stock jest of Taylor's camps at the time was to ask, with mock solemnity, "when did you hear from General Wool?" the soldiers being amused by the report that he was marching somewhere in the wilderness searching for General Taylor.[23] General Wool, in point of fact, had marched far, and he had sought permission to put himself in supporting distance of Taylor's army, but he had not been wandering.

He had left San Antonio de Bexar upon his assigned mission of going to Chihuahua, just as Monterey fell. His column consisted of portions of the Sixth Infantry and of the Second Dragoons, regulars; the six-gun regular field battery of Captain John M. Washington; the Arkansas regiment of cavalry commanded by Colonel Archibald Yell; the First Illinois Regiment, commanded by Colonel John J. Hardin, former Whig Congressman whose seat in the House of Representatives had been taken by his Whig friend, Abraham Lincoln; and the Second Illinois, commanded by Colonel William H. Bissell, future representative in Congress and governor of Illinois. The column had been assembling at San Antonio since orders were issued in June but the troops had a long way to come to get to the starting point. The battery came overland all the way from Carlisle Barracks in Pennsylvania; the Arkansas cavalry and the regulars from Fort Smith, Arkansas, and Fort Gibson, Indian Territory; and the two Illinois regiments by steamboat to New Orleans, by ship to Port La Vaca on Matagorda Bay, and thence overland nearly 150 miles—two weeks' haul for loaded wagons in wet weather—to San Antonio. Two other regiments, the Tennessee and Kentucky cavalry, originally intended for Wool, marched overland from their home states, also, but before reaching San Antonio were diverted to the lower Rio Grande.

Supplies came by the long and difficult route through Port La Vaca, but General Wool had been forehanded in the matter of timely requisition of the wagons needed for the haul from the port to San Antonio, and so despite mix-ups in shipping wagon parts, he was sufficiently served with transportation.[24]

General Wool himself reached San Antonio in mid-August. Six weeks later, with his preparations as complete as he could make them, he marched during the last week of September with just under 2,000 men, leaving a strong rear party to follow with additional supplies. After an eleven-day march, the little column reached the riverbank opposite the Mexican town of Presidio Rio Grande. The river here was nearly 300 yards wide and more than four feet deep, with a rapid current, but again, as in the matter of wagons, General Wool had made timely preparation. Captain William D. Fraser, his engineer officer, had brought along the pontoons and framed timbers for a so-called "flying bridge," prepared at San Antonio, and on October 12, three days after reaching the river, the army with all its wheeled and animal transport marched across dry-shod.[25]

One of the engineer officers with the column was Lieutenant William B. Franklin who, in December 1862, was to march his divisions across pontoon bridges spanning a Virginia stream, the Rappahannock, to the slaughter at Fredericksburg. Doubtless watching the crossing of the Rio Grande—as he was to watch Franklin's crossing at Fredericksburg—was the future Confederate commander, Captain Robert E. Lee of the Corps of Engineers, who had joined Wool's staff only four days before the start of the march.

The crossing of the Rio Grande was unopposed but on the south bank General Wool was met by a Mexican officer with news of the fall of Monterey and the signing of the armistice. Construing the armistice terms as permitting an advance as far as Monclova, Wool erected bridgehead fortifications at Presidio, left parties to protect the crossing for his supply trains, and marched on. On the nineteenth, he was at San José, seventy-five miles south of the Rio Grande, with forty-eight days' rations on hand and the expectation of procuring more from the country as he went along, although he was without hard cash and could not use paper money.[26]

Monclova, a town of some 8,000 and the former capital of Coahuila y Tejas when those areas were combined in one state, was situated some 200 miles south of the river. Reaching there on October 29, Wool was halted by the armistice terms. The delay of nearly four weeks he improved by further drilling his troops and organizing his services, and by scouting the routes toward Chihuahua. The only practicable route, it developed, was by way of Parras, ninety miles west of Saltillo. Finding that he would be compelled to pass so close to the main army, Wool came to the sensible conclusion that his troops would be more useful there than they would in faraway Chihuahua. His message to General Taylor, requesting authority thus to alter his plans, was received at Monterey on November 8.

General Taylor issued orders for Wool to advance to Parras, abandon his long line of communication through San Antonio and Port La Vaca, and set up a new one through the Rio Grande and Camargo. With these new dispositions, General Taylor reported that the direct route from Mexico by way of San Luis Potosí was covered by Worth at Saltillo, and "the other route" would be covered by the forces at Parras, which in case of active operations toward the interior would "be in position to march on San Luis, Zacatecas or Durango."[27]

After receiving permission to change his base and his destination, General Wool brought forward his rear parties and his supplies en route and, on November 24, marched on. Eleven days later and 180 miles farther into the enemy's country, he brought his command of some 3,000 to rest at Parras, having marched more than 500 miles from San Antonio without seeing a hostile party in arms or firing a shot at an enemy. The column, in fact, according to Captain George W. Hughes, had met at the hands of the Mexicans "nothing but kindness and hospitality."

This lack of armed opposition did not indicate, however, that General Wool had no difficulties other than those of distance and terrain. Relations between his soldiers and the Mexican population had the same explosive possibilities as in the main army, but Wool seems to have had better success in preserving discipline and good order.

His achievement of discipline was the more remarkable in view of the tensions between himself and some of his officers. He had had to discipline Colonel William S. Harney, regular officer commanding the mounted troops, for undertaking an unauthorized and near-disastrous minor expedition beyond the Rio Grande at a time when the troops were supposed to be gathering at San Antonio. He was intensely disliked by his infantry brigadier, the volunteer General James Shields, who sought and secured transfer to get out from under Wool's command. He clashed with Archibald Yell, former governor of Arkansas and the colorful commander of the cavalry from that state. To Josiah Gregg, chronicler of the commerce of the prairies, who accompanied Yell's regiment on the expedition, Wool seemed overly preoccupied with "military forms and ceremonies," indeed "decidedly old-womanish."

To such antipathies were added the ire and enmity of some of the soldiers, who had joined the army to fight Mexicans and found it hard to understand why their commander should object to their doing so. One sergeant wrote home from Parras in disgust that the Illinois volunteers "had met no enemy, yet . . . that will meet us in fight but when they can get two or three of our men alone they will club on them and have used some of them pretty rough, but we the volunteers from Illinois and Arkansas intend to give them the Devil every chance . . . in spite of the old Woolly Devil. . . . I do not believe we will ever be in a fight, or if we do it will be brought on by someone else beside Gen. Wooll for . . . since we have been here he has showed more friendship to the Mexicans than he does to the Volunteers."

"Old Granny Wool," the same sergeant wrote on another occasion, "will not allow us to impose on them [the Mexicans] in the least . . . he shows them more friendship than he does us."[28] Wool possessed, indeed, none of the air and little of the attributes of either political or military popularity, but in all the war no soldiers were better cared for, none suffered less from camp diseases, none were better behaved and none fought better than his.

While General Taylor was arranging for Wool at Parras and Worth at Saltillo to form the right of his intended line, the United States Navy moved in and occupied its left, the port of Tampico.

The occupation of Tampico was the first break of consequence in the navy's weary task of blockading the Mexican Gulf coast—duty which, for the most part, consisted of chasing the vessels which continued to carry on the small Mexican trade with the world overseas, notifying neutral vessels of the existence of the blockade, and endorsing the fact of such notification on their ship's papers. Major difficulties in the way of landing operations were a lack of suitable steamers, suitable gunboats and suitable equipment for landing parties, and the weather of the Mexican Gulf with its frequent and unpredictable "northers."

It was "a few days of settled weather" which had induced Commodore Conner to make his first landing attempt against the river and town of Alvarado, back in August, and it was weather which had had much to do with its failure. On October 15 the navy had made another attempt at Alvarado, and had again failed. The steamers which were to tow gunboats across the bar and into the river proved to be too weak to buck the current. One steamer grounded, throwing the gunboats which it had in tow into "the greatest disorder"; the *Mississippi* which was to remain outside and bombard the forts at the river's mouth could not get in close enough to do its work—all of which Commodore Conner reported "with deep mortification."[29]

Undaunted by the second failure at Alvarado, the *Mississippi* and most of the small vessels of the squadron were sent south on the very next day to make an attempt upon the river, province and town of Tabasco. Commanding the expedition was Commodore Matthew Calbraith Perry—younger brother of Perry of Lake Erie and destined to fame of his own as Perry of Japan. Arrived off the bar of the Tabasco, on October 23, the commodore transferred his flag to the small steamer *Vixen,* which entered the river with sailing vessels and barges in tow. The commercial town of Frontera, near the mouth of the river, was captured, along with two steamers, without opposition. On the following day the expedition, making use of the captured steamers, started for the provincial capital of San Juan Bautista de Tabasco, seventy-five miles upriver. After steaming for a day and a night, the invading force reached the city—still without effective opposition— on the morning of the twenty-fifth. Captain French Forrest—whose experience in this tropical river was a foretaste of future prolonged and extended operations with Union gunboats on the rivers of the Mississippi Valley—was landed a mile below the town, with a detachment of 200 sailors and marines, and the flotilla moved up to "half musket shot" from the city, before a summons to surrender was sent in. The governor, General Don Juan Bautista Tracones, proudly refused to capitulate but took no effective steps for defense. Thinking that the refusal to surrender was more in bravado than in earnest, the commodore ordered one ship only to fire at the flagstaff. After the third shot, the flag disappeared. Upon inquiry, it developed that the

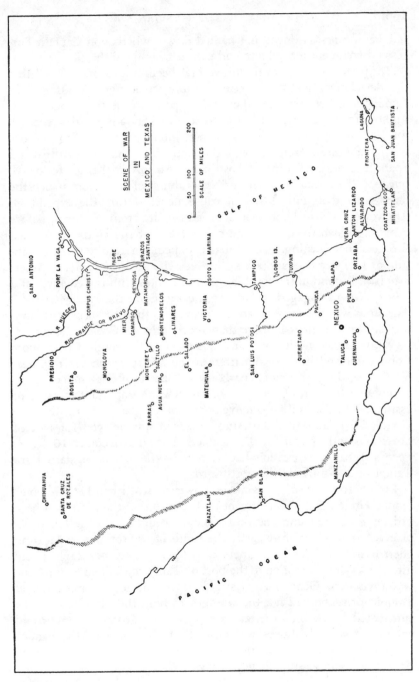

SCENE OF WAR
IN
MEXICO AND TEXAS

SCALE OF MILES

GULF OF MEXICO

PACIFIC OCEAN

185

flag had been shot down, not hauled down, whereupon Captain Forrest's detachment moved into and partially occupied the city.

"Apprehending, from the proverbial heedlessness of sailors," that
the detachment might suffer in possible street fighting after dark,
Commodore Perry recalled the landing party to the ships, but lay all
night before the city, ready to return fire. Shooting did not begin
until morning, however, and was soon interrupted by a flag of truce
bearing a message from the neutral merchants of the town, British and
Spanish, urging cessation of hostilities. An informal truce followed,
but soon there came another furious outburst of fire, from which the
navy suffered its only losses of consequence during the expedition.
The vessels returned and soon silenced the fire from the town, before
dropping downstream with the prizes taken at the landing, to reach
Frontera that evening. The Tabasco expedition resulted in the capture of two steamers and six sailing vessels, Mexican, and an American bark "found in treasonable communication with the enemy," and
a brig "found engaged in landing a cargo upon the enemy's coast."
The affair was the more notable, however, as the first successful landing effort of the navy in more than six months' service on the coast.[30]

While his second-in-command was away in the south, Commodore
Conner received at his headquarters anchorage at Anton Lizardo, near
Vera Cruz, the Secretary of the Navy's dispatch of September 22, or-
dering that the port of Tampico be taken as an important measure of
assistance to "a military movement contemplated from the Rio
Grande."[31] The start from Anton Lizardo was delayed for lack of
provisions and of coal for the steamers, but on November 10—after
Perry's Tabasco expedition had rejoined—the squadron started for
Tampico, 200 miles to the northward.

Even before the start was made, however, word had been received
from a United States secret agent at Tampico that the place had been
ordered evacuated, and that no resistance would be made. The order
of evacuation was at least partly the result of the capture by Mexican
guerrillas of the War Department dispatch of September 2 which had
directed Taylor's attention to the port of Tampico. When Santa Anna
was advised by General Anastasio Parrodi, the local commander at
Tampico, that he had not the strength to hold the place against the
anticipated attack, he ordered its evacuation. Troops, supplies and
equipment were, so far as was possible, to be taken up the Panuco
River and thence by way of the pass at Tula to San Luis, where Santa
Anna was accumulating his new army.

When this order was received at Tampico, on October 14, there was a storm of local protest. The government at the capital, moreover, seemed loath to see Tampico abandoned, possibly because of the successful resistance which it had offered to the royal Spanish forces seeking reconquest of Mexico in 1829. But Santa Anna, whose own first military reputation of consequence was founded on the defense of Tampico against the Spanish, peremptorily repeated his order for immediate evacuation. In the haste which resulted, there was indiscriminate waste and loss of matériel. Much was thrown in the river, some destroyed, and only part sent up the river. The evacuation was complete by October 27—more than two weeks before the arrival of the naval squadron.[32]

Commodore Conner, however, had no word of the completion of the evacuation when he reached the mouth of the Panuco. Consequently, when the vessels headed into the river, on November 14, they did so prepared to overcome whatever resistance might be offered—steamers towing gunboats, followed by ships' boats carrying landing parties. Before reaching the town, two leagues up from the mouth of the stream, the landing forces were met by a deputation from the city government which had come forth to make surrender. The surrender was accepted without formal capitulation but with the understanding that the inhabitants and their private property would be protected while arms and public property would be turned in. Finding that much of the armament had been sent away up the river, the commodore dispatched Commander Josiah Tattnall to locate it and either bring it back or destroy it. The commander—whose later fame rests largely on his declaration that "blood is thicker than water," made when he went to the aid of a British ship assailed by Chinese pirates, and whose naval career was to end as commodore of the Confederate States Navy—found it necessary to make two trips far up the Panuco to carry out his orders.[33]

Having taken Tampico, the navy felt that, with its crews already shorthanded, it could not spare enough men to garrison it for any length of time. Commodore Perry, therefore, was sent on to the Brazos, 200 miles to the north, to report the capture and to arrange for occupation by the army.

Major General Patterson, commanding on the lower Rio Grande under Taylor, was prompt to act. Six companies of regular artillery serving as infantry and the Alabama regiment of volunteers were dispatched by sea, and plans were made to add a brigade of volunteer infantry. Commodore Perry meanwhile steamed on to New Orleans, where he reported the Tampico situation to Governor Isaac Johnson of Louisiana, to Quartermaster General Jesup, who was in New Orleans at the time, and to Brigadier General George Brooke, the regular army commander at that point. Arrangements were made to divert 400 mounted riflemen destined for the Rio Grande to the new objective at the mouth of the Panuco. This force was increased by subsequent orders from the War Department in Washington, transferring artillery companies at Fort Columbus and Tampa Bay to Tampico.[34]

General Taylor approved of Patterson's original dispositions, and announced that he would send a brigadier general, probably Shields, who had left Wool and was with Taylor at Monterey, to command at Tampico. But when the general learned, two days later, that Patterson proposed to send additional troops, he dispatched a "special express" to "arrest this fatal indiscretion." His suspension of Patterson's orders was due, partly, to his feeling that no greater garrison was required to hold a post which the enemy had voluntarily abandoned, and partly because the proposed movement interfered with plans to "concentrate a respectable force at Victoria," the inland capital of the state of Tamaulipas.

Taylor's reaction to Patterson's proposal to send more troops to Tampico was mildness itself compared to his feelings when he learned of the action taken at New Orleans to divert troops originally intended for the Rio Grande to garrison newly captured Tampico. If, he furiously wrote the Adjutant General of the Army, "officers at a distance, totally ignorant of my views and incurring no responsibility for the failure of operations" were to intercept forces intended for him, he had "no assurance that any reinforcements or supplies will reach me through New Orleans. . . . With such proceedings . . . I cannot be held responsible for the efficient prosecution of the objects of the government here.

"While I am considered competent to exercise the chief command in the field," he continued, "it is no more than reasonable that subordinates and above all, officers not serving with the army against Mexico, should be compelled to keep in their proper places, and not expose to hazard, by mischievous meddling, the success of military operations involving the reputation of the army and the country."

And while he was unbosoming himself on this new grievance, the aroused commander in the field went back once more to an older one. General Patterson's "departure from the full and precise instructions . . . given him," he protested, was "a legitimate result of the position of quasi-independence given to that officer by the Department of War" when it corresponded with him directly. As to that, however, Patterson himself had an almost immediate and exceedingly neat riposte—for Taylor was guilty of the same conduct of which he complained by corresponding directly, and with far less justification, with Patterson's subordinate, Colonel Baker. ". . . I neither sent up nor approved any application of Colonel Baker to go to Washington," Patterson protested. "His correspondence with head-quarters was direct, and did not pass through the usual channel. . . . I venture to request that hereafter all correspondence with officers under my command be passed through the usual channel."[35]

To such tensions between Taylor and his second-in-command there soon were to be added even greater tensions between Taylor and the General in Chief of the Army, who, on November 24, left Washington to take direct command of the principal forces in Mexico.

----

[1] Ex. Doc. 60, H. R., 30th Cong., 1st sess., p. 360.

[2] Kenly, *Maryland Volunteer*, pp. 151-152.

[3] Giddings, *Sketches*, p. 232.

[4] McClellan, *Mexican War Diary*, p. 18.

[5] Meade, *Life and Letters*, I, 147, 161.

[6] Ex. Doc. 60, H. R., 30th Cong., 1st sess., pp. 424, 430-431, 508; Giddings, *Sketches*, pp. 221, 222.

[7] Henry, *Campaign Sketches*, p. 222; Ex. Doc. 60, H. R., 30th Cong., 1st sess., pp. 508-509.

[8] Meade, *Life and Letters*, I, 162-163.

[9] Ex. Doc. 60, H. R., 30th Cong., 1st sess., p. 512.

[10] Meade, *Life and Letters*, I, pp. 161-162.

[11] Giddings, *Sketches*, pp. 220, 232, 233.

[12] Grant, *Memoirs*, I, 118.

[13] Ex. Doc. 4, H. R., 29th Cong., 2nd sess., pp. 55-56; Ex. Doc. 60, H. R., 30th Cong., 1st sess., pp. 369-370.

[14] Henry, *Campaign Sketches*, pp. 217, 222, 226.

[15] Robinson, *Reminiscences*, p. 174; Kenly, *Maryland Volunteer*, p. 153; Meade, *Life and Letters*, I, 146.

[16] Henry, *Campaign Sketches*, pp. 218-219.

[17] Giddings, *Sketches*, p. 240; Robinson, *Reminiscences*, pp. 175, 180, 182; Henry, *Campaign Sketches*, I, 146.

[18] Kenly, *Maryland Volunteer*, pp. 154, 158-160; Henry, *Campaign Sketches*, p. 254; Giddings, *Sketches*, pp. 225-226; Spell, "Anglo-Saxon Press," *American History Review*, October 1932.

[19] Henry, *Campaign Sketches*, p. 226; Giddings, *Sketches*, p. 229; Kenly, *Maryland Volunteer*, pp. 155-156.

[20] Same, p. 161; French, *Two Wars*, p. 68; Ex. Doc. 60, H. R., 30th Cong., 1st sess., pp. 433-435.

[21] Ramsey (ed.), *The Other Side*, p. 83; Ex. Doc. 60, H. R., 30th Cong., 1st sess., p. 351; Ex. Doc. 4, H. R., 29th Cong., 2nd sess., p. 82.

[22] Same, pp. 377, 436, 439.

[23] Kenly, *Maryland Volunteer*, pp. 166-167.

[24] Ex. Doc. 60, 30th Cong., 1st sess., pp. 328, 426-429.

[25] Baylies, Francis, *A Narrative of Major General Wool's Campaign in Mexico in the Year 1846, 1847 and 1848* (Albany, 1851), pp. 12, 13; Ex. Doc. 32, Sen., 31st Cong., 1st sess. (Hughes, Capt. George W., Topographical Engineers, *Memoir . . . of March . . . of General Wool . . .),* pp. 15-18.

[26] Same, pp. 18-23; Ex. Doc. 4, H. R., 29th Cong., 2nd sess., pp. 108-109. Keeping the United States forces in hard cash was a problem throughout the war. It was necessary more than once to transfer coin, the only money usable in Mexico, from New York to New Orleans. Transferring $503,500 in November cost $3,950.60; $1,300,000 in December, $9,000. Pub. Doc. 111, Sen., 29th Cong., 2nd sess., p. 2.

[27] Ex. Doc. 60, 30th Cong., 1st sess., pp. 361, 377, 433.

[28] Fulton, Maurice G. (ed.), *Diary and Letters of Josiah Gregg* (Norman, 1941), I, 260, 263; Henderson, Alfred J., "A Morgan County Volunteer in the Mexican War," *Journal of the Illinois State Historical Society* (Springfield), Vol. XLI, No. 4 (December 1948), pp. 392, 394; Ex. Doc. 32, Sen., 31st Cong., p. 33.

[29] Ex. Doc. 4, H. R., 29th Cong., 2nd sess., pp. 381, 630-633; Conner, *Home Squadron*, pp. 7-8; Semmes, *Service Afloat and Ashore*, pp. 89-90.

[30] Ex. Doc. 4, H. R., 29th Cong., 2nd sess., pp. 632-639; Ex. Doc. 1, H. R., 30th Cong., 2nd sess., pp. 1165-1170; Conner, *Home Squadron*, pp. 7-8; Semmes, *Service*, pp. 89, 90.

[31] Conner, *Home Squadron*, p. 34.

[32] Ex. Doc. 1, H. R., 30th Cong., 2nd sess., pp. 1171-1174; Ramsey (ed.), *The Other Side*, pp. 100-105.

[33] Same, pp. 105-107; Ex. Doc. 1, H. R., 30th Cong., 2nd sess., pp. 1174-1175.

[34] Ex. Doc. 60, H. R., 30th Cong., 1st sess., pp. 379-382, 480-482.

[35] Same, pp. 381, 384. Colonel Baker, who was still a member of Congress from Illinois, was granted leave of absence to attend the second session of the 29th Congress. Appearing in Congress in full uniform, he made an earnest and impassioned appeal for cessation of partisan wrangling and action on questions of supply and support to the army in Mexico. Two days later, on December 30, 1846, he resigned his seat and returned to the front. Beveridge, *Lincoln*, I, 417.

General Taylor writing to the War Department.

CHAPTER 12

Marches and Countermarches

PERHAPS mindful of the untoward consequences of his delayed departure from Washington at the time of his earlier designation to the Mexican command, General Scott left the capital on the fifth morning after the President told him that he was to command the Vera Cruz expedition. But despite his "hurry of preparation" the general had "many long personal interviews on military matters" with the President, and also found time to write a "circular to the leading Whigs in Congress . . . to say how handsomely [he] had been treated by the President and Secretary of War."

On the last day of his stay the new commander drew up, at the request of the Secretary of War, suggestions for a letter of instructions from the Secretary to himself. "The President, respecting your judgment," the suggested letter ran, "is pleased with the assurances you have given" as to the importance of prompt movement and the willingness expressed to get under way for Vera Cruz with even as few as 8,000 men. The day was to come when General Scott would complain that he had been allowed "only four days" in Washington "when twenty might have been most advantageously spent in the great bureaux" of the War Department. At the time, however, in the suggested instructions to himself, the general advised Secretary Marcy that he had "in a very few days . . . laid a sufficient base" for the expedition and thought "it best to proceed at once to the southwest. . . ."[1]

Secretary Marcy did not adopt the suggested letter but, on the same day, issued a brief and general letter of instruction, leaving to Scott the widest discretion. "It is not proposed to control your operations by definite and positive instructions," the letter ran, "but you are left to prosecute them as your judgment, under a full review of all the

191

circumstances, shall dictate. The work is before you, and the means provided, or to be provided, for accomplishing it, are committed to you, in the full confidence that you will use them to the best advantage." Exception was afterward taken to this grant of discretion on the ground that it was noncommittal and intended to place on the general the responsibility in case of failure, while reserving to the administration the opportunity to claim the credit for success. It is difficult to read such a meaning into the letter, nor does any such view of it seem to have been entertained at the time of its receipt. On the contrary, General Scott, as he afterward wrote, "left Washington highly flattered with the confidence and kindness the President had just shown me."[2]

From the day of the general's departure from Washington on November 24, his movements were dogged with exasperating delay, his plans balked by misunderstanding and mischance, and his sanguine spirit beset by "cruel uncertainties." He elected to go to New Orleans by way of New York, where he arrived "at a late hour of the night" of the twenty-fifth, as he wrote General Taylor, "more than half sick of a cold." He left New York on November 30 for what ordinarily would have been a voyage of about twelve days. Instead, head winds so delayed his ship that it was not until December 19—almost four weeks after leaving Washington and at least two weeks later than if he had gone direct—that he reached New Orleans.[3]

There he spent four crowded days. His schedule included consultations with General Brooke, commanding the western division of the army, with Governor Isaac Johnson of Louisiana, and with merchant-ship captains from whom he learned of an anchorage at the Lobos Islands, sixty miles south of Tampico, where his transports might rendezvous. He corresponded with the War Department, and with Commodore Conner of the navy on measures for their joint operation. And one evening—the only one when he was not "locked up, at work"—he dined with his friend Henry Clay, who was sojourning at New Orleans.[4]

There also the general was confronted with the painful fact that the secrecy with which it had been sought to surround his expedition had already been breached by the publication in *La Patria,* a New Orleans Spanish-language newspaper, of a garbled and inaccurate but revealing account of the expedition against Vera Cruz. Responsibility for this publication, duly repeated in papers farther north, was laid by the President on the general who was in New Orleans. The plan of campaign, the President believed, "could only have gotten to the public through Gen'l Scott. . . . He has from inordinate vanity or some other cause given it out."

The President's belief—neither just nor in keeping with the confidence which Scott felt had been assured him—may have sprung, in part, from the fact that only Polk's own prudential caution had kept the general from outlining the Vera Cruz plans in his letter telling Taylor that he was coming to Mexico. In far larger part, however, it grew out of Polk's general state of mind as to his new field commander. He "had been compelled to send Gen'l Scott to take command of the army," he explained to one senator, "as a choice of evils, he being the only man in the army who by his rank could command Taylor." Polk's belief about the New Orleans publication of plans merely intensified the opinion he had already formed that "neither Taylor nor Scott are fit for the command of the army."[5]

Feeling as he did, Polk continued his efforts to secure "a commander in whom I have confidence"—Thomas H. Benton. Scott's ship was hardly out of New York harbor before the President repeated to Benton his offer of appointment as lieutenant general and renewed his effort to secure Congressional legislation authorizing such a post for the Missouri senator. The effort was to fail, by a narrow margin, quite as much because of senatorial antagonism to Benton as because of its inherent unwisdom. But the fact that the effort was made was, quite naturally, to envenom all the relations between the President and his commander in the field. When the general first heard of it, just as he was about to embark at New Orleans for the Brazos, he received the news with incredulity. "If the rank were asked for," he assured his informant, "it could only—remembering Mr. Polk's assurance of support and reward—be intended for me on the report of my first success." But with later and incontrovertible information came disillusionment and bitterness.[6]

Scott sailed from New Orleans on the day before Christmas, 1846, one day after he had expected to arrive at Camargo, according to his letter of November 25 to Taylor. In that letter, sent from New York, Scott had omitted direct mention of Vera Cruz, as "not being prudent at this distance," but had assured Taylor that he was "not coming to supersede you in the immediate command on the line of operations rendered illustrious by you and your gallant army. My proposed theatre is different. You may imagine it. . . ."

"But, my dear general," the letter continued in the same propitiatory strain, "I shall be obliged to take from you most of the gallant officers and men (regulars and volunteers) whom you have so long and so nobly commanded. I am afraid that I shall, by imperious necessity—the approach of yellow fever on the gulf coast—reduce you, for a time, to stand on the defensive. This will be infinitely painful to you, and for that reason distressing to me. But I rely upon your patriotism to submit to the temporary sacrifice with cheerfulness."

No definite suggestion for a meeting of the two generals was made in the first letter, Taylor being told only that Scott was coming to Camargo "in order to be within easy corresponding distance from you." In a second letter, however, dispatched from New Orleans on December 20, Scott was more definite and specific both about his plans and about a personal meeting with Taylor at Camargo or lower down the Rio Grande.[7]

As one of the mischances of the campaign, this second letter was never received by Taylor and there was no meeting of the two generals at Camargo or anywhere else. Failure of the letter to reach Taylor is attributed by Scott in his autobiography to the "gross neglect of the officer who bore it" in losing three days' time, and also to a "strange digression" made in the meantime by Taylor "toward Tampico." It was also said in the autobiography that this dispatch "most confidential, and so marked, outside and in" was opened "at the volunteer headquarters, Monterey . . . freely read and discussed by numbers—all not in a condition to be wise or discreet." The general's recollection is at fault as to this particular dispatch but, as appears from the contemporary record, another and even more detailed and more important dispatch of January 3, 1847, was so treated.[8]

Even with the utmost diligence on the part of the courier, however, a communication sent from New Orleans as late as December 20 could not have brought about a meeting of Scott and Taylor at Camargo at the time appointed, for Taylor had left his headquarters at Monterey on December 15—before he had received Scott's letter sent from New York—on what developed into a complicated series of marches and countermarches in southern Tamaulipas which effectually put him out of touch with the arriving commander.

The original plan for this extensive and resultless maneuver was outlined by Taylor in a letter of December 8. The main Mexican force, he reported, was at San Luis Potosí, "a position almost equally distant from the points of the line" between Parras and Tampico. This fact, Taylor added, would give the Mexicans "a very great advantage over us, were it not for the nature of the country and the communications—the region between San Luis and the mountains being scantily supplied with water and subsistence, and the road by Saltillo and Monterey being the only practicable route for artillery across the mountains."

Such a situation—especially after the occupation of Tampico from the sea—would have seemed to call for keeping the American forces concentrated on the "only practicable route for artillery," whether for defense or for offense. Instead, General Taylor "deemed it more than ever important" to occupy Victoria, capital of the state of Tamaulipas. Among the stated reasons for the importance of such an occupation was the fact that "it threatens the flank of the Mexican army should it advance from San Luis"—though it is not clear how such a threat could be effective through a country described as virtually impassable, nor how it could in any way compensate for the weakening of the main force by the dispersion involved in the march to Victoria.

Nevertheless, plans went forward for the march. Worth was to remain at Saltillo, Wool at Parras, and Major General William O. Butler, commanding the reserve, at Monterey, whence Taylor himself was to march with Twiggs's regular and Quitman's volunteer brigades. This column was to meet, at Montemorelos, sixty-eight miles southeast of Monterey, another brigade under Riley, which was to march there from Camargo. The combined column was to march on to effect a junction, before Victoria, with Patterson's column of three regiments of infantry and the newly arrived Tennessee regiment of horse, marching direct from Matamoros.

The movement started on December 13. On the seventeenth, the junction was made at Montemorelos, but on that very evening four hard-riding dragoons overtook Taylor with a dispatch from Worth, at Saltillo, reporting that Santa Anna was taking advantage of the division of the United States forces to make a rapid march from San Luis Potosí to attack, in turn, the small garrisons at Saltillo and Parras. To meet this threat, Taylor turned back with his regulars, ordering Brigadier General Quitman to continue the march with the volunteer troops to the junction with Patterson at Victoria.[9]

At the same time that Worth had sent word to Taylor of Santa Anna's reported advance, he had advised Butler at Monterey and Wool at Parras. Both had promptly started to his assistance—Wool, indeed, being under way within two and one half hours after receiving

Worth's call. Had Santa Anna left San Luis on the sixth, as was reported, Wool's small force would have been in a perilous position, since they were not only some 120 miles from the nearest United States force but would also have to march for the last twenty of those miles on the same road which would be used by advancing Mexicans. It would have been entirely possible for Santa Anna to thrust a force between Wool and Worth and destroy them individually and in detail.

With all haste, therefore, Wool set out by forced marches. With all the haste of his departure, however, he left behind only fourteen soldiers too sick to march, and brought with him all of his 350 wagons, carrying sixty days' supplies for his entire command. On the fourth day—having made more than thirty miles over mountain roads on each of two successive days, and having so conducted his march that "not a broken wagon, or a dead animal, or a stragller" was left behind—Wool passed the hacienda La Encantada, where the Parras road came into the road from San Luis to Saltillo, and was safely between Santa Anna and Worth. On the next day, December 21, he was at Saltillo. General Butler, meanwhile, had come forward from Monterey, and General Taylor—riding with a dragoon escort ahead of his troops—had passed Monterey on the way to Saltillo, when he was met by a dispatch from that point saying that Santa Anna was not coming, after all.[10]

Ordering Butler to remain at Saltillo in general command, Taylor turned once more to Victoria, marching from Monterey with Twiggs's division on December 23. The march continued through Christmas— the day being marked by hard marching and, in some commands, "a little egg-nog." On the day after Christmas the column again reached Montemorelos. By that time, Scott's letter of November 25 sent from New York had been received, and within twenty-four hours, as the march continued, the camp was alive with rumors—"nothing official"—that Scott was coming to Mexico, and that he was to head an expedition for Vera Cruz for which he would take a large part of Taylor's army.[11]

Meanwhile, Quitman and the volunteers, who had not been called upon to make the countermarch to Monterey and return, had kept steadily on their way and, on December 29, had occupied the capital of Tamaulipas without resistance and with considerable ceremony. The ceremony included lowering the Mexican and raising the United States flag in the plaza, accompanied by delivery of the keys of the city, and enlivened by music from the band which, however, was soon drowned by the braying of the local jackasses and the roar of laughter among the troops which that braying provoked.

On January 4, General Taylor and the regulars arrived in the morning, and, in the afternoon, General Patterson and the volunteers who had left Matamoros on December 23—the same day on which Twiggs's men made their second start from Monterey. And so, early in January, Taylor had succeeded in concentrating nearly 6,000 men—almost half his disposable force—at a city unimportant in itself, which was ten days' march from either Monterey, Matamoros or Tampico, and from which it was perfectly impracticable to march against any considerable body of Mexicans. "For what object, no one knows, is so large a force assembled at this point," wrote one thoughtful lieutenant.[12]

After less than ten days at Victoria the "state of the supplies" made it necessary to move the command. On January 12, orders were issued for the evacuation of the city. General Patterson was to take his own forces and those of Generals Twiggs and Quitman—a total of 4,733 officers and men—on to Tampico, while General Taylor, with Captain May's squadron of dragoons, Colonel Jefferson Davis' regiment of Mississippi Rifles, and the light batteries of Captains Sherman and Bragg, was to return to Monterey. No troops were to be left in garrison at Victoria.[13]

General Scott, meanwhile, had arrived at the Brazos two days after Christmas, had found there no word from Taylor, and had hastened up the Rio Grande to Camargo, which he reached on January 3, 1847. Finding it impossible to get in direct touch with Taylor for consultation about the division of troops between the two theaters of action, Scott issued orders direct to General Butler, commanding in the absence of Taylor on the Camargo-Monterey-Saltillo line, for the dispatch of the troops which would be required for the descent upon Vera Cruz. Copies of the orders to Butler were sent to Taylor, with due apologies for the "necessary interference with his general command."

The fatality which pursued Scott's efforts to reach a working basis of understanding with Taylor attached to this letter also. Butler's copy went direct to him at Saltillo. Taylor's copy was forwarded by way of Monterey, where it was opened, read and discussed at the headquarters of Brigadier General Marshall, and then bundled up and forwarded to Taylor by the hand of Lieutenant John A. Richey, with an escort of ten men. On the way, Lieutenant Richey entered the village of Villa Gran alone, to procure provisions, and while there was lassoed and murdered. The dispatches he bore were captured and, it was assumed by the United States commanders, forwarded to Santa Anna at San Luis Potosí.[14]

A duplicate of the letter of January 3, however, did reach Taylor at Victoria on January 14, the day after the evacuation of that city had started. Its receipt produced—perhaps provoked would be the more descriptive word—two letters from Taylor. One, strictly official, was addressed to the commanding general's chief of staff; the other, personal, was addressed to Scott direct. The official letter noted the departure of the troops for Tampico and reserved comment upon the defensive line which it was proposed Taylor should hold until he could get back to Monterey and see what Butler had done under the orders sent to him direct.

In his unofficial letter to Scott, Taylor declared that he would have made "no complaint" if he had been "at once relieved of the whole command" but that, as it was, "almost every man of my regular force and half the volunteers (now in respectable discipline)" had been taken from him, leaving him with "less than a thousand regulars and a volunteer force partly of new levies to hold a defensive line, while a large army of more than twenty thousand men is in my front." To this complaint about the division of troops—throughout the correspondence between Scott and Taylor there is apparent on both sides a sort of proprietary attitude toward the troops under their command— there was added another, more personal in tone. "I feel," Taylor wrote, "that I have lost the confidence of the government, or it would not have suffered me to remain, up to this time, ignorant of its intentions. . . . But, however much I may feel personally mortified and outraged . . . I will carry out in good faith . . . the views of the government, though I may be sacrificed in the effort."[15]

The letter contained the germ of what was to prove to be a winning issue in Presidential politics. Taylor's objections to the military force and mission assigned him did not accord with his own previous recommendations for the Vera Cruz expedition to be undertaken with 25,000 men of whom at least 10,000 should be regulars, and for assuming a defensive position in northern Mexico. But in the suggestion that he was to be "sacrificed" to the ambition of others, doubtless sincerely believed, there was an appeal more potent than military logic in advancing the cause of a candidate for the Presidency—which was what Taylor, despite his protestations to the contrary, became before the month was out. To the "plaudits of the people for bravery and skill," as Lieutenant Meade wrote his wife, there would be added "their sympathy for the injustice" which their favorite had suffered. The injustice, in the minds of Taylor's officers and of many others, was that "the administration, alarmed at his growing popularity . . . hoping to divide or parallel his fame with another, sent Gen. Scott with such an inadequate force that he was obliged to deprive Gen. Taylor of troops."[16] With more complete information now available it is apparent that the feeling was unfounded but, with the knowledge of surface happenings only, and in the prevailing state of mind, the assumption was not unnatural.

Scott was to write afterward that the order for transfer of troops "began to sour his [Taylor's] mind in proportion as he became more and more prominent as a candidate for the Presidency." At the time, however, he responded with a conciliatory and explanatory letter. "There are some expressions in your letters," he wrote, "which, as I wish to forget them, I shall not specify or recall. . . . If I had been within easy reach of you . . . I should . . . have consulted you fully on all points. . . . As it was, I had to act promptly, and, to a considerable extent, in the dark. . . . I hope I have left, or shall leave you, including the new volunteers who will soon be up, a competent force to defend the head of your line (Monterey) and its communications. . . . To enable you to do this more certainly, I must ask you to abandon Saltillo, and to make no detachments, except for *reconnoissances* and immediate defence, much beyond Monterey. I know this to be the wish of the government, founded on reasons in which I concur."[17]

Having thus done what he could to placate the implacable Taylor and to promote the safety of the command left with him, General Scott returned to the Brazos to engage in the immensely laborious task of organizing the first major amphibious operation ever undertaken by American forces. Troops were coming not only from Taylor's army but also from the United States, where nine new volunteer regiments were being organized. Supplies had to be provided and transportation arranged, even to such details as ordering that ships coming out to the Mexican coast should bring with them a sixty days' supply of firewood and Mississippi River water in casks, sufficient not only for their own crews but for the additional men and horses who were to be embarked at the Brazos or Tampico.

The original plan for the expedition had contemplated embarkation about the middle of January. Orders for the detachment of troops did not reach Butler at Saltillo, however, until the afternoon of January 8. Worth, who was to command the forces sent from there, was exceedingly prompt in his departure, and had everything moving by morning of the tenth. But it was a matter of two weeks' marching to the point of embarkation, so that, even though he made an "admirable movement," Worth, with the head of his division, did not arrive at the mouth of the river until January 22, the same day on which the first of the new volunteers from the States arrived off the bar of the Brazos. "I have not heard a word of the ordnance and ordnance stores, and other siege materials, since I left Washington," Scott wrote on the twenty-fourth. "I trust that most of them are near at hand." At any rate, he expressed the intention to commence embarkation "the moment that the extra water casks, from New Orleans, arrive and can be filled," which he hoped would be by the end of the month.[18]

Before leaving the Brazos, however, General Scott had to take time to straighten out the affairs of Colonel William S. Harney, who refused to be separated from the command of his regiment, the Second Dragoons, in favor of Major Edwin V. Sumner, whom Scott considered "a much safer and more efficient commander." The affair went to a court-martial and also came to the attention of President Polk and his Cabinet. The President violently disapproved the order of transfer, attributing it to the fact that Harney was a Democrat in politics, and was a personal friend and appointee of President Jackson. "I have myself been wholly uninfluenced by any reference to the political opinions of the officers of the Army in the conduct of the war," the President confided to his diary, and no doubt believed his own statement. "It has not been so with the Federal ["Federal" being, in Polk's vocabulary, sometimes synonymous with Whig] commanders in the field," he added, with the resolution "that Col. Harney shall not be sacrificed to propitiate the personal and political malice of Gen'l Scott." Far from showing malice, however, Scott had taken the unusual step of suggesting that Harney himself name the officers who were to try him on charges of disobedience of orders and insubordinate conduct, and when the court found him guilty and sentenced him to be reprimanded, he had not only remitted the sentence but, finally, restored him to command—all before the papers in the case had even reached Washington.[19]

Amid such vexations General Scott continued with his preparations. By February 4, one of the ships bringing out the specially designed and built landing boats was off the bar at the Brazos, but "not one" transport had arrived, nor had anything been heard of any ship with ordnance or siege materials. Troops had begun to arrive by sea, however, and had been ordered on to the appointed rendezvous at the Lobos Islands, and General Patterson had reported that, after a march of ten days from Victoria, his column had reached Tampico on January 23, 24 and 25, bringing the force there—with General Shields's garrison—up to nearly 7,000 men.

On February 9, the anxious Scott had received confirmation of the capture of his dispatches of January 3 by the Mexicans. Believing, therefore, that his "plans, views, and means, are now as well known at San Luis de Potosí, Mexico and Vera Cruz, as at these headquarters" he was all the more anxious to get under way as promptly and with as strong a force as possible. Commodore Conner, from the fleet anchorage at Anton Lizardo near Vera Cruz, was telling him that now was "the most favorable time" for the attack but the transports had not arrived—"detained, first, for the want of extra water casks" and then "for want of seamen" at New Orleans. Quartermaster officers were doing their best to supply deficiencies by charter of local vessels—enough to carry 3,750 men by crowding. Two new volunteer regiments from Pennsylvania, and one each from New York, South Carolina and Louisiana had proceeded already to the Lobos Islands. Sixty-five of the 141 landing boats ordered had been received, and the general was ready to "make the descent near Vera Cruz if not another should arrive" but he could not leave "until some of the cruel uncertainties" as to transports and other supplies should be relieved.

A howling "norther" blew in for three days to prolong the general's uncertainties but finally, on February 15, he got under way, leaving Worth to complete the embarkation at the Brazos.[20]

Three days later the commanding general came up the Panuco, with the regiments encamped on the riverbank near Tampico firing salutes as his steamer passed, and the artillery in the town itself "thundering out a louder welcome" as the escort troops went through a carefully rehearsed ceremony.

In the three months of its occupation by United States forces Tampico had begun to take on something of an American complexion. Regimental bands took turns in playing in the Plaza, where their music reminded Captain Robert Anderson, as he wrote his wife, of earlier days when he had been stationed at Fort Moultrie in Charleston harbor—where he would be stationed once more in the time of crisis following the secession of South Carolina. A company of actors were playing nightly at the "American Theatre" to crowded houses which were kept only moderately quiet by the "fear of the bayonets of the guard." There was a weekly newspaper, the *Tampico Sentinel,* and the usual assortment of eating, drinking, and gambling establishments bearing such appealing names as "The Rough and Ready Restaurant." Most of the soldiers found that pulque "was not sufficiently strong for them to overcome their repugnance to its odor," and the sale of spirituous liquors was prohibited by General Patterson. But there were "traveling groceries," prepared to sell a dram of mescal or aguardiente from a canteen for a real, or bit, the eighth part of a dollar. Patronage of these walking saloons was brisk, because the soldiers were more than usually in funds since a goodly portion of the army "made a pay day" for two months while at Tampico. But with it all, it was reported, "few crimes were committed—scarcely any murders or stabbing, so common near Matamoros and in the valley of the Rio Grande."[21]

During his short stay at Tampico General Scott made arrangements for leaving a garrison consisting of the Louisiana regiment and the Baltimore-Washington battalion of volunteers, under Colonel Gates of the regular artillery, and for the embarkation of the remainder of the troops who were to follow him, as soon as shipping was available, to the Lobos rendezvous. And then, on February 20, after a stay of but thirty hours, the commanding general sailed on.[22]

But during his brief stay he did one other thing which marked his stay at Tampico as notable. He issued, on February 19, his General Order No. 20. This order, subsequently reissued at Vera Cruz, Puebla and Mexico City, extended the jurisdiction of military courts to cover crimes not defined in the Articles of War of the sort which, had the army been at home, would have been punishable by ordinary civil courts. The purpose—and in large measure, the result—of the general's order was to prevent the atrocities which had marked the passage of Taylor's army through the country.

Observing the difficulties in which Taylor found himself for lack of such jurisdiction, Scott had drawn up a *projet* for such an order as early as October, even before he was ordered to Mexico. He mentioned the matter to Marcy but, according to Scott's autobiography, the Secretary made no comment, then or ever, except a "startle at the title" of the proposed "martial law order" which was "soon silently returned, as too explosive for safe handling." Subsequently, Scott wrote, the Attorney General asked for a copy of the proposed order but, after reading it, "was stricken with legal dumbness. All the authorities were evidently alarmed at the proposition to establish martial law, even in a foreign country, occupied by American troops."

The general's recollection, written nearly twenty years after the event, became the basis for statements in subsequent works to the effect that "the Polk administration refused to take responsibility" and was "afraid to use martial law even in Mexico," preferring to let Scott, as a Whig, shoulder the public displeasure which was feared. Such statements overlook, however, as General Scott must also have overlooked, the fact that the report of the Secretary of War of December 5, 1846, transmitted to Congress by the President with his annual message, strongly recommended passage of legislation for the establishment of martial law in foreign lands to cover offenses "which are not by express provisions of law within the jurisdiction of any military tribunal."

"Without some authority to punish such crimes," the Secretary wrote, "great injury will necessarily result. . . . I therefore recommend that courts-martial, or some military tribunal to be organized by the general in command, should be vested by express provision of law, with authority to try offenses committed beyond the limits of the United States . . . where there are no civil or criminal courts, or none but those of the enemy, to which the offenders can be delivered up for trial and punishment."

On February 15—the day on which Scott left the Brazos—Secretary Marcy wrote him that "the chairman of the committee of the Senate . . . did not consider legislation necessary, as the right to punish such cases necessarily resulted from the condition of things when an army is prosecuting hostilities in an enemy's country."[23] This was likewise the general tenor of the debate on the subject in the House of Representatives, where James A. Seddon, a new member from Virginia—now better remembered as Secretary of War of the Confederate States—forcefully expressed the views of most of his colleagues that the obligation to establish and enforce a code of law lay on the conqueror. "The worst of all conditions for a people," young Seddon said, "is to be without government at all—a prey to anarchy and confusion, with their rights, their property, and their persons, at the mercy of the ruffian, or the ravisher, whose excesses no law restrains and no justice punishes. For a conqueror to overthrow an existing policy, and leave a submissive people to such horrors, would be such a tyranny as no principle of humanity or law could tolerate."[24]

General Scott, however, when he took the bold step of issuing General Order No. 20 at Tampico on his own responsibility as the commander in the field—"the conqueror"—had no way of knowing that his course had the support of both the administration, which had recommended legislation, and of Congress, which did not feel that legislation was necessary. Without waiting for such word, Winfield Scott issued his own order—and so doing, not only added to the measure of his stature as man and soldier but also laid the foundations of American military government.[25]

[1] Ex. Doc. 60, H. R., 30th Cong., 1st sess., pp. 1218-1219; Scott, *Memoirs*, II, 399.

[2] Ex. Doc. 60, H. R., 30th Cong., 1st sess., pp. 372, 1219.

[3] Same, pp. 374, 838-839, 891, 894.

[4] Same, pp. 838-843; Elliott, *Scott*, pp. 445-446.

[5] Quaife (ed.), *Polk's Diary*, II, 277, 327-328, 393-394; Nevins (ed.), *Polk*, p. 185.

[6] Scott, *Memoirs*, II, 400; Quaife (ed.), *Polk's Diary*, II, 261-262, 268-270, 273, 275, 277, 281-282, 286, 292-293, 302, 304, 347, 356; Nevins (ed.), *Polk*, pp. 176, 178. Polk discussed the lieutenant generalcy with Senator Cass, who reported that he consulted others, all of whom were in opposition to the idea. Senator John C. Calhoun was strongly opposed and Polk ascribed the defeat of the bill in the Senate to "Mr. Calhoun and two or three Democratic Senators, aided by the united Federal vote." A month later, on February 26, the bill passed the House, 112 to 87, but was not acted on favorably by the Senate.

[7] Ex. Doc. 60, H. R., 30th Cong., 1st sess., pp. 373-374, 839-840.

[8] Same, pp. 857-859; Scott, *Memoirs*, II, 401, 402.

[9] Ex. Doc. 60, H. R., 30th Cong., 1st sess., pp. 379-382, 385; Claiborne, *Quitman*, I, 277-283.

[10] Ex. Doc. 60, H. R., 30th Cong., 1st sess., pp. 385-386; Ex. Doc. 32, Sen., 31st Cong., 1st sess., pp. 34, 61-62; Henry, *Campaign Sketches*, p. 273; French, *Two Wars*, p. 70; Baylies, *Narrative*, pp. 20-23.

[11] Ex. Doc. 60, H. R., 30th Cong., 1st sess., p. 387, 515; Henry, *Campaign Sketches*, pp. 277, 279; French, *Two Wars*, pp. 69-70.

[12] Ex. Doc. 60, H. R., 30th Cong., 1st sess., pp. 387-389; French, *Two Wars*, p. 20; Meade, *Life and Letters*, I, 173.

[13] Ex. Doc. 60, H. R., 30th Cong., 1st sess., pp. 861-862.

[14] Same, pp. 851, 876, 890, 893, 1098-1099, 1101, 1151-1153, 1159-1160.

[15] Same, pp. 861-863, 1097-1098, 1157-1159.

[16] Same, p. 353; Smith, *War with Mexico*, I, 368, 547; Meade, *Life and Letters*, I, 175; French, *Two Wars*, p. 72. General Taylor's attitude toward the Presidency is indicated in Samson (ed.), *Zachary Taylor's Letters*, pp. 19, 76, 99, 103, 105-110, 113.

[17] Ex. Doc. 60, H. R., 30th Cong., 1st sess., pp. 864, 1161-1162; Scott, *Memoirs*, II, 405.

[18] Ex. Doc. 60, H. R., 30th Cong., 1st sess., pp. 855-861, 865.

[19] Same, pp. 866, 870-871, 874-875, 885-889; Quaife (ed.), *Polk's Diary*, II, 384-386; Nevins (ed.), *Polk*, pp. 197-199.

[20] Ex. Doc. 60, H. R., 30th Cong., 1st sess., pp. 875-877, 891-894, 896-899, 1166, 1167.

21 *Autobiography of an English Soldier in the United States Army* (New York, 1853), pp. 137-141; Anderson, *Artillery Officer*, pp. 15, 18, 28, 30; Kenly, *Maryland Volunteer*, pp. 238-240; Furber, George C., *The Twelve Months Volunteer; or Journal of a Private in the Tennessee Regiment of Cavalry* (Cincinnati, 1848), pp. 402-403, 413, 419-422, 424, 434. Private Furber, who had marched with his regiment overland all the way from Tennessee to Tampico, grew almost lyrical over the setting of the city near the mouth of the Panuco, "in the midst of as lovely a country as is to be found on the globe; where we were furnished with every comfort, every convenience, that soldiers in a foreign land could expect or ask for" (p. 393).

22 Ex. Doc. 60, H. R., 30th Cong., 1st sess., pp. 900-902.

23 Same, pp. 873-874, 1264-1266; Ex. Doc. 4, H. R., 29th Cong., 2nd sess., pp. 55-56; Scott, *Memoirs,* II, 392-395.

24 Quoted in Gabriel, Ralph H., "American Experience with Military Government," *American Historical Review,* Vol. XLIX, No. 3 (July 1944), p. 632. In this article Professor Gabriel interestingly discusses General Order No. 20 as the genesis of American military government. The comments upon the timidity of the Polk administration, quoted above, are from the same article. The text of G. O. 20 appears in Smith, *War with Mexico,* II, 455-456. Professor Smith also follows Scott's statements as to Marcy's reception of his idea, remarking that "the idea of putting constraint on the free American voter probably struck Marcy with terror." It is noted, nevertheless, that "the crying need of some adequate method for punishing American soldiers in foreign parts compelled Marcy in December to recommend that Congress authorize a military tribunal; but that body also doubtless had an eye to votes, and took no action" (II, 220). The course of neither Marcy nor Congress seems to warrant the strictures on them, based on uncritical acceptance of Scott's subsequent recollections. The order as republished at Mexico City appears in Scott, *Memoirs,* II, 540-549.

25 Scott's martial-law order had been anticipated to a certain extent, however, by General Shields, commanding at Tampico, who had set up a "court" rather than a military commission. This court was actually trying cases when the new order was issued. Its membership included the editor of the *Sentinel* newspaper and a former sutler of the Eighth Infantry. Anderson, *Artillery Officer,* pp. 38-40.

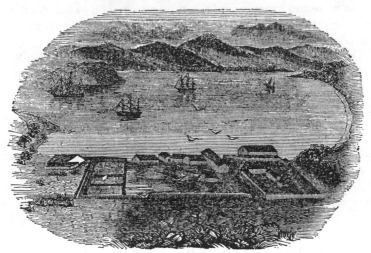

Anchorage at Yerba Buena.

CHAPTER 13

California—Revolt and Reconquest

NEWS of neither the armistice which followed the fall of Monterey, nor the new design to make Vera Cruz the main military objective, nor the fact that California had already been taken by the United States Navy—in fact, no news from the world outside his own command—had reached General Stephen W. Kearny when he set out from Santa Fe on the second stage of his march from the Missouri to the Pacific.

Two of the five weeks in which Kearny had been in possession of New Mexico had been spent in a march of reconnaissance of the regions down the Rio Grande, from which he returned on September 16 to Santa Fe. The inhabitants, he reported, were thoroughly well disposed to the new government, so much so that the commander whom he would leave behind when he marched on to the West would have "nothing to attend to but to secure the inhabitants from further depredations from the Navajoe and Eutaw Indians."

The "territory being now so perfectly quiet," General Kearny turned his attention to preparation for the march to his ultimate goal of California. The preparations included, on the civil side, setting up on September 22 a new territorial government, complete with its organic law and bill of rights, its executive, legislative and judicial departments, a body of civil and criminal statutes, and a full complement of civil officers, all duly enumerated in parallel columns of English and Spanish, turned out on the one poor printing press found in Santa Fe. The laws thus proclaimed—prepared by Colonel Doniphan and Private Willard P. Hall of the mounted Missouri regiment—were based on the existing Mexican laws, modified by those of Missouri, Texas and Louisiana.

The first governor of the new Territory of New Mexico was Charles

Bent, of the family whose fort was such a center of frontier activity. The other officers included both New Mexicans and "Americans" resident in the territory, a fact which raised difficulties. Judge Otero of the Superior Court, for example, spoke no English and the District Attorney, Francis P. Blair, Jr., spoke no Spanish.[1]

Military preparations included erection on a hillside overlooking the new territorial capital of Santa Fe of a substantial earthwork, christened Fort Marcy, on which the soldiers labored under the direction of Lieutenant Jeremy F. Gilmer—the same who later, as major general and chief of engineers for the Confederate States, was to build other fortifications which would fly a flag as yet unborn.

Colonel Sterling Price, bringing out the second contingent of Missouri volunteers, had not yet arrived, but it was arranged that Doniphan would remain in command until he should come, when Doniphan was to march on to Chihuahua to report to General Wool who, it was assumed, would certainly be there before him.

Marching toward New Mexico, also, was the newly recruited battalion of volunteers from the Mormon encampments about Council Bluffs, Iowa. Not knowing when to expect the arrival of these reinforcements, and knowing that the government was anxious that he reach California as promptly as possible, Kearny determined to leave orders for the Mormon Battalion to follow his trail, and to set out himself with 300 of his dragoons, under the immediate command of Major E. V. Sumner.

So, on September 25—ten days after his return from the down-river districts and four days after proclaiming the new territorial government, and, as it happened, on the day on which Taylor's troops occupied Monterey in Mexico—General Kearny and his dragoons struck out for the Pacific.[2]

For two weeks they marched down the Del Norte. On October 3 word was received that Sterling Price had arrived at Santa Fe, and one uncertainty was removed from the general's mind. Three days later, while the command was still following the river valley south, Kearny met a small, quiet-spoken man with a "keen hazel eye" riding east. He was Kit Carson, the great "mountain man" who had shown many of the wilderness ways to "the Pathfinder"—who is better described in Allan Nevins' phrase as "Frémont the Pathmarker."

Carson had been sent by Frémont from California to take to Washington the great news of the occupation of that province. He had started with fifteen men, including six Delaware Indian scouts, and with fifty animals. The rigors of the trail had broken down many of his animals, some of which he had had to leave behind and others he had traded with the Apaches, through whose country he came, giving two of his worn-out horses for one of the Apache ponies. He had approached the New Mexican settlements with as much trepidation as Christopher Carson ever felt, or at least with due caution, because until a few days before he met Kearny he had not learned of the United States occupation of Santa Fe and the territory.

From that point of view, Carson's meeting with Kearny must have been a relief but from another standpoint it must have been a keen disappointment, for Kearny insisted that Carson turn back and guide his command over the way by which he had just come. Carson urged his pledge to go to Washington with the letters entrusted to his care. Kearny, promising to relieve him of the responsibility and send the dispatches on by a safe hand, insisted. Carson yielded, with the more reluctance because it meant giving up for another year his chance to see the wife whom he had left at Taos, and on October 7 "turned his face to the west again."

With the news in hand that "California had surrendered and that the American flag floated in every port," Kearny decided that 200 of his 300 dragoons should be sent back, under Sumner, while he went ahead with a hundred troopers under Captain Benjamin Moore, accompanied by a party of topographical engineers and guided by a detachment of the indispensable "mountain men."

On the ninth, from a point 200 miles south of Santa Fe, the wagons were sent back and the column halted to await the arrival of pack mules. On the thirteenth, the mules came up, the baggage was repacked, the last mail to be received was read and answered, and on October 14 the little command marched on. One more day they followed the Rio Grande del Norte downstream and then, on the fifteenth they turned westward. "Thenceforth a new road was to be explored."[3]

Five days later, after passing abandoned copper mines which had been worked by the Indians, the troop crossed the continental divide and made camp on the headwaters of the Gila. That night, in a communicative mood, Carson "remarked that he never knew how fine a weapon the bow and arrow was until he had had them fired at him in the night"—a bit of lore from the frontier experience of the great hunter and scout which was duly noted in the diary of Captain A. R. Johnston of the dragoons.

For more than a month the party made its toilsome way down the valley of the Gila. They passed Indian ruins, with pottery, which excited the interest of men whose main interest was to make the marches from water hole to water hole—some of them as much as forty-five miles apart, with a dry and grassless camp between. They passed well to the north of the settlement of "Tucsoon," and entered the Country of the Pima and the Maricopa, friendly Indians with whom they traded for food and animals.[4]

On the night of November 22, almost two months out of Santa Fe, they made camp near the mouth of the Gila, where it falls into the Colorado. That night fires were observed across the bottoms of the Gila. Lieutenant Emory, with twenty men, sent to observe more closely, found a party of Californians driving four or five hundred horses to Sonora. One of the party proved to be a bearer of letters as well—and in the letters there was news of the events which had taken place in California after Carson's departure, and while Kearny was marching west. Instead of finding a California peacefully occupied by United States forces, Kearny's handful of dragoons, on their worn and exhausted mules, were marching into the midst of a temporarily successful counterrevolution.[5]

The new government of California, proclaimed by Commodore Stockton from the capital at Ciudad de Los Angeles on August 17, had lasted peacefully and without interruption for just one month and one week. During that time the commodore had made plans to turn over the government to Major Frémont, who was to increase his California Battalion to 300 men, and to station garrisons of from twenty-five to fifty men each at Los Angeles, San Diego, Santa Barbara, Monterey and San Francisco. That being done, Frémont was to join the commodore at San Francisco on October 25, when he was to be named as governor, and Captain Gillespie of the Marine Corps as secretary, of the new territory.[6]

Meanwhile, the commodore proclaimed on paper "all the ports, harbors, bays, outlets and inlets, on the west coast of Mexico, south of San Diego, to be in a state of vigorous blockade." To enforce such a sweeping declaration he had but two vessels available. The *Warren*, Commander Joseph B. Hull, was sent to Mazatlán, from which harbor its small boats boldly cut out, captured and brought off the one Mexican warship on the west coast, the armed brig *Malek Adel*. The *Cyane* was sent to San Blas and to Guaymas, which was briefly occupied, and engaged in blockade duty along the coast of Lower California—a foretaste, on a most limited scale, of the duty which its commander, become Rear Admiral Samuel F. Du Pont, was later to undertake on a grand scale off the south Atlantic coast of the Confederate States.

Commodore Stockton, however, planned more than a blockade. He purposed, as soon as he should turn the government over to Frémont, "to leave the desk and the camp, and take to the ship and the sea," having in mind his plan to sail his squadron to Acapulco, capture that port, and march thence to Mexico City with the idea, as he told Frémont, that he might find a way "to shake hands with General Taylor at the gates of Mexico."[7]

Pursuant to these plans, the commodore sailed north from San Pedro in the *Congress* at the beginning of September, and Major Frémont proceeded overland to his former field of operations and recruiting ground among the Americans in the valley of the Sacramento, to raise men, if possible, for the Acapulco expedition. Captain Gillespie, made military commandant of the southern department, was left in charge at Los Angeles, under instructions from Stockton to maintain martial law, including both the curfew and the prohibition against bearing arms which were so galling to the Californians, but to temper the rigors of the law with special written permissions to "persons known to be friendly to the government."

The elections called for September 15 were held and "as far as heard from" resulted in the choice of "the proper officers," including Chaplain Colton of the *Congress,* elected alcalde of Monterey. The people, Stockton reported on the eighteenth, were "getting over their first alarm" and all was "going on as well as we ought to desire." Five days later the uprising began in Los Angeles.[8]

The reasons ascribed for it, according to one Mexican account, were the "patriotic fire which burned in the hearts of the majority of the citizens," especially in the district which is now known as Southern California, and the "impolitic and despotic conduct of the military authorities." Frémont ascribed it, in part, to resentment at what he called "police regulations." General Kearny wrote—although it was after he had quarreled with Stockton and Frémont—that the Californians had "been most cruelly and shamefully abused by our own people" and that "had they not resisted, they would have been unworthy the names of men."

The first disturbance was in the early morning hours of September

23, when a party of Angeleños, led by Don Cerulvo Varela, captain of auxiliaries, attacked the quarters of the tiny United States garrison. The attack was easily repulsed, but it was the signal for more serious disturbances. On the next day Captain José María Flores of the regular army, who had represented General Castro in the abortive efforts to negotiate with Stockton prior to the surrender of Los Angeles, established his camp a mile or so from the American quarters, rallied some 500 men about him, gathered arms and ammunition which had been in hiding, and "proclaimed the liberty and independence of the country, in the very city occupied by the enemy."[9]

By the twenty-fifth—the day on which Kearny started his march from Santa Fe—Gillespie and his handful of men were under siege. On the following day Lieutenant Wilson and a party were surrounded and compelled to surrender to a force led by Captain Varela and Lieutenant Diego Sepulveda. Four days later, on September 30, Gillespie capitulated under terms which permitted him to march out, with arms and ammunition, to San Pedro. The Mexican understanding of the terms of capitulation was that Gillespie and his men would there embark for Monterey and remove themselves from the scene of action. Gillespie's own understanding of the terms was merely that he should retire to San Pedro, which understanding he satisfied by boarding the United States merchant ship *Vandalia* which remained in the harbor.[10]

Word of the insurrection in Southern California—which spread to San Diego and Santa Barbara with the dispatch of forces from Los Angeles—reached Commodore Stockton at San Francisco at the beginning of October. Captain Mervine, sent south with the *Savannah,* anchored on October 6 at San Pedro, where he was joined by Gillespie and his party. Sailors and marines from the *Savannah* landed on the seventh and, in the face of opposition, advanced some five miles inland before halting for the night. On the morning of the eighth, after more fighting with elusive Mexican cavalry which hovered around and harassed his force but which could not be brought to grips, Captain Mervine retired to his ship, with a loss of a dozen men.

Vastly encouraged by this further success against the United States arms, the legislative body of California met on October 29 and elected Flores to the combined office of governor and *comandante general.* From San Luis Obispo south, California was once more in the hands of the native Californians.

At the end of October Stockton himself returned to the south, reinforced Mervine, landed at San Pedro, seemed about to march upon Los Angeles but changed his plans, re-embarked, and sailed away for San Diego, which in the meanwhile had been reoccupied by Captain Merritt and a detachment of the California Battalion. Reoccupied San Diego, however, was besieged from the land side by the Flores forces, so that Stockton was compelled to bring in provisions by sea from Lower California.[11]

In this posture affairs remained for a month—a month during which Flores was undertaking, with small success, to organize a government and to equip and supply an army; Stockton was preparing to resume land operations from San Diego as a base; Frémont was strengthening his position in the north, preparatory to moving against the Californian forces in the south; and Kearny's dragoons were making their toilsome way across what is now Arizona.

Kearny entered what is now California when he forded the broad Colorado on November 25. During the two days before, having learned from the captured letters of the altered state of affairs in California, he had been replacing the mules his men were riding—some of which had come more than 1,800 miles, and many of which were failing—with horses taken from the intercepted Mexican *caballada*. From the western bank of the river the column marched fifteen waterless miles and then found an old Indian well, dug it out to the depth of nine feet, and carefully doled out the precious ooze of water to man and beast. On the next three days a march of ninety miles from water to water was made across the area which modern large-scale irrigation has made a vast garden, before striking Cariso—or "Cane"—Creek. The command followed up the dry, sandy bed of the creek, with failing animals "sinking with thirst" and furnishing a "feast day for the wolves" as they fell and had to be left behind. Even the fat mares and colts which were driven along for food—the last beef having been slaughtered ten days before—were lost on this dreadful desert *jornada*.

On the thirtieth, finding a stretch of grass along the narrow valley—"it would be considered a poor camp on the Arkansas"—the command halted to give the animals a chance to graze. As they toiled on, they had "still to look for the glowing pictures drawn of California. As yet, barrenness and desolation hold their reign"—but finally, on the second of December, the summit of the coastal range was crossed and the column entered "the beautiful valley of the Agua Caliente, waving with yellow grass," down which they marched to the "magnificent hot spring" from which the valley took its name. That night, and the next day, camp was made on the near-by rancheria belonging to an American named Warner. Mr. Warner was himself away from home, but his fat sheep appeased hunger, and the pools below his spring, where natural hot and cold water could be mixed to the desired temperature, gave grateful relief to skins burned by the sun and caked with the salt of sweat and sand. "A day will come, no doubt," wrote Lieutenant Emory with prophetic touch, "when the invalid and pleasure seeking portion of the white race will assemble here to drink and bathe in these waters." Warner's, in the opinion of another of Kearny's soldiers, offered "nothing like the luxuriant growth of the prairies of Missouri" and "would be considered a poor location in the United States," but was grateful, nevertheless, to the eye of one who had just crossed the desert.

That night by the hand of an English settler, E. Stokes, Kearny sent word of his arrival to Stockton at San Diego. After a day's rest, on December 4, he resumed his march, making thirteen miles in a heavy rain, to pitch camp that night at the Stokes ranch. In the absence of the owner, the ranch was in charge of a deserter from an English merchantman, known to his Spanish neighbors simply as "Señor Beel." The señor made hospitable use of the limited resources of the rancheria for the comfort of the strangers, who, on the fifth, marched on in the rain to arrive, after nightfall, at the rancheria Santa María. There the first contact was made with the forces of the navy when Captain Gillespie, accompanied by Lieutenant Edward Fitzgerald Beale and Passed Midshipman J. M. Duncan, with a party of thirty-five men, arrived from San Diego with dispatches from Stockton for Kearny.[12]

Word was received there, also, that the enemy was in force nine miles distant. Two more miles were marched before halting, when a grassless camp was made in a canyon. Lieutenant Hammond, sent forward to reconnoiter the position of the enemy, was discovered and the enemy alerted. It was decided to attack and force a passsage. The call to horse was sounded at 2:00 A.M. and the march began.

At daybreak of December 6, at the Indian village of San Pascual, General Kearny's troops—having marched all the way from Fort Leavenworth to within forty miles of the Pacific without firing a shot at an armed enemy—had their first fight. The attack upon the Mexicans, commanded by Andres Pico, brother of the former governor, was unnecessary, badly conceived, and not well executed, except in the matter of headlong bravery. The advance, consisting of a dozen men under Captain A. R. Johnston, charged. The Mexicans feigned retreat and the advance was separated from the main body. Then the Mexicans turned upon their attackers and soon the whole force was engaged in hand-to-hand conflict, in which the three small howitzers of Kearny's forces were useless and firearms of any sort were little used.

"As day dawned, the smoke cleared away" and the Mexican forces withdrew—a circumstance upon which Kearny based his belief that the battle of San Pascual was a victory for United States arms. But if it were a victory, it was both dearly bought and little regarded. Eighteen of the little command were dead, including Captains Moore and Johnston and Lieutenant Hammond of the dragoons, and François Menard, one of the "mountain men" who accompanied the soldiers— all but two killed by the saber or the lance—and thirteen were wounded. Among the wounded were Captain Gillespie and General Kearny himself. The Mexicans had broken off contact but they hovered about the dismal bivouac of the Americans, where, all during the day of the sixth, the one surgeon worked at dressing wounds.

"When night closed in," wrote Lieutenant Emory, "the bodies of the dead were buried under a willow to the east of our camp, with no other accompaniment than the howling of the myriads of wolves attracted by the smell. Thus were put to rest together, and forever, a band of brave and heroic men" who on the long march of 2,000 miles had come to know and depend on one another. The survivors were truly forlorn—"provisions exhausted, horses dead, mules on their last legs, and men . . . worn down and emaciated," as well as surrounded by active and vigorous enemies.[13]

On December 7 the march was resumed with the wounded carried on travois ambulances made of poles dragged along the ground behind mules—excruciating contrivances devised by the three mountain men remaining but the best that could be done in the absence of wheeled vehicles. With the wounded dragged in the center, the column made its painful way to the San Bernardo ranch, where the horses were watered and chickens were caught and killed for the sick. A mile beyond, after a brush with the enemy parties hovering about, Kearny's men became convinced that no further progress could be made. Camp was made for the night and, as it turned out, the next day also. Holes were bored for water, the fattest of the mules were killed for meat, and time was passed in anxious lookout for the return of Alexis

Godey, the mountain man who had started, two days before, to make his way to San Diego and bring back relief.

Night falling on the eighth without relief, the indomitable Kit Carson, the gallant Lieutenant Beale of the navy, and an equally gallant but forever anonymous Indian, volunteered to undertake the twenty-nine-mile trip through enemy-held country to seek assistance—a journey that was to involve two nights passing through or between enemy positions, sometimes crawling in the cactus, with a day between spent in hiding.

While the relief party was making its perilous and painful way to San Diego, the command held its position. More of the wounded died. The hovering assailants sent a stampede of wild horses against the encampment but the Americans, instead of stampeding, captured two or three of the fattest of the horses and reduced them to rations. Finally, on the night of the tenth, affairs being desperate and no relief in sight, orders were issued to resume the march the next morning.

But during the night American-speaking voices were heard in the dark, as Lieutenant Andrew F. V. Gray of the navy, sent out from San Diego in response to the two calls for help, arrived with a party of a hundred bluejackets and eighty marines from Stockton's ships.

With the coming of morning the march of the reinforced command was resumed and before night Kearny's men were to glimpse the Pacific—for most of them, the first sight of the sea. On the next day, December 12, they marched into the little town of San Diego—a group of handsome mission buildings, deserted; a calaboose and a few adobe dwellings, two or three of which had plank floors; the hide houses where the one article of trade of the surrounding territory was stored to await the coming of ships; and, riding at anchor in the fine bay, the United States frigate *Congress* and the sloop-of-war *Portsmouth*.[14]

Kearny's men had ended their long march to the Pacific but they had not completed their assigned task. San Diego was the only position in Southern California held by United States forces. These forces had been there for five weeks but, awaiting the return of Frémont and his mounted battalion from the north, had undertaken no aggressive move. Plans were on foot for an advance either as a diversion to favor Frémont's anticipated movement or, as Kearny urged and as was finally done, a movement overland directly against Los Angeles—but nearly three weeks more were to pass before the movement was ready.

On the morning of December 29 the advance began—fifty-seven of Kearny's dragoons, forty-five sailors acting as artillery to handle six small guns, 397 sailors and marines acting as infantry, sixty volunteers, and a wagon train of one four-wheel carriage and ten oxcarts. Kearny was in direct command of the column but Stockton was commander in chief of the whole operation—a relationship from which future conflict was to arise.

On January 2, 1847, the column halted for the day at the deserted mission of San Luis Rey—the magnitude, convenience and durability of whose buildings, it was noted, would do credit to any country—because the sailor-infantrymen were "suffering dreadfully from sore feet." Two days later a flag of truce was met, bearing a proposition from Governor-Comandante Flores that there be no fighting and that the fate of California be settled by the general outcome of the war. Stockton declined to treat with Flores on the ground that he had taken and broken an oath of allegiance to the United States, and the column marched on. On the fifth, it was at the mission San Juan Capistrano, and on January 8 it met its first opposition at the crossing of the San Gabriel River, some twelve miles from Los Angeles.

Flores undertook, without success, to dispute the passage of the knee-deep ford by the fire of sharpshooters and small cannon. Stockton's men splashed their way across, formed in a rough square on the farther bank, and—after an hour's labor to drag the guns and carts across the quicksand bottom of the river—opened a cannonade upon the Mexican position, followed by a charge made under the battle cry "New Orleans!" in memory of Jackson's great victory on another eighth of January thirty-two years earlier. Flores' men did not stand to receive the charge but abandoned their position.

On the next morning, the ninth, the United States forces resumed the advance across the wide plain between the San Gabriel and the little city. Halfway to Los Angeles there was another brush with the defending forces, starting with long-range and ineffective artillery fire, followed by scattering cavalry charges on flank and rear. Repulse of the charges, and the withdrawal of Flores and his forces northward to the vicinity of the present-day Pasadena, brought an end to the fighting for Los Angeles.

It was yet but midafternoon and the town lay open to entrance less than five miles away. The United States commanders, however, realizing the difficulty of controlling men entering, just as night was falling, a town where the supply of aguardiente was plentiful, remained where they were and did not march into the City of the Angels until the following morning. On that day, January 10, 1847, the flag which had been lowered upon Captain Gillespie's capitulation more than three months before, was raised once more in the California capital.[15]

During those three months little had been heard in Southern California of Frémont and his forces. He had started south once but had turned back when he learned at Santa Barbara of the repulse of Captain Mervine between San Pedro and Los Angeles. Through the remainder of October and in November Frémont had recruited his forces to a strength of 400 mounted riflemen. Finally, at the beginning of December, he had started south again. At San Luis Obispo Frémont captured Don Jesus Pico, cousin of Andres and of the former Governor Pío Pico; tried him for violation of the oath of allegiance to the United States which he and most of the other California leaders had taken; sentenced him to death and pardoned him—a proceeding which, as a whole, made a grateful friend of Don Jesus, who accompanied Frémont south to play a part in the final pacification.

From San Luis Obispo, apparently fearing an ambush along the coast road, Frémont detoured across the mountains, and then back in a terrible December crossing in which more than a hundred horses were lost. At Santa Barbara he sojourned a week, all of which delayed his approach from the north until after Stockton and Kearny, coming up from the south, had scattered armed opposition.

Near the mission in the San Fernando Valley, north of Los Angeles, Frémont met a remnant of the scattered forces under Andres Pico, and there, on January 13, four days after the last fighting and three days after the occupation of the city, he entered into the Treaty of Cahuenga under the terms of which the insurgents were free to go or to stay in the country as they pleased, were excused from taking any oath of allegiance while the war lasted, were to be protected in person and property, and were guaranteed the same rights and privileges as citizens of the United States.

Commodore Stockton, who had declined to grant such terms only four days before when he still faced an enemy in arms, hesitated to accept the treaty made by his subordinate but, after reflection, wisely decided that this was the way of peace and reconciliation and adopted as his own the terms granted by Frémont.

The settlement thus brought about did indeed prove to be the end of contention between the men from the United States and the men from California, the little brush on the afternoon of January 9, 1847, being "the last exertion made by the sons of California, for the liberty and independence of their country whose defense will always do them honor."[16]

Further contentions—and they came almost at once—were among the conquerors. General Kearny, acting under the instructions from the War Department with which he had left Fort Leavenworth more than six months before, promptly claimed the right and duty to establish the new government of California. Commodore Stockton, acting under the letters of instruction which the Navy Department had sent to his predecessor in command, as positively asserted a like right and duty in himself. Stockton, with the ships' companies and the California Mounted Battalion—which was a "navy" organization—had by far the greater force back of him. He suspended Kearny from all military command other than over the dragoons which he had brought with him and, on January 16, named Frémont as governor, as he had originally planned to do three months before. The young army officer appointed by an officer of the navy, despite the presence and against the orders of an army officer of superior rank, was caught in the middle of a conflict of orders, a rivalry of services, and a clash of personalities. But he had worked with and liked Stockton and he knew and did not like Kearny, and so, with but slight hesitation, he accepted appointment at Stockton's hands.

Stockton and Frémont had a double basis for their action, in the orders from the Secretary of the Navy and in their interpretation of the orders from the Secretary of War exhibited by Kearny. Their position, as it may be derived from subsequent statements, was that Stockton had "conquered the country . . . [and] established a civil government"; that his right to do so was "incident to the conquest . . . under the law of nations"; that Kearny had been sent out first to conquer the country and then organize a government; that in consequence of meeting Carson with the news of the conquest he had reduced his force to a mere bodyguard with which to cross the desert; that he had come into the settlements in such condition that he not only could not conquer them, but could not even have reached them without timely aid sent out by Stockton; and that his instructions, because of the development of unanticipated events, had become obsolete and no longer binding and effective.[17]

Kearny, not wishing to precipitate an open collision at this critical time, remained silent and departed for San Diego, where he expected the arrival of the Mormon Battalion which was following the dragoons, marching by a longer but somewhat less difficult route. The battalion, some 350 strong, arrived on January 29.[18] Two days later, leaving Lieutenant Colonel Philip St. George Cooke in command at San Diego, the general sailed for Monterey. There, Stockton having departed, he found Commodore W. Branford Shubrick, who had just arrived from the United States in the razee *Independence,* in command of naval forces in California waters.

Shubrick recognized the validity of Kearny's instructions from the War Department as to military command ashore, but when it came to the question of civil government, he had instructions of later date from Secretary of the Navy George Bancroft, addressed to Commodore Sloat, that the civil government made necessary by occupation of California "should be established under your protection."

This conflict of instructions between the two departments was resolved upon the arrival, on February 13, of Colonel Richard B. Mason, who had left Washington in November and proceeded by way of the Isthmus of Panama, bearing instructions from both Secretary Marcy and Secretary John Y. Mason, who had succeeded Bancroft at the Navy Department. Direction of land operations and of "the administrative functions of government," the instructions read, should be in the hands of the senior army officer present, while port regulations were to be the function of the navy.

With such explicit instructions—which also emphasized the importance of "harmony" between the two "arms of one body"—Commodore Shubrick relinquished control to Kearny, and joined with him in issuing, on March 1, a circular defining their respective duties, which Kearny followed with a proclamation setting up the new government with Monterey as its capital. From his southern capital of Los Angeles, however, Lieutenant Colonel Frémont—who apparently had not been furnished with a copy of the latest instructions from Washington—continued to assert his authority as governor, and declined to carry out a military order from General Kearny that he turn over command of the southern military district to Cooke and bring north to Monterey or Yerba Buena for discharge such men of his irregularly enlisted California Battalion as might decline to be mustered in as volunteers under the existing law.

Directing his second-in-command to honor no orders from Cooke or anyone else other than himself, Frémont rode north to see Kearny—

a "most extraordinary ride," he was to call it, and it was, for with no companions other than his friend Don Jesus Pico and his colored servant Jacob Dodson, he covered more than 400 miles in less than three and a half days. Arriving at Monterey on March 25, he found there not only Kearny but another in the succession of naval commanders—Commodore James Biddle, who had arrived on March 2 from China by way of Japan, where he had paused for an early and unsuccessful attempt to open that country to Western commerce. The new naval commander accepted Kearny's authority, also, and there was nothing left for Frémont but to return to Los Angeles, which he did in the same dramatic fashion and at the same breakneck and breath-taking speed. Altogether he and his companions rode more than 800 miles in eight days.

More controversy followed, carried on both at Monterey and Los Angeles and at long range between them, and including even an impending duel between Frémont and Mason, with double-barreled shotguns and buckshot cartridges. Finally, with the long-delayed arrival of Colonel Stevenson's regiment of New York volunteers, Kearny brought the difficulties to a conclusion, insofar as the government of California was concerned, by making Colonel Mason governor. On May 31, Kearny left the coast by way of the South Pass route for Fort Leavenworth and Washington, taking Frémont with him under conditions which were galling to the proud and independent spirit of the intrepid explorer.[19]

Back in the States, charges of mutiny, disobedience of orders and conduct prejudicial to the public service were filed against Frémont. He was tried before a court-martial whose sittings began with November 1847 and ended with the last day of January 1848. The defendant was represented by his distinguished father-in-law, Senator Benton, and his brother-in-law, William Cary Jones. The case was, in every sense of the word, a *cause célèbre,* the subject of then almost unprecedented publicity and political pressures. At the end of the trial the court found Frémont guilty of all three charges and sentenced him to dismissal from the service, with a majority recommendation for executive clemency.

The record in the case—it fills almost 450 pages of small print—reached the White House early in February. There it was the subject of careful, indeed anxious, consideration, even to the extent of occupying the attention of an extraordinary meeting of the Cabinet on a Sunday night. All members of the Cabinet were agreed that the disobedience and prejudicial conduct charges had been sustained, but that there was doubt as to the charge of mutiny. All were agreed, also, that there were mitigating circumstances, and most of the Cabinet agreed that Polk should approve the sentence except as to mutiny, and should at the same time remit the penalty and restore Frémont to duty—which was done.

Such a discharge of a "painful and responsible duty," as Polk described it, was in no wise satisfactory to Frémont, or to his wife Jessie Benton, or to her imperious father, Senator Benton. Frémont promptly resigned from the army, refusing to accept the implication of guilt in the President's pardon. Benton, after twenty years as head of the Military Affairs Committee of the Senate, resigned his chairmanship and, in effect, declared implacable war upon the War Department, which he held responsible for the charges against his son-in-law, whose real offense, the Senator wrote, was that he had not only "entered the army without passing through the gate of the Military Academy" but had "become distinguished" through his explorations and services.

"From the day I approved the sentence in Col. Fremont's case," President Polk ruefully remarked in his diary, Senator Benton became "exceedingly hostile."[20] By that time—the date was February 16, 1848—hostilities between the United States and Mexico had come to an end, and in faraway California, the land which in their separate ways both Frémont and Kearny had helped to add to the territory of the United States, the millwright James Marshall, repairing the race of Sutter's sawmill, had already found flakes of gold.

---

1 Ex. Doc. 60, H. R., 30th Cong., 1st sess., pp. 174-229. One typographical difficulty in the printing of the new constitution and laws was the lack of a "W" in the Spanish language and consequently in the type font which was used. It was surmounted by setting two "V's" side by side. Private Hall, one of the authors of the organic laws and statutes, received notice two days before their promulgation that he had been elected to Congress from Missouri. The notice came through an express sent forward by Colonel Sterling Price seeking provisions to replenish the nearly exhausted commissary of his column of Missourians which was advancing by the Cimmaron cutoff of the Santa Fe Trail. Hughes, *Doniphan's Expedition*, pp. 121, 127-128 (Connelley ed., pp. 241-242, 251). Hughes's statement about the Spanish type font is declared by Douglas C. McMurtrie, the eminent historian of printing, to be in error. The font did have "W's," McMurtrie shows in "The History of Early Printing in New Mexico." Bieber (ed.), *Southwest Historical Series* III, p. 222*n*, 242*n*.

2 Ex. Doc. 60, H. R., 30th Cong., 1st sess., pp. 174-175; Ex. Doc. 41, H. R., 30th Cong., 1st sess., Emory's notes, p. 45.

3 Same, pp. 45, 49, 53-56, 60, 567, 572-576.

[4] Same, pp. 60, 64-65, 67-68, 84, 86-88, 577, 579; Ex. Doc. 1, Sen., 30th Cong., 1st sess., pp. 513-514.

[5] Ex. Doc. 41, H. R., 30th Cong., 1st sess., pp. 95-97, 608-609.

[6] Ex. Doc. 4, H. R., 29th Cong., 2nd sess., pp. 668-672, 675; Ex. Doc. 60, H. R., 30th Cong., 1st sess., pp. 265-270.

[7] Ex. Doc. 4, H. R., 29th Cong., 2nd sess., p. 670, 673-675; Ex. Doc. 70, H. R., 30th Cong., 1st sess., p. 46; Ex. Doc. 1, H. R., 30th Cong., 2nd sess., p. 1045; Ex. Doc. 33, Sen., 30th Cong., 1st sess., p. 182; Frémont, Memoirs, I, 569; Du Pont, Rear Admiral Samuel F., Official Dispatches and Letters of Rear Admiral Du Pont (Wilmington, Delaware, 1883), pp. 9-17; Stockton, Life, Appendix A, p. 4.

[8] Ex. Doc. 70, H. R., 30th Cong., 1st sess., pp. 38-39, 43-44.

[9] Same, pp. 40-41; Ramsey (ed.), The Other Side, pp. 407-408; Ex. Doc. 33, Sen., 30th Cong., 1st sess., p. 97; Frémont, Memoirs, I, 573, 574.

[10] Smith, War with Mexico, I, 338-340; Hughes, Doniphan's Expedition, p. 235 (Connelley ed., p. 343).

[11] Ex. Doc. 1, H. R., 30th Cong., 2nd sess., pp. 1045-1047; Smith, War with Mexico, I, 340; Ramsey (ed.), The Other Side, pp. 409-410.

[12] Ex. Doc. 40, H. R., 30th Cong., 1st sess., pp. 95-97, 99, 101-107, 610-614; Ex. Doc. 33, Sen., 30th Cong., 1st sess., pp. 186-187; Ex. Doc. 1, Sen., 30th Cong., 1st sess., pp. 513-514; Ex. Doc. 1, H. R., 30th Cong., 2nd sess., pp. 1048-1050.

[13] Same, pp. 514-516; Hughes, Doniphan's Expedition, pp. 226-230 (Connelley ed., pp. 334-339); Ex. Doc. 41, H. R., 30th Cong., 1st sess., pp. 108-109.

[14] Ex. Doc. 41, H. R., 30th Cong., 1st sess., pp. 109-113; Ex. Doc. 1, H. R., 30th Cong., 2nd sess., pp. 515, 1051.

[15] Same, pp. 1051-1052; Ex. Doc. 41, H. R., 30th Cong., 1st sess., pp. 115-121; Ex. Doc. 33, Sen., 30th Cong., 1st sess., pp. 61, 70-71, 188-193; Ex. Doc. 1, Sen., 30th Cong., 1st sess., p. 517; Hughes, Doniphan's Expedition, pp. 236-240 (Connelley ed., pp. 348-350). Captain Gillespie, wounded at San Pascual, was wounded again in the last fight before Los Angeles.

[16] Ex. Doc. 1, H. R., 30th Cong., 2nd sess., p. 1067; Smith, War with Mexico, I, 345-346; Sen., Doc. 33, 30th Cong., 1st sess., pp. 183-184; Ramsey (ed.), The Other Side, p. 413; Frémont, Memoirs, I, 598, 599, 652, 653; Stockton, Life, Appendix, p. 9; Nevins, Frémont, Pathmarker, pp. 293-300. The commissioners for negotiation of the Treaty of Cahuenga were, on behalf of Frémont, P. B. Reading, Louis McLane and William Henry Russell, of Fulton, Missouri, sometimes confused with William Russell of Lexington, Missouri, a partner in the great wagon-freighting firm of Waddel, Majors and Russell; on behalf of Andres Pico, J. A. Carrillo and O. Olvera—the last a name perpetuated in the well-known Los Angeles street. Hughes, Doniphan's Expedition, pp. 240-242 (Connelley ed., pp. 348-350).

[17] Ex. Doc. 60, H. R., 30th Cong., 1st sess., pp. 154, 231, 233, 235-237; Ex. Doc. 33, Sen., 30th Cong., 1st sess., pp. 6, 9, 10, 69, 79-80, 90, 94-95, 118, 175, 410-411; Stockton, Life, Appendix, p. 11; Nevins, Frémont, Pathmarker, pp. 306-314.

[18] The march of the Mormon Battalion is described in detail by Philip St. George Cooke, who took command at Santa Fe, in his report made from San Luis Rey, California, on February 5, 1847, published in Ex. Doc. 41, H. R., 30th Cong., 1st sess., pp. 551-563. The battalion arrived at Santa Fe, under command of First Lieutenant A. J. Smith, between October 9 and 12, 1846. It was there reorganized by weeding out the sick, eighty-six men, who with some twenty-five women and children, were sent back under escort to a camp on the Arkansas "at a small settlement close to the mountains, called Pueblo." (Cooke, Conquest of New Mexico and California, p. 91). The wives of two captains and three sergeants, however, having their own wagons, mules and provisions, were permitted to accompany the expedition. Before leaving the Del Norte, fifty-eight more men were sent back as unfit for the grueling march

ahead. The route followed was well to the south of that of Kearny's dragoons and passed through the settlement of "Tueson, Sonora." Cooke, with his wagons, had extreme difficulty in the long waterless crossing from the Colorado River until he met running water in the bed of the Carizita. The animals went fifty hours without water, the last half-ration of flour was eaten, and the men were "staggering utterly exhausted" before they were able to cross the summit of the divide above Agua Caliente. And, with it all, the battalion arrived too late to have any part in the final pacification of California.

[19] Ex. Doc. 1, Sen., 30th Cong., 1st sess., pp. 947, 948; Ex. Doc. 60, H. R., 30th Cong., 1st sess., pp. 163-165, 238, 247-249; Ex. Doc. 33, Sen., 30th Cong., 1st sess., pp. 12-14, 96-97, 100, 106, 108, 144-145, 153-154, 190, 198, 296, 422, 427; Hughes, *Doniphan's Expedition*, pp. 249-254 (Connelley ed., pp. 355-358); Nevins, *Frémont, Pathmarker*, pp. 320-326. The movements and negotiations of the various participants were brought out in detail at the trial of Colonel Frémont, reported in Sen. Doc. 33, 30th Cong., 1st sess.

[20] Benton, *Thirty Years' View*, II, 715-719; Quaife (ed.), *Polk's Diary*, III, 120-123, 168, 175-177, 180, 197-198, 204-206, 324, 335-338, 340; IV, 227, 330.

Battle of San Pasqual.

CHAPTER 14

The March of Doniphan's Thousand

WHILE Kearny and his dragoons, Stockton and his sailors and marines, and Frémont and his mounted rifle volunteers were engaged in the final pacification of California, the troops in New Mexico were called on to struggle with pacification problems of a different sort.

Before leaving New Mexico, Kearny had issued instructions that as soon as Colonel Sterling Price's new Second Missouri Mounted Volunteers should arrive, Colonel Doniphan was to go out into the vast tableland between the Rio Grande del Norte and the Colorado, from which the dreaded incursions of the Navajos and the Utes were made against the New Mexican settlements, there to recover prisoners and restore property taken by the Indians, and to take security for their future conduct—all before entering on compliance with the orders of September 23 to go to Chihuahua to join General Wool.[1]

Before the end of October, columns of the mounted Missourians were threading their way through the Indian country, clear across the continental watershed into the valleys of the San Juan and the Little Colorado. They traveled light, without tents or wagons. Winter coming on in the high altitudes of the plateau, the men suffered much from exposure but they did succeed in bringing together at the Ojo Oso, or Bear Spring—the site of the present Fort Wingate—a notable gathering of Navajo chiefs to discuss a treaty not only with their old enemies, the New Mexicans, but with the "New Men," as they called the North Americans who had come in from the East.

You Americans, one chief declared, "have a strange cause for war against the Navajos . . . for fighting the New Mexicans on the west, while you do the same thing in the east. . . . This is our war." Whether the warriors ever understood the reasoning of the new white men who

224

sought to protect those against whom they had so lately warred, they accepted the situation as it was presented to them and, on November 22, fourteen of the principal chiefs entered into a treaty of peace, trade and mutual protection. The treaty was sealed by gifts, those of the Navajo being blankets which were dispatched by Doniphan to Washington as evidence of their taste in design and their skill in manufacture.[2]

By mid-December Doniphan's regiment was again assembled, and encamped in the valley of the Rio Grande at Valverde—where, fifteen years later, the first New Mexican battle between the forces of the United States and those of the Confederacy would be fought. Valverde had been the most southerly settlement in the province but in 1846 it had long been abandoned because of Indian depredation. The Indians were supposedly pacified, however, and the New Mexicans of the Rio Abajo district, down the river from Santa Fe, seemed to have accepted the new regime in good spirit. That they had already begun to consider themselves citizens of the United States was indicated by the query put to an American officer by one of the local alcaldes, whether *"El Senor Don St. Iago Polk no esta el Presidente de nuestra república."*

At Valverde, Doniphan found encamped also the traders with 315 wagons of goods which could be sold in Chihuahua, ordinarily, for anywhere from three to eight or ten times their purchase price in St. Louis. Against this, however, there had to be charged, even in ordinary times, the heavy Mexican duties and the high cost of freighting, estimated at $360 a ton. And these were not ordinary times, for the traders had been waiting at Valverde since October, while the mounting expenses of delay ate into anticipated profits.[3]

Before arriving at the Valverde rendezvous, Doniphan had sent back to Sterling Price at Santa Fe for a battalion of light artillery which had been left there. Earlier, without orders from Doniphan, Price had sent forward Lieutenant Colonel D. D. Mitchell of his regiment with Captain Hudson's "Chihuahua Rangers," one hundred strong. With their arrival, Doniphan had 856 men, not including the traders and their teamsters and helpers—enough, in the opinion of almost every man of the 856, to "whip anything in or this side of Chihuahua."[4]

Major William Gilpin—the same who was to become the first governor of the Territory of Colorado, and whose name is perpetuated in the smallest and one of the most rugged of the counties of that state—led off with the first detachment of 300 men on December 14. Two days later, he was followed by Lieutenant Colonel Congreve Jackson with another 200, and on the nineteenth by Doniphan himself with the remainder of the command. The traders and their wagons, meanwhile, moved in the intervals between the marching groups.

Nine miles south of Valverde, the river and the road to El Paso diverged. Crowded by bare mountains, the river swung westward in a great bow; straight across the bend like the string to the bow ran the road across ninety waterless miles—the dreaded Jornada del Muerto. This Journey of the Dead, as it had come to be called by the traders, gave its name of *jornada* to every waterless stretch across which the men from the United States had to march in their Mexican campaigns—and there were many such—but this one was notable both as the first to be encountered and as the accepted boundary between the states of New Mexico and Chihuahua. In all the ninety miles there was but one small waterhole. To lack of water, there was added suffering from cold, for it was now mid-December, the Rio Grande was running with ice, the bare elevated plain across which the road ran was swept by piercing winds, and even if there had been time for the usual halts around the grateful warmth of campfires, there was no wood with which to make them. "No food—no fire—no sleep—very cold" was one soldier's description of a night's halt.

Three days it took each unit of the command to cross, but by December 22, the whole command was through the *jornada* and reunited at the little Mexican town of Doña Ana, a dozen miles below the lower end, where there were forage for the animals and corn meal and dried fruit for the men. Here, for a day, the command "feasted and rested." Here, also, information was received that Mexican forces, with artillery, were gathering at El Paso del Norte to dispute the passage of the invaders from the north.[5]

The troops so assembled, according to an account from Mexican sources, numbered up to 2,000, including dragoons from the interior and local levies, with four pieces of artillery. Upon receiving word that the Americans had reached Doña Ana, according to this account, the colonel commanding was attacked by a malady diagnosed by his surgeon as a brain fever which both compelled the colonel's return south and required the continued attendance of the doctor. The command devolved upon Lieutenant Colonel Luis Vidal, who moved out a short distance upstream from El Paso and halted to fortify. From this position, on December 24, he sent forward Lieutenant Colonel Antonio Ponce, with his own squadron of perhaps 500 dragoons reinforced by a somewhat larger number of local infantry, and with one small howitzer, to meet and destroy the advancing Americans.[6]

On the same day that Ponce moved north, Doniphan resumed his southward march. Continuing on the next morning, he had made eighteen miles by midafternoon when the head of the column began to go into camp in a level open space alongside the smaller arm of the Rio Grande where it was divided by a little island—El Brazito, it was called by the Americans, or, by the Mexicans, Temascolitos. The men of the advance scattered to their camping chores—gathering wood for cooking, seeking fresh grass for the animals, and taking them to water, all done probably with a little more of the skylarking spirit than usual, for the day was Christmas. With the advance so engaged, and while the rear units were scattered for miles back along the road, Colonel Ponce scored an almost perfect surprise.

The Mexicans were not discovered until they were less than a mile away, and already forming in line of battle to advance. With the Mexicans almost upon them, the 500 men who were on hand began to run for their arms and to fall in to meet the enemy's advancing line. But instead of pressing home his attack without delay, the Mexican commander halted and sent forward a mounted messenger, under a black flag bearing the motto *Libertad ó Muerto,* to demand that the American commander come to the Mexican lines for parley. Upon refusal, the Mexican herald announced that the Mexicans would charge and take him, neither asking nor giving quarter, and gracefully galloped back to his position. To this bit of histrionics, the reply of Doniphan was "more abrupt than decorous—to charge and be damned."

The Mexicans charged, opening fire as they reached a distance of about a quarter of a mile. Under instructions, the American line held its fire until the Mexicans were within 150 yards, when the Missourians opened with deadly volleys. As the repeated fire at short range checked the charge, the Mexican dragoons sheered off to the right toward the park of the wagon trains. There they were met by a hot fire from the teamsters, to which was added the effect of an intrepid charge from the flank by eighteen of the Missourians who had secured their mounts, led by Captain John W. Reid.

Less than half an hour after the fight began, it was over. The Mexicans were in full retreat, with a loss, as reported by Doniphan, of forty-three killed and a larger, but not definitely known, number wounded. The American loss was seven wounded, none fatally—a result which was attributed to the Mexicans firing too high.[7]

On the next morning, the column moved forward on the twenty-five-mile march from Brazito to El Paso—a very different sort of column from the one which had straggled over miles of road into camp on the day before. Baggage, provision and ammunition wagons, and the merchant train were closed up, with strong guards front and rear and flankers well out, all moving cautiously forward. The march of the day was fifteen miles, and that night Doniphan sent back to Santa Fe to hasten forward the artillery which he thought that he might need for the taking of El Paso.

But the Mexican defenders had either dispersed or departed for the south, and on the afternoon of December 27, after inconclusive negotiations with the municipal authorities, Doniphan's men bivouacked near the public plaza of El Paso del Norte—not situated at the location of the present Texas city of that name but across the river at the present Ciudad Juárez, Chihuahua. There the men settled down to wait for the arrival of the artillery from Santa Fe.

The men "found El Paso different from anything in New Mexico or the United States, with its *acequias* . . . its fruit trees and shrubbery, its vineyards and orchards," its choice fruits and wines, and, after a little while, its "dons and señoritas," its fandangos, and its square "like a market place, the scene of perpetual gambling" with both "Spaniards & American soldiers blocking up the streets at monte-dealing." The "sport of gambling" ran so high, indeed, that Colonel Doniphan had to put a stop to it on the streets, as he had previously prohibited the sale of spirituous liquors, and as he subsequently forbade "horse & mule racing & Fandangoes." But the El Paso wines, famed throughout that part of the world, were "very abundant and cheap," and "dissipation," one observer thought, was "carried to a great excess." After one lieutenant had stabbed another in an affray, it was observed that "the officers mostly have been too Licentious in their conduct," but on the whole there seem to have been friendly and satisfactory relations between the soldiers and the eight or ten thousand people of the pleasant irrigated upland valley that stretched for twenty-odd miles downstream from the mountain gorge—the "Gate of the North" which gave the area its name.[8]

By that time—early January 1847—reports of unrest and incipient revolt at Santa Fe had trickled down to the command isolated at El

Paso. Receiving word in mid-December of attempts to arouse the people of New Mexico against the new order, Colonel Price and Governor Charles Bent quickly rounded up seven of the secondary leaders but failed to apprehend the supposed principals, Tomás Ortiz and Diego Archuleta. The movement was believed to be confined to the four northern counties of the territory, and the action taken was thought—erroneously as the event proved—to have ended any attempt at organized resistance.

In January 1847, Governor Bent went himself into the northern counties above Santa Fe, accompanied by five of his officials, New Mexicans as well as Americans. At the village of San Fernando de Taos, on the nineteenth, the governor and his party were surrounded, captured, and "put to death with all the horrible details of savage barbarity," according to the report of Donaciano Vigil, the secretary of the territory who became acting governor. On the same day, and as part of the same plan for a general uprising, seven Americans were murdered at the Arroyo Honda and two others at the Rio Colorado, north of Taos. "It appeared to be the object of the insurrectionists," Colonel Price reported, "to put to death every American and every Mexican who had accepted office under the American government."

As soon as word of the uprising in the north reached Santa Fe, Colonel Price ordered up troops from the Rio Abajo district about Albuquerque, which had remained quiet, and Acting Governor Vigil addressed a fervent proclamation to the people, denouncing the insurrectionists for their "barbarous assassination" and their general policy of disturbance and hatred. On January 23, Price marched north with 352 men and four small mountain howitzers. Meanwhile, the New Mexicans and Pueblo Indians who were making common cause in the revolt marched south toward Santa Fe.

The first clash was on the afternoon of the twenty-fourth, when, after a sharp fight with loss on both sides, Price drove the native forces from the village of La Cañada. After two days there, he moved on up the Rio Grande to Luceros, where, on the twenty-eighth, he was joined by the troops which had made a forced march from the region about Albuquerque. With his number raised to nearly 500, Price flanked the rebels and forced his way through the pass of Embudo and crossed the high mountains in snow as much as two feet deep into the valley of Taos.

There they overtook the remains of the main insurgent force in the Pueblo de Taos. On the afternoon of February 3, they opened fire on the great enclosure with "its two large buildings of irregular, pyramidal form rising to the height of seven or eight stories," and its adjoining church. From a distance of 250 yards the fire was ineffective against the massive walls, as it proved to be again on the morning of the fourth. Toward noon it was decided to storm the building but it was not until nearly night, and after the guns had been run up to within ten yards of the walls, that the defenses were breached and the defenders driven out.

The loss of the United States forces that afternoon was seven killed and forty-five wounded. The loss of the defenders was about 150 killed, wounded unknown. On the morning of the fifth, having fought with obstinate bravery, the remaining defenders surrendered. Two of the principal leaders, Jesús Tafoya and Pablo Chavez, had fallen in the action; a third, Manuel Cortés, made his escape; a fourth, Pablo Montoya, was tried the next day by court-martial and, on the seventh, was hanged.[9]

At the same time as the rising in the valley of the Rio Grande, the villages east of the Sangre de Cristo range were likewise called on to rise against the invaders. Las Vegas refused to rise but at the village of Mora, on the upper waters of the Canadian, five Americans were killed. From Las Vegas, where a number of grazing parties and other Americans east of the mountains had gathered for safety, Captain J. R. Hendley led a detachment against Mora and there, while fighting in the streets as the Americans were "burning and tearing down houses," he was killed. In the fight, fifteen New Mexicans were killed and a like number wounded, and the little town was all but destroyed.[10]

The bloodless conquest of New Mexico by Kearny, in August, had become by January and February a bloody affair of assassinations and reprisals, with stern repressive measures to restore American authority in the districts north and east of Santa Fe. By March, however, government had been restored to the extent that the prisoners taken in the suppression of the revolt were turned over to the civil courts set up under Kearny's authority. Twenty-five of them were discharged, the grand jury not finding sufficient evidence to indict them. Four were indicted for treason against the United States and at the March term of court one was tried and convicted. Other prisoners were to be tried subsequently before the territorial court for the murder of Governor Bent. Meanwhile, in the case of the one prisoner convicted of treason, sentence was suspended until word could be had from Washington whether, in point of fact or law, such a charge could be sustained against any native New Mexican whose United States citizenship was derived from nothing more than General Kearny's proclamation of annexation. Acting Governor Donaciano Vigil and United States District Attorney Frank P. Blair submitted the question. President Polk's decision, made known to the military commander at Santa Fe, was that neither the rights nor the obligations of United States citizenship could be so summarily created. Those guilty of murder, or of instigating others to that crime, might be punished by either civil or military authority, but there could be no treason against the United States on the part of those who owed it no allegiance. It was the President's "decided wish," therefore, that the sentence pronounced on Antonio María Trujillo, whose case had been presented to him, be remitted.[11]

There were to be more disorders in New Mexico, and on the long trails across the plains and mountains traveled by soldier and civilian on the way to and from that outpost territory. There was to be, also, severe criticism of the state of discipline and order among the soldiers stationed there. But there were to be no more organized and concerted insurrections after the bloody suppression of the uprising of January 1847.

On the first day of February 1847, the long-awaited artillery from Santa Fe, under Major Meriwether Lewis Clark with Captain Richard H. Weightman in direct command of the six-piece battery and the 117 men, met a joyous reception as it marched into El Paso. Because of apprehensions of unrest, the start from Santa Fe had been delayed until early January, and even then the number of guns sent had been reduced. The winter march down the river, across the *jornada* and through the lower settlements had taken almost a month of hardship and toil—but the guns had come through and the long wait at El Paso, which had begun to irk soldiers of as "restless and roving disposition" as marked Doniphan's men, was nearly at an end.

After a week of busy preparation, on February 8, the "whole Army, Artillery, Escort, Volunteers, hospital Train, & commissary Train, a promiscuous host," set out for Chihuahua. The military part of the "promiscuous host" consisted of 924 men, to whom there were to be added, three days later, a small two-company battalion of volunteers from the hands employed by the traders. By this time Doniphan had had more definite news—although still not official—that he would not find General Wool at Chihuahua. With this thousand or so men, therefore, he was deliberately marching another 250 miles into the country of the enemy, with intent to capture and occupy the populous capital city of a major Mexican state, with every likelihood of meeting opposition in superior force, and without the slightest possibility of aid or reinforcement from any quarter. Few bolder decisions have been made than to go forward, and few have been more triumphantly justified by results.

The first enemy to be overcome was distance, much of it through waterless wastes. The first of these was struck on the sixth day out. As they started into this sixty-five-mile stretch, men filled even their saber scabbards with the precious liquid, letting the blades hang naked at their sides. The march was the more difficult because much of the way was in deep sand, through which it was necessary to double, and even quadruple, the teams and even then to have a dozen or more men turning at wheels sunk nearly to the hub in soft sand. On the third day, at the first water, "horse, mule & man vied with each other in drinking out of the same puddles." The teams and teamsters, which had been left ten miles behind to struggle on to water if they could make it after lightening the loads by throwing away several thousand pounds of supplies, were saved by a copious shower coming on at nightfall from which "both men and animals were filled."

On the fifth day after passing their first waterless stretch, the command halted for a few hours at the Ojo Caliente, in preparation for another forty-five-mile *jornada* just ahead—an opportunity which the colonel and many of his men improved by bathing in the warm, clear waters flowing from the spring. That afternoon, the twenty-first, they marched on to make a cold and waterless camp after nightfall.

The next day—one on which battle was being joined at the hacienda of Buena Vista, 600 miles to the southeast—men and animals struggled through waterless stretches to another cheerless camp. On the twenty-third, another bold spring was reached, but the twenty-fourth was another day of marching to a waterless camp. Toward noon of the twenty-fifth, the advance struck water at the Laguna Encenillas, twenty miles long and three miles wide, but someone was careless with fire and let it get away into the grass. Before long another fire which had got away two nights before was seen approaching on the wings of wind from the north—a rolling, crackling, raging wall of flame, ten to twenty feet high, gaining strength with every puff of the rising wind.

The drivers of the wagons—especially those carrying ammunition—lashed their teams, but the frenzied horses needed no urging to escape the advancing flames. Unable to keep ahead, some of the wagons and artillery were driven into the waters of the lake, while the men who had already reached its shore frantically set about to trample down firebreaks and set backfires. A patch of burned and blackened earth was created, around which the fire swept, and within which the exhausted men and animals made camp, grateful enough to be secure from the flames which raged past them, but discomforted by the clouds of ashes and dust blowing about.

Two more days the regiment marched, after its battle with fire at the lake, and finally, on Sunday, February 28—three weeks out from El Paso—it came face to face with the enemy.[12]

Since November, when Angel Trias had become governor of the state of Chihuahua, active preparations for its defense had been under way. General José A. Heredia had been sent north to take over the military command. Cannon had been cast at a local foundry, arms had been repaired, clothing provided, and soldiers enrolled—all steps which, by their very taking, had generated a degree of enthusiasm and confidence. Scouting parties had observed the advance of Doniphan's men, and fortifications had been erected where the El Paso road crossed the Rio Sacramento, some eighteen miles north of the city of Chihuahua.[13]

The point of resistance was well chosen. Approaching from the north, the road on which the Americans were marching, and probably the only road practicable for wagons, dropped down first to cross the broad dry bed of the Arroyo Seco; rose to surmount an elevated tongue of land between the arroyo and the Sacramento; and dropped again to cross that stream at a narrow gap commanded by heights projecting to the riverbank—all in a space of less than four miles, constricted between ranges of mountains bordering the valley on the east and the west. The Mexican fortifications were so sited as to cover all approaches—a row of works on the north side of the tongue of land, on a hill known as the Cerro Frijoles, facing north; a row of redoubts for guns with breastworks for infantry stretching from this bastion across the elevated tongue of land to the north bank of the Sacramento, facing west; a strong work at the Hacienda Sacramento, on the south side of the stream. These works were furnished with ten guns, besides smaller pieces described as culverins, and were garrisoned by a force of 2,000, according to Mexican accounts, and of from 3,500 to 5,000, according to the accounts of the Americans.

Arrived at the north bank of the Arroyo Seco in midafternoon of February 28, after a waterless march of fifteen miles, Doniphan paused. That day, he had formed the 400 wagons, military and mercantile, in four parallel columns of 100 wagons each, with the troops and artillery marching in the spaces between, and with three companies of cavalry in front, screening the movement. After a brief survey of the situation, the American formation wheeled right, up the north bank of the arroyo to a point beyond the range of the defenders' cannon, where it turned left and dropped into the deep and steep hollow of the arroyo. Teams and wagons, forced over the edge of the fifty-foot-high banks, slid down into the dry stream bed, scrambled and dragged their way up its south slope, came out on the elevated tongue of land between the two streams, turned left—and were in formation, facing the Mexican position.

Misjudging the portent of Doniphan's movement, the Mexican commander had failed to sally from his position and strike while the American force was involved in the struggle to cross the arroyo. When he did advance, the American line was formed, the wagons were up, and the artillery was ready to open a brisk and effective fire which drove back the advance of the Mexican cavalry. For nearly an hour there was cannonading on both sides, followed by an advance of the Americans to within a quarter mile of the Mexican fortifications. Here there was a halt while two guns under Weightman and three companies of cavalry were ordered to charge the central redoubt of the Mexicans. Through some misunderstanding only one company charged, but the guns were unlimbered and went into action scarcely fifty yards from the Mexican line. There was a short sharp struggle until the remaining companies came into action, when the rest of the American line swept forward from right to left, against the other redoubts, and soon drove out the Mexican defenders.

Some of the defenders fled down the Sacramento toward Chihuahua; others crossed the stream to join in the continuing defense of the position on the south bank. With the other positions cleared, the American artillery was turned upon this work, which, just before sunset, was charged and carried, by horse and foot. The battle had lasted, from the time of the first shot, not more than three hours. In all the firing and fighting the American loss was but one killed— Major Samuel Owens, commanding the provisional battalion of the merchants, struck down in an intrepid charge—and eleven wounded.

The Mexican loss, according to Doniphan's report, was about 300 killed and as many more wounded.

In all the incredible saga of Doniphan's march nothing is more incredible than the Battle of Sacramento, in which a numerically superior force was driven from well-located and prepared positions, almost without loss to the attackers. Whatever other reasons there may have been for such a result, one reason was the decisive superiority in effective fire power which the United States forces so quickly secured and consistently maintained.[14]

On the day after the battle the city of Chihuahua, having been abandoned by the Mexican military, was occupied by Lieutenant Colonel Mitchell and an advance party of 150 men, who bivouacked that night in the tree-shaded Alameda, at the foot of the monument to Hidalgo, whose Grito de Dolores touched off the long revolt against Spanish rule in Mexico and whose career ended before a firing squad there. On the second of March Doniphan entered the city, at the head of a force which he himself described as "rough, ragged and ready."

Despite his smashing victory at Sacramento, Doniphan was in a position which he described as "ticklish." He not only was not in touch with any other American force, he did not even know where any other one was. He had heard, though he was not sure, that General Wool, to whom he had been ordered to report, was "shut up at Saltillo by Santa Anna." His "little army," he wrote, was "out of reach of help, and it would be as unsafe to go backward as forward," wherefore, he concluded, "high spirits and a bold front, is perhaps the best and safest policy." Proclamations were issued, public property possessed, artillery planted to command the approaches to the plaza, and the Americans settled down to the role of an occupying force, even to the extent of the establishment of a bilingual newspaper, the *Anglo-Saxon,* which began publication as early as March 13.

Receiving word through Mexican sources that a battle had been fought at Buena Vista, and correctly divining the result, Doniphan first fired a national salute of twenty-eight guns in honor of victory, and followed it up, on March 20, by dispatching to General Wool a report of his situation, by the hand of J. L. Collins, a trader and "amateur soldier" who had fought at Sacramento, with an escort of a dozen men. "My position here," the doughty Doniphan wrote, "is exceedingly embarrassing . . . most of the men . . . have been in service since the 1st of June, and have never received one cent of pay. Their marches have been hard . . . so that they are literally without horses, clothes, or money—nothing but arms and a disposition to use them. . . . They are volunteers . . . wholly unfit to garrison a town or city . . . and will soon be wholly ruined by improper indulgences"— wherefore, the colonel concluded, he would like to be ordered to give up the garrison job and join the main body of the army.[15]

After a perilous and toilsome journey of two weeks, marching at night through more than 600 miles of enemy-held territory where rifles were the only "passports," Collins' little party reached General Wool's camp on April 2. There they rested a week, while the dispatches they brought were forwarded to Taylor at Monterey, and until the receipt of orders from the general that Doniphan should bring his men to the main army, whence—their twelve months' enlistments being nearly up—they would proceed to New Orleans for discharge and pay.

To strengthen the party for the return journey to Chihuahua, a company of Arkansas cavalry was detailed, under command of Captain Albert Pike—subsequently to command Indian troops for the Confederacy but destined to wider fame for his contributions to the philosophy of the Scottish Rite of the Masonic order. Accompanying the return party, also, was the noted author of *Commerce of the Prairies,* Josiah Gregg, who, with Pike and John T. Hughes, historian of the Doniphan expedition and a member of Collins' party, constituted what was perhaps the most distinguished literary trio to make any of the marches of the Mexican War.[16]

Arriving at Chihuahua on April 25, the couriers found that the army there had received erroneous information that the dispatch bearers were killed or captured, and was already preparing to make the same movement which had been ordered. That day the artillery and one battalion set out for Saltillo. Three days later, on April 28, after fifty-nine days of occupation of the city, the last of Doniphan's troops marched out of Chihuahua.

On May 22 they were reviewed at Buena Vista, where, as it turned out, the brilliantly uniformed General Wool and his staff were inspected by the Missourians with quite as much interest as the reviewing officers had in the already legendary marchers and fighters who had just come in from Chihuahua. Five days later they were reviewed by General Taylor at the American camp at the Walnut Springs, out of Monterey, and passed on down to the Rio Grande, to take steamboat to the Brazos and to sail across the Gulf to New Orleans. There, still "rough and ready" and as "ragged" as ever, they received their discharges and—after twelve months of service—their first pay. From New Orleans Doniphan's Thousand proceeded, as individuals and without orders, back to Missouri—to complete early in July a year's journey of more than 5,000 miles of toil and peril which, then and since, has aptly been likened to the Anabasis of the Ten Thousand of Xenophon.[17]

[1] Ex. Doc. 56, H. R., 30th Cong., 1st sess., p. 318; Hughes, *Doniphan's Expedition,* pp. 143-144 (Connelley ed., pp. 206-207).

[2] Ex. Doc. 1, Sen., 30th Cong., 1st sess., p. 496; Hughes, *Doniphan's Expedition,* Chapters VIII-XI.

[3] Ex. Doc. 41, H. R., 30th Cong., 1st sess., pp. 499-501, 506; Bieber (ed.), *Southwest Historical Series,* IV, 216; Hughes, *Doniphan's Expedition,* pp. 255-256 (Connelley ed., pp. 360-365).

[4] Same, pp. 255-257 (Connelley ed., pp. 360-366); Bieber (ed.), *Southwest Historical Series,* III, 279-292, IV, 214.

[5] Ex. Doc. 1, Sen., 30th Cong., 1st sess., p. 497; Hughes, *Doniphan's Expedition,* pp. 257-258 (Connelley ed., pp. 86, 367-369); Bieber (ed.), *Southwest Historical Series,* IV, 215-226.

[6] Ramsey (ed.), *The Other Side,* pp. 168-169.

[7] Ex. Doc. 1, Sen., 30th Cong., 1st sess., pp. 497-498; Ex. Doc. 56, H. R., 30th Cong., 1st sess., p. 318; Hughes, *Doniphan's Expedition,* pp. 259-267 (Connelley ed., pp. 369-378); Bieber (ed.), *Southwest Historical Series,* III, 300-309, IV, 227-237.

[8] Hughes, *Doniphan's Expedition,* pp. 267-285 (Connelley ed., pp. 88-97, 378-394); Bieber (ed.), *Southwest Historical Series,* III, 309-317, 323-324, IV, 237-244.

[9] Ex. Doc. 1, Sen., 30th Cong., 1st sess., pp. 520-530; Ex. Doc. 70, H. R., 30th Cong., 1st sess., pp. 17-24; Hughes, *Doniphan's Expedition,* pp. 389-396, 398 (Connelley ed., pp. 90, 511-516).

[10] Ex. Doc. 1, Sen., 30th Cong., 1st sess., pp. 531-533; Hughes, *Doniphan's Expedition,* pp. 396-397 (Connelley ed., pp. 517-518).

[11] Ex. Doc. 70, H. R., 30th Cong., 1st sess., pp. 24-35.

[12] Ex. Doc. 1, Sen., 30th Cong., 1st sess., p. 499; Hughes, *Doniphan's Expedition,* pp. 286-301 (Connelley ed., pp. 97-103, 395-406); Bieber (ed.), *Southwest Historical Series,* III, 325-343, IV, 246-259.

[13] Ramsey (ed.), *The Other Side,* pp. 167-168, 172-174.

[14] Ex. Doc. 1, Sen., 30th Cong., 1st sess., pp. 499-513; Ramsey (ed.), *The Other Side,* pp. 174-178; Hughes, *Doniphan's Expedition,* pp. 301-315 (Connelley ed., pp. 103, 407-443); Bieber (ed.), *Southwest Historical Series,* III, 344-351, IV, 259-269.

[15] Ex. Doc. 60, H. R., 30th Cong., 1st sess., pp. 1128-1129; Hughes, *Doniphan's Expedition,* pp. 325-339 (Connelley ed., pp. 104-108, 449-455); Bieber (ed.), *Southwest Historical Series,* III, 353-363, IV, pp. 270-276.

[16] Ex. Doc. 56, H. R., 30th Cong., 1st sess., pp. 317-319, 326, 334; Ex. Doc. 60, H. R., 30th Cong., 1st sess., pp. 1143-1145; Hughes, *Doniphan's Expedition,* pp. 339-348 (Connelley ed., pp. 108, 458-463); Fulton (ed.), *Gregg's Diary,* 89-100.

[17] Same, pp. 349-380 (Connelley ed., pp. 109-111, 464-498); Fulton (ed.), *Gregg's Diary,* pp. 107-130.

CHAPTER 15

Buena Vista

DURING all the weeks in which the Government of the United States was determining to shift the weight of its attack from the north to the beaches of Vera Cruz, and while Scott was vainly trying to come up with Taylor to arrange a division of forces, Santa Anna had been engaged, with great energy, in accumulating at San Luis Potosí a force with which to strike the invader.

In the matter of the financial sinews of war he had had the greatest difficulties. During the earlier weeks Santa Anna was nominally no more than the commander of the army, leaving to José Mariano Salas, in the exercise of the executive authority conferred upon him by the August revolution, the task of finding funds. The response to eloquent appeals for voluntary contributions proved to be quite insufficient, so late in November, Salas decreed that the government would tap the resources of the Church by means of drafts to the total amount of $2,000,000 drawn on the several bishops, payable in two years and subject to immediate discount by persons designated and required to purchase them. The bishops, however, were slow to accept such drafts, and the designated purchasers were quite as reluctant to cash them—and there matters stood when the new Mexican Congress met on December 6, 1846.

The new Congress, created under the pronunciamiento of the August revolution, elected Santa Anna President, and as his Vice-President, Valentin Gómez Farías, leader of the *Puros,* as the simon-pure Federalists or anti-Centralists were called. Santa Anna accepted the office thus conferred on him but, absorbed in military matters, did not return from San Luis to Mexico to take the oath of office—thereby leaving on the erect and unbending shoulders of Farías, the ancient enemy of the clerical party, the dangerously unpopular task of raising the money which the general in the north sternly demanded.

238

By January, Farías was reduced to the last expedient—forcible seizure and sale or mortgage of the properties of the Church to the amount of as much as $15,000,000. A measure authorizing such a step was presented to Congress on January 7. On the morning of the tenth, after continuous session during nearly three days and nights, it was passed. On the next day, signed by Farías as Acting President, it became law. Enforcement of the law, however, proved even more difficult than its passage. At noon of the very day on which the measure became law, Church authorities issued a strong and solemn protest calling down ecclesiastical penalties on the heads both of those who sought to seize the Church properties and of those who might become purchasers of property so seized. When the government undertook enforcement of the act, it was met with resistance, both passive and active, extending even to rioting in the streets, while few persons could be found to advance money on properties so secured.

To add to the embarrassments of the Farías government, Santa Anna, the President-designate who had approved the measure when it was passed early in January, turned against it before the end of the month, urging that the law be modified and some other means be found for raising the money which—he continued to insist—must be had for his Army of the North and the defense of the nation. Thus encouraged, the clerical party in Congress secured the passage, early in February, of a measure which in terms gave the government "extraordinary powers" for the raising of funds. In its more practical effect, however, it was a partial repeal and suspension of the operation of the law of January 11 for the seizure of estates of the Church.[1]

Despite difficulties, dissensions and even disasters, however, neither the Mexican Congress, nor the executive, nor the general in chief relaxed in the least their fierce resolve to resist invasion, and to repel anything resembling proposals for peace. Partly, this was due to innate resentment; partly, to the hope for a reverse to United States arms as they advanced into Mexico, with lengthening lines of communication and supply.

Upon the "first disaster," Lieutenant Meade wrote home,

[Mexico] expects a *pronunciamento* on the part of the Whigs and Northern Democrats, forcing the Government to withdraw the troops and propose more lenient terms. In this idea . . . she is . . . fortified . . . by the speeches in Congress of some of the Whigs, and the tone of many newspapers of the Whig press. . . . Do not think this idea is absurd; it is true.

To those who viewed the American political scene from a distance, a Whig pronunciamento at the first reverse to American arms might well have seemed a reasonable prospect. In the elections of November 1846 the Whigs had won a majority of the seats in the next House of Representatives. They had won on a variety of issues, of which the most effective was probably Polk's veto of the popular rivers and harbors appropriation bill. The most conspicuous of the issues, however, was denunciation of "Mr. Polk's War." When the old Congress, the Twenty-ninth, met on December 7, 1846, for its second and closing session, and the administration presented its measures for raising men and money for the prosecution of the war, Whig political strategy and Abolitionist sentiment combined to produce a perfect torrent of vituperative oratory.

The denunciations of an "unholy war" were partisan, rather than sectional. Meredith P. Gentry, a Tennessee slaveowner who in after years would serve as a member of the Congress of the Confederate States, denounced Polk as a "petty usurper." Garrett Davis of Kentucky, to become a staunch Union leader, inquired by "what imperial or regal authority his majesty undertook to act." Robert Toombs, Georgia slaveowner and future Secretary of State of the Confederacy, charged the President with "usurping the war-making power" in invading and seizing Mexican territory. Thomas L. Corwin of Ohio, combining strong antislavery sentiment with his party affiliations, attained the heights—or depths—of intemperate abuse when he declared that "this desolating war" was brought on by American invasion of Mexico, and added, "If I were a Mexican I would tell you, 'Have you not room in your own country to bury your dead men? If you come into mine, we will greet you with bloody hands, and welcome you to hospitable graves.' "[2]

This particular outburst could not have reached Santa Anna at San Luis Potosí, but he and other Mexicans in authority were sufficiently familiar with the indications of American dissension to cause them, probably, to exaggerate its significance, and to raise up in their minds unrealistic anticipations of the results of a victory—if one could but be gained.

The Mexican commander in chief had particular reasons for seeking such a victory at the earliest date. There had been whispers about his loyalty to the Mexican cause when the United States permitted his passage through the blockading fleet. His more recent orders to

Ampudia to fall back from Saltillo after the loss of Monterey, and to Parrodi to evacuate Tampico, had revived and strengthened the same suspicion. The best way to rebut such whispers—and more than whispers—was to seek, and destroy, the enemy.

There is no direct evidence that the captured copy of Scott's letter of January 3 to Taylor, in which the entire American plan of campaign was outlined, was received by Santa Anna, and the Mexican commander might not have known of the impending descent upon Vera Cruz.[3] He was, however, sufficiently well informed of the strength and positions of General Taylor in his immediate front, through the wide-ranging activities of his cavalry corps which both effectively screened his own movements and gobbled up scouting parties sent out by American commanders.

The first such party to meet this fate was one dispatched by General Wool to investigate rumors of the approach of the Mexicans. Major Solon Borland of Colonel Yell's Arkansas regiment of cavalry, was dispatched on January 18, with orders to go as far as La Encarnación, fifty-five miles below Saltillo, to find out whether the enemy had come to that point, and to return and report. Finding no troops there, Major Borland enlarged on his orders and sent back to Colonel Yell for reinforcements with which to go on to El Salado, fifty miles or so farther on. Before hearing from Yell, he received unexpected reinforcements when Major John P. Gaines and Captain Cassius M. Clay, of the Kentucky cavalry, arrived with another party on a scout. The combined force of some eighty men started, on January 22, for El Salado but, it coming on to rain, the party decided to return and spend the night more comfortably in the buildings of the ranch at La Encarnación. There, at dawn, they awoke from a refreshing and unguarded sleep to find themselves surrounded by an estimated 3,000 of General J. V. Miñon's Mexican cavalry. Their resulting capture was not because of "lack of courage," one contemporary noted, but from their "recklessness of danger."

When neither Major Borland nor Major Gaines returned, Captain William J. Heady of the Kentucky cavalry was sent out with a party of nineteen to find what had become of them. This party, according to a pamphlet written by one of its members and published in Louisville after the war, put out sentries. General Wool in his report says it did not. But regardless of this detail it found itself, on the morning of January 27, surrounded by overwhelming force to which it was compelled to surrender, likewise without firing a shot. General Wool

reported his difficulties in "inducing the volunteers to obey orders" as
to putting out sentinels and guarding against surprise. He had no
idea that Saltillo or Buena Vista would be attacked, he said, but felt
that if they continued to go "to sleep without a sentinel or picket"
the reconnoitering parties would be in danger. Meanwhile, the prisoners, with the exception of the scout and interpreter Daniel Drake
Henrie who escaped with news of their capture, were on their way
south, first to San Luis Potosí and then to the capital, where they were
to become supporting evidence of Santa Anna's subsequent claims of
victory, and finally to Toluca, where they were sent to prevent recap-
ture.[4]

News of the capture of the reconnitering parties, which reached
General Taylor at his headquarters at Monterey on January 30, caused
him to move forward to Saltillo. He took with him the same troops
that had escorted him on the return from Victoria to Monterey—
Lieutenant Colonel May's squadron of dragoons, the batteries of Captains Thomas W. Sherman and Braxton Bragg, and the regiment of
Mississippi Rifles commanded by the general's onetime son-in-law,
Colonel Jefferson Davis. Arriving at Saltillo on February 2, the general decided, as a measure of restoring the confidence of the volunteers and of the inhabitants of Saltillo, to move his troops and his
headquarters still farther toward the enemy. On February 5, therefore, he advanced eighteen miles to Agua Nueva.

Taylor was subject to severe criticism for disregarding the expressed
wish of the administration and what he termed the "advice" of Scott
to evacuate Saltillo, hold nothing beyond Monterey, and stand on a
"strict defensive." Taylor's own reasons for not doing as he was told,
as given in his letter of February 7 to the Adjutant General of the
Army, were that such a retrograde movement would have had a "per-
nicious moral effect upon volunteer troops," and that there were
"powerful military reasons" for occupying the southern, rather than
the northern, end of the pass of Rinconada. He explained:

The scarcity of water and supplies for a long distance in front com-
pels the enemy either to risk an engagement in the field or to hold
himself aloof from us; while, if we fell back upon Monterey, he could
establish himself strong at Saltillo, and be in position to annoy more
effectually our flanks and our communications.

To these reasons expressed by the commander, Major Isaac I.
Stevens—the same who, as a major general of the Union Army would

die on the same Virginia field on which Philip Kearny would meet death—adds another. Taylor, he says in his balanced study of the battles in Northern Mexico, was wise in not giving Santa Anna the opportunity to manufacture the enormous prestige which he could have built from a retirement, even a voluntary retirement, of the American forces from their advanced position at Buena Vista.

Actually, however, General Taylor was not greatly concerned over the possibility of a Mexican advance. The frequent alarms about the advance of Santa Anna, he assured the Adjutant General, seemed to be "without substantial foundation," and no "serious demonstration in this direction" was considered likely. A week later, on the fourteenth, he was equally skeptical as to the probability of a Mexican movement against him—more than two weeks after the movement had started and when, indeed, the Mexican army was already at El Salado, only eighty miles away.[5]

The Mexican march started from San Luis Potosí on January 27, with units departing daily until February 2, when the headquarters moved out. Baggage was reduced to little more than the men could carry—but General Santa Anna explained in his ringing proclamation of the march against the enemy that "the Mexican soldier is well known for his frugality and capability of sufferance. . . . Today you commence your march, through a thinly settled country, without supplies and without provisions; but you may be assured that very quickly you will be in possession of those of your enemy, and of his riches; and with them, all your wants will superabundantly supplied." With such promises, and not much else, Santa Anna's force of some 20,000 men and twenty guns took up the trying march to "wipe away from our soil the vain-glorious foreigner who has dared to pollute it with his presence."

The march, in a February of more than usually bitter weather and through a high plateau country of sparse supplies and scant water, proved to be indeed a terrible trial for the army, "not only the soldiers, but the women who followed . . . with their killing burdens of wood." Men deserted and men died, but with it all, by February 20 the whole force was assembled at La Encarnación—only thirty-five miles from the American camp at Agua Nueva.[6]

First intimation of the approach of the Mexican army was had from the indefatigable Major Ben McCulloch of the Texas Rangers, whose men reported a cavalry force of unknown strength at La Encarnación. On February 20, Lieutenant Colonel May and a party of the regular dragoons were sent on a reconnaissance across the mountain range bounding on the east the valley in which Agua Nueva lay. The dragoons experienced some of the same ill fortune that had dogged the volunteers, when Lieutenant Samuel D. Sturgis and an orderly were surrounded and captured as they reached the summit of a range of hills. The capture, however, revealed the presence of enemy force, which was confirmed by observation of fires and dust.

The same afternoon McCulloch went back to La Encarnación, to see what could be seen. By midnight, he had scouted the campfires and knew that a large force was before him. To get the information to Taylor as promptly as possible, he sent back all his men but one, who remained with him within the Mexican lines. At daybreak he made an accurate estimate of Santa Anna's forces and made his escape, to ride to Agua Nueva with the news by the afternoon of February 21.

On the night which Ben McCulloch so coolly passed within the Mexican lines, orders were issued for the final stage of the march, to start at eleven o'clock in the morning of the twenty-first with intent to strike the Americans by surprise at Agua Nueva on the following morning. Rations were issued for three days, with no fires or cooking to be permitted on the night of the twenty-first, nor any military music. The movement of the morning of the twenty-second was to be made "in profound silence." Very special attention was to be paid to the matter of water. Troops were to drink all they could before starting, and to carry all they could on the march—for the next water was to be had only after the defeat of the Americans at Agua Nueva.[7]

So the waterless march of thirty-five miles was organized, to reach the anticipated scene of battle in the early morning of February 22. But, instead of surprising unsuspecting Americans at Agua Nueva, the advancing Mexicans found an abandoned campsite, which gave every evidence of having been quitted in haste. At the last moment the dogma that retrograde movements were damaging to the morale of volunteer troops was given up, and a hasty retirement from Agua Nueva was ordered. The camp there, Taylor reported, could be turned on either flank by the enemy's "greatly superior . . . cavalry"; so he had determined, during the morning of the twenty-first, to retire eleven miles and there await an attack.

Colonel Yell's Arkansas regiment was left behind to bring back the considerable amount of supplies which could not be hauled off that day but, toward midnight, Yell's pickets were driven in and he, too, abandoned Agua Nueva, burning the buildings, the stacks of grain, and the other supplies which had not been loaded into transport wagons. There was ample evidence in the looks of things for Santa Anna's too-ready assumption upon his arrival that the abandonment of Agua Nueva had been a flight, and for the eagerness with which he drove forward his men, after their all-afternoon and all-night march, to overtake and crush the fleeing Yanquis. He did not even allow the cavalry in the advance, famishing for water as they were, an opportunity to drink and refill their canteens. At last, so it seemed, victory over a fleeing enemy was in reach.[8]

The position to which the United States forces had retired, and in which they had been placed by General Wool while General Taylor went on seven miles farther to see about the immediate defenses of Saltillo, was described by Taylor as a line of "remarkable strength." It lay three miles south of the hacienda Buena Vista, near the head of a narrow valley through which the road from San Luis to Saltillo ran. The valley drained northward toward Saltillo but, in February, the channels and washes through which the mountain torrents ran in the wet season were deep, steep-banked, dry gullies, making, on the wider eastern side of the valley, a herringbone pattern of ridges and gullies extending from the mountain on the southeast to the narrow passage of the road on the northwest. The situation has not been better described than it is in General Taylor's own report of the battle:

The road at this point becomes a narrow defile, the valley on its right being rendered quite impracticable for artillery by a system of deep and impassable gullies, while on the left a succession of rugged ridges and precipitous ravines extends far back towards the mountain which bounds the valley. The features of the ground were such as nearly to paralyze the artillery and cavalry of the enemy, while his infantry could not derive all the advantage of its numerical superiority. In this position we prepared to receive him.

The site, well-named La Angostura or "The Narrows," had been chosen as the place of battle by General Wool, who did not scorn to make defensive preparations in advance. He had gone so far, in fact, as to strengthen the position across and on the right of the road by having a small ditch dug and a parapet thrown up, leaving a narrow passage which could be closed by running into it two wagons loaded with stones. He had, moreover, left pickets out at the Encantada ranch, three and one half miles to the south, who in midmorning of

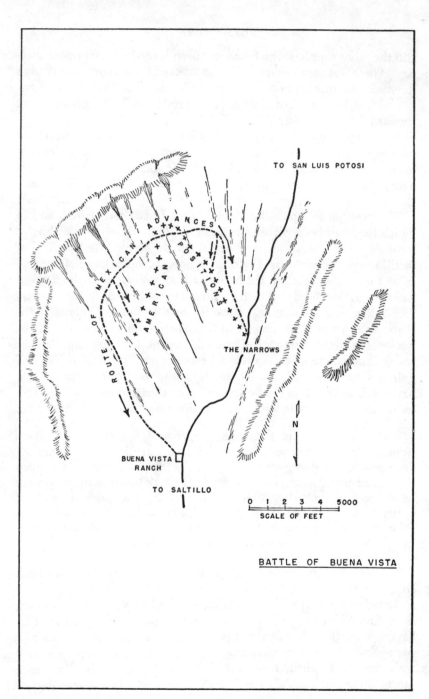

BATTLE OF BUENA VISTA

Washington's Birthday reported that the enemy was advancing. Wool, notifying the commanding general at Saltillo, brought forward the troops at Buena Vista and began to put them in position.

At what it was believed would be the key position, where the road passed through the Narrows between the network of gullies on the right and the plateau intersected with ravines on the left, General Wool placed the battery of Captain J. M. Washington, which had marched from Pennsylvania to San Antonio de Bexar, and from there all the long miles through Monclova and Parras, and had yet to fire a shot at an enemy—a battery which, before the fight was over, was to justify its long tedious march. On both sides of the battery were the troops of the First Illinois, Colonel John J. Hardin. To their right was Colonel William McKee's Second Kentucky. To the left there was not a continuous line—not enough troops for that—but a series of detached positions: first, Colonel William Bissell's Second Illinois, then Brigadier General Joseph Lane's Indiana brigade, with a squadron of regular dragoons in reserve behind them, and then, clear over by the mountain which bounded the valley on the left, or east, the Kentucky and Arkansas cavalry regiments and a battalion of Indiana infantry, under command of Colonel Humphrey Marshall of Kentucky.

With the return of General Taylor from Saltillo, bringing with him May's dragoons, Davis' Mississippi Rifles, and the batteries of Sherman and Bragg, these troops were placed in reserve, except that Bragg's battery was advanced with the Kentucky infantry to a position on the extreme right.

The total strength of the American force was 4,759—of whom only the 700 or so troops who had accompanied the commanding general to Saltillo on the night of the twenty-first, and returned with him on the morning of the twenty-second, had smelled hostile powder.[9]

Against this force there was to be thrown a command which, according to Santa Anna's report, had numbered 19,525 when it left San Luis Potosí and which, allowing for all the detachments and the attrition of the terrible march to the field of battle, probably still numbered over 15,000—to whom there should be added the cavalry forces of General Miñon operating on the flanks and constantly threatening to take the American position in the rear. The odds, though, were less desperate than they seem. The Mexican force had just made a most extraordinary march of more than forty-five miles in less than twenty-four hours, with little food, less water and no real rest. Many units were composed of unwilling soldiers, pressed into service, and were badly armed and ill equipped besides. Only the magic name and the driving force of Santa Anna, indeed, could have brought them so far.[10]

About eleven in the morning of February 22, Santa Anna sent forward under flag of truce a summons to Taylor to "surrender at discretion" if he would avoid "suffering a rout and being cut to pieces" by the "twenty thousand men" surrounding him. An hour was allowed for consideration but Taylor needed no more time than was necessary to have the message translated and for his chief of staff, Major Bliss, to reduce his explosive oral answer to a polite note "begging leave to say that I decline acceding to your request"—an 1847 equivalent of a later American general's "Nuts!"[11]

While these polite preliminaries were under way, and for an hour or two thereafter, the little American army watched the Mexicans— truly an army with banners—march up and spread across the valley. Finally, near three o'clock in the afternoon, the Mexican artillery opened. It was another hour, however, before the Mexican right, under Pedro Ampudia, advanced with apparent intent to gain the flanks of the mountain above the lightly held American left. There, on the mountainside, inconclusive maneuver and skirmishing continued until after dark, when Colonel Marshall's defending detachment was ordered down into the valley for the night.[12]

That night the troops on both sides lay on their arms where they stood, without fires, shivering in the icy cold winds of a February night in a mountain valley, 6,000 feet above the sea. That night, also, General Taylor, convinced that the main battle would not take place until the next day, took the Mississippi Rifle regiment and May's dragoons with him back to Saltillo, about whose defense he had become concerned when it was reported that Miñon's cavalry had made its way through a pass to the east of the city into the valley behind the American army. Leaving six companies of Mississippi and Illinois troops, with three pieces of artillery, to protect his rear and defend the city—which they proved sufficiently able to do—General Taylor went forward again, on the morning of February 23, taking the other troops with him.[13]

The action of that desperate day had well begun before the general arrived at the position of La Angostura. At dawn the Mexican force was discovered to have gained the very top of the mountain which Marshall had vacated, under orders, after the action of the day before; to have planted a battery on its slopes within long range of the American left; and to have, indeed, passed around and beyond that flank. "Everything now indicated that the main attack would be against our left," and Wool began shifting forces—the Second Kentucky infantry and Bragg's battery sent from the right, and Sherman's battery from reserve, to the left center; and a battalion of Illinois riflemen sent to reinforce Marshall, who held the extreme left.

The first major attack was made by the divisions of Manuel Lombardini and Francisco Pacheco against the left center of the American position. To meet the attack, it was intended to advance the Second Indiana regiment nearer to the brow of the slope up which the Mex-.cans were moving. They were to accompany three guns from Washington's battery commanded by Lieutenant John Paul Jones O'Brien. O'Brien and his guns dashed forward, unlimbered and went into action within musket range of the advancing Mexican infantry, and under flanking fire of a battery. Looking back for the infantry which was supposed to have accompanied him, he found that "instead of advancing" it had, in the language of its brigade commander, "retired in some disorder." Other reports were that the regiment, after standing long enough to deliver twenty-one rounds of fire, broke under the combined effect of a tremendous cross fire from flank and front and an ill-advised order to "cease fire and retreat." Having done so, most of the men—though not all—did not stop until they reached the haven of the Buena Vista ranch. Part of the regiment, rallied by its Colonel Bowles—who had given the unfortunate order—remained on the field and in the fight. O'Brien stayed where he was, firing away until he "had not a cannoneer to work the guns" and was just about to be overwhelmed by the Mexican advance when he limbered up and withdrew two of his three pieces, leaving behind one for which all the horses had been killed.

About the same time as the break in the left center of the position, the forces on the extreme left flank were being driven off and away from the mountainside—"I could see no infantry belonging to our army, and the progress of the enemy seemed unresisted, if not resistless," Colonel Marshall reported—thus opening the way for Mexican forces to by-pass the Angostura position and move along the east side of the valley toward Buena Vista.

The retirement of these two commands on the left uncovered the position of Colonel Bissell's Second Illinois infantry which, being entirely unsupported by troops other than a section of artillery, was compelled to fall back but in good order. The continued advance of the Mexican lancers and infantry, however, brought them against the strong point toward the American right, where the attack was broken up by the "rapidity and precision of the fire" of Washington's battery.[14]

The American position of the morning, except for this strong point, had been turned and breached. No longer was there even the semblance of a line across the head of the valley facing south. The American right still looked to the south, but the center and the left had been bent back and faced east. "The enemy was now pouring masses of infantry and cavalry along the base of the mountain on our left, and was gaining our rear in great force," recorded General Taylor. "At this moment I arrived upon the field." On his arrival, General Wool wrote, Taylor "took his position in the center of the field of battle, where he could see and direct the operations of the day." And where, moreover, he could be seen by his hard-pressed soldiers, imperturbably seated on "Old Whitey," a solid rock of calm courage.[15]

The Mississippi Rifles which Taylor brought back with him from Saltillo went into action at this juncture and, for a season, held the Mexican infantry advance in check near the center of the field. Meanwhile, however, the Mexican cavalry had passed beyond, toward the Buena Vista ranch buildings in the rear. To meet this threat there was hastily assembled a composite command—D. H. Rucker's regular dragoons and Albert Pike's Arkansas squadron, both under May; Marshall's and Yell's regiments; a section of guns under Lieutenant John F. Reynolds; and a motley detachment gathered up by Major John Munroe, chief of artillery, from the several hundred stragglers and fugitives from various commands who had drifted to the rear during the morning. As the Mexican cavalry charged toward the ranch buildings, from the east, they were met by a countercharge which split the column. After a melee, in which Archibald Yell lost his life, the two wings of the Mexican command fell away, under fire from men on the roofs and behind the walls of the ranch, one in the direction from which it had come, the other to pass on to the west and so to ride clear around the United States position before reaching the Mexican camps.[16]

The Mississippi regiment was soon called on to meet an even heavier charge but this time it had help—J. H. Lane's Third Indiana regiment, those parts of the Second Indiana which had kept the field, and Captain Sherman with one of his howitzers. A strong body of lancers

rode out from the flank of the mountain and across one of the plateaus
between the gullies which cut into the American position, preparing
to charge the infantry, stationed a little way in advance of Buena
Vista. The launching of the charge was delayed a little while by fire
from the guns of Braxton Bragg, who had moved back from the right
and front to be closer to the center of the fighting. As the Mexican
lancers advanced, the Mississippi and Indiana infantry formed into a
line presenting to the enemy a re-entering angle, and stood awaiting
his charge. Coming toward that firm and immovable line, the charge
slowed down until, just as it entered the jaws of the angle, it was moving at no more than a walk. And then the angle came to life, with a
cross fire from both sides so destructive that the head of the column
withered, and the lancers broke and were driven from the field—an
action which was to become famous as the "V" of Buena Vista, and
one which, with the subsequent actions of the day, did much to cement
that military friendship between Jefferson Davis and Braxton Bragg
which was to have fateful bearing on the fortunes of the Confederacy.[17]

With the repulse of the lancers, the Mexicans who had penetrated
the American positions on the left were in full retreat along the foot
of the mountain, under the repeated and continued fire of the American batteries. Then it was, when affairs seemed to have turned toward
American success, that through some misunderstanding which has
never been fully explained, a flag of truce passed between the two
armies and, for a season, firing was suspended. By the time it became
apparent that neither side was ready to give up and that there was in
fact no reason for suspension of hostilities, the disorganized bodies of
troops on the Mexican right had regained the main body and, as the
hillsides were pelted with a driving shower of rain, preparations were
under way for the final effort of the day, with the available cavalry
and infantry massed under General Francisco Perez for one more
attack.

This last effort was made by the Mexicans—all day they had taken
the initiative and forced the fighting—against what had been, in the
morning, the American center and was now the left. The American
infantry on that part of the line—the two Illinois regiments and the
Second Kentucky—were in process of deployment when the new
charge struck. Once again, the charge of an advancing army was to
be met by no more than a handful of guns—at first, indeed, only a
section under Lieutenant O'Brien and a single gun under Lieutenant

George H. Thomas. At the last moment, before the advancing charge swarmed over him, Thomas managed to withdraw his gun. O'Brien, with every cannoneer gone, abandoned his guns only when the Mexicans were within yards of his muzzles. "I could have saved the guns . . ." he reported, "but in such case, the day might, perhaps, have been lost."

"This was the hottest as well as the most critical part of the action," General Wool reported. "At the moment when our troops were about giving away"—Colonel Hardin of the First Illinois was dead, Colonel McKee of the Second Kentucky was dead, his lieutenant colonel, son and namesake of Henry Clay, was dead, many another soldier was dead—the fortunes of the day were turned once more by the artillery. Captains Bragg and Sherman, with jaded horses and exhausted men, forced their way forward through and around the gullies, came into action from the rear "most opportunely," and drove back the enemy almost from "the muzzles of their pieces." Close behind the field artillery came infantry reinforcements on the run— the troops which had formed the sides of the "V", the rifles from Mississippi and the Third Indiana, whose Lieutenant James Taggart was the last man to fall in the close fighting at Buena Vista. And, about the same time, the Mexican lancers who had taken the Kentucky and Illinois infantry in flank and driven them down the ravine in front of Washington's battery, came under the fire of those well-served guns—and, at close of day, were turned back.[18]

"Without our artillery," wrote General Wool, "we could not have maintained our position a single hour." The handful of artillerists to whom such credit was given were, indeed, a brilliant and devoted corps. They ranged in age from Captain Washington, who had entered the Military Academy in 1814, to Second Lieutenants Darius Couch and Francis Bryan, who had graduated just in time to get into the war. Couch, the only officer of Washington's battery who survived to serve in the War between the States became a corps commander of the Army of the Potomac. Braxton Bragg became a general of the Confederate States; his lieutenant, Charles Kilburn, a Union brigadier general. Thomas W. Sherman became a United States major general, and every one of the four officers who served under him at Buena Vista attained like rank in one or the other army—in the Union Army, John F. Reynolds, who met death on the first day at Gettysburg, and George H. Thomas, the Rock of Chickamauga and the victor at Nashville; in the Confederate Army, Samuel

G. French, who was wounded at Buena Vista, and Robert S. Garnett, who was to be the first Confederate general officer killed in battle.

To the services of the batteries handled by these officers, General Wool said, "we are mainly indebted for the great victory. . . ." But on the night of February 23, 1847, no one—not even the indomitable Taylor—was sure that there had been a victory. Buena Vista, as one Mexican writer noted, was not one battle but a succession of separate fights. The Mexicans, as they figured it, had won "three partial triumphs, but not a complete victory." Insofar as relative strength and position went, the two armies stood on the night of the twenty-third, just about where they had been that morning. Once more the United States troops lay on their arms, without fires, without even taking the harness off the artillery horses, anticipating a renewal of the desperate struggle, hoping for the arrival of a small reinforcement which was on its way forward from the pass of the Rinconada on the other side of Saltillo, determined to resist whatever further attacks there might be, but with no thought of themselves attacking.

But when morning came, Santa Anna's host was gone—most of them, in fact, being all the way back to Agua Nueva before the Americans discovered their departure. "The great disparity of numbers and the exhaustion of our troops," wrote Taylor, "rendered it inexpedient and hazardous to attempt pursuit." It was the evening of the twenty-sixth before Santa Anna left Agua Nueva for the thirty-five-mile march across the plain to La Encarnación—a night march which even without pursuit had in it enough of horror and human suffering to make it, in the opinion of a Mexican officer, one which "might with reason be designated as the *noche triste.*" Santa Anna himself hurried ahead while his miserable soldiers plodded on, losing men by sickness, death and desertion until, when San Luis was reached at last, the command mustered barely more than half the number who had marched out only a little more than a month before.[19]

The American loss in the fighting at Buena Vista had been heavy— 267 killed, 456 wounded, 23 missing—a total of 746 casualties. The heaviest losses had been, as usual, in the infantry, with the Second Illinois and the Second Indiana reporting the heaviest regimental losses. The loss of the Mexicans, as the attackers, was far heavier— not less than five times as many in absolute number and twice as heavy in percentage of those engaged. General Santa Anna had signally failed to gain the victory he so desperately needed but, as he marched his men back over the terrible track to San Luis Potosí in a retreat as fatal, some Mexicans said, as "a complete rout on the field of battle," he did the next best thing—he announced one to the waiting capital and the nation, supporting his announcement with the prisoners taken at La Encarnación and O'Brien's captured guns.[20]

The first reports which reached the United States were disturbing rumors of defeat. Part of Santa Anna's plan had been to send a cavalry force against the American line of communication and supply. One such raiding force, under General Urrea, struck the line between Monterey and Camargo, destroyed wagon trains, killing escorts and drivers, and for a season blocked all passage.[21] It was not until March 20 that any intimation of the battle of Buena Vista reached Washington, in the form of vague rumors published in the New Orleans newspapers, which created "painful apprehensions for the safety" of the American forces. These apprehensions were deepened by further reports, and by a call from Colonel Curtis, commanding the Ohio regiment which garrisoned Camargo, for a reinforcement of 50,000 men for the Rio Grande. Polk considered the rumors greatly exaggerated but nevertheless hastened to dispatch to the Rio Grande the 2,000 or so men who had enlisted in the ten new regiments of "Regulars," so-called, which had been intended for the support of Scott's operations. These were, indeed, the only reinforcements immediately available for either commander. The President had asked, in December, for the legislation necessary for the enlargement of the Regular Army by ten regiments. For more than six weeks, the President noted, Congress had "engaged in discussing the abstract question of slavery & gravely considering whether it shall exist in a territory which we have not yet acquired & may never acquire from Mexico"—a discussion excited by renewed efforts to add the Wilmot Proviso to the appropriations sought. Almost despairing of action on the Ten-Regiment Bill, the President had written, on February 4, "when it will pass, God only knows," but a week later it had been acted on by both Houses, signed by the President, and become law.[22]

But—a fact which seemed hard to learn—passing a law did not create regiments, although it did bring forth, immediately, great swarms of applicants for commissions as officers. "The City is crowded with young men, many of them loafers without merit, seeking military appointments," Polk noted a week after the bill passed. ". . . I could soon have an army of officers, such as they would be, if I could ap-point all the applicants. . . . I have pushed them off and fought them off with both hands like a man fighting fire." Even after the session of Congress closed on March 4, the President was visited by "a crowd of persons, chiefly young men, seeking captaincies and lieutenancies in the army." The army officers thought that the new Regular regiments should be organized and trained in the United States before being sent out, but the President, feeling that "if this were done they would not be on the theater of action until mid-summer," decided to send them out to the Brazos by companies, as soon as they could be got up to the strength of sixty-four men each. To receive and organize them there, George Cadwalader, an able Philadelphia lawyer, was appointed brigadier general—a post in which he was to serve acceptably. It was these men, on whose reinforcement Scott was relying, who were temporarily diverted to Taylor's command upon receipt of the rumors of great loss and possible disaster beyond Saltillo.

And then, on April 1, the long delayed dispatches from General Taylor were received in Washington, with the great news of Buena Vista. Lieutenant Meade, who was not at Buena Vista, expressed the national estimate of Buena Vista as the greatest "feat ever yet performed by our arms, or which ever will be." Another aspect of the national response to the victory was reflected by Theodore O'Hara in his elegiac poem with its well remembered stanza:

> On Fame's eternal camping-ground
> Their silent tents are spread,
> And Glory guards, with solemn round,
> The bivouac of the dead.

The news of Buena Vista meant, too—though no one could have known it at the time—that except for the long tedium of garrison duty broken only by occasional guerrilla actions against wagon trains and isolated parties, the war in the north was over.[23]

Not only that, the Presidential election of 1848 had been settled. Polk was correct in his opinion that many valuable lives would have been saved had General Taylor obeyed his instructions to stand on the defensive at Monterey and its near-by passes. He was correct in his estimate that American victory was due to "the indomitable & intrepid bravery of the officers and men" rather than to superior generalship. But such considerations weighed not at all with the rejoicing public— nor, for that matter, with the soldiers who had seen Zachary Taylor at Buena Vista, and from seeing him had drawn fresh store of indomitable resolution. A great battle had been fought and won against what seemed to be fearsome odds. It had been fought by a general after the soldiers' and the people's own hearts; one who, the soldiers and the people believed, had been the victim of jealous and spiteful discrimination, and who, despite all handicaps and in the face of all odds, had won. Winning, he had won not only a battle but the Presidency of the United States.

And, though no one would realize the fact for yet another dozen years, Buena Vista had set the feet of Colonel Jefferson Davis, whose Mississippi Rifles had done so much, who had himself suffered a serious wound, and who was second only to Taylor as the hero of the day, on the path which was to lead through the Senate and the Cabinet of the United States to the Presidency of another nation—the Confederate States of America.

---

[1] Ramsey (ed.), *The Other Side*, pp. 149-154; Rives, *U. S. and Mexico*, II, 308-320; Smith, *War with Mexico*, II, 7-12.

[2] Meade, *Life and Letters*, I, 180-181; *Congressional Globe*, 29th Cong., 2nd sess., pp. 211-218. For more extended treatment of the political situation during the closing session of the 29th Congress, see McCormac, *James K. Polk*, pp. 457-471, and Beveridge, *Lincoln*, I, 415-420.

[3] Both Scott and Taylor were convinced that Santa Anna had received the captured dispatch, and each one was sure that with this information of American plans in hand Santa Anna would turn against him. Santa Anna himself does not mention in his reports, or in his subsequent writings, that he received the dispatch. General French writes that Colonel Agustin Iturbide, son of the Mexican emperor and an officer of the Mexican army whom French met after the war, told him that Santa Anna did receive the dispatches and decided to attack the weakened Taylor first, defeat him, and then turn to defend the capital against Scott's advance from Vera Cruz. French, *Two Wars*, p. 71.

[4] *Encarnacion Prisoners . . . By a Prisoner* (Louisville, 1848), pp. 34-42, 73, 74; Baylies, *Narrative*, p. 25; Ex. Doc. 60, H. R., 30th Cong., 1st sess., pp. 1106-1109. One of the Encarnación prisoners, Major Gaines, became governor of Oregon; another, Major Borland, senator from Arkansas, United States minister accredited to the republics of Central America, and subsequently, a Confederate brigadier. A third, Lieutenant T. J. Churchill, likewise become a Confederate brigadier, was to surrender the fort at Arkansas Post, with five thousand men, to a Union expedition under General McClernand.

[5] Stevens, Isaac I., *Campaigns of the Rio Grande and of Mexico: With Notices of The Recent Work of Major Ripley* (New York, 1851), pp. 39, 40; Smith, Isaac, *Reminiscences of a Campaign in Mexico . . .* (Indianapolis, 1848), p. 66; Ex. Doc. 60, H. R., 30th Cong., 1st sess., pp. 849, 864, 1106, 1109-1111, 1113.

[6] Ex. Doc. 1, Sen., 30th Cong., 1st sess., pp. 153-156; Ramsey (ed.), *The Other Side*, pp. 114-120.

[7] Same, pp. 120-121; Ripley, *War with Mexico*, I, 383-385; Webb, *Texas Rangers*, pp. 112-113; Ex. Doc. 1, Sen., 30th Cong., 1st sess., p. 132. Earlier, on the march to Victoria, Lieutenant Sturgis had been cut off in a defile through which he was es-

corting the baggage train but had escaped capture and rejoined his command. Lieutenant Colonel May preferred charges against him, but Sturgis came out of the trial with credit to himself and an acquittal from the court. Ex. Doc. 60, H. R., 30th Cong., 1st sess., pp. 1095-1097; Maury, *Recollections*, p. 31. As a brigadier general of the Union Army he was to have an active and varied, but not always fortunate or successful, career in the War of Secession.

8 Ramsey (ed.), *The Other Side*, pp. 121-122; Carleton, James Henry, *The Battle of Buena Vista* (New York, 1848), pp. 11-26.

9 Ex. Doc. 1, Sen., 30th Cong., 1st sess., pp. 132, 142, 145, 146; Baylies, *Narrative*, pp. 23, 27; Ex. Doc. 32, Sen., 31st Cong., 1st sess., p. 38.

10 Ramsey (ed.), *The Other Side*, pp. 94-98, reports Santa Anna's army at San Luis as numbering 21,553 officers and men, to whom were added the brigade of Parrodi, 1,000 men, which joined at Matehuala, on the march forward. From this should be subtracted the severe losses of the rapid march. Santa Anna's own figures indicate that he left San Luis with 19,525 men, to whom were added the detachment picked up at Matehuala, and from whom there were to be subtracted cavalry detachments under Miñon and Urrea, and the heavy losses of the march, reducing the force to a little more than 15,000 by the time it reached Encarnación. However, the Miñon command came into the action of February 22-23, threatening Saltillo and detaining part of the American force there, so that it may be figured that the Mexican forces in the field of operations at Buena Vista numbered something more than 16,000. Rives, *U. S. and Mexico*, II, 362-363.

11 Ex. Doc. 1, Sen., 30th Cong., 1st sess., p. 98; French, *Two Wars*, p. 77.

12 Ramsey (ed.), *The Other Side*, pp. 122-123; Ex. Doc. 1, Sen., 30th Cong., 1st sess., pp. 146, 165.

13 French, *Two Wars*, p. 78; Ex. Doc. 1, Sen., 30th Cong., 1st sess., pp. 133, 205-209. The latter pages give the reports of Lieutenant Colonel W. B. Warren of the First Illinois, left in command at Saltillo, and of Captain L. B. Webster and Lieutenant W. B. Shover, of the artillery. One of the officers who held the cathedral behind barricaded streets was Captain B. M. Prentiss of the Illinois regiment, the same who as General Prentiss, U. S. V., was to do so much to save the day at Shiloh by his stubborn defense of the "Hornet's Nest."

14 Ex. Doc. 1, Sen., 30th Cong., 1st sess., pp. 134, 147, 160, 167, 172, 176-179, 182, 186-187, 190; Ramsey (ed.), *The Other Side*, pp. 124-125.

15 Ex. Doc. 1, Sen., 30th Cong., 1st sess., pp. 134, 147; Smith, *Reminiscences*, pp. 50, 51, 66.

16 Ramsey (ed.), *The Other Side*, p. 125; Ex. Doc. 1, Sen., 30th Cong., 1st sess., pp. 134-135, 148, 162-163, 167-168, 172-173, 179-180, 182, 187, 190-193, 197-199.

17 Ex. Doc. 1, Sen., 30th Cong., 1st sess., pp. 135, 182-184, 187-188, 193-194, 201-202, 204; Smith, *Reminiscences*, pp. 51, 52, 74, 75.

18 Ramsey (ed.), *The Other Side*, pp. 126-127; Ex. Doc. 1, Sen., 30th Cong., 1st sess., pp. 136-137, 148-149, 160-161, 170-171, 174-175, 177, 188, 194, 202, 205; Smith, *Reminiscences*, p. 53.

19 Same, pp. 137, 150, 203; Rives, *U. S. and Mexico*, II, 360.

20 Ex. Doc. 1, Sen., 30th Cong., 1st sess., p. 143; Rives, *U. S. and Mexico*, II, 363-365; Ramsey (ed.), *The Other Side*, p. 141.

21 Ex. Doc. 1, Sen., 30th Cong., 1st sess., pp. 210-215.

22 Ex. Doc. 60, H. R., 30th Cong., 1st sess., pp. 1123-1124, 1241-1243; Quaife (ed.), *Polk's Diary*, II, 304, 340, 375, 434-435, 438, 441.

23 Quaife (ed), *Polk's Diary*, II, 382-383, 408-409, 428-429, 433-434, 438, 444, 449, 451-452, 462, 479-480; Nevins (ed.), *Polk*, p. 197; Meade, *Life and Letters*, I, 193.

CHAPTER 16

D-Day, 1847

O
N February 21, 1847—the day on which Santa Anna's army was marching to meet Taylor at Buena Vista—General Scott at long last reached Lobos Island, the appointed rendezvous for his troops and transports.

Waiting for him at Lobos, either ashore on the tiny island or in ships anchored in its lee, Scott found part of a Mississippi regiment, which was supposed to have gone to the Brazos, and part of a Louisiana regiment, the remainder of which had been wrecked on the shore south of Tampico, where, however, it had escaped both the perils of the sea and attempted capture by the Mexican garrison of Tuxpan. Awaiting the general, also, were regiments from New York and South Carolina, and two from Pennsylvania—the first volunteers to arrive at the seat of war from states east of the Appalachians.

Worth with his regulars was delayed at the Brazos for lack of transports; Twiggs's regulars and Patterson's volunteers from Tampico were yet to come; the horse artillery batteries, the regular dragoons and the Tennessee regiment of cavalry intended for the expedition had not sailed; two thirds of the ordnance stores called for had not arrived, and only half of the specially designed surfboats were at hand. And, to complete the catalogue of the general's vexations, smallpox had broken out among the soldiers of the Second Pennsylvania regiment. To prevent the spread of the scourge, the men who had been exposed were unloaded to a quarantine camp on the beach, with actual cases isolated on the infected ship. The steps taken were successful but, for a season, the situation threatened further delay. Taking all these things into account, the harried general was to write, a week after arriving at the Lobos rendezvous, that "perhaps no expedition was ever so unaccountably delayed—by no want of foresight, arrangement or energy on my part, as I dare affirm. . . ."[1]

258

But during the time the general was at Lobos, ships arrived daily from Atlantic and Gulf ports, bringing supplies and equipment; transports from the Brazos and Tampico were "coming down before the gale like race horses," until to one young Pennsylvania private who had left his job of canal boating to go to the war, the Lobos anchorage "looked like a wilderness of spars and rigging."[2]

On the morning of March 2 the designated flag gave the signal for which the whole fleet was impatiently waiting—"All vessels; proceed to Anton Lizardo!" The steamer *Massachusetts,* with the general's blue, red-centered flag flying at the main-topmasthead, and with the stately figure of the general himself on the deck, threaded its way through the fleet, cheered by the vessels as it passed. The other steamers, "on board which are the Generals and their staffs, paddled off to the southeast and were soon out of sight," while the sailing ships set about the business of making headway against a light wind, dead ahead. By afternoon, the wind rose, the sails were spread, and the whole fleet—eighty or more sail—stood away to the southward, a "glorious spectacle, one which few men ever see, such as I never expect to look upon again," wrote Captain Ephraim Kirby Smith, so soon to lose his life at Molino del Rey. On the night of the third, the southerly breeze shifted to the north and rose to a gale, before which the sailing vessels scudded away down the 180 miles to Vera Cruz.

Commodore Conner had stationed naval vessels at the Isla Verde, five miles seaward from the city, to receive and assist the arriving ships in finding their way into the naval anchorage at Anton Lizardo, a dozen miles farther down. About noon of March 5 the naval watchers saw the army fleet "coming down before the wind . . . more vessels than we could count . . . ship after ship, crowded with enthusiastic soldiers." By the next afternoon all were in and anchored between Salmedina Island and the mainland at Point Anton Lizardo.[3]

On that day Commodore Conner took Scott and all his generals, with their staffs, in the little steamer *Petrita*—one of those captured by Perry on the Tabasco expedition—to reconnoiter the Vera Cruz area from the sea. As the steamer turned the point of the long reef on which the castle of San Juan de Ulúa stands, the castle opened fire and promptly bracketed the target with shell, but failed to score a hit. "We were in a ridiculous position," wrote Scott's Inspector General, Ethan Allen Hitchcock—"in danger with no adequate object, without means of defense, with all our officers of rank on board." And, though no one could then have anticipated it, not only the "rank" of

Scott's army but, among their staffs, no small part of the future "rank" of the armies of the Union and of the Confederacy.[4]

On this same day of March 6, through a British man-of-war which was in touch with the city, the Americans were furnished with copies of the Vera Cruz newspaper, *El Locomotor*—so-called, perhaps, because the Mexican Republic's first railroad was then being started from Vera Cruz, although it had not yet acquired a locomotive engine and was using four-footed horsepower. *El Locomotor* contained two items of news which—if true—had most direct bearing on the enterprise in hand.

The item of most immediate interest was an announcement from General Santa Anna of a great victory over Taylor in the north. He had met Taylor, he reported to his government, strongly posted at a pass in front of Saltillo; had attacked him on the twenty-second and twenty-third of February; had lost 1,000 killed and wounded in the attack but had inflicted upon Taylor a loss twice as great; had held the field after two days of fighting; and was retiring only because of the state of his supplies and the necessity of giving proper attention to his wounded.

The response of the Americans off Vera Cruz to such claims was the same as that of Doniphan and his men at Chihuahua—disbelief amounting to conviction that Taylor had won a victory. They doubtless were glad to learn, also, that Santa Anna would not be on the beach at Vera Cruz to oppose their landing. It does not appear, however, that General Scott received the information noted by other Americans on this date or, if he did, it did not displace in his mind the fixed conviction that Santa Anna, knowing of the coming attack against Vera Cruz, would certainly march to resist this most imminent threat to the vitals of his nation. "Ignorant of President Santa Anna's desperate march over the desert upon Major-General Taylor," he wrote later, "we did not doubt meeting at our landing the most formidable struggle of the war. No precaution therefore was neglected."[5]

There was in the same issue of *El Locomotor* another item of news which, if it were properly evaluated, might have given encouragement to the seemingly desperate venture of putting ashore an army on an open beach. Another revolution, it was announced, had broken out in Mexico, precipitated by refusal of troops of the National Guard to leave the capital and march to the defense of Vera Cruz.

This order by the government of Vice-President Farías, and the refusal of the Independencia battalion to march, was the immediately inciting cause of the latest pronunciamento, but back of it there was a long and involved story of political intrigue. The underlying cause was the struggle over the attempt to enforce the newly enacted law levying on the estates of the Church for the financial resources necessary to prosecute the war. Acting President Farías, anticlerical leader and apparently almost as anxious to carry out measures against the clericals as he was to defeat the invaders, was determined to enforce the statute. Against his determination the opposition secured the adherence and support of the National Guard in the capital—the battalions Independencia, Bravo, Hidalgo and Victoria, which, as a group, in contradistinction from and opposition to the "Puros" of Farías, acquired the nickname of "Polkos" from the "musical strain which converted the polka into a hymn of the Guard."

Not feeling strong enough to disarm the Polko battalions, Farías—who like all Mexico was by this time informed of the impending descent upon Vera Cruz—ordered the march to the threatened city. The Guards refused to leave, and took up defensive positions in the capital. Efforts were made by the government to disarm them. Revolt followed, on February 27—while Scott was at Lobos and Santa Anna was marching back from La Encarnación—with pronunciamentos and occupation of strong points in the city by both sides, and a deal of firing back and forth. The firing was "wholly ineffectual, for both parties kept their respective positions, very few were killed or wounded, and more injuries were received by the people, who from necessity or curiosity passed through the streets." After a few days of this desultory and ineffective musketry "an armistice of two hours a day was agreed upon by both parties, during which the soldiers not only went out to provide necessaries, but a kind of promenade was formed along the lines. . . . After a lapse of fifteen days, neither of the opposing bands had any prospect of conquering or being conquered and the peaceful inhabitants of the city were in a state of desperation."[6]

These facts—or so much of them as was reported in the Vera Cruz newspaper—were either unknown to, or little noted by, the army and navy commanders whose immediate task it was to put the expedition ashore. As to that, General Scott and Commodore Conner quickly agreed on the time, the place and the method. With the yellow-fever season just ahead, and renewal of the northers an ever-present possibility, it was clear that the landing should be made at the first possible moment. The place chosen was the beach opposite Sacrificios Island, some two and one half miles from the city, and out of range of its guns and those of the castle.

The method of making the landing was the product of joint thinking and planning by army and navy. Fortunately, a precise technical narrative of what was done, and how, was prepared by a passed midshipman blessed with the spirit of professional inquiry. This document, prepared by a young man who was to become Rear Admiral William G. Temple, United States Navy, may be regarded as the unofficial forerunner of the studies by the historical staffs attached to military headquarters and units in the Second World War. It reposed in the archives for more than forty years until, just before the war with Spain, it was brought out and published, to stand as the best record of the first major joint amphibious operation of the navy and army of the United States.[7]

The foundation of the operation was surfboats, built to the specifications of the Quartermaster Department, and brought out to Mexico in "nests" of three. The boats had both ends pointed alike, so as to move handily in both directions, and were nearly flat-bottomed. The bottom boat of each nest was forty feet long, twelve feet wide, and four feet deep, and each of the others was, successively, nearly two feet shorter and one foot narrower, so that it would fit inside the boat below.[8] Forty-seven such nests, or 141 boats, were contracted for, with a premium to be paid for speed, and a corresponding penalty for delay, in their completion. Despite all efforts at speed, however, only sixty-five boats reached the Mexican coast in time to be of use in landing troops.

As the ships bearing them arrived, the boats were unloaded, inspected, fully prepared for service and hauled up on the beach on the landward side of Salmedina Island, facing Anton Lizardo. There they were arranged by divisions, and numbered.

This, however, was but the beginning. The original plan had been to disembark the soldiers from transports to surfboats at the place where the landing was to be made. Because of the inevitable confusion which would have resulted from an attempt to crowd so many transports into this constricted area, Commodore Conner suggested a better plan—to transfer the soldiers from transports to naval vessels for the movement from Anton Lizardo to Sacrificios, and there to make the transfer into the surfboats. The plan was adopted, with Captain French Forrest of the *Raritan* assigned to superintend the details of its execution.

The landing, planned for March 8, was deferred for a day because of a threatened norther. The storm failed to materialize, and at sunrise on March 9, 1847—the first "D-day" for American armed services on a foreign shore—the movement was launched.

Under the direction of officers sent ashore on the island the day before, naval boats' crews promptly launched the surfboats from their numbered places on the beach at Salmedina, and used them to transfer the troops from the anchored transports to the ships which were to take them to Sacrificios, each man carrying greatcoat, haversack with bread and meat (cooked) for two days, and canteen of water, in addition to his arms and ammunition. Available for the movement to Sacrificios there were ten sailing vessels and four steamships of the navy, and five army steamers. The frigates *Raritan* and *Potomac,* largest of the naval vessels, took aboard some 2,500 men each; the sloops *Albany* and *St. Mary's,* about 900 each; the smaller vessels in proportion. Accompanying each ship carrying troops was a steamer, towing its assigned surfboats. The transfer was accomplished in excellent order, and by eleven o'clock the fleet, with its long strings of surfboats in tow, was on its way to Sacrificios.

By midafternoon Commander Josiah Tattnall, with his "Mosquito fleet" of small steamers, stood into the channel behind the island of Sacrificios and anchored in line parallel to the shore, at good grape-shot range, to cover the landing. The ships carrying the troops dropped anchor behind the covering line of Tattnall's flotilla, and the surfboats, in assigned order, came alongside to take off the men of the first assault wave. Each surfboat could carry, besides its naval complement of eight, from forty to fifty soldiers—a half company. As each boat was loaded, it fell into position in the shelter of its mother ship, formed according to regiments and companies, in the prescribed order of battle.

While all this ordered bustle of preparation went on, "the day continued as clear as it had begun, and the sea-breeze, as it died gradually away, left behind it a glazed and unruffled sea." The magnificent snow-capped mountain of Orizaba—the "Peak of the Star"—came out of the haze, with almost startling sharpness. "The walls of the town and castle, the domes of the churches, and the rigging and mast-heads of the foreign men-of-war, anchored at Sacrificios, all filled with curious and eager spectators," noted Lieutenant Raphael Semmes of the navy—the same who, in another war, was to fight the *Kearsarge* until his *Alabama* sank under him, while like crowds of "curious and eager spectators" watched from the hills about Cherbourg.[9]

At last, with everything in readiness, just as the afternoon sun was beginning to sink behind the great eighteen-thousand-foot mass of Orizaba, the signal gun was fired from Scott's headquarters ship. The surfboats cast off from their ships and from one another, moved forward into position, squared away in "line abreast," and, with every oarsman straining, dashed for the beach, struck the line of breakers and went in on the rollers. The soldiers jumped overboard, holding their muskets high, to splash their way ashore onto the sand beach, form in line of skirmishers, and charge to the crest of the first line of sand dunes.

And all the while, not a shot had been fired!

The first line ashore—Worth's regulars—consisted of the Second and Third Artillery, serving as infantry; the Fourth, Fifth, Sixth and Eighth regiments of infantry; a company of Louisiana volunteers and another from Kentucky; the army's one and only company of combat engineers, newly formed and glorying in the name of Sappers, Miners and Pontoniers; and "a handsome detachment" of 180 marines, under Captain Alvin Edson.

With this line safely ashore, and pushing out to the crest of the dunes to protect further landings, the boat crews pulled back to the vessels off shore, to take aboard the second assault wave—the two regiments each of Pennsylvania and Tennessee volunteers, which made up Pillow's brigade, and the South Carolina regiment, these being all of Patterson's volunteers who had yet reached the rendezvous, although others were to arrive and land in time to take part in the siege.

Before ten o'clock at night the third landing had been made— Twiggs's "brigade" of regulars, composed of Persifor Smith's mounted riflemen, dismounted, the First and Fourth regiments of artillery serving as infantry, and the First, Second, Third and Seventh regiments of infantry.

All in all, more than 10,000 men were put ashore over the beach that evening, without confusion, accident, or loss—thanks to careful planning and to close co-operation between navy and army, and thanks, too, to the failure of the Mexican commander at Vera Cruz to take advantage of the best opportunity he would ever have to resist the invaders.

The landing on the beach was the most difficult step, but it was only a beginning. In front of Scott was a city, ringed by nine forts, with curtain walls between, and covered on the seaward side by the great pile of San Juan de Ulúa, within easy cannon range across the harbor. The total garrison of city and castle numbered more than 4,000; the total armament included more than 200 guns; the supply of ammunition was ample; the determination of garrison and popu- lace, as was to be shown by the fortitude with which they soon with- stood bombardment, was strong. But—possibly because of the news of revolts at the capital—the spirit of energetic and enterprising de- fense was lacking.

No resistance of consequence was offered while Scott, beginning on March 10, enlarged his beachhead, started putting ashore his ordnance and supplies, and began to draw his lines about the city. On the next night, there came the first of a series of northers which effectively cut off the men on shore from all communication with the ships for the greater part of the following week. During this time the extension of the lines went ahead—Worth's regulars holding the right, begin- ning at the place of landing; Patterson's volunteers—with reinforce- ments which had arrived and landed on March 10—in the center; and Twiggs's regulars extending the line of investment on around to the sea again at Vergara, two and one half miles up the beach from Vera Cruz, which was reached and occupied by midday of the twelfth.[10]

During this period of sealing off Vera Cruz by land as well as by sea there was sporadic fire from the castle and the forts about the city and an occasional brush with parties outside the walls. The most serious obstacles, though, were northers. These furious storms, blow- ing almost without interruption for days on end, not only prevented the landing of the necessary guns and supplies, but also drove more than a score of ships ashore and scattered surfboats and small craft for miles down the beach. In the lulls between storms, however, the landing work went on with a will until the beach behind Sacrificios, covered with piles of stores and crowded with men, seemed to one soldier from an inland river town "like the levee of a vast commercial city."

The northers not only imposed delays and shortages upon the growing number of men ashore, particularly because they made it impossible to land draft animals and pack mules to move what supplies were on the beach, but they also filled the air with stinging, blinding sand, picked up and driven by the wind. Sand, indeed, was one of the trials of the siege, to say nothing of a peculiarly voracious breed of sand fleas. "How they live in that dry sand no one knows," wrote young Lieutenant Dabney H. Maury, future major general, C.S.A. "They don't live very high, though, for they are ever ready for a change of diet." Line soldiers, Maury wrote, had to endure the fleas as best they could, but two young officers of engineers "slept in canvas bags drawn tight around their necks, having previously greased themselves all over with salt pork." The officers who took such drastic steps to defeat the fleas were Lieutenant Gustavus W. Smith, in command of the company of combat engineers, and Lieutenant George B. McClellan, his second-in-command, who on a day in 1862 would find themselves facing each other across the battle lines about Richmond, one commanding the defenders, the other, the attacking army.[11]

On March 15, while the northers still blew, the whole army and the squadron were heartened by the announcement in general orders that "authentic information," even though not yet official, had been received of "a great and glorious victory" by General Taylor at Buena Vista. To at least one volunteer officer it seemed, however, that the rejoicing of the regulars was at least tinged with disappointment that Buena Vista had been mainly a volunteer fight. "The whole of the officers of the regular army," wrote Colonel William B. Campbell of the First Tennessee, "seem to regret that the battle of Buena Vista was fought by volunteers . . . and seem not to rejoice in the success of our arms in the hands of any but regulars." To which he added, in a letter to his uncle the governor of Virginia, "while the command and control of the army and all its departments is in the hands of Regular officers, justice will never be done to the volunteers."[12]

While the soldiers battled with sand and wind, insects and thorny chapparal, hunger and thirst, such camp diseases as diarrhea, and all the other discomforts of camping out in the sand dunes, General Scott had to determine how Vera Cruz was to be reduced. The approach of the yellow-fever season ruled out the possibility of reduction by starvation. Taking the place by assault was urged on Scott by "several Generals and Colonels—among them General Patterson," who "solicited the privilege of leading storming parties." Among the men who had been with Worth at Monterey, Lieutenant Cadmus

Wilcox noted, there was impatience that Vera Cruz was not to be stormed as Monterey had been. But Scott, believing that the place could be reduced by regular siege operations with sufficient promptness, and with very moderate loss, decided on taking the city and castle by what he described as "headwork, the slow, scientific process."[13]

On March 18, therefore, as soon as the storms abated enough to permit the landing of heavy ordnance, regular siege works were undertaken. The siege of Vera Cruz, the men soon found, was a supply job, in which Commodore Conner and the naval squadron were "indefatigable" in their assistance. It was an engineer's job, too, requiring skillful location of batteries and their approaches, and prodigious labor in their construction in shifting, drifting sand. And, finally, when the navy had put the materials ashore, and the engineers had done their work, it was a gunner's job, in which the heavy metal sent ashore by the ships and manned by navy crews in daily rotation supplied the power and weight which were lacking in the army's light siege train.

Landing went on without interruption except for the weather. The defending fortifications sought, by a spirited but ineffectual fire, to interfere with the building of the batteries which the engineers laid out, and the emplacement in them of the army and navy guns. But despite such efforts, some of the American batteries were ready to open fire on March 22, and that afternoon General Scott summoned the city to surrender—a summons which was promptly and positively declined.

The American land batteries opened fire and the smaller vessels of the fleet under Tattnall, by arrangement previously made, stood close inshore and pounded the southerly end of the city fortifications—so close, indeed, as to bring the vessels within effective range of the guns of the castle. Commodore Perry—who had relieved Commodore Conner in command of the squadron only the day before—was compelled to recall the intrepid flotilla "from a position too daringly assumed."[14]

On the twenty-third another norther arrived and cut off the landing of the shot and shell necessary to keep up the rate of fire from the land batteries. The storm slackened on the morning of the twenty-fourth, however, and landing of ammunition was resumed. That day, also, No. 5, known as the Naval Battery, went into action for the first time. Its firing changed the nature of the bombardment from a rather ineffectual shelling with light metal to a smashing, terribly effective fire, which was to open breaches in the walls on both sides of the Santa Barbara Fort. No. 4—the last battery to be completed—opened up on the morning of the twenty-fifth, and all the batteries were in "awful activity," while the defenders returned a "spirited and obstinate" fire from guns which were both well-served and far heavier in caliber and greater in number than the attacking batteries.[15]

On the twenty-fourth, the British, French, Spanish and Prussian consuls in Vera Cruz, moved by "the frightful results of the bombardment," collectively addressed to Scott an appeal for a suspension of hostilities and a truce for the removal of the foreign families and the Mexican women and children from the city.

The general, who received the note late that night, replied on the twenty-fifth, reminding the consuls that on the day after the landing he had offered them opportunity and safeguards to escape the siege, that this opportunity had been kept open until the twenty-third, and that before opening fire he had appealed to the governor to spare the women and children by surrendering the city. Now, he concluded, the only proposition for truce which he could consider must come from the Mexican commander himself as a preliminary to surrender. General Juan Morales, the commander of both city and castle, falling sick at the moment, or perhaps feigning sickness, the consuls presented this reply to his successor in command, General José Juan de Landero. The new commander, on the next day, replied directly to Scott that he would not "hesitate . . . to enter into an honorable accommodation . . ." for which purpose he suggested the naming of commissioners to meet and treat.

Commissioners were accordingly appointed, and firing was suspended. For the Mexican commander the negotiators were Colonels Villanueva and Herrera, and the distinguished lieutenant colonel of engineers, Manuel Robles; for the American commander, Generals Worth and Pillow and Colonel Totten, to whom was added subsequently—after the storm then raging had subsided enough to allow communication with the fleet—Captain John H. Aulick of the frigate *Potomac,* representing Commodore Perry. The commissioners met outside the walls, at the Punta de Hornos, where after some preliminary disagreement and reporting back and forth, they arrived at an acceptable capitulation on the night of Saturday, March 27. The terms were approved by both commanders on the twenty-eighth—as it happened, one year to the day after Taylor's command reached the north bank of the Rio Grande at Matamoros.

Under the terms agreed on, the garrison was to march out with the honors of war, and lay down its arms, after which they were to be released on parole given by the officers on behalf of themselves and their men not to serve again until duly exchanged. To these strictly military terms were added two others—protection to persons and private property in the city, including fair compensation for the use of buildings occupied by the American army, and a guarantee of "absolute freedom of religious worship and ceremonies."[16]

On March 29, at ten o'clock in the morning, the formal surrender took place. The Mexican flags flying above the forts of Santiago and Concepcion and the castle of San Juan came fluttering down, as their batteries fired a national salute. As the Mexican troops cleared the city, the American flags rose on the same staffs, and batteries, afloat and ashore, roared out a salute. Out from the Merced gate marched the garrison, into a field where groups representative of the squadron and of the several army units, and also spectators from the foreign shipping lying off the harbor, were gathered to watch General Worth receive the surrender. The Mexican soldiers marched to the designated point, stacked their muskets, hung over them their bayonet scabbards and cartridge boxes, and trudged away homeward, many of them accompanied by women, "loaded like a mule" with all manner of household articles and with amazed and wondering children by their sides. From the American host there was not, during all the long process of disbanding an army, a single cheer. The Mexican soldiers in their hour of surrender received, as one of their writers proudly noted, "the honor due to their valor and misfortunes—the respect of the conqueror. Not a look was given them by the enemy's soldiers which could be interpreted into an insult."[17]

General Scott had won his base of operations at a cost of fewer than 100 casualties, of whom nineteen were killed. However, it was said, not only in Mexico but also in the United States and Europe, that the victory had resulted from his "inhumanity" in bombarding the city into submission. Vera Cruz was a fortified city—the most heavily fortified on the American continent—which had refused to surrender and expressed a determination to resist, no matter what the method of attack might be. In the taking of such a place there was bound to be loss and suffering, but it is hard to see what else Scott might have done which would have imposed less loss upon the civilian population. The losses suffered are undoubtedly exaggerated in the inflamed contemporary accounts—some estimates running into the hundreds— but the British naval commander, whose information and opportunity to judge were excellent, wrote that the defending army had about eighty killed, and that civilian deaths numbered about 100.[18]

The news of Scott's occupation of Vera Cruz reached the United States barely more than a week behind the delayed report of Taylor's great victory in the north. In the popular estimation, at least, Vera Cruz was overshadowed and outshone by the drama of Buena Vista. Contributing to this, no doubt, was the subconscious feeling that the capture of Vera Cruz could not have been such a great feat after all, because the American losses were so light—less than one fifth the loss at the storming of Monterey, less than one tenth the loss on the field of Buena Vista.[19]

---

[1] Ex. Doc. 60, H. R., 30th Cong., 1st sess., pp. 896-898, 902-903.

[2] Kirby Smith, *To Mexico*, p. 106; Oswandel, J. Jacob, *Notes of the Mexican War* (Philadelphia, 1885), p. 61.

[3] Croffut (ed.), *Fifty Years*, p. 237; Oswandel, *Notes*, p. 63; Parker, *Recollections of a Naval Officer*, p. 82; Conner, *Home Squadron*, pp. 63-64; Kirby Smith, *To Mexico*, pp. 109-110. Captain Kirby Smith's younger brother Edmund, who was to become a general and commander of the Trans-Mississippi Department in the Confederate service, was in the same fleet.

[4] Croffut (ed.), *Fifty Years*, p. 237; Kirby Smith, *To Mexico*, p. 112; Conner, *Home Squadron*, p. 64. In the numerous accounts of this incident the name of the vessel is given variously as the *Secretary* or the *Champion*, as well as the *Petrita*.

[5] Kirby Smith, *To Mexico*, p. 111; Meade, *Life and Letters*, I, pp. 188-190; Anderson, Robert, *Letters of An Artillery Officer in The Mexican War* (New York, 1911), p. 66-67; Scott, *Memoirs*, II, 414.

[6] Ramsey (ed.), *The Other Side*, pp. 149-166, 248; Rives, *U. S. and Mexico*, II, 314-323.

[7] Commodore Conner's report is in Ex. Doc. 1, H. R., 30th Cong., 2nd sess. pp. 1177-1179. Publication of Admiral Temple's "Memoir of the Landing of the United States Troops at Vera Cruz in 1847" was due to Mr. P. S. P. Conner, son of Commodore Conner, who, with permission of the Navy Department, published it in his *Home Squadron Under Commodore Conner* (Philadelphia, 1896). Mr. Conner was justifiably concerned at the misunderstanding of the relief of the commodore from command by Commodore Perry at the crisis of the siege of Vera Cruz, and at the failure to give recognition to the part played by his father in the planning and execution of the landing. In his work, therefore, he collected much pertinent material, including, fortunately, the memoir of the former midshipman. Details of the landing arrangements, where not otherwise noted, are from his memoir.

[8] Lieutenant Totten of the navy had a hand in the design of the surfboats, and they were constructed under the "supervision of naval officers," according to General Scott's correspondence. Ex. Doc. 60, H. R., 30th Cong., 1st sess., pp. 847, 865.

[9] Semmes, *Service Afloat and Ashore*, pp. 126-127.

[10] Ex. Doc. 1, Sen., 30th Cong., 1st sess., pp. 216-217, 220.

[11] Parker, *Recollections*, pp. 86-87; Furber, *Twelve Months Volunteer*, p. 505;

Maury, Dabney H., *Recollections of a Virginian* (New York, 1894), p. 34; *English Soldier in U. S. Army,* pp. 150-161.

[12] Ex. Doc. 1, Sen., 30th Cong., 1st sess., p. 221. The orders were forwarded to Taylor with a note of hearty congratulations (Ex. Doc. 56, H. R., 30th Cong., 1st sess., p. 359); Sioussat (ed.), *Campbell Letters,* p. 166.

[13] Wilcox, *Mexican War,* p. 262; Scott, *Memoirs,* II, pp. 423-425.

[14] Ex. Doc. 1, H. R., 30th Cong., 2nd sess., pp. 1179-1180; Ex. Doc. 1, Sen., 30th Cong., 1st sess., pp. 224, 240. Commodore Conner had served nearly a year beyond the customary three-year limit in command and was in wretched health. He was responsible, however, for the excellent planning and co-operation of the navy with Scott. Ex. Doc. 1, Sen., 30th Cong., 1st sess., p. 223. The newly arrived soldiers noted on the twenty-first "much ceremony and firing salutes during the day, on account of change of commanders." Furber, *Twelve Months Volunteer,* p. 508.

[15] Ex. Doc. 1, H. R., 30th Cong., 2nd sess., pp. 1180-1185; Ex. Doc. 1, Sen., 30th Cong., 1st sess., p. 226.

[16] Same, pp. 228-238.

[17] Ramsey (ed.), *The Other Side,* pp. 196-197; Ripley, *War with Mexico,* II, 42; Semmes, *Service Afloat and Ashore,* pp. 145-146; Furber, *Twelve Months Volunteer,* pp. 555-560.

[18] Smith, *War with Mexico,* pp. 33, 340-341.

[19] General Scott seems to have felt keenly this public reaction, although he had anticipated, and had told his "little cabinet," what it would be. "I know our countrymen will hardly acknowledge a victory unaccompanied by a long butcher's bill," he said to his advisers, but nevertheless decided to "take the city with the least possible loss of life." Later, when he heard about the popular reaction at home, he owned that his "poor human nature was piqued for a moment" but he came to accept it. "Mortifications are profitable to sufferers," he noted, "and I record mine to teach aspirants to fame to cultivate humility; for blessed is the man who expects little, and can gracefully submit to less." Scott, *Memoirs,* II, 424-425.

Vera Cruz.

CHAPTER 17

Cerro Gordo and the March to the Plateau

IMMEDIATELY upon the occupation of Vera Cruz, energetic steps were taken to establish government in the city, to reassure the inhabitants, to open and regulate the use of the port, to hasten the landing of arriving troops and supplies, and to collect land transportation for the marches ahead.

There were but two days left of the month of March when the city surrendered, and it was feared that by the middle of April the dread *vomito,* or yellow fever, might make its appearance. It was of the utmost urgency, therefore, that whatever was to be done should be done promptly, and that the body of the army should escape from the *tierra caliente* of the coastal country to the *tierra templada* of the highlands.

But with all the haste to get away, it was necessary to leave behind a well-ordered and secure base through which all future supplies and reinforcements might pass. To that end General Order No. 20, the martial-law order first issued at Tampico, was reissued for the governance of Americans, "without disturbing the ordinary functions of the civil magistracy, as between Mexicans and Mexicans." Civilian arms were collected, however, and civilians were restricted to daylight hours for entering and leaving the city. Soldiers, other than the guards, were not allowed in the city except on pass, and then only in daylight and, in most cases, in parties of not more than ten from a company, accompanied by a noncommissioned officer.

Pulperías were closed, except on special license with a 6:00 P.M. closing hour. Prices of foodstuffs and other necessaries were regulated, as vendors reappeared in the markets. Ten thousand rations of bread, meat and beans were distributed among the poor. Wages were paid to laborers engaged in clearing away the debris of the bombardment and cleaning up the city. A scale of duties was prescribed under which the merchant ships in the port were permitted to introduce goods into the city, with the amounts collected "to be applied to the benefit of the sick and wounded of the army, the squadron, and the indigent inhabitants of Vera Cruz."

The Cruzaño shops began to reopen as confidence was re-established, and the army, as usual, was promptly followed into Vera Cruz by enterprising American civilians, authorized and unauthorized. Within three days after entrance into the city five persons had been licensed to keep *fondas* or cafés, and on April 3, less than one week after the occupation, the inevitable newspaper, *The American Eagle,* issued from a Mexican printing office, was on the streets at one "bit," or twelve and one half cents, per copy.[1]

Not even the most single-minded determination, however, nor the most energetic measures, could completely preserve order in a city occupied by an invading army. On April 1 the general issued general orders expressing his "cruel disappointment" at the conduct of "a few worthless soldiers, both regulars and volunteers." By the fifth, however, the military commissions set up for the trial of offenses against the Mexican population had begun to impose fines and imprisonment, and on the tenth an American camp follower tried by military commission and found guilty of rape, was publicly hanged. The execution, the first of its sort, was viewed by a "large concourse of people," according to the account in the Vera Cruz *Eagle,* which felt that it would "no doubt prove a salutary lesson to many." Before leaving Vera Cruz, General Scott could report that the "inhabitants . . . are beginning to be assured of protection, and to be cheerful," and Private Oswandel of the First Pennsylvania regiment could note a "wonderful change."[2]

Along with all his business at Vera Cruz, General Scott was engaged in efforts to secure the draft and pack animals so urgently needed for his march. It had been planned all along to get the larger part of them from the country, and this became more than ever necessary because of the large number of horses and mules shipped from the States which had been lost in the forty or more vessels wrecked or driven ashore by the northers. One likely source of supply of horses was thought to be the Alvarado River Valley, some forty-five miles southeast of Vera Cruz. The navy had its reasons, also, for special attention to the port of Alvarado in view of earlier failures to occupy it, and the fact that the river afforded the best near-by source of fresh water.

Consequently, on the afternoon of the day after Vera Cruz was occupied a joint navy-army expedition set out to take Alvarado—Quitman's brigade of Georgia, Alabama and South Carolina troops, and
Commodore Perry with a good part of the fleet. The concerted plan
of action was that the navy should withhold its attack until the army
was in position to prevent the horses which were sought from being
run off into the interior. On the evening of April 1, however, as Quitman approached the town by land, he was met by a note from Midshipman Temple that the town had surrendered to the steamer
Scourge, Lieutenant Charles G. Hunter commanding.

The *Scourge,* mounting one gun and carrying forty men, had been
sent ahead by the commodore with orders to reconnoiter the mouth of
the river but to do no more. Approaching the bar, Lieutenant Hunter
decided to give the Alvarado fort a round or two. The Mexican commander, knowing that Vera Cruz and its mighty castle had fallen,
construed this attention as a demand for surrender, with which he
promptly complied. Hunter left a midshipman and five men to occupy Alvarado, and took his steamer on upriver to extend his captures
to the inland town of Tlacotalpam—so that when the commodore and
his squadron arrived, they were greeted by the sight of the American
flag flying at the mouth of the river and the sound of Hunter and his
one gun banging away upstream.

Furious at the way the young lieutenant had exceeded his orders
and had flushed the covey before Quitman was in position to round
up the horses, Perry put him in arrest and preferred charges. A court-
martial sustained the charges and sentenced the lieutenant to be reprimanded, the reprimand to be read from the quarter-deck of every
vessel in the squadron—all of which, when word of it got back to the
United States, had the natural effect of making a popular hero of
"Alvarado" Hunter, the lieutenant who played the April-fool joke
on commodore and general by taking the town with one gun and not
a single marine.[3]

The port of Tuxpan, to the north of Vera Cruz, was the next immediate object of Commodore Perry's attention. In preparation, the
squadron rendezvoused at near-by Lobos Island for a day or so of
landing exercises on the beach. This time no overeager lieutenant
sailed in ahead of the squadron, which was just as well because there
was a brisk fire from the forts—armed, to a considerable extent, with
guns salvaged from the United States ship *Truxtun* which had struck
and foundered on the bar the year before. Fifteen hundred sailors and
marines, transferred from the ships to smaller vessels which could pass

the bar, made their way up the river. Resistance faded when strong landing parties went ashore—the boats in the lead being those of Commander Franklin Buchanan, who had just joined the fleet after completing a tour of duty as the first superintendent of the new Naval Academy at Annapolis, and who, in time, was to become first in rank in the Confederate Navy and to command in action both the ironclad *Virginia,* better known under its earlier name of *Merrimac,* and the ram *Tennessee* which fought Farragut's fleet in Mobile Bay. With the disappearance of its defenders, Tuxpan, last port of consequence save one on the Gulf coast of Mexico, yielded to the navy.[4]

While Quitman was on his way back from the trying, and for the time fruitless, march to Alvarado, General Scott received news of the course of events in the Mexican capital since the outbreak of the Polko revolt. News of this uprising against the authority of Acting President Farías had reached Santa Anna at San Luis Potosí, just after he had received there a triumphal welcome upon his return from the "victory" of Buena Vista. Santa Anna had started south on March 14, preceded by glowing accounts of his victory, and followed by some of his best troops with whom, apparently, he intended to go to the support of Farías, and to put down the Polkos. At Querétaro he received another triumphal welcome, and received, also, deputations from the contending parties in the capital city. Other messengers met him as he continued his triumphal progress southward until, by the time he reached Guadalupe Hidalgo, just outside the capital—where a Te Deum was sung for his "victory"—he had come to the conclusion that Farías must go, and that once more the savior of the situation must be none other than Antonio López de Santa Anna.

Holding this conviction, he refused to enter the city until peace was restored between the contending factions, whereupon deputations from Congress waited upon him at his retreat. There, on March 21— the day before Scott began the bombardment of Vera Cruz—he took the oath of office and assumed the authority of President. A week later he was given virtually unlimited power in domestic affairs, including even the power to increase the demands on the Church or, in his discretion, to decree the repeal of the offending laws under which Farías had sought to take over ecclesiastical estates. The latter, Santa Anna promptly did, after receiving assurances of "voluntary" Church contributions said to have amounted to as much as $2,000,000.

But the news from Vera Cruz was such that obviously the President and general must soon go to the new military front in the east, and his departure would leave Vice-President Farías in charge at the seat of government. There being no other way to remove that stubbornly honest man, he was, by a slender majority in Congress, legislated out of office. By an act of April 1 the Vice-Presidency was abolished and the office of substitute or interim President was created. To this new and temporary office, Pedro Maria Anaya was elected. As General Scott reported to Secretary Marcy from Vera Cruz on the fifth, Santa Anna was once more "in full possession of the executive authority. . . . There is no longer an opposing party in arms."[5]

General Scott reported, also, that he thought it "quite probable" that there might be an effective peace movement among the substantial portions of the Mexican population if there were "American commissioners at the headquarters of this army," prepared to treat with Mexican commissioners on "terms just and honorable to both republics." His letter continued:[6]

To several of the prisoners of war of high rank [taken at Vera Cruz] . . . I took care to say that I had not been clothed with diplomatic functions, but thought it probable that I should soon be joined by American commissioners . . . to be in position and readiness to receive overtures from Mexican commissioners, and that, in the meantime, the army would continue to advance, presenting at once the olive branch and the sword.

The general was overoptimistic in his hopes of Mexican readiness to discuss terms of peace, for the Mexican Congress, while granting to the new President sweeping powers in domestic affairs, had pointedly not granted to him the powers which would be essential to making peace.

General Scott was not alone either in his idea of possible Mexican willingness to agree to end the war, or of the desirability of having with the army a commissioner prepared to treat. On April 10, the very day on which news of the occupation of Vera Cruz reached Washington by a "Telegraphic dispatch from the office of the Baltimore *Sun,*" which enterprising paper had received the news by special express from Pensacola, President Polk and his Cabinet came to the same conclusion—that there should be a commissioner at army headquarters in Mexico. The "great difficulty" was in the selection of such a diplomatic representative. General Scott himself might have been considered, in the light of his diplomatic success in the settlement of the dispute over the boundary between the State of Maine and the Province of New Brunswick, but of course he was not. The obvious choice of President and Cabinet was the Secretary of State, James Buchanan. He would have been willing to go had there been any assurance that the Mexicans would receive him, but in view of that uncertainty it was apparent that an official of his distinguished rank should not be sent.

Mr. Buchanan suggested, instead, Nicholas P. Trist, who with the title of chief clerk, was actually the second in rank in the State Department. He was West Point-educated, had studied law under Thomas Jefferson and married that statesman's granddaughter, had served as private secretary to President Jackson, had been United States consul at Havana for eight years, and was presumably "perfectly familiar with the Spanish character and language." The suggestion was accepted by every member of the Cabinet. Mr. Trist was sent for, the mission was outlined to him, and he agreed to undertake it. Secretary Buchanan was requested to draw up, for his guidance, a project for a treaty, with necessary instructions for variations to meet contingencies.

The draft of a treaty was submitted to the full Cabinet at a meeting on the thirteenth, which lasted five hours, except for a brief intermission in which the President and his ministers met "Gen'l Tom Thumb" who had called at the White House. With modifications suggested at this meeting, it was discussed again at a four-hour meeting on the same evening, and was approved. The Secretaries of War and the Navy were requested to prepare suitable orders to the commanders in Mexico.

All these documents were drafted and once more considered at a special Cabinet meeting on April 15. That night the President delivered to Mr. Trist his letter of appointment and "had a full conversation with him." On the morrow Mr. Trist set out on his mission to the headquarters of the army in Mexico. The mission was supposed to be held closely secret. Four days after his departure the whole story was published "with remarkable accuracy & particularity" in the columns of the *New York Herald*—a most inauspicious beginning for a mission which, after personal bickerings which would have been comic but for their seriousness, was finally to result in a treaty of peace made by a commissioner whose powers had been revoked.[7]

While all these preparations for peace were afoot in anticipation of, and accord with, Scott's suggestion, the general was moving heaven, earth and the Quartermaster Department in his efforts to get his troops out of the fever-ridden *tierra caliente* before the *vomito* should strike. The immediate destination was Jalapa, seventy-five miles from Vera Cruz and more than 4,000 feet above the sea. The immediate difficulty—no serious Mexican opposition was anticipated—was the lack of wheeled and animal transport. By reducing baggage to the minimum, however, and by having the men carry forty rounds of ammunition and four days' rations on their persons, it seemed by April 6 that it would be possible to start the movement.[8]

Before starting, there was a reorganization of the army into divisions of two brigades each—Worth's First Division, with its brigades commanded by Colonel John Garland and Colonel N. S. Clarke; and Twiggs's Second Division, with brigades under Brevet Brigadier General Persifor F. Smith and Colonel Bennett Riley.

Twiggs's division led out, marching on April 8. The road to be followed was that of Cortes—the great highway, graded, paved and guttered, which the Spaniards had built and used for three centuries, but which, in 1847, was fallen sadly into disrepair. The way had been vividly described by Madame Calderon de la Barca, the Scottish-born wife of the first Ambassador from the King of Spain to the Republic of Mexico, whose published letters were used by General Scott both as intelligence reports on things Mexican and as the 1847 equivalent of the pamphlets issued during a later war to acquaint American soldiers with the characteristics of the countries and the peoples whom they would meet.

The first few leagues of the way, Madame Calderon had written, were "nothing but sand—sand—as far as the eye could reach," and so Twiggs's men were to find it, as they started out to try to keep up with "Old Davy"—or rather, with his horse, which set the pace as the general rode at the head of a column of foot soldiers. "At length hills of sand" gave way to a "wilderness of trees and flowers"—but by the time Twiggs's men reached that stage of the march the combination of bad footing, blazing heat, the camp diarrhea from which many of the command were suffering, and a rate of march set by a horse, had proved to be too much even for the veterans of the hard marches in Northern Mexico. By noon of the first day's march, the roadside was strewed with equipment and even clothing which men had thrown away to lighten the load, and the scanty shade of the palmetto bushes which were the principal vegetation of this stretch were dotted with prostrated soldiers. At the sunset roll call that evening nearly one third of the division were missing, and seventy-five still had not come up two days later.

The march of the second day was conducted at a more reasonable pace and with more frequent halts. It was on the graded and paved road, "now going to ruin" but still a better road than most of the American soldiers had seen. The march was through "leagues of natural garden," and all of it, on both sides of the road, the personal and private property of General Santa Anna, whose estates extended from near Vera Cruz nearly to Jalapa, virtually without a break. On this day the soldiers passed, and some of them visited, Manga de Clavo, the general's home place in the *tierra caliente*. On the third day out the column passed another of Santa Anna's homes, and reached, and admired, the magnificent stone-arch National Bridge across the Antigua—a bridge which had not unreasonably been described as "worthy of the best days of Rome," in a setting which brought to mind the beauty spots of home. One soldier saw in it reminders of the river glens of his native Scotland; to a Marylander it brought back Harper's Ferry; to a Pennsylvania soldier, the stone bridge over Conestoga Creek near Lancaster.

One more day Twiggs's command marched—and all the while, one day's march behind, came Patterson's volunteer division, less the brigade of Quitman. At noon of April 11, Twiggs reached another and lesser stone-arch bridge across the Rio del Plan, at the village of Plan del Rio, where, in times of peace, the passengers in the diligences bound for Mexico stopped the night before beginning the serious ascent into the highlands.[9]

Meanwhile, back in Vera Cruz, General Scott had dispatched another expedition—all army this time—into the valley of the Alvarado, seeking to increase the horse supply so that Worth's division and the remainder of Patterson's might be put on the road to Jalapa. On the ninth—the day Patterson set out to follow Twiggs—the general in chief received information that Santa Anna was at Jalapa with a force of 6,000 men.[10]

Though heavily discounted both by him and by the commanders of the marching column, the information which had reached Scott was uncommonly accurate. Santa Anna was at Jalapa, and did have about 6,000 men, with more coming. He had left the capital on April 2— Good Friday—after issuing a resounding proclamation in which he announced his determination "to die fighting" rather than to see "the American hosts proudly tread the capital." With this and other fervid exhortations to do or die in defiance of the invader, he had managed to infuse into army and people something of his own energy and activity, and had actually been able to assemble another fighting force.

The backbone of the force with which Santa Anna purposed to resist the invader as he sought to rise from the lowlands up the slopes of the tremendous mountain wall which faced him at Vera Cruz, was the brigades of Generals Ciriaco Vasquez and Pedro Ampudia. These troops had made the march from San Luis Potosí to La Angostura, had fought bravely at Buena Vista, had suffered on the retreat to San Luis, and had marched for Mexico, following their chieftain. At his order they had turned off before reaching the capital, and by way of Zumpango, San Juan Teotihuacan, Otumba, Huamantla and Perote, had marched to Jalapa—altogether a march of more than a thousand miles. "Mexican troops," Major I. I. Stevens observed, "are indeed remarkable for their rapid marches, and their patient endurance of hunger and fatigue," and these were truly veteran troops.

The new President of Mexico had reached Jalapa on April 5. Engineer officers had reconnoitered passes and positions of defense both above and below that city. The general decided that the advance of the Americans should be checked so far down the slopes of the Cordillera that they would be compelled to remain at levels where they would be in reach of the *vomito*. Climate being there a matter of altitude, such a position was to be found only a little more than twenty miles to the east but nearly half a mile lower in altitude, at the pass of Cerro Gordo. This, then, was the position chosen for defense, where, for a week before the American attack, the Mexicans had been furiously fortifying.[11]

The first contact between the advancing Americans and the defenders of the Mexican highlands was at the village of Plan del Rio on the afternoon of Sunday, April 11, when a party of lancers retired before the advance of Twiggs's division. On the next day a strong reconnaissance force pushed on up the national road into the rugged country where its serious climb to the heights begins, with Captain Joseph E. Johnston in advance. There Captain Johnston—he had just been appointed lieutenant colonel of the new regiment of Voltiguers then being formed—was seriously wounded. Wounds in action were misfortunes which would pursue him through his whole military career, even after he had become a general of the Confederate States Army.

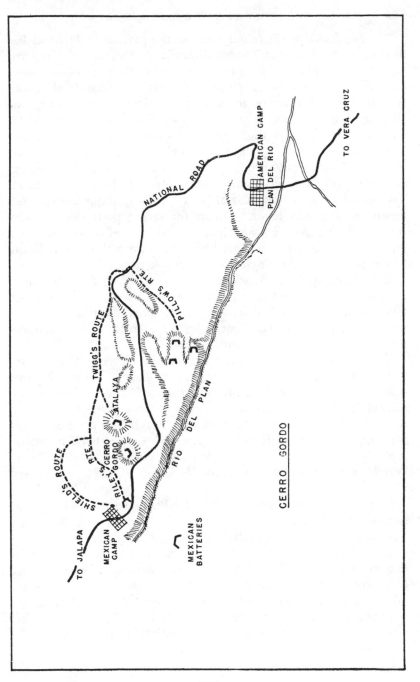

CERRO GORDO

TO VERA CRUZ

AMERICAN CAMP

PLAN DEL RIO

NATIONAL ROAD

PILLOW'S RTE.

TWIGG'S ROUTE

SHIELD'S ROUTE

RILEY'S RTE.

CERRO GORDO

ATALAYA

RIO DEL PLAN

TO JALAPA

MEXICAN CAMP

MEXICAN
BATTERIES

The Mexicans, it was found, were in the pass above Plan del Rio in considerable force but Twiggs determined to attack them in fortified position, without waiting for the arrival of the rest of the army—or of commanders who ranked him. Orders were accordingly issued for a four-o'clock attack on the morning of the thirteenth. The same evening, however, the volunteer brigades of Pillow and Shields marched into Plan del Rio. Their commanders expressed a desire to participate in the fight but did not believe that their men, having marched all day, could make an attack at four o'clock in the morning. A day's postponement seemed reasonable to Brigadier General Twiggs, who was in command of both divisions, Major General Patterson being on sick report. Orders for such a postponement were received during the night—with considerable relief on the part of a good many soldiers who had not looked forward with any enthusiasm to the prospect of the single-division attack planned.[12]

Before the postponed attack could be launched on the morning of the fourteenth, Major General Patterson had risen from his sickbed, taken command of both divisions, and ordered a further postponement to await the arrival of General Scott who, with Worth's division, was coming from Vera Cruz with all haste.

Word had come to General Scott, on the eleventh, that the divisions which he had started on the climb to Jalapa were running into obstacles, in the shape of a Mexican force of 4,000. This he considered "rather an exaggerated account" of the enemy's force but, as he wrote Secretary Marcy, "by working all night" he planned to "go forward, personally, early in the morning." On the twelfth, accordingly, he set out, and at noon of April 14 was at Plan del Rio, with Worth's division coming on behind.[13]

Crossing the bridge over the Rio del Plan, the national highway turns sharp left, or westward, to run roughly parallel with the stream. The little river, flowing east, has cut its way through the rocky escarpment of the lowest bench of the Cordillera in a steep, deep, narrow canyon, or barranca. The road, winding to surmount the same bench of the mountain, turns away from the river below the mouth of the canyon to run first northwest, then southwest, and to return to the river at a point some two miles beyond, and at a height of 500 feet above the bed of the stream. In the elliptical space between the course of the stream and the northward swing of the road there is a ridge, running about a mile to the east and there jutting out into the valley below in three promontories, or points, with ravines between. On each of these jutting points the Mexicans had erected batteries, constituting the strong right of their position.

Just north of the point where the road returned to the rim of the canyon above the river rose a great conical hill, sometimes called El Telegrafo because it was surmounted with the remains of one of the old line of visual telegraph towers once used to communicate between Vera Cruz and Mexico, but more commonly known as Cerro Gordo—which is to say, "Big Hill." Half a mile to the northeast of Cerro Gordo was another hill, Atalaya, nearly as high and as steep. The highway, up which men coming from the coastal country must toil, lay between these two hills and the fortified ridge which was the Mexican right. A battery was placed at the head of this stretch of highway, commanding it for the distance of more than half a mile. Another battery was placed at the main Mexican camp, at the ranch Cerro Gordo, half a mile to the west of this point. And dominating the whole position were the guns atop the 700-foot cone of Cerro Gordo itself.

One drawback to the Mexican position was the lack of water, which could be had only from the stream far down in the depths of the canyon—but then the canyon covered the entire south side of the position, and the question of water supply was solved by bringing it all the way from Santa Anna's upland home of Encero, ten miles above, in a ditch dug by the army. It was objected, also, that there was no definite protection of the north side of the position but to Santa Anna it seemed that there was sufficient protection in ridges and ravines so rugged, and thickets so impenetrable, that not even a rabbit would be able to make his way up on that side. The position seemed so formidable, indeed, that when the Americans made no move to attack by the sixteenth, "it was even imagined," says a Mexican account, "that intimidated by the position of our army, they would not make an attack, but would retire. . . ."[14]

During the days of seeming inaction, however, the Americans were anything but idle. Young engineer officers—among them Lieutenants Beauregard and Zealous B. Tower—had reconnoitered the Mexican front. These reconnaissances were continued and extended far out to the right, in the region through which rabbits were not supposed to be able to pass, by a forty-year-old captain of engineers, Robert E. Lee—the only junior officer of Taylor's army for whose services Scott had asked by name. On the fifteenth, Captain Lee made his way, with all precaution, clear beyond the Mexican left flank. There he all but fell into the hands of the Mexican soldiery, and escaped detection and capture only by lying for hours hidden behind a fallen log, motionless, barely breathing, not daring so much as to scratch where the teeming insects crawled and bit. It was not until after dark that he could leave his log—on which Mexican soldiers had sat and conversed even while he lay hidden—and make his way back through the thickets and ravines by which he had come. On the sixteenth, with the help of a party of pioneers under Lieutenant John G. Foster—he would, in time, as the Union commander in eastern North Carolina, threaten the vital rail line supplying Lee's army about Richmond—Captain Lee retraced his steps, cutting out a path, still "without alarming the enemy."[15]

On the seventeenth, Scott began to move his troops into position for the operation which the reconnaissance had indicated. Twiggs's division, guided by Lee, advanced by the path which the pioneer party had cut the day before "over chasms so steep," as Lieutenant U. S. Grant would recall, "that men could barely climb them. Animals could not. . . . Artillery was let down the steep slopes by hand, the men engaged attaching a strong rope to the rear axle and letting the gun down, a piece at a time, while the men at the ropes kept their ground on top, paying out gradually, while a few at the front directed the course of the piece. In like manner the guns were drawn by hand up the opposite slopes."[16]

Toward noon of the seventeenth, as Twiggs's men were making their toilsome way along the path, their movement was discovered from the hill Atalaya. An infantry company under Lieutenant Frank Gardner—the same who was to defend so stubbornly the Confederate fortress of Port Hudson on the Mississippi—was dispatched to seize the top of the hill. There was a sharp struggle for the crest, with both sides feeding in forces. Finally the United States troops under Colonel Harney, acting brigade commander, swept over and around the hill and, carried forward by their "zeal and impetuosity," went beyond it and even started up the slopes of Cerro Gordo itself. There being no sufficient force available to bring such an attack home, the problem came to be how to break off the engagement and get the exposed men—who were suffering losses beyond anything they could inflict—back to the comparative safety of a saucerlike depression on top of Atalaya. Any thought of counterattack by the Mexicans was quickly broken up, however, by the fire of the rifles and of light artillery on the hill, under Lieutenant Jesse L. Reno—who, fifteen years later, was to meet death while leading his men against the heights of South Mountain in Maryland, held by men in gray.[17]

To reinforce Twiggs, Scott dispatched the volunteer brigade commanded by James Shields, but by the time it could reach the scene of action the day was spent and the action broken off—a result which misled the Mexican commander into thinking that there had been an American repulse and that the victory was his. That night, however, Twiggs's men held their positions for the battle of the following day, while Shields's men—two regiments from Illinois and one from New York—labored mightily, under the direction of Captain Lee, in helping to bring forward three of the heavy 24-pounders of Captain Steptoe's battery for emplacement on the crest of Atalaya.[18]

During the night, also, General Scott issued his orders for the attack of the eighteenth. Twiggs's division, reinforced by Shields, was "to move forward before daylight, and take up position across the national road in the enemy's rear, so as to cut off a retreat towards Jalapa." Pillow's brigade was to get into position to attack the Mexican right—the three batteries on the eastern end of the ridge between road and river—and, as soon as they heard Twiggs's guns to their right, were to "pierce the enemy's line of batteries" and, "once in rear of that line," to turn to the right or left, or both, and attack them in reverse.

Worth, whose division had come up in the early morning of the seventeenth, was to follow in the track of Twiggs's advance, and all troops were to be vigorous in pursuit.[19]

On Sunday morning, the eighteenth, Twiggs sent the brigades of Riley and Shields, under the guidance of Captain Lee, well out to the right, or westward, to strike the Jalapa Road at, or above, the Mexican camp. Harney, from his position on the crest of Atalaya, was to move directly across the hollow between that hill and Cerro Gordo against the Mexican position on its crest. As Riley and Shields made their difficult way to the positions directed, the guns on the two hilltops opened an artillery duel. Shields continued on his appointed way to strike the Mexican camp, but Riley was diverted to his left, so as to cross the western flank of Cerro Gordo. There his little column divided—part moving up the hill to take the Mexican position on the summit in reverse, part continuing on its way against the battery at the Mexican camp in the plain below.

At about seven in the morning—before Shields or Riley had reached the road beyond Cerro Gordo—Harney's men charged. Down Atalaya's slopes they dashed, across the intervening hollow, up the slopes of Cerro Gordo, firing at will as they went. Seventy yards short of the crest, being much blown by the climb, the men halted, lay down for a few moments to catch breath, and then, with redheaded Harney calling them on, they rushed the breastworks, and were over the crest. There the brave Mexican General Vasquez was killed, and the battery was overrun, as Sergeant Thomas Henry, of the Seventh Infantry, ran up the United States flag on the summit, and as Captain John Magruder of the artillery turned the Mexican guns upon the fleeing enemy, who plunged down the southerly slopes of the hill toward the road.

With Harney's men bursting upon them from one direction, and Riley's from another, and with their own batteries turned on them from above, the Mexican left began to give way—just as Shields's brigade came crashing out of the thickets into the cleared space about their camps. The batteries there greeted Shields with a blast—grapeshot passed clear through the body of that intrepid leader in a wound which was supposed to be, but was not, mortal—and momentarily checked the advance of the brigade. Colonel Baker of the Illinois troops sprang to the front, and the men charged ahead, as the Mexican force gave way.[20]

Meanwhile, a mile and more to the east, the battle on the Mexican right had never really got started. Pillow's brigade, which had spent the night in the camps at Plan del Rio, had three miles to march before it reached the place where it was to turn off the national road, filing to the left through a narrow track into a tangle of thickets and hollows, in front of and below the three Mexican batteries. What with delay and confusion in the march, and the difficulties of terrain, Twiggs's guns had begun to speak long before the brigade was in position to attack. The assault was to have been delivered by two storming parties, each made up of one Pennsylvania and one Tennessee regiment. In the confusion of the approach march, however, the paired regiments were separated, and before any of them were in position, the regiment in front—Colonel William Haskell's Second Tennessee—came under heavy fire as it made its way along the path. In disorder, but with determined bravery, most of the regiment attempted to crash its way through the thickets and brush entanglements between it and the Mexican battery, but was driven back with heavy loss—the heaviest loss of any American regiment on the field that day. Before the supporting Pennsylvanians could be got into position, or the other storming party which had farther to go could be made ready to charge, the battle was over. The Mexicans, cut off to the westward by Twiggs's advance, were flying white flags of surrender, and General Pillow—who had suffered a wound in the arm—suspended the assault.[21]

By a little after ten o'clock in the morning the fighting was over on both wings, Santa Anna and such of his generals and staff as could accompany him had fled, and most of the Mexican soldiers had surrendered or were desperately trying to follow their leaders in flight.

The American loss was light—sixty-three killed, 337 wounded. The Mexican loss is conjectural, there being no one left to make reports, or to whom reports might be made. Inspector General Hitchcock reported the capture of five general officers, one of whom, the gallant La Vega, had been captured at Resaca and exchanged; 199 officers of other ranks; and 2,837 rank and file, the number with which the escorting parties got back to Plan del Rio. At least, 1,000 others, he thought, had made their escape from the guards on the way to the point where they were to be paroled, not to serve again during the war unless exchanged. Being unable to transport the forty-three guns captured in the several Mexican batteries, the Americans rendered them unserviceable and abandoned them.[22]

At least half of the Mexican army, however, escaped capture, and went streaming westward up the highway toward Jalapa, with the American forces pelting along in pursuit. With the start which the Mexicans had, no great number were overtaken and captured before the pursuit ended, for the day, at Santa Anna's upland home of Encero, short of Jalapa. The master of Encero had made his escape, but his traveling carriage and his baggage wagon, with a military chest containing coin for the payment of his soldiers, had been captured. Of all the captures made that day, the highest degree of interest was shown in a wooden leg supposed to have been his, taken by the Fourth Illinois, and long exhibited in the State Capitol at Springfield. So great was the interest in this personal item, in fact, that "enterprising Yankees for some months continued to exhibit veritable wooden legs of 'Santa Anna' through the towns and cities of the States."[23]

On the nineteenth, fresh from the horrors of a battlefield, the Americans marched into Jalapa—capital city of the State of Vera Cruz and, by every account, one of the beauty spots of Mexico and the world. The city—"the most beautiful spot that any of us ever saw"—

lay in a great amphitheater of mountains, with the snowy peak of Orizaba thirty miles away but seeming close at hand, and the Cofre de Perote, frequently snow-clad also, rising just behind the city. With its 4,250 feet of elevation above the sea, Jalapa enjoyed the "softest and most equable climate." Its immediate environs were, to one soldier, "more like the Garden of Eden" than anything else he could think of, with the flowers and fruits of both tropic and temperate clime, while, looking to the eastward over the tropical country, one could see, on a clear day, the blue of the sea forty miles away in an air line.

Jalapa was not only occupied but, within two weeks or less, temporarily "Americanized." The publican and the shopkeeper followed the army, and "even the daguerreotype man was giving permanence to the beauties of the fair Jalapeñas." There was a theatrical troupe, whose performances were attended by a dense throng of soldiers, teamsters and loafers, as one observer described them—and there was, of course, a newspaper, this time *The American Star*, which the enterprising Mr. Peoples brought out within a week of the arrival of the army.[24]

Worth's division, however, did no more than pause in Jalapa. Taking the lead, they marched on, up the great highway—"the finest road I have ever seen," one officer noted—which twisted and turned to surmount the massive front of the Mexican plateau that loomed ahead. Ten miles beyond, the "terrible pass" of La Joya was found abandoned, its fortifications incomplete, its guns spiked. Another ten miles, and the summit—more than 8,000 feet—was reached at Las Vigas, where camp was made the night of April 21, and where many a man regretted the absence of the greatcoat or blanket which he had left behind in the heat of the tropics, only a few miles back.

On the morning of April 22 the march was continued for another dozen miles across the great plain behind the snowy peaks of Orizaba and the Cofre de Perote, and at noon Worth occupied, without resistance, the old stone fortress of San Carlos de Perote, where in other years the Texan prisoners taken by Mexico had been confined. The retreating commander had left behind a commissioner to deliver to the advancing Americans the forbidding rectangular pile of masonry, moated and bastioned, with quarters for a garrison of 2,000 men and with an armament of sixty-six guns and much ordnance matériel, for all of which Colonel Velasquez took careful receipt from Captains DeHart and Lee.[25]

Only a little more than six weeks before Scott and his men had been on shipboard. And now they had won a firm foothold on the great interior plateau of Mexico, more than a mile and half above the sea—and within 200 miles of the capital.

---

[1] Ex. Doc. 60, H. R., 30th Cong., 1st sess., pp. 910, 930-934; Anderson, *Artillery Officer*, pp. 111-112, 119; Furber, *Twelve Months Volunteer*, pp. 563-564; Oswandel, *Notes*, pp. 101, 103; Spell, "The Anglo-Saxon Press." Before the end of the American occupation of Vera Cruz, there were to be four other newspapers established, the *Chronicle*, the *Sun of Anahuac*, the *Genius of Liberty* and the *Free American*. Causes of newspaper mortality were lack of patronage in some cases, clashes with military authority in others.

[2] Ex. Doc. 60, H. R., 30th Cong., 1st sess., pp. 910-911, 914, 935-936; Vera Cruz *Eagle*, July 13, 1847; Oswandel, *Notes*, p. 105. Some of the regular officers did not agree with the commanding general that both regular and volunteer soldiers were involved in disorders. "Of course not the slightest excess was committed by any of the Regulars," wrote Lieutenant McClellan. *Mexican War Diary*, p. 91. "If the Volunteers were at home we could so govern our soldiers as to check outrages now hourly committed," wrote Captain Robert Anderson. *Artillery Officer*, p. 112.

[3] Ex. Doc. 1, Sen., 30th Cong., 1st sess., p. 547; Ex. Doc. 60, H. R., 30th Cong., 1st sess., pp. 911, 917-918; Semmes, *Service Afloat and Ashore*, pp. 147-148; Parker, *Recollections*, pp. 103-106; Ex. Doc. 1, H. R., 30th Cong., 2nd sess., p. 1190.

[4] Ex. Doc. 1, H. R., 30th Cong., 2nd sess., pp. 1192-1203; Semmes, *Service Afloat and Ashore*, pp. 150-155; Parker, *Recollections*, pp. 106-107; Lewis, Charles Lee, *Admiral Franklin Buchanan* (Baltimore, 1929), pp. 115-118. Buchanan was the only man to hold the rank of admiral in the Confederate Navy.

[5] Ex. Doc. 60, H. R., 30th Cong., 1st sess., pp. 908-909, 1125-1126; Ramsey (ed.), *The Other Side*, pp. 142-146; Ripley, *War with Mexico*, II, 391-394; Smith, *War with Mexico*, II, 13-16.

[6] Ex. Doc. 60, H. R., 30th Cong., 1st sess., p. 909.

[7] Quaife (ed.), *Polk's Diary*, II, 465-468, 471-487; McCormac, *James K. Polk*, pp. 488-493; Ex. Doc. 52, Sen., 30th Cong., 1st sess., pp. 81-89.

[8] Ex. Doc. 60, H. R., 30th Cong., 1st sess., pp. 913, 921.

[9] Ex. Doc. 60, H. R., 30th Cong., 1st sess., p. 928; *English Soldier in U. S. Army*, pp. 167-171; Oswandel, *Notes*, pp. 108-109; Robinson, *Reminiscences*, pp. 238-240; Semmes, *Service Afloat and Ashore*, pp. 170-174. The description of the road by Madame de la Barca is in her Fifth Letter. Santa Anna's estates were vast in extent—nearly 500,000 acres—but much of the land was of small value. In 1845 he had offered to sell his three haciendas of Manga de Clavo, Paso de Varas and Encero for 280,000 pesos, with no takers. Calcott, *Santa Anna*, pp. 217-218.

[10] Ex. Doc. 60, H. R., 30th Cong., 1st sess., pp. 928, 936, 939-940.

[11] Ex. Doc. 1, Sen., 30th Cong., 1st sess., pp. 259-261; Ramsey (ed.), *The Other Side*, pp. 146-148, 198-200.

[12] Ex. Doc. 1, Sen., 30th Cong., 1st sess., pp. 274-275; *English Soldier in U. S. Army*, pp. 174-175; Robinson, *Reminiscences*, pp. 240-248; Stevens, *Campaigns*, p. 18.

[13] Ex. Doc. 60, H. R., 30th Cong., 1st sess., p. 929.

[14] Ramsey (ed.), *The Other Side*, p. 205.

[15] Scott, *Memoirs*, II, 432; Furber, *Twelve Months Volunteer*, pp. 600-601; Ex. Doc. 1, Sen., 30th Cong., 1st sess., p. 261. In Freeman, Douglas S., *R. E. Lee*, I, 218, it is stated that "there is no evidence to bear out the tradition that Scott par-

ticularly requested that Lee be sent to him." But see Ex. Doc. 56, H. R., 30th Cong., 1st sess., p. 346, Scott to Taylor, January 6, 1847: "Of the officers of engineers, topographical engineers, and ordnance, with you, or under your command, I propose to take only Captain R. Lee, of the first named corps. Colonel Totten, who will be with me, desires him, and I shall write to have him sent down from Saltillo." The account of Lee's hiding behind the log is from Freeman, *R. E. Lee,* I, 238-241. From the day of Cerro Gordo, Captain Lee was a marked man in the army.

16 Grant, U. S., *Memoirs,* I, 132-133.

17 Ex. Doc. 1, Sen., 30th Cong., 1st sess., pp. 275, 279-280, 283-284, 286, 291; Ramsey (ed.), *The Other Side,* pp. 205-206.

18 Ex. Doc. 1, Sen., 30th Cong., 1st sess., pp. 262, 275, 278, 290, 293, 298.

19 Same, pp. 258-259.

20 Same, pp. 262, 275-276, 279-283, 285-286, 288-294, 298-300; Wilcox, *Mexican War,* pp. 288-289.

21 Ex. Doc. 1, Sen., 30th Cong., 1st sess., pp. 296-298. Lieutenant McClellan's *Diary,* pp. 79-90, gives a vivid, circumstantial, confused and probably prejudiced picture of the affair. The lieutenant, just out of West Point, was exceedingly scornful of volunteer troops in general, as well as those to whom he was assigned that day in particular. The losses of the Second Tennessee were seventeen killed, fifty wounded— one fourth of the total killed and one sixth the wounded in the whole army for two days of fighting. Through typographical error the printed reports attribute most of these losses to the Kentucky company or the First Tennessee.

22 Ex. Doc. 1, Sen., 30th Cong., 1st sess., pp. 275-277, 280-290, 298-299; Ex. Doc. 60, H. R., 30th Cong., 1st sess., p. 1089; Croffut (ed.), *Fifty Years,* p. 253.

23 *English Soldier in U. S. Army,* p. 197.

24 *English Soldier in U. S. Army,* pp. 203-205; Kirby Smith, *To Mexico,* p. 139; Oswandel, *Notes,* pp. 136, 140, 142, 145-146; Robinson, *Reminiscences,* pp. 257-259; Semmes, *Service Afloat and Ashore,* pp. 186-187, 189, 191; Furber, *Twelve Months Volunteer,* pp. 603-604.

25 Ex. Doc. 60, H. R., 30th Cong., 1st sess., pp. 948-949; Ex. Doc. 1, Sen., 30th Cong., 1st sess., 262, 300-302; Ramsey (ed.), *The Other Side,* pp. 220-221; Anderson, *Artillery Officer,* pp. 141-144. The steeper part of the 8,000-foot climb from sea level to the plateau was above Jalapa but there, also, was the better road. An American railway engineer, locating a line over the same terrain forty years later, paid a "tribute of admiration and respect to the unknown engineer, whoever he was . . . who laid out" the highway. "From a point near Jalapa to the summit," he added— a rise of nearly 4,000 feet—"there is not a break in the steady ascent. . . . If a Spanish soldier in 1530 could put something like a six per cent highway grade down that mountain slope, an American engineer in 1881 ought to get a two per cent railroad line down it, or take off his hat to his predecessor." Wellington, Arthur M., *The Economic Theory of the Location of Railways* (New York, 1887), p. 941 (6th Edition, 1900).

CHAPTER 18

Pause at Puebla

"MEXICO has no longer an army," General Scott wrote from Jalapa to General Taylor, on April 24. After what had happened at Buena Vista and Cerro Gordo, the assumption was reasonable and, for the moment, substantially correct. The fourth army which Mexico had put in the field against the United States had been utterly broken and scattered. General Santa Anna himself had made his way southward from the field of Cerro Gordo as a fugitive, to reach the city of Orizaba. There, however, even as Scott was writing Taylor, he had begun to gather up the scattered soldiery, to recruit new commands, and to organize for continued resistance.[1]

News of the crushing defeat at Cerro Gordo, reaching Mexico on the twentieth, was presented to Congress by the Ministry with a recommendation that the "extraordinary powers" heretofore granted to the government be limited "in such manner as to prevent it from making peace." At ten o'clock that night, accordingly, the Congress decreed that while the "supreme government of the union has power to take the necessary measures to carry on the war" it could not "make a peace with the United States." Every individual, moreover, who might in any way, officially or unofficially, publicly or privately, "treat with the government of the United States" was declared to be a traitor to Mexico. Anticipating that its own continued sessions might become impossible, the Congress created a commission of senior members to act as a council of government, to name a temporary President in case of vacancy—it not being known at the capital whether Santa Anna had escaped capture or where he might be—and to conduct the next national election for President.[2]

The nature of the resistance immediately contemplated is indicated

by the proclamation of former President Salas, published on the next
day, reciting that he had received authority to raise a guerrilla corps
"with which to attack and destroy the invaders, in every manner imag-
inable," and inviting citizens to enroll themselves for a "warfare of
vengeance—war without pity, unto death!"[3]

Except for such proclamations and appeals there was, for the moment, nothing between Scott and the Mexican capital but distance.
But despite the lack of organized opposition, the American commander could not at once advance in force. "We are obliged to look
to the rear," he wrote Taylor. "The yellow fever at Vera Cruz, and
on the road, fifty miles this way, may soon cut us off from our depot.
Deep sand, disease, and bands of exasperated rancheros, constitute
difficulties. With an inadequate train we are endeavoring to get here
[Jalapa] *essentials* before heat and disease cut us off from Vera Cruz.
Our cavalry is already meagre, and from escorting, becoming daily
more so." Part of the inadequacy in transportation was due to a lack
of teamsters and qualified wagon masters—such men being, in those
days, employed civilians rather than military personnel—to handle the
wagons and animals which were accumulating in Vera Cruz in sufficient numbers.[4]

One persistent shortage which plagued Scott and other commanders in Mexico, then and later, was the lack of money with which to
pay the troops and purchase supplies. The difficulty was not the pov-
erty of the United States Government but the inadequacy of its arrangements for the transfer of funds in coin—the only sort of money
usable in Mexico. Paydays for the soldiers, supposed to come every
other month, frequently had to be passed over until paymasters were
in funds. But while soldiers could be compelled to wait for their
money, quartermasters and commissaries could not keep the army supplied with those items which had to be secured locally unless they had
funds, and in coin. Such funds could be secured, usually, from merchants with foreign connections—notably, in the case of Scott's army,
Louis Hargous, American merchant of Vera Cruz. But the system of
drafts on local sources failed more than once, and paymasters had to
divert funds to the purchasing officers of the government, so that even
if the soldiers could not be paid, they and their animals might be fed.
Even so, there were times when it appeared that the American commander might be reduced to seizing supplies or making a forced loan
on the Mexicans. The system of drafts was to be supplemented,
though too late to be of much use to Scott, by an arrangement entered

into between the Treasury Department and August Belmont, agent of the Rothschilds of London, by which that firm undertook to make available funds for the use of the army in Mexico.[5]

Late in March, during the week in which Vera Cruz fell, President Polk concluded that the time had come to exercise the right of an occupying power to shift the costs of occupation to the country occupied, first by raising the blockade of Mexican ports and opening them to the commerce of the world upon the payment of a scale of duties to be worked out by the Treasury Department, and collected at the ports by the army or navy commanders; and second, by levying contributions upon the country if, in the judgment of the commanders in the field, such a step would not imperil the army's supply and subsistence.

Scott had been two weeks at Jalapa before these instructions reached him. The instructions as to collection of duty he simply passed back to the commanding officers at the ports of Vera Cruz and Tampico, being himself "too distant from the coast, and too much occupied with the business of the campaign" to attend to the matter. As to levying contribution upon the country, he promptly exercised the discretion given him—as Taylor had done before—by not doing it. "If it be expected at Washington, as is now apprehended," he wrote, "that this army is to support itself by forced contributions levied upon the country, we may ruin and exasperate the inhabitants, and starve ourselves; for it is certain that they would sooner remove or destroy the products of their farms, than allow them to fall into our hands without compensation. Not a ration for man or horse would be brought in, except by the bayonet, which would oblige the troops to spread themselves out many leagues . . . in search of subsistence, and to stop all military operations."[6]

Scott was the more emphatic because of his acute shortage of man power. His plan of advance and supply on leaving Vera Cruz had been to have each successive detachment of new troops as they arrived act as escorts for the necessary wagon trains going to the army in the highlands. One week after arriving at Jalapa, however, he received Secretary Marcy's letter telling him that it had been necessary to divert Cadwalader and the "new" regulars to Northern Mexico. The Secretary explained the reasons for the diversion, as the facts were then understood in Washington. From his experience in the War Department dealing at long range with Taylor, Scott should have realized and appreciated that the administration was doing the best it could with the means at hand to meet the situation as it was apprehended. But by this time Scott had developed an attitude toward Washington and all its works much the same as that which, when displayed by Taylor, he had condemned. Reinforcements were being withheld from him, he began to believe, with deliberate intent to sacrifice him and his forces—though just what any government might hope to gain from such a step, even if it had been willing to take it, is beyond rational comprehension.

But the responsibilities on Scott were many and crushing, and his shortages and deficiencies varied and exasperating. One that was weighing on him when he received word that Cadwalader and the "new" regulars would not arrive as scheduled—they were on the way, but he did not know it—was the problem of what to do with the twelve-months volunteers. Their year's term of service would expire, for the different regiments, at various dates between the end of May and July. Efforts to induce the old volunteers, "now become respectable in discipline and efficiency," to re-enlist for the period of the war were so little successful that out of the whole seven regiments but one company could be secured, under the leadership of Captain C. Roberdeau Wheat of the Tennessee cavalry.[7] Fifteen years later, after following William Walker in Nicaragua, campaigning with Garibaldi in Italy, and soldiering in many another foreign land, Major Bob Wheat was to yield his life leading another ardent battalion, the Louisiana Tigers, against the Federal lines about Richmond during the Seven Days.[8]

In this state of affairs, with a month or six weeks of service left for the seven regiments of old volunteers, General Scott's first thought was to advance while the disorganization and despair following Cerro Gordo were still on the enemy. In fact, march orders were issued on April 30, to take effect "soon after the arrival of trains now coming up from Vera Cruz." Objection was strongly urged, however, that to march the old volunteers farther into Mexico, and hold them in service until the end of their terms of enlistment, would make it necessary for them to pass out of the country through Vera Cruz, on their way home, at what it was feared would be the height of the "deadly sickly" yellow-fever season. The argument prevailed with the general, who on May 3 notified Colonel Henry Wilson, commanding at Vera Cruz, to have transports ready for 3,000 men—the number to which the rigors of a year's campaigning had reduced the seven regiments.

On the following day orders were issued for the departure of the infantry regiments from Alabama and Georgia, the two from Illinois and the two from Tennessee, and the Tennessee cavalry regiment, with independent companies from Louisiana and Kentucky. Two days later, amid scenes of general rejoicing on the part of those who were leaving and envious regret on the part of those whose terms of service were for the war, the old volunteers marched out down the road up which they had come only a little more than two weeks before. In command was Major General Patterson. Accompanying the column was Gideon Pillow, newly appointed a major general, who was going home to bring out a division of the new regulars being recruited in the States under the Ten-Regiment law. The twelve-months volunteers had "seen the elephant," as the slang of the day went, and they were willing to give up to old regulars and new recruits alike their chance of "reveling in the Halls of the Montezumas."[9]

The volunteer troops remaining—the Pennsylvania, New York and South Carolina regiments recruited under the call of November 1846—were assigned to John A. Quitman, likewise newly appointed to the rank of major general. Leaving the Second Pennsylvania regiment, with a company of artillery, to garrison Jalapa, Quitman marched forward on May 7, to join Worth at Perote. There, Worth was to take command of the column, leave one of Quitman's regiments in garrison at the fortress, and with his own division and the two remaining regiments of Quitman's, to march on to Puebla.[10]

That night—May 7—there clattered into the narrow streets of Jalapa a detachment of forty cavalry, carrying a letter for the commanding general. The letter was from Nicholas P. Trist. Mr. Trist had traveled from Washington under the assumed name of "Doctor Tarreau," and in the character of a French merchant going to Mexico. At New Orleans, as he had explained in most elaborate detail to Secretary Buchanan, he had lodged at a "French auberge, of the economical order," rather than stopping at the hotel St. Louis or St. Charles where he would have met, "within the first five minutes, someone who would be sure" to recognize him and pierce the veil of secrecy which was supposed to surround his movements. From New Orleans, where he had made himself sufficiently conspicuous by his solicitude in the selection of the government vessel that was to bear him in haste across the Gulf, he had sailed for Vera Cruz in the revenue cutter *Ewing*. During his voyage of eight days his conception of the urgency and magnitude of his mission grew.

Arriving at Vera Cruz on May 6—the day the old volunteers started down the mountain from Jalapa—he found that a large train was to go up to Scott's headquarters on the second day thereafter. He could have waited and gone up with the train, or he could have secured from Colonel Wilson a cavalry escort to take him up the mountain ahead of the train. Either course would have complied with his instructions to proceed to General Scott's headquarters, make his presence known, explain his mission, and call on the general for the specified aid in carrying it out. He did neither. He wrote a letter, and insisted that it be sent forthwith up the mountain.[11]

With his letter he enclosed one from Secretary of War Marcy, addressed to Scott. Marcy's letter would have been sufficiently clear, when read in connection with what was in Marcy's mind and the President's mind, and what was in the papers which Trist did not send to Scott. But none of these things which he was supposed to communicate did Mr. Trist pass on to Scott—merely a sealed dispatch addressed to the Mexican Minister of Foreign Affairs, which Marcy's letter told Scott to transmit to that official, with information that "Mr. Trist, an officer from our department of foreign affairs, next in rank to its chief," was at army headquarters.

As to Mr. Trist's status, the general was told that he "was clothed with such diplomatic powers as will authorize him to enter into arrangements with the government of Mexico for the suspension of hostilities." This statement was expressly qualified, however, by a double condition—first, hostilities should be suspended only on notice from Trist that "the contingency has occurred, in consequence of which the President is willing that further active military operations should cease"; and second, that even then the final judge of whether to suspend hostilities, insofar as it involved retreat from, or occupation of, any position deemed necessary "to the health or safety of the troops," was to be the commanding general himself.[12]

Such qualifications, however, were entirely lost on Scott, who in the inflamed state of his feelings could see nothing except that, as he immediately wrote Trist with a copy to Marcy, he had been sent a "communication . . . (sealed!)" for the Mexican minister, and that the "Secretary of War proposes to degrade me, by requiring that I, the commander of this army, shall defer to you, the chief clerk of the Department of State, the question of continuing or discontinuing hostilities."

As to the "(sealed!)" communication the general "very much

doubted" whether he should "so far commit the honor" of the government as to have anything to do with forwarding it to the minister of a government which was even then denouncing "as a traitor any Mexican functionary who shall entertain propositions for peace, or even an armistice."

The question of an armistice, the general wrote with eloquent indignation, "is, most peculiarly, a *military* question, appertaining of necessity . . . to the commander of the invading forces; consequently, if you are not clothed with military rank over me, as well as with diplomatic functions, I shall demand . . . that, in your negotiations, if the enemy should entertain your overtures, you refer that question to me. . . . The safety of this army demands no less, and I am responsible for that safety, until duly superseded or recalled."[13]

Had Trist followed his instructions and shown Scott the copies of the letter to the Mexican minister and of the proposed treaty which he carried for that purpose, the misunderstanding need not have occurred. The draft of the treaty would have shown him that the "contingency" referred to in Marcy's letter, on which Trist was to notify the general that the President was willing to have hostilities suspended, was nothing less than the ratification by Mexico of a treaty of peace. The letter to the Mexican Foreign Affairs minister, which Scott was called on to forward, was a reply to one of February 22, in which the Mexican Government had repelled an earlier peace overture of the United States unless, as a condition preliminary to any discussion, the blockade of Mexican ports were raised and the territory of the republic completely evacuated. Mr. Buchanan's response to this virtual refusal to consider peace proposals—which Trist was supposed to have shown Scott—was that "the President will not again renew the offer to negotiate," but that, to insure that the "evils of the war shall not be protracted one day longer than shall be rendered absolutely necessary by the Mexican republic" he was sending to the headquarters of the army an official "invested with full powers to conclude a definite treaty of peace" whenever the Mexican states were ready to do so.[14]

General Scott's reply, on its way down the mountain, met Mr. Trist on his way up. Mr. Trist felt it his "duty at once" to make "a written correction of the misconceptions" which, he told the general, "have taken possession of your imagination." Accordingly, he spent "nearly the whole night" toiling away at a letter—or, perhaps, it would be more correct to say, in the joy of composition, for Mr. Trist, like

General Scott, took pen in hand gladly. One night, however, was not sufficient for the completion of the task, and it was not, in fact, until he had actually been in Jalapa for six days that Mr. Trist completed his thirty-page masterpiece of epistolary ineptitude.[15]

Scattered through its thirty pages of irrelevant observations and elaborate and heavy-handed sarcasms there was a little light on the nature and limitations of his mission—but before receiving Mr. Trist's explanations, General Scott was doing some letter writing on his own account, this time direct to the Secretary of War with a copy to Trist. Opening up the subject on May 20, the general said: "Mr. Trist arrived here on the 14th instant. He has not done me the honor to call upon me. Possibly he has thought the compliment of a first visit was due to him! . . . I understand your letter to me of the 14th ultimo as not only taking from me, the commander of an army under the most critical circumstances, all voice or advice in agreeing to a truce with the enemy, but as an attempt to place me under the military command of Mr. Trist. . . ."

The general expressed his willingness to obey the orders of the President "directly, or through any authorized channel" but entreated that he "be spared the personal dishonor of being again required to obey the orders of the chief clerk of the State Department. . . ."[16]

On the next day, May 21, Mr. Trist's thirty-page effusion was delivered to the general. Busy with affairs "of much higher importance," Scott "did not allow the seal . . . to be broken till the evening of the 22nd," when with disdainful formality the packet was opened in the "presence of many staff officers." The general did not read the letter then, nor does it appear from the record that he ever read the whole of it—which was probably just as well from the standpoint of the blood pressure of the American commander in Mexico.[17]

The business on which General Scott was so engaged was the advance of the army to Puebla, then the second city of Mexico. In anticipation of this advance, and partly in preparation for it, the general issued from Jalapa, on May 11, a proclamation from *"El General-en-gefe de los Egércitos de los Estados-Unidos de America, a la nacion Megicana."* The proclamation was issued, after some hesitancy on the part of the general, at the suggestion of the Bishop of Puebla, who sent a confidential agent to Jalapa to urge that it be done, and to advise as to its form and content. The document recited at length, and in language as conciliatory as the subject matter permitted, the causes and the course of the war, the mistakes and misdeeds of the Mexican rulers, and especially of Santa Anna, and the reasons for peace and friendship between the two peoples. The proclamation warned that "the system of forming guerilla parties" would "produce only evils to this country, and none to our army," and closed with the announcement:[18]

I shall march with this army upon Puebla and Mexico. I do not conceal this from you. From those capitals I may again address you. We desire peace, friendship, and union; it is for you to choose whether you prefer continued hostilities.

The advance thus announced to the Mexican people had already started. Worth marched from Perote with his own division on May 8, to be followed a day later by Quitman's force, less the First Pennsylvania, which was left, with one company of artillery, to garrison the fortress. On the twelfth, the advance cleared the pass of El Pinal, without opposition, to come out on a vast level plain from which there rose mighty ridges and isolated mountains. Ahead to the west, there were the giant snow-clad peak of Popocatapetl, nearly 18,000 feet high, and the long ridge of Ixticcihuatl, the "Sleeping Woman" under her blanket of white. Behind them there still were to be seen the mighty cone of Orizaba and, near by, the peak Malinche, itself nearly 15,000 feet high. "The soldiers marched often in silence," one of them wrote, "awed by the grandeur of their surroundings."

On the fourteenth, having reason to anticipate that there would be no opposition to his occupation of Puebla, General Worth halted for the day at Amozoque, twelve miles outside the city, to give the men a chance to clean up and brush up, in order that they might make a favorable impression as they entered Puebla early on the following morning. As they were doing what they could to make themselves and their accouterments presentable, a drummer boy who had wandered out beyond the pickets came running in with word that the enemy was approaching. Galloping forward, officers discovered, indeed, that a force of enemy cavalry, estimated at from 2,000 to 3,000 men, was marching toward them from the direction of Puebla.[19]

The force, though that was of course not known at the moment, was part of that which Santa Anna had assembled and was commanded by Santa Anna himself. During the three weeks while Scott waited at

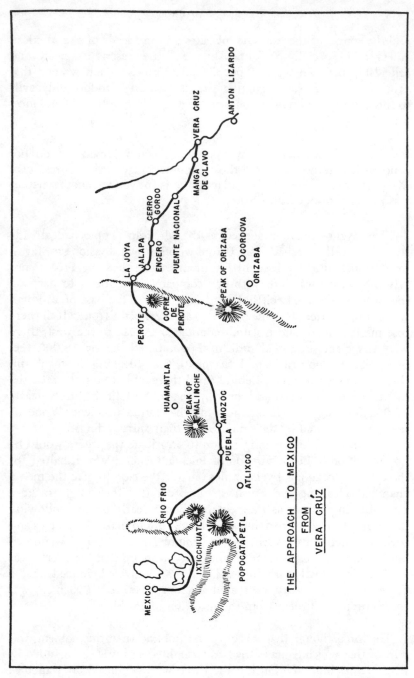

THE APPROACH TO MEXICO
FROM
VERA CRUZ

Jalapa and Perote for supplies coming up from Vera Cruz, the Mexican general had formed at Orizaba two battalions of 1,500 men each from the remains of the infantry which had scattered after Cerro Gordo. There he was joined, also, by about 1,000 new troops from the State of Oaxaca, to the southward, and from there he directed Canalizo, commanding the cavalry which had escaped from Cerro Gordo, to take post at San Andres Chalcimocula, forty miles farther up, and on the central plateau. In his flight Santa Anna had come to rest in a position from which he could strike the American line of communications in flank, either below Jalapa or above Perote.

His restless impatience, however, would not permit him to remain in a position which might well have forced Scott to the embarrassing step of turning aside from his movement on Mexico to march halfway down the Cordillera to reach Santa Anna at Orizaba. Instead, the Mexican commander threw himself into Puebla. There he sought, in vain, to arouse something of the same spirit with which that city had resisted his own attacks during the civil wars. Disappointed in his desire to obtain men, money and ammunition, and in his hope to rouse the people of Puebla, Santa Anna dispatched his infantry to Mexico, and with his cavalry moved out to meet the American advance, with what purpose it is hard to see. It was this command which caused the beating of the long roll in Worth's bivouac at Amozoque.

The United States infantry fell into line, men and officers gathering up their arms in haste as they got into position. Duncan's light artillery opened upon the approaching column. Under its fire the Mexican cavalry sheered away to their left, or north, and passed around Worth's position, apparently heading toward Quitman's troops, who were marching a few miles in the rear. Warned by the sound of the cannonade, Quitman was ready, and once more the Mexican horsemen shied away, to lose themselves behind the near-by spurs of the mountains, and to return by a wide circuit to the gates of Puebla late that afternoon.

Finding that the city would not resist the entrance of Worth's column, Santa Anna and his cavalry marched away from Puebla, at four in the morning of May 15, to follow the infantry to Mexico.[20]

At dawn of the same day Worth's men, most of whom had stood by for a night march and lain out in the rain all during the night, marched through ankle-deep mud for Puebla. As they marched, a deputation from the *ayuntamiento* of the city met Worth, who accepted their capitulation on terms which were more liberal than those granted by Scott at Vera Cruz and which, in fact, contravened the martial-law order by permitting Mexican authorities to try and determine controversies between Americans and Mexicans, as well as between Mexicans and Mexicans.

Two miles from the city all the troops were closed up, the baggage trains put in the rear, and with colors displayed and bands playing, and "Young Cortes"—as some of the soldiers called Worth—at the head of the column, the doughty little army of 4,000 mud-spattered Americans marched into Puebla. With its 75,000 population, this was by far the most important Mexican city, and the finest, which any of them had seen. Indeed, there were those who felt that there was "nothing to compare with it in the United States."

"Our little army of four thousand was completely lost in the crowds that pressed around us, examining us pretty much as they would animals in a menagerie," wrote Captain Kirby Smith. As they marched by the government palace—Puebla is the capital of the state of the same name—the Americans received the salute of the municipal troops, before turning into the central plaza, alongside the great cathedral. There, while waiting for the billeting officers to complete the assignment of quarters, they stacked arms, and many of them, much fatigued by the events of the past two days, quietly lay down beside the stacked muskets and went to sleep—to the utter amazement of the throngs, already astonished at the unmartial aspect of the dread soldiery from the north.

"Our reception was respectfully and coldly courteous, but without the slightest cordiality," General Worth reported to his chief that night. But two days later the general and his staff, with the commanders of brigades and regiments, called on the bishop, by whom they "were very affably received," and who returned the call in an hour. In another two days Worth was able to report to Scott, still at Jalapa, that there was "every disposition to sell" supplies to the Americans, but that to secure them there "must be some semblance of coercion" which he could not apply for lack of cavalry to cover the country and "allay the fears of holders." Besides being short of cavalry, he was "greatly straitened for funds" but thought that "through certain *high moral* influences" he might "get along" until Scott came up. Meanwhile, he reported, Scott's proclamation of May 11 was in great demand. He had had a third edition of it struck off, and was besieged for copies. "It takes admirably," he commented, "and has produced more decided effects than all the blows from Palo Alto to Cerro Gordo"—an estimate of the power of his proclamation with which many observers would not have agreed, but which pleased Scott nevertheless.

But whatever the effect of Scott's proclamation, the two weeks of General Worth's command at Puebla was a season of alarms and uneasiness. "During his brief command," matter-of-fact Lieutenant U. S. Grant was to write afterward, "he had the enemy hovering around the city. . . . On one occasion, General Worth had the troops in line, under arms, all day, with three days' cooked rations in their haversacks. He galloped from one command to another proclaiming the near proximity of Santa Anna with an army vastly superior to his own."[21]

General Scott was not long in coming. Two large trains of supplies, altogether nearly 400 wagons and more than 1,000 loaded pack mules, had come up from Vera Cruz to Jalapa by May 20. Two days later, Twiggs's division left Jalapa for Puebla. With an escort of four companies of dragoons, General Scott passed to the front and entered Puebla on May 28, to be followed by Twiggs's men on the next day. With the exception of garrisons at Vera Cruz, Jalapa and Perote, the army was concentrated at its point of farthest advance—an army of fewer than 6,000 effectives, with a sick list of more than 1,000.

But small as the force was, in a city with a population of more than ten times its number, the army and its camp followers soon set up their "Little America." The troops were disposed in barracks and buildings in and about the city. When they had spending money—which was not always, what with the infrequency and irregularity of paydays—they drank and they gambled and, contrary to orders, some of them stayed out of quarters after tattoo and, occasionally, one of them would be found in the morning robbed, or perhaps stabbed. But there seems to have been less of this sort of disorder than in some of the places occupied earlier, perhaps because of the increasing discipline among the troops and perhaps because, in a city of the size and importance of Puebla, there were other ways for passing the time.

The soldiers enjoyed the novelty of the *neverias,* where ice cream and sherbets, cooled with snow brought from the mountains, were served. They enjoyed visiting the *paseos* or public gardens or promenades of the city, where army bands played of an evening, and where, after it had been discovered how little there was to fear from the invaders, the fair and the fashionable of Puebla took their evening strolls, or, perhaps, a few circuits under the trees on horseback. The Americans, by this time, had become accustomed to the cigarito, although from the particularity with which they described it in their letters home it was evidently unknown, or at least a rare novelty, in the States. They had even become accustomed to the use of the cigarito by the Mexican ladies, but in the evening mounted promenades at Puebla they found a real novelty—"Mexican ladies riding a-straddle on horseback." It was "quite a common practice," one officer wrote, to see "a young lady surrounded by three of four of her beaux, chatting and laughing with them as unconcernedly as if both of her nether limbs had been on the same side of her saddle!" But the writer, though he could not bring himself to refer to the lady's nether limbs as legs, was broad-minded enough to note that "her appearance was in all respects perfectly modest . . . so that the only indecency existed entirely in the imagination of the beholder, and not in anything he saw."

The soldiers thronged, also, to the theater where the enterprising Messrs. Wells and Hart presented such dramas as *Rob Roy, Timour the Tartar, The Soldier Returns from the War,* and even *Romeo and Juliet* and *Hamlet.* And the soldiers bought copies of the bilingual *The American Star—No. 2,* which made the first of its regular appearances on June 12. The lack of "w's" in the type fonts of the Spanish printing office from which the paper was issued produced such typographical twisters as this opening sentence in an article in the second issue:[22]

I vvill begin and vvill end vvith nothing but facts vvell vvorth your attention.

In mid-June there was a flurry of excitement when General Worth issued to the men of his division a scare circular, warning that he had received trustworthy information that the Mexican market men and women were mixing poison with the food sold to American soldiers, and urging his men to stick to their government rations and not buy food in the markets. Such a circular, if well-founded, should have gone to all the troops. If ill-founded, as this one was, it should not have been issued at all. This was the view Scott took of it, when he had Worth call in all copies which could be rounded up.

The incident caused Worth to demand, and insist on, a court of inquiry to pass on his action in issuing the "poison" circular and also in accepting the capitulation of the city authorities of Puebla which Scott had, in effect, disapproved without specific mention by the device of republishing for the government of the troops and the city his General Order No. 20—the martial-law order. The court of inquiry found Worth in error, and subject to censure, in both actions. Scott, out of consideration for his lifelong friend, made the censure light and gave it minimum publicity by having it read only to division and brigade commanders and chiefs of the staff departments with the army.

But even so, Worth was aggrieved and from that time forward limited his intercourse with his chief and old-time friend to matters strictly official. Another had been added to the list of feuds within the army. At Puebla, also, another disagreement arose as to relative rank between Worth and Quitman, although Scott's patient and considerate handling of Quitman's claims under his new rank of major general kept this particular difference of opinion from developing the impassioned animosity of a service feud.[23]

On May 29, the day after Scott arrived in Puebla, he took pen in hand to express to Mr. Trist the "contempt and scorn" he felt for what he described as his "farrago of insolence, conceit and arrogance." The general wrote:

The Jacobin convention of France never sent to one of its armies in the field a more amiable and accomplished instrument. If you were armed with an ambulatory guillotine you would be the personification of Danton, Marat, and St. Just, all in one.

On June 4, the general sent a copy of his rejoinder to Trist to the Secretary of War, with a letter in a vein reminiscent of his "fire in the rear" letter of the year before. To Secretary Marcy he said:

Considering the many cruel disappointments and mortifications I have been made to feel since I left Washington, or the total want of support and sympathy on the part of the War Department which I have so long experienced, I beg to be recalled from this army the moment it may be safe for any person to embark at Vera Cruz, which I suppose will be early in November. Probably all field operations will be over long before that time.[24]

Mr. Trist, who had moved forward to Puebla with the military family of General Persifor Smith to which he was attached for quarters and rations, had not confined his efforts entirely to "demolishing" Scott, as he put it. Recalling the interest in the restoration of peace expressed by the British government, he succeeded, by what means does not now appear, in getting through a note to Charles Bankhead, the British Minister at Mexico. The note advised Mr. Bankhead of the presence of an American commissioner with the army, and of his desire to have a letter delivered to the Mexican Minister of Foreign Affairs. Would the British Legation undertake its delivery?

Rather than replying in writing, Mr. Bankhead sent his attaché, Edward Thornton, who afterward, as Sir Edward, would serve for fourteen years as British Minister at Washington and would act as a member of the joint high commission on the *Alabama* claims. Thornton, making his way through the bandit-infested country between Mexico and Puebla, found it necessary to see Trist and Scott separately, for the two Americans still were not on speaking terms. After seeing them, he undertook the delivery of Trist's note to the Mexicans, and on June 11 returned to Mexico, bearing the packet.[25]

Meanwhile, back in Washington, the first round of notes between Scott and Trist had arrived, and had produced reactions quite different from those which their writers might have fondly imagined. Marcy wrote on May 31, explaining to Scott his obvious misconceptions as to Trist's mission. He was not too concerned, however, for it was felt that the matter would be straightened out as soon as Trist and Scott saw each other, for it never occurred to anyone that they would not do so. But when the second round of letters reached Washington, it was obvious that some sort of ridiculous situation had developed which might well have serious consequences.

The subject was serious enough to be discussed at the Cabinet meeting of June 12. At the same meeting, the Secretary of the Navy produced another batch of contentious correspondence between Scott, Commodore Perry, and Lieutenant Raphael Semmes, who was acting as Perry's representative. Perry had sent Semmes forward to army headquarters to seek contact with the Mexicans to discuss the release of Passed Midshipman Rogers whom the Mexicans had captured. Scott refused to forward Perry's papers, as previously he had refused to forward Trist's communication. The double refusal roused the wrath of President Polk, who wrote in his diary:

Gen'l Scott arrogates to himself the right to be the only proper channel through which the U. S. government can properly communicate with the Government of Mexico on any subject. . . . an assumption wholly unwarrantable & which I will not tolerate.

When the subject was again before the Cabinet three days later, the President had not abated his anger at Scott's course. He feared that "the golden moment to make a peace . . . may be lost because of Gen'l Scott's arrogance and inordinate vanity" but, before taking the contemplated step of recalling him from his command, the cautious President decided to await developments. Meanwhile, the Secretary of War and the Secretary of State wrote their respective subordinates strongly worded admonitions against the apparent lack of "cordial co-operation" and against the continuance of "personal altercations."

When the matter again came before the Cabinet nearly a month later, on July 9, Mr. Trist's thirty-page outpouring and General Scott's scornful reply had been received. "Gen'l Scott has written very foolish & bitter letters to Mr. Trist & Mr. Trist has written as foolish a letter to him," President Polk noted. "Between them the orders of the Secretary of War & the Secretary of State have been disregarded; and the danger has become imminent that because of the personal controversy between these self-important personages, the golden moment for concluding a peace with Mexico may have passed." The President asked the Cabinet for advice on the recall of both officers. It was the unanimous view of the members that, with the army far into the enemy's country, such a recall would be inadvisable. The President somewhat unwillingly concurred, and the final unanimous action of the Cabinet, which may well stand as a just judgment of the controversy, was that the Secretaries of War and State should address dispatches to their respective subordinates strongly condemning their course, and that "both despatches should command them to cease their correspondence and personal controversy, and to act in harmony, each in his respective sphere, in obeying the orders, and carrying out the views of the Government."[26]

Meanwhile, in Mexico, the two embattled correspondents had, in fact, laid down their pens and begun to act together. A predisposing cause for the assumption of official intercourse between them was probably the good offices of Persifor Smith, judge turned soldier who had the respect and liking of both civilian and soldier, regular and volunteer. The immediate cause, however, was the return of Mr. Thornton of the British Embassy from Mexico. Mr. Thornton had reported to his chief his conversations with Scott and Trist, and also the fact that they were not speaking to each other. The British Minister, having sounded out General Santa Anna and found that he would receive Secretary Buchanan's letter, had delivered it informally to Domingo Ibarra, the new Mexican foreign minister. The latter, in a polite note, advised Buchanan that he had informed President Santa Anna of the contents of the dispatch, and that it would be transmitted by him to "the sovereign congress of the nation," in whose hands the decision rested. This note, dated June 22, young Mr. Thornton took to Puebla, where he arrived on the twenty-fourth. Once more the British diplomat had to call on both Trist and Scott, and tell them separately that Santa Anna would submit the American note to his Congress, as soon as a special session with a quorum could be assembled.

On the following day Trist wrote Scott a brief and businesslike note, notifying him of his readiness to respond to the indicated willingness of the Mexicans to treat, and enclosing a copy of his commission. Scott acknowledged the note, and official intercourse began between them. A few days later Trist fell sick in his quarters, about the time that the American garrison was showing Puebla how the Fourth of July should be celebrated. Hearing of his illness, General Scott rummaged his mess chest to find a box of guava marmalade which, on July 6, he sent to General Smith with the suggestion that the physician might not consider it improper as part of the diet of his "sick companion." The sick companion responded at once, and in kind, to the friendly overture. Before the month was out, Mr. Trist wrote his chief that he had "entirely misconceived" the general's character and conduct, that any publication of the correspondence between them would be a "cause of the most serious regret," and that he would like "to be permitted to withdraw it from the files of the department."

General Scott wrote Secretary Marcy of the "happy change in my relations, both official and private, with Mr. Trist," and expressed his entire willingness "that all I have heretofore written to the department about Mr. Trist should be suppressed." This, he declared, was due to his "present esteem for that gentleman," but insofar as relations between himself and the War Department went, he added, "I ask no favor, and desire none. . . . Justice to myself, however tardy, I shall take care to have done."[27]

---

[1] Ex. Doc. 60, H. R., 30th Cong., 1st sess., p. 948-951; Ramsey (ed.), *The Other Side*, pp. 214-221.

[2] Ex. Doc. 60, H. R., 30th Cong., 1st sess., pp. 951-952.

[3] Same, pp. 945, 951.

[4] Same, pp. 949, 966. The wounded from Cerro Gordo, who had been collected at the village of Plan del Rio, were brought up to Jalapa with the first train to come up from Vera Cruz. Oswandel, *Notes*, p. 147.

[5] Ex. Doc. 60, H. R., 30th Cong., 1st sess., pp. 929, 939, 994, 1004, 1012-1013, 1224; Croffut (ed.), *Fifty Years*, pp. 256, 258; Anderson, *Artillery Officer*, p. 225; Semmes, *Service Afloat and Ashore*, p. 279; *English Soldier in U. S. Army*, p. 213; Oswandel, *Notes*, pp. 62, 149, 154-155, 172-173, 238. The American difficulties over funds became known to the Mexicans, through publication of a letter taken from the person of a special messenger from Washington. Such information may have helped to stiffen resistance at critical times.

[6] Ex. Doc. 1, Sen., 30th Cong., 1st sess., pp. 552-590; Ex. Doc. 60, H. R., 30th Cong., 1st sess., pp. 958-959, 963, 994.

[7] Ex. Doc. 60, H. R., 30th Cong., 1st sess., pp. 906, 944; Quaife (ed.), *Polk's Diary*, II, 250; Nevins (ed.), *Polk*, p. 174.

[8] Ex. Doc. 60, H. R., 30th Cong., 1st sess., pp. 910, 966, 993; Wilcox, *Mexican War*, p. 305; Taylor, Richard, *Destruction and Reconstruction* (New York, 1879), pp. 25-26.

[9] Ex. Doc. 60, H. R., 30th Cong., 1st sess., pp. 910, 954-957; Semmes, *Service Afloat and Ashore*, pp. 208-209; Croffut (ed.), *Fifty Years*, p. 255; Furber, *Twelve Months Volunteer*, p. 613; Oswandel, *Notes*, pp. 157-158.

[10] Ex. Doc. 60, H. R., 30th Cong., 1st sess., pp. 957-958.

[11] Ex. Doc. 52, Sen., 30th Cong., 1st sess., pp. 150-156. Most of the Buchanan-Trist-Marcy-Scott correspondence appears also in Ex. Doc. 56, H. R., 30th Cong., 1st sess., pp. 130-131, 148-156, 165-192; and in Ex. Doc. 60, H. R., 30th Cong., 1st sess., pp. 940-941, 958-966, 975-1002.

[12] Ex. Doc. 52, 30th Cong., 1st sess., pp. 118-119.

[13] Same, pp. 120-121, 157-159.

[14] Ex. Doc. 1, Sen., 30th Cong., 1st sess., pp. 36-40. As a result of another visit of A. J. Atocha, the same through whom the passage of Santa Anna through the blockade had been negotiated, Secretary Buchanan had, on January 18, 1847, suggested to the Mexican Minister of Foreign Relations the appointment of commissioners to meet at Havana or Jalapa (this being before the United States landing and occupation of that city) to consider peace. The Mexican minister José Maria Ortiz Monasterio to whom the proposal was handed by Atocha replied as indicated, on February 22. Secretary Buchanan's letter of April 15 was in response to this reply.

Still another peace effort of this period was that conducted through Moses Y. Beach, publisher of the New York *Sun*. Mr. Beach, being about to go to Mexico on private business, suggested that he might accomplish something in that direction. He was accordingly constituted a secret agent of the United States, without diplomatic powers but informed as to the nature of a treaty which would be acceptable. Beach arrived in Mexico at the end of January 1847, and was there during the period of the revolt against the Farías government in February and March. Just before Santa Anna reoccupied the capital, he made his escape via Tampico. On May 10 he called at the

White House and gave President Polk "valuable information." His mission is discussed in Smith, *War with Mexico,* II, 11-14, 331-332.

[15] Ex. Doc. 52, Sen., 30th Cong., 1st sess., pp. 159-168.

[16] Same, pp. 126-127.

[17] Same, pp. 172-173.

[18] Ex. Doc. 60, H. R., pp. 968-974.

[19] Wilcox, *Mexican War,* pp. 308-309; Ripley, *War with Mexico,* II, 108-110; Kirby Smith, *To Mexico,* p. 162.

[20] Ex. Doc. 60, H. R., 30th Cong., 1st sess., pp. 994-995; Ramsey (ed.), *The Other Side,* pp. 221-226.

[21] Ex. Doc. 65, Sen., 30th Cong., 1st sess., p. 527; Ex. Doc. 60, H. R., 30th Cong., 1st sess., pp. 967-968, 993-995; Anderson, *Artillery Officer,* pp. 170, 174-176; Wilcox, *Mexican War,* pp. 310-312; Ripley, *War with Mexico,* II, 113-115; Kirby Smith, *To Mexico,* pp. 156, 167-168; Scott, *Memoirs,* II, 549; Semmes, *Service Afloat and Ashore,* pp. 211-214; Grant, *Memoirs,* I, 136.

[22] Ex. Doc. 60, H. R., 30th Cong., 1st sess., pp. 993-994; Semmes, *Service Afloat and Ashore,* pp. 214-215, 229, 237-239, 253-254, 265-266, 270-271; Anderson, *Artillery Officer,* pp. 202-203, 208, 216, 220; Kirby Smith, *To Mexico,* pp. 165, 176; Oswandel, *Notes,* pp. 221, 223-227, 229, 236; Croffut (ed.), *Fifty Years,* pp. 262-263.

[23] Ex. Doc. 65, Sen., 30th Cong., 1st sess., pp. 527-528; Anderson, *Artillery Officer,* pp. 226-228, 236; Ex. Doc. 60, H. R., 30th Cong., 1st sess., pp. 1021-1027.

[24] Ex. Doc. 52, Sen., 30th Cong., 1st sess., pp. 129-131, 172-173; Ex. Doc. 60, H. R., 30th Cong., 1st sess., p. 994; McCormac, *James K. Polk,* p. 498n. Chapter XX of this work contains an excellent treatment of the Scott-Trist correspondence.

[25] Ex. Doc. 52, Sen., 30th Cong., 1st sess., pp. 178-185.

[26] Same, pp. 112-117, 121-124, 127-129, 131-135; Quaife (ed.), *Polk's Diary,* III, 57-59, 62-63, 75-79, 83-86; Nevins (ed.), *Polk,* pp. 242-245, 247-248; Ex. Doc. 60, H. R., 30th Cong., 1st sess., pp. 977-992.

[27] Ex. Doc. 60, H. R., 30th Cong., pp. 830-831, 1011; Ex. Doc. 52, Sen., 30th Cong., 1st sess., pp. 178-185; Ex. Doc. 1, Sen., 30th Cong., 1st sess., pp. 40-41.

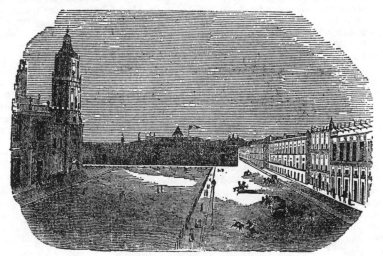

Grand Plaza in the City of Mexico.

CHAPTER 19

The Valley of Mexico

I T was in July 1845 that General Taylor moved to interpose his
army between the Republic of Texas and the war which Mexico
had threatened as a consequence of its annexation to the United
States. A year later, the first battles had been fought, Taylor was
moving his Army of Occupation up the Rio Grande, Kearny's Army
of the West was on the march to Santa Fe, and Sloat's Pacific squadron
had occupied Monterey in California. Another year, and midsummer
of 1847 found United States forces in possession of Mexican places
and ports all the way from San Francisco Bay to the Laguna de Ter-
minos, lying between the Mexican State of Tabasco and the peninsula
of Yucatán.

Throughout the history of the Mexican republic Yucatán had maintained a position of semi-independence. Between 1839 and 1843, in
fact, the State had been in open secession, in the course of which it
had entered into a financial and naval alliance with the Republic of
Texas, with which it conducted joint naval operations against Mexico.[1] In recognition of the tenuous relation between the peninsula and
the rest of Mexico, the United States had at first exempted Yucatán
from the blockade. But when the government came to believe that
this "generous course . . . had been abused," the naval commanders
were instructed to regard Yucatán as an integral part of Mexico. A
brief occupation of El Carmen Island, which controlled the outlet of
the Laguna, followed in December 1846.[2]

In the summer of 1847, after the capture of Vera Cruz, Alvarado
and Tuxpan, Commodore Perry turned his attention again to the ports
of southeastern Mexico. On May 12, without opposition, he entered
the river Coatzacoalcos on the Isthmus of Tehuantepec, where he
left one vessel, and went on to the river Tabasco, or Grijalva, where

311

he left another at the port of Frontera. From there he sailed on to the port of Laguna, on Carmen Island, which he again occupied—this time for the duration of the war. Part of his force he sent on eastward to the port of Campeche. With the rest he returned by the way he had come. He touched at Frontera and, on the twenty-first, sailed up the Coatzacoalcos to receive the formal surrender of the inland city of Minatitlan, before returning to the familiar anchorage at Anton Lizardo.

Three weeks later, the squadron was back at the mouth of the Tabasco, which it entered on June 14, to go again to the state capital of San Juan Bautista. With the broad pennant of the commodore flying on the lead vessel, and with each of the four light-draft steamers towing smaller sailing craft and a string of ten to twenty small boats from the ships, the expedition strung out along the river for six miles. Frequent stops to clear away obstructions in the narrow river, or to answer fire from its jungle banks, slowed the aquatic procession on its ninety-mile journey, but on the sixteenth, the commodore, with 1,500 men and seven field pieces, took possession once more of the capital city of Tabasco. Six days later, leaving a small garrison to hold the place, the procession of boats departed downstream. Another month of trials and difficulties, especially from tropical sickness, convinced the commodore that the occupation of the remote inland city was not worth what it was costing, and on July 22 the Tabasco garrison was withdrawn, although the occupation of Frontera, at the mouth of the river, continued.[3]

With every Mexican Gulf port from Soto la Marina, north of Tampico, to Yucatán under occupation or close blockade, Commodore Perry issued orders on August 18 that all vessels other than army transports arriving at Mexican ports must be visited by a guard boat with a boarding party, to detect and prevent "irregularities." The particular "irregularity" which produced the order was the secret landing at Vera Cruz from a British mail steamer of the exiled ex-President Paredes, who had had so much to do with starting the war and whose return, it was feared, might prolong it.[4]

On the Pacific side, the squadron—commanded in the summer and fall of 1847 by Commodore W. Branford Shubrick, after the departure of both Stockton and Biddle for the States—had the far more difficult task of blockading more than 4,000 miles of coast line, operating from a base at Monterey which was itself a thousand miles from the nearest port to be blockaded. Stockton had sought to establish a blockade of the whole coast by proclamation but Secretary Mason, adhering to the policy insisted upon by the United States in earlier disputes with European maritime powers, ruled that no port was to be regarded as under blockade unless a force was actually present or temporarily driven away by stress of weather, intending to return. Shubrick had not nearly enough ships to enforce that sort of blockade, and not nearly enough men to land and occupy the principal ports, even if there had been no resistance. Intermittent blockades were established, however, at Mazatlán, the principal port on the west coast at that time, and occasionally at other ports. La Paz, the territorial capital near the tip of the long peninsula of Baja California, was occupied with a garrison of three companies of troops from the New York regiment which had volunteered for west coast duty.[5]

In the north, in New Mexico, Sterling Price was having difficulties, also. Marauding bands raided his grazing parties on the waters of the Canadian, cutting out or stampeding the animals. The companies whose twelve-months enlistment was nearly up went home. With his forces reduced, the air was filled with reports of an invasion from Chihuahua, or another revolt in New Mexico. Although doubting these rumors, the commander accepted as an undeniable fact the resentment and hatred of the New Mexicans toward the occupying forces, and felt it necessary to concentrate his reduced command at Santa Fe, at least pending the arrival of reinforcements.[6]

Difficulties of somewhat the same sort were experienced by General Taylor, also. His long line of communications was harassed by Mexican cavalry forces for a season, and then by smaller bands of guerilleros, or perhaps just plain plunderers. "Occasional acts of violence" toward the Mexicans, which Taylor attributed to the volunteer troops, continued. General Wool felt that much of the trouble was caused by American deserters, guilty of crimes against the inhabitants. "It is these parties," he said, "that make guerrillas." Another observer, Captain Hughes, laid most of the trouble to "some of the quartermaster's men" who were not subject to martial law, and particularly to "desperate adventurers called by the army 'outsiders,' who made war on their own hook."

Teamsters driving the American wagon trains were, in some cases, "inhumanly murdered." In retaliation, in one case, parties unknown perpetrated what the general described as an "atrocious massacre" in a village whose surviving inhabitants were afraid to testify, for fear of further reprisals. As an indemnity for the forty or more Americans murdered upon the capture of a wagon train at Marin, Taylor levied contribution upon the states of Nuevo León and Tamaulipas, requiring each district or *juzgado* to pay, in cash or kind, its proper share.

As their enlistments approached an end, the twelve-months volunteers serving under Taylor were just as unanimous in their determination to take their discharges and go home as were the men under Scott. The Saltillo *Picket Guard* of May 21, 1947, satisfied its readers' "Curiosity as to Voltigeurs" by describing this new sort of regiment as a "little army in itself, horse, foot, and artillery," with 500 infantrymen, 500 dragoons who could take up the infantry behind them in rapid movements, and a battery of light field pieces. But the paper satisfied a much more eager curiosity by announcing that the two Illinois regiments and the two Indiana regiments stationed at Saltillo would be gone in a few days. The three Kentucky and two Ohio regiments were already gone. The Mississippi, Louisiana and Arkansas regiments were going, also, and the mounted Texans. The services of the Texas cavalry were described by the general as "of the highest importance," but he begged "that no more mounted troops be sent me from Texas." They "have scarcely made one expedition," he wrote, "without unwarrantably killing a Mexican."

By the end of June, the twelve-months volunteers were gone, and the new "for the war" troops were coming in—regiments of volunteers from Virginia, Massachusetts, and North Carolina, and another from Mississippi; and three of the new regular regiments raised for the period of the war, and "regular" in little but name. The new troops were concentrated in a supposedly healthy camp of instruction on the Rio Grande at Mier, rather than at Camargo where losses had been so great in the previous summer, but even so, before the summer was out a full one fourth of the troops, new and old, were disabled by disease.

With a force of only a little more than 6,000 men, Taylor recommended that he do no more than hold a defensive line and "throw all the remaining troops into the other column" advancing upon Mexico. In line with the recommendation, Brigadier General Joe Lane, with the Ohio and Indiana regiments, and Brigadier General Caleb Cushing, with the Massachusetts regiment and the new Sixteenth regulars, were ordered in August to Vera Cruz. Brigadier General Enos Hopping—another of the new generals appointed from civil life—remained at Mier, commanding, until his death in September, the two new regular regiments.[7]

Inland operations were undertaken by the army at Tampico when Colonel L. G. De Russey started toward Huejutla, where American prisoners were reported to be held. On July 12, the fourth day of his march, he ran into opposition at the Rio Calaboso and, after a lively affray, fell back to the town of Tantuyac. There, having used up the regular ammunition for his one light gun, he seized powder and ball in the town and, using champagne bottles as containers and sand as packing, made up a supply of effective ammunition. Five days later, having fought off attackers and forced his way through ambushes, he reached Tampico, with the loss of more than ten per cent of the small force with which he had ventured into the interior. The prisoners at Huejutla, enlisted men who had been captured at Encarnación in February, were not released until after the fall of the city of Mexico.[8]

But with all the activity around the edges of Mexico, by mid-summer of 1847 the war had come to a focus in the very heart of the country, where Scott at Puebla faced the problem of "conquering a peace," and Santa Anna at Mexico faced the problem of negotiating one, if he could do so without losing his position and power, or if he could not, fighting to save the capital.

Santa Anna's position after his defeat at Cerro Gordo and his failure at Puebla was precarious in the extreme—except for the fact that the wide-spread opposition to him had failed to develop a leader who could unify and direct it. Upon his approach to Mexico, on May 17, he was once more met by a deputation from Congress—this time to urge that he not resume the Presidential office. Being so urged, he sent in a letter renouncing the office for the remainder of the short term to which he had been elected, and leaving the control of civil affairs in the hands of his interim substitute, Anaya. But almost before the messengers bearing the letter were under way, he changed his mind and followed on into the city, where, two days later, he announced that he would once more sacrifice his inclination to retire from public affairs by consenting to re-assume the office of President.

This he accordingly did, on May 22, taking the oath under the Constitution of 1824, which had been restored by the *Acta de Reformas* of May 18. In an accompanying proclamation he called upon "all classes of society and all individuals" for co-operation, directing special attention to the clergy, who, it was said, could not "in conscience consent to the domination of a people who admit, as a dogma of their policy, the toleration of all religious sects." The Church was therefore called upon to "sacrifice a portion of its property" in order to save the rest and "preserve . . . the privileges which our laws respect and which those of the United States do not allow."[9]

On May 28, however, Santa Anna once more made formal renunciation of the Presidency. Because the peace party knew of his "determination . . . to fight to the death," he said, it was a matter of public notoriety that revolutions were forming against him. "It is also notorious," he added, "that the enemy does not dare to advance from Puebla . . . unless he is aided by a revolutionary movement of this capital. This revolutionary movement I can ward off by a word; and this word it is my duty to utter, as the last and most efficacious service which it is left me to render. It is the formal renunciation, which I make by the present note, of the presidency of the republic. . . ."

The public and Congressional response to this moving entreaty being less than enthusiastic, five days later, on June 2, the President once more sacrificed himself by withdrawing his resignation. "What a life of sacrifice is the General's," commented the *Monitor Republicano*, "a sacrifice to take power, to resign, to resume; ultimate sacrifice; ultimate final; ultimate more final; ultimate most final; ultimate the very finalest . . ."[10]

While preparations for defense were being driven forward with the energy for which Santa Anna was famous, the possibilities of a negotiated peace were likewise being explored. It was not until July 13, however, that a quorum of the Mexican Congress could be secured for the consideration of Secretary Buchanan's note delivered nearly a month before. When a quorum was at last secured, there remained as an obstacle to negotiation the Congressional decree of April 20 that any Mexican treating with the Americans would be deemed guilty of treason. The President sought repeal of this decree but the Congress, preferring to let Santa Anna take the full responsibility for opening negotiations, called attention to the subsequent restoration, by the act of May 18, of the Constitution of 1824. That instrument of government provided that the executive should in the first instance conduct foreign relations and negotiate treaties, which, it was felt, made the decree of April 20 inoperative. But Santa Anna, not being minded to bear alone the odium of proposing peace, insisted upon clear-cut action, either repealing or re-affirming the decree—which action he never got from a Congress equally determined not to act in any such unequivocal fashion.[11]

Such deterrents to public negotiation, however, did not prevent negotiations in private. Santa Anna, it was reported to Trist and through him to Scott, was disposed to peace but could not make, or carry through, a treaty without having at hand means to "satisfy" certain individuals. English merchants at the capital were reported as saying "that a peace can be had for a little money," and the English and Spanish ministers were said to be of the opinion that "a bribe is absolutely indispensable." The agents with whom Mr. Trist was in communication represented this to him as a "custom universally obtaining in Mexico."

On the evening of July 16, at Puebla, General Scott assembled his general officers, except Worth with whom personal relations were at an end, and P. F. Smith, who was sick, to "post them up" on the situation, both as to reinforcements on the way up from Vera Cruz and as to the negotiations anticipated at Mexico. Outlining the word that had come through Trist, Scott said that he had dispatched $10,000 from his secret service fund to "a particular individual in the government (not Santa Anna) and that one million had been placed in Mexico, not to pass under the orders of Santa Anna till the treaty shall be formally ratified." Scott's position, as stated then and afterward, was that he had "never tempted the honor, conscience, or patriotism of any man, but held it as lawful in morals as in war to purchase valuable information or services voluntarily tendered me."

The officers present were given an opportunity to express themselves, although the step had already been taken. Pillow, with whom Scott and Trist had consulted earlier because of his close connection and friendship with the President, favored the measure. Quitman, while decidedly approving the motives which led to the action taken, didn't like what had been done. Twiggs was for it. Shields expressed doubts and misgivings but no final opinion. The discussion closed before Cadwalader could express himself.

The steps taken, whether approved or disapproved, turned out to have no effect upon the course of events, for before the end of July word came back from Mexico that Santa Anna could not get Congress to repeal the obstructive decree of April 20, and was unwilling to act without its repeal. It was suggested, therefore, that Scott advance from Puebla and that he would be met by a flag of truce before he reached the outskirts of the capital. Scott replied, in effect, that he "would advance upon the capital, and would either defeat the enemy in view of the city, if they would give him battle, or he would take a strong position from the enemy, and then, if he could restrain the enthusiasm of his troops, he would halt outside of the city and take measures to give those in the city an opportunity to save the capital by making a peace."[12]

Any hope of peace by negotiation without more fighting and further victories was ended by July 27, when Santa Anna's old antagonist, General Gabriel Valencia, arrived at the capital with the Army of the North, from San Luis Potosi. The arrival of these veterans of the Rio Grande and the Angostura raised the hopes of the defenders, while nothing would have suited the leader of this most important remaining Mexican force better than to lead a revolution against anything savoring of presidential proposals for peace.

With all the various peace feelers and negotiations, public and private, there was no slackening in preparation on the part of the defenders of Mexico, nor any delay in movement on the part of Scott.

The American commander was waiting for reinforcements of men and supplies to arrive at Vera Cruz, and to make their way up the 200 miles of guerrilla-infested mountain road to Puebla. The same solicitude that had been shown for the health of the twelve-months volunteers going home for discharge could not be applied to the new recruits and the new organizations. They not only had to pass through Vera Cruz in the "deadly sickly" season of midsummer, but in most cases had to remain there for days, and in some cases for weeks, awaiting the accumulation of a sufficient train and escort to fight its way up to head of the column at Puebla.

The first train to start up after the occupation of Puebla got under way on June 2, under command of Colonel J. S. McIntosh, with nearly 700 recruits, more than 400 pack mules and 700 draft and riding animals, and with 128 wagons, including ten loaded with silver coin for the army—a fact which was published in the Vera Cruz newspaper and "noised abroad from Vera Cruz to Mexico." The recruits were green, sick and unpaid. The teamsters were in a state of suppressed mutiny. Almost from the start, the train was beset by hovering attackers. Four days out, it stalled to wait for the arrival of General Cadwalader with reinforcements. Coming up with 500 men, Cadwalader resumed the march on June 11, but soon had to force his way across the National Bridge, losing thirty-two men—an operation in which Lieutenant George Maney, future general officer of the Confederate States, and Lieutenant Hooker, who was to become known as "Fighting Joe," were distinguished.

Jalapa was reached on June 15. There the column halted three days, to recruit the animals. The Jalapa garrison joined the column when it marched on to Perote, carrying the sick who could be moved and leaving the others in the care of the Jalapa townspeople, who most faithfully executed their trust. Upon reaching Perote, Cadwalader received orders from Major General Gideon J. Pillow, on his way up from below with 1,500 men, to wait for him. On July 1, two weeks out from Vera Cruz, Pillow reached Perote, and the combined columns—by now numbering more than 4,000 men and 500 wagons—marched on to arrive in Puebla on July 8.[13]

With the arrival of these reinforcements, Scott now had at the head of his column something more than 10,000 men, of whom more than 2,000 were on sick report. As he was preparing to move forward with this force, word came up from below that 2,400 men under Brigadier General Franklin Pierce had left Vera Cruz on July 19. It was decided to await their arrival.

General Pierce's troops were new regulars, many of them recruited in New England. The general himself—one of the three officers of the Mexican War who would become Presidents of the United States—was a graduate of Bowdoin College, where he had been a college mate of Henry Wadsworth Longfellow and Sargent S. Prentiss and a close friend of Nathaniel Hawthorne. By the time he was thirty-eight years old he had established himself as a lawyer in New Hampshire, had served four years in the national House of Representatives and five years in the Senate of the United States, from which he had resigned to resume the private practice of law. The sincerity of his withdrawal was attested by subsequent refusal both of an appointment to the Senate and one to President Polk's Cabinet as Attorney General. With the coming of the war, his lifelong interest in things military led him to enlist as a private in the first companies raised in New Hampshire. He soon became colonel, and, in March 1847, was one of the new generals made by the President. Five years later, in 1852, as the nominee of the Democratic party for President, he would run against and overwhelmingly defeat his old chief, General Scott, nominee of the Whigs.

Pierce's movement up from Vera Cruz was handled with unusual competence. Although he had had to wait almost a month for sufficient wheeled and animal transport for his force, he lost but one man on the coast from the *vomito,* and none by disease on the march. His march was interrupted by the destruction of the bridges over the San

Juan and the Rio del Plan, and he was five times attacked, but came through without undue delay or loss of consequence, to arrive at Puebla on the evening of August 6.[14]

On August 7, 1847, the morning after Franklin Pierce arrived with the last reinforcements known to be on the way, General Scott started his march to the Valley of Mexico.

"Like Cortez," he had earlier written to the Secretary of War, "finding myself isolated and abandoned, and again like him, always afraid that the next ship or messenger might recall or further cripple me, I resolved no longer to depend on Vera Cruz, or home, but to render my little army *a self-sustaining machine.*" The "machine," after leaving behind at Puebla more than 1,800 sick in hospitals and a garrison of 400 men under Colonel Thomas Childs, numbered only 10,738 men of all arms. With them, Scott set forth to conquer a city of 200,000 people, protected by mighty mountains, by lakes and marshes, and by fortified hills, and defended by an army which Scott estimated to be not less than three times his own in number. "A single defeat," as one Mexican writer noted, "would be sufficient for the destruction of the American troops," while the defenders "might suffer several without deciding the fate of the contest." An eminent neutral, the Duke of Wellington, who followed Scott's progress from afar, is quoted as having said, when he learned that he had started for the Valley of Mexico, "Scott is lost. . . . He can't take the city, and he can't fall back upon his base."[15]

The first division of the American army to get under way—preceded by Harney's dragoons—was that of Twiggs. Its two brigades—P. F. Smith's and Bennett Riley's veteran regulars—assembled in the grand plaza at Puebla early in the morning of August 7, gave a mighty "Cerro Gordo shout" as they started, and led out on the way toward the tremendous mountain wall which guarded the Valley of Mexico.

A day later, about five hours' march as the day's movements were regulated, came Quitman's division, which included Shields's brigade of New York and South Carolina volunteers, and a brigade made up of parts of the Second Pennsylvania and a battalion of 300 marines, the brigade commander being Lieutenant Colonel S. E. Watson, U.S.M.C.

Another day, and Worth marched with his division—the veteran regular brigades of Colonel John Garland and Colonel N. S. Clarke. Still another day, and on the tenth, Pillow's division—Pierce with a

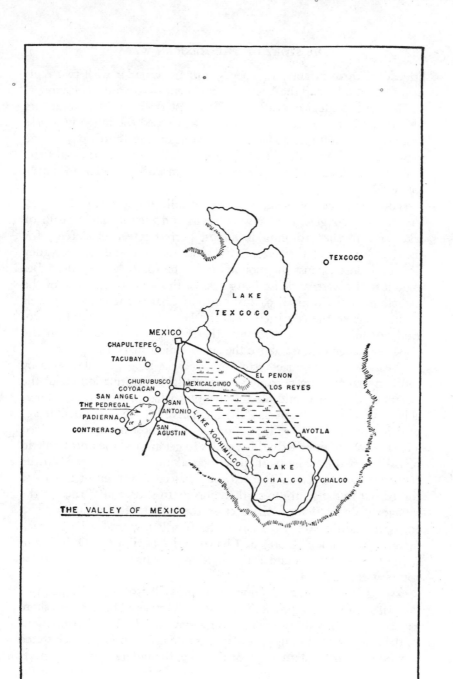

TEXCOCO

LAKE
TEXCOCO

MEXICO
CHAPULTEPEC
TACUBAYA

CHURUBUSCO
COYOACAN   MEXICALCINGO   EL PENON
SAN ANGEL   LOS REYES
THE PEDREGAL
PADIERNA   SAN
CONTRERAS   ANTONIO   AYOTLA
                  SAN
                  AGUSTIN   LAKE XOCHIMILCO

                                        LAKE
                                        CHALCO   CHALCO

THE VALLEY OF MEXICO

brigade of three infantry regiments, and Cadwalader with two regiments of infantry and the Voltigeur regiment—closed the column.

The road to Mexico struck out northwest from Puebla, wound its way up the northern flank of Ixticcihuatl, crossed the range in a pass more than 10,000 feet above the sea, and, on the fourth day of the march, opened out into the magnificent Valley of Mexico—a scene which has delighted all manner of men, from world travelers to simple soldiers.

Half a mile below them, and twenty miles away to the west, lay the city they sought. But between them and the city lay a chain of lakes and marshes, forming an almost perfect screen of defense for the city. Nearest of the lakes, in the southeastern corner of the valley floor and close against the mountains on the south, was Chalco. Beyond it to the west, and also lying against the spurs of the base of the mountains, was Xochimilco. Just north of Chalco, and extending well to the north of the city itself, was the largest of the lakes, Texcoco. And nowhere between them was there firm passage except on the causeways, mounded up above the surrounding marshes.

The American engineers had improved the long wait at Puebla by collecting from every possible source available information about the terrain of the valley, and plotting it upon what proved to be a tolerably accurate map. From this, there appeared to be four possible approaches to the city from the southeast. The most northerly involved a long march of more than thirty miles to get around the northern end of Lake Texcoco. The most direct was along the main road, on the causeway between Lakes Texcoco and Chalco. A variant of this route turned out to the south, to skirt the northern shores of Chalco to the village of Mexicalcingo, there cross the outlet of Xochimilco, and then turn northward to the city. The fourth involved a long march around the southern shores of Chalco and Xochimilco. Only reconnaissances on the ground could determine which, if any, of these routes was practicable.

Twiggs's division filed down into the valley on the afternoon of August 11, and encamped at the village of Ayotla, on the northern shore of Lake Chalco. During the next three days, while the other divisions of the army were closing up and going into camp in villages clustered around the northeastern angle of the lake, the indefatigable engineers were at their work of finding out what was in front, and how best the army might march—and fight—its way to Mexico.

For two days, Major John L. Smith, the senior engineer officer with the army—he had served in the War of 1812—and his eager juniors, Captains Robert Lee and James L. Mason, and Lieutenants Pierre Beauregard, George McClellan, Zealous B. Tower and Isaac I. Stevens, probed the approaches and defenses. The long route around Lake Texcoco was soon eliminated as wholly impracticable, and attention was concentrated on the two possibilities in the area between Texcoco and the more southerly lakes.

"The reconnaissances of the 12th and 13th," Captain Lee wrote in a private letter, "satisfied us of the strength of the enemy's defences in our front. Their principal defence was at El Peñon, commanding the causeway between the lakes of Tezcuco [sic] and Chalco. The hill of El Peñon is about three hundred feet high. . . . It stands in the waters of Lake Tezcuco. Its base is surrounded by a dry trench, and its sides arranged with breastworks from its base to its crest. It was armed with thirty pieces of cannon, and defended by 7,000 men. . . . The causeway passed directly by its base; the waters of the lake washed each side of the causeway for two miles in front, and the whole distance, seven miles, to the city. There was a battery on the causeway, about four hundred yards in advance of the Peñon; another by its side; a third about a mile in front of the entrance to the city, and a fourth at the entrance."

The Peñon, it was concluded by the general, "might have been carried" but only at a price which the American army could not afford to pay."

"About two miles in front of the Peñon," Captain Lee wrote, "a road branched off to the left, and crossed the outlet of Lake Hochimillico [sic], at the village of Mexicalcingo, six miles from the main road. This village, surrounded by a marsh, was enveloped in batteries, and only approached over a paved causeway, a mile in length; beyond, the causeway continued through the marsh for two miles farther, and opened upon terra firma at the village of Churubusco. . . ."

The general's conclusion as to the route across the outlet of Lake Xochimilco at Mexicalcingo was that "it might have been easy (masking the Peñon) to force the passage"—an opinion with which many of his officers disagreed—but that having done so, "we should have found ourselves . . . on a narrow causeway, flanked to the right and left by water, or boggy grounds," and still four miles from a practicable route to the city.[16]

On August 14, General Worth sent out from his camp at Chalco a strong reconnoitering party under Lieutenant Colonel Duncan of the artillery, to report on the practicability of the route to the south of Lakes Chalco and Xochimilco. Marching halfway along the south shore, Duncan reported back, in the early afternoon, that he found the road rough but practicable for artillery and trains. This information was sent on to Scott at Ayotla ten miles away. With all the information in hand, Scott abandoned any plan to attack the Peñon and returned to "the project, long entertained, of turning the strong eastern defences of the city, by passing around south of Lakes Chalco and Jochilmilco [sic], at the foot of the hills and mountains, so as to reach" the village of San Agustin, on terra firma south of the city.[17]

"By a sudden inversion," the army reversed its movement—Worth leading off from the village of Chalco on the morning of August 15, to pass around the lake by the south and to be followed closely by Pillow and Quitman on the same day. Twiggs's division was left at Ayotla, to keep up as long as possible the appearance of a possible advance upon the Peñon, and then to bring up the rear, moving on the sixteenth.

The march was delayed for the greater part of one day by reports of a strong cavalry attack upon Twiggs, which turned out to have been strong in numbers only, with a few rounds from the artillery settling the argument. Besides the possibilities of attack in the rear, there was some uneasiness because the Americans were marching around the outside of the arc of a circle, across which the enemy could move directly—which, in fact, the energetic Santa Anna did.

But the march was still opposed by no more than light skirmishing parties easily brushed aside by the cavalry when, on August 17, the advance occupied the village of San Agustin, better known under its Aztec name, which it bears today, of Tlalpan. San Agustin lay nine miles from the city, on the great highroad to Acapulco over which, in vice-regal times, had passed the cargoes of Mexican silver for the Orient and the silks and brocades which the Manila galleons brought back in return. Running north toward the city, the road skirted for a mile or so the eastern edge of the Pedregal—literally a "stony place"—a lava field whose broken and tortured surface reminded a naval officer of a "tempest-tossed sea, instantly transformed into stone." Thence the road ran dead level, on a causeway raised above the surrounding marshes, "neither turning to the right hand nor to the left," as it had been described by old Bernal Diaz when Cortes made his entrance upon it to the Aztec capital.[18]

The defenders of the city had fortified what Madame Calderon described as the "noble hacienda" of San Antonio, two and one half miles north of San Agustin. A little more than two miles farther north, where the canalized Rio Churubusco crossed the road at right angles, the bridge had been fortified, and also the heavy-walled convent of San Mateo—persistently referred to in the American reports as San Pablo.

From Churubusco, a local road ran to the southwest through Coyoacan, skirting the northern end of the Pedregal, passing San Angel and continuing up the Magdalena brook along the western edge of the lava field. The road ran past the ranches of Ansaldo and Padierna to, and beyond, the village of Contreras, where it ended as a mule track on the slopes of Mt. Ajusco, from whose long-extinct crater the lava of the Pedregal had poured.

Looking from the south, where the Americans stood, the two roads formed a rough inverted "Y," with the stem toward the city and the two legs passing on either side of the supposedly impassable lava field. With excellent strategic sense, Santa Anna determined to post his defending forces in the region where the two legs of the Y split, from which he could shift his forces readily, and by short routes, to either the San Agustin-San Antonio road on which Scott then was, or to the San Angel-Contreras road if by any chance Scott should be able to push a force across the Pedregal and advance that way. By thus massing his forces at San Antonio, Coyoacan and San Angel, all within a space of four miles, and with supporting troops at Churubusco no more than two miles away, he would be in excellent position to meet whatever might come.

Santa Anna's forces, according to his official report, numbered 20,000, with ninety guns. His original dispositions had been made almost entirely upon the assumption that Scott would advance from the east. Valencia's army had been posted north and east of Lake Texcoco, either to resist any advance in that direction or to fall upon Scott's right and rear should he attempt an attack on the Peñon. Nicolás Bravo was given command in the Mexicalcingo-Churubusco region, and Manuel Rincon at the Peñon. The general in chief took his post there, also, with his second-in-command, former President Herrera.

There was a deal of disappointment among the Mexicans when Scott was so disobliging as not to go up against the position prepared for him but the resourceful Santa Anna began, at once, to shift his forces to meet the new threat from the south. His own headquarters were moved to the convent of San Mateo at Churubusco. Coyoacan

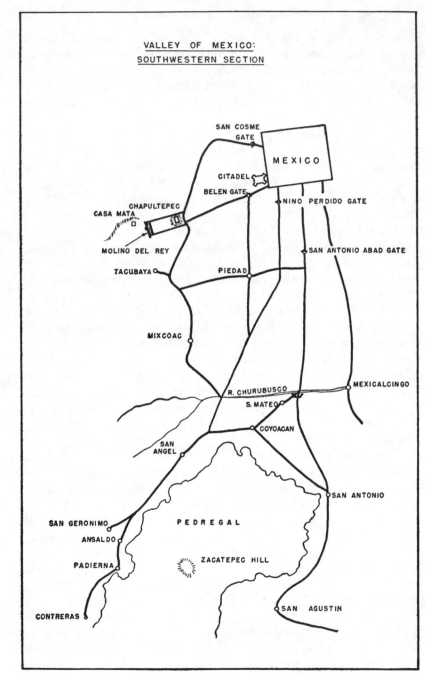

VALLEY OF MEXICO:
SOUTHWESTERN SECTION

SAN COSME GATE

MEXICO

CITADEL

BELEN GATE

NINO PERDIDO GATE

CHAPULTEPEC

CASA MATA

MOLINO DEL REY

SAN ANTONIO ABAD GATE

TACUBAYA

PIEDAD

MIXCOAC

R. CHURUBUSCO

MEXICALCINGO

S. MATEO

COYOACAN

SAN ANGEL

SAN ANTONIO

SAN GERONIMO

PEDREGAL

ANSALDO

ZACATEPEC HILL

PADIERNA

CONTRERAS

SAN AGUSTIN

326

was reinforced by a "splendid brigade" of 3,000 under Francisco Pérez. Most of the Peñon garrison was moved into the same area. Valencia's army marched around through the city itself and out to the south to take post at San Angel. Before Scott's forces were all in hand at San Agustin, Santa Anna had his forces concentrated "so that they could operate advantageously and promptly," and so placed as to give him every advantage of position.[19]

On August 18, with all his troops and his train of 1,000 wagons at or near San Agustin, Scott started once more the reconnaissance of Mexican positions. Worth's division advanced toward San Antonio, while Captain Mason and Lieutenants Beauregard and Tower pushed forward under the escort of Captain Seth Thornton of the dragoons— the same whose ambush and capture on the Rio Grande had been the immediate cause of the American declaration of war. By melancholy coincidence, the first cannon ball fired from San Antonio struck and killed the unfortunate captain, first to fall in the battles for the city of Mexico. The engineers developed the fact that San Antonio could be approached from in front only on a narrow causeway, from the right only through boggy ground, and from the left only through the jagged rocks and across the cavities and crevasses of the lava field. General Worth, therefore, was ordered not to attack, but merely to threaten San Antonio.[20]

Some other way would have to be found.

---

[1] Robinson, William M., "The Sea Dogs of Texas," The Military Engineer, Vol. XXVIII, No. 162 (November-December, 1936), pp. 453-457; Rives, U. S. and Mexico, I, 451-452, 462-463.

[2] Ex. Doc. 1, H. R., 30th Cong., 2nd sess., pp. 1175-1177; Ex. Doc. 1, Sen., 29th Cong., 2nd sess., p. 382.

[3] Ex. Doc. 1, H. R., 30th Cong., 2nd sess., pp. 1204-1233; Wilcox, Mexican War; Smith, War with Mexico, II, 201-205. The first vessel to force its way past the obstructions in the river below Tabasco was the Spitfire, commanded by Sydney Smith Lee, brother of Robert E. Lee (Washington Union, August 27, 1847). Subsequently, as a captain in the Confederate States Navy, Smith Lee would command the defenses on the James River below Richmond.

[4] Ex. Doc. 60, H. R., 30th Cong., 1st sess., pp. 787-798; Quaife (ed.), Polk's Diary, III, 152. The return of Paredes made little more than a ripple upon the surface of Mexican affairs. After the withdrawal of the Americans he took part in a revolt led by Padre Cenobio Jarauta against Sr. Herrera, who became President of Mexico after the end of the war. General Paredes' second revolution against Herrera did not have the success of his first in 1845, but he escaped capture and execution and was granted amnesty before his death in 1849.

[5] Ex. Doc. 1, Sen., 30th Cong., 1st sess., pp. 1303-1304; Ex. Doc. 1, H. R., 30th Cong., 2nd sess., pp. 1055-1065. The occupation of Lower California was undertaken "under the Treaty of Cahuenga."

6 Ex. Doc. 1, Sen., 30th Cong., 1st sess., pp. 534-538.

7 Ex. Doc. 60, H. R., 30th Cong., 1st sess., pp. 1123-1124, 1134-1135, 1138-1143, 1146-1148, 1175-1178, 1180, 1187, 1188, 1195-1197, 1199; Baylies, *Narrative*, p. 57; Ex. Doc. 32, Sen., 31st Cong., 1st sess., pp. 43-44.

8 Washington *Union*, August 13, 1847; *Encarnacion Prisoners*, pp. 70, 71.

9 Ex. Doc. 65, Sen., 30th Cong., 1st sess., p. 533; Rives, *U. S. and Mexico*, II, 436-438.

10 Ex. Doc. 52, Sen., 30th Cong., 1st sess., p. 177; Ramsey (ed.), *The Other Side*, pp. 236-237; Smith, *War with Mexico*, pp. 84-85.

11 Ex. Doc. 52, Sen., 30th Cong., 1st sess., pp. 177, 302-306; Rives, *U. S. and Mexico*, II, 436-447; Ripley, *War with Mexico*, II, 148-163; Semmes, *Service Afloat and Ashore*, pp. 309-310.

12 Ex. Doc. 60, H. R., 30th Cong., 1st sess., p. 1085; Ex. Doc. 65, Sen., 30th Cong., 1st sess., p. 524; Croffut (ed.), *Fifty Years*, pp. 266-269.

13 Ex. Doc. 1, Sen., 30th Cong., 1st sess., Appendix, pp. 4-9, 11-14, 16, 19-21; Ripley, *War with Mexico*, II, 130-139.

14 Ex. Doc. 60, H. R., 30th Cong., 1st sess., p. 1013; Ex. Doc. 1, Sen., 30th Cong., 1st sess., Appendix, pp. 25-26; Ripley, *War with Mexico*, pp. 164-166; Hawthorne, Nathaniel, *The Life of Franklin Pierce* (Boston, 1852), pp. 68-94; Nichols, Roy Franklin, *Franklin Pierce: Young Hickory of the Granite Hills* (Philadelphia, 1931), pp. 151-159. While a representative in Congress, Pierce opposed appropriations for the Military Academy at West Point. His experiences and observations in the war caused him to reverse his attitude (Nichols, *Pierce*, p. 174).

15 Ex. Doc. 1, Sen., 30th Cong., 1st sess., pp. 384, 471; Ex. Doc. 60, H. R., 30th Cong., 1st sess., p. 1223; Ramsey (ed.), *The Other Side*, p. 241; Scott, *Memoirs*, II, 466.

16 Ex. Doc. 65, Sen., 30th Cong., 1st sess., pp. 461-462; Ex. Doc. 1, Sen., 30th Cong., 1st sess., p. 303.

17 In the violent internal disagreements which disrupted the American command after victory, it became a point of controversy whether Scott would, or would not, have attacked via Mexicalcingo if it had not been for the Duncan reconnaissance south of Chalco. There seems to be no doubt that orders were given for such an attack, but it was afterward explained that they were tentative and in part intended to keep the Mexicans in doubt. Inspector General Hitchcock wrote, in the course of the controversy, that "to conceal his objects and purposes from the enemy . . . the General was obliged to conceal them from most of his own officers. . . ." Contemporaneously, however, in his journal entry of August 15, Hitchcock noted that "the General intended to threaten a display before it [the Peñon] and then suddenly fall upon the batteries at Mexicalcingo. He was perfectly confident of success." Scott acted as if this was to be his plan but obviously he kept his mind open for all the information which came in. Ex. Doc. 65, Sen., 30th Cong., 1st sess., pp. 522-526; Croffut (ed.), *Fifty Years*, p. 274; Ex. Doc. 1, Sen., 30th Cong., 1st sess., p. 303; Ex. Doc. 52, Sen., 29th Cong., 2nd sess., pp. 187-188; Ripley, *War with Mexico*, II, 188-203; Semmes, *Service Afloat and Ashore*, pp. 351-358. Lieutenants Ripley and Semmes were convinced that only the Chalco reconnaissance, sent out by Worth, prevented the attack between the lakes. Neither, of course, was in position to know what was in the commanding general's mind other than as it was made apparent by his acts.

18 Ex. Doc. 1, Sen., 30th Cong., 1st sess., pp. 303-304, Appendix, pp. 37-38; Semmes, *Service Afloat and Ashore*, pp. 370-375, 377, 393; Ripley, *War with Mexico*, II, 209.

19 Ex. Doc. 65, Sen., 30th Cong., 1st sess., pp. 533-536; Ramsey (ed.), *The Other Side*, pp. 259-267.

20 Ex. Doc. 1, Sen., 30th Cong., 1st sess., p. 304.

CHAPTER 20

Double Victory and an Armistice

ON the same day on which reconnaissance toward San Antonio showed the impracticability of a direct advance upon Mexico by the Acapulco causeway, Captain Lee was probing the possibilities of crossing the Pedregal to place a force on the road to San Angel. A passable track ran into the lava as far as a little farm whose name of Peña Pobre indicates its poor and stony character. Beyond Peña Pobre, Lee and his escort made their way to the piled-up mass of volcanic rock known as the hill of Zacatepec. While the engineer was making his observations from the hill, the escort in front of him had a brush with Mexican pickets—a fact which confirmed the estimate that there was across the Pedregal some sort of path which was practicable for foot soldiers, and which, with labor, might be made practicable for wheeled vehicles.[1]

The Mexican soldiers who had penetrated the lava field from the west were from General Valencia's Army of the North. On the day before, August 17, this veteran corps had arrived at San Angel from its earlier position northeast of the capital. On that evening, Valencia, feeling that his position at San Angel was exposed and indefensible, asked for permission to withdraw nearer to the city if he could not be heavily reinforced. Santa Anna repeated his order to remain at San Angel, with permission to retire toward Tacubaya if he received positive information of an American advance. But by morning of the eighteenth, Valencia's conception of his position and its possibilities had changed. He desired neither to hold his ground as ordered, nor to retire as permitted, but to advance. Accordingly he moved southwestward from San Angel on the road to Contreras. Before reaching that village—which was to give its name to American ac-

329

counts of the coming battle though it was occupied by neither army and saw nothing of the fighting—he found a position which, he believed, would insure a victory redounding to the special and particular glory of Valencia.

Four miles directly west of the American headquarters at San Agustin, and at the far end of the partially reconnoitered pathway across the Pedregal was the ranch of Padierna which, as the nearest identified point of the terrain, was to give its name to Mexican accounts of the battle. The ranch lay below the western edge of the lava field, on a slope which led down to the Magdalena brook. Beyond the ranch was the deep, rugged, and all but impassable ravine cut by the torrent, and beyond that, the road. West of the road a bold hill rose to a height well above the level of the lava field. On the eastern slopes of this hill, though not extending clear to its crest, Valencia placed his troops in an entrenched camp.

To him there, Santa Anna sent an order on the evening of August 18, to bring his troops back to the main army "at dawn tomorrow morning." But that was the afternoon on which Valencia's pickets had the brush with Captain Lee's escort. The escort, its mission completed, withdrew. To Valencia this was an earnest of victory and confirmation of his superior strategic sense in moving away from the rest of the army. To Santa Anna's order to return to the concentration of troops in the angle between the Acapulco and Contreras roads, where forces might be shifted quickly and easily to meet the American advance no matter by which road it might come, Valencia's reply was that neither his patriotism nor his "conscience as a military man" would permit him to obey.

Confronted with Valencia's insubordination, and wishing "to avoid a rupture in front of the enemy," Santa Anna contented himself with a reply, on the same evening, that Valencia's conduct was not approved but that he could do as he pleased and take the responsibility for the consequences—so that, from the beginning, the Mexicans had two commanders in the same theater of action.[2]

With the reports of the reconnaissances of the eighteenth in hand, General Scott issued his orders for the next day's work. Worth's division was to hold its position in front of San Antonio until further instructions. Quitman's division was to remain in reserve at San Agustin, guarding the train and supplies. Pillow's division, under the supervision of engineer officers, was "to open a practicable road, to the extent of about two miles, for the siege and other trains, in the direction of San Angel." Twiggs's division was "to advance . . . about two miles on the same track, and cover Pillow's division." Nothing was said about fighting a battle, other than the direction that the wagons would be left at San Agustin until the pass of San Antonio could be turned and forced. The orders were to open a road. The fighting which followed grew out of the necessities of road building rather than from any developed plan of bringing the Mexicans to battle.[3]

As a matter of fact, the American commanders knew little of the terrain ahead of them—no more, in fact, than could be gathered by long-range observation from the hill of Zacatepec. They could see, to their left, the ridge on which Valencia's troops and guns were stationed and, well away to their right, the village of San Angel. From knowledge of the direction of stream flow and from the appearance of the ground, they could deduce that there was a depression, or ravine, between them. They could see a church tower and roofs embowered in the trees in the bottom of the depression, approximately halfway between the high ground on which Valencia stood and the heights toward San Angel. The name of the village was San Gerónimo, and it lay beyond the ranch Ansaldo—though the two names were to be hopelessly confused in the American reports, and both were to be confused with Contreras as "the village, hamlet, or hacienda, called, indifferently, Contreras, Ansaldo, San Gerónimo." Indeed, the American unfamiliarity with the Spanish place names was such that one officer reported that he "arrived at ———— (small town)," from which he "proceeded to ———— (another small town)," while another simply lumped the whole area under the name "El Contrario."[4]

The road being built on the morning of August 19 was aimed directly toward the ranch Padierna, the only route which seemed to offer possibilities of being made practicable for wagons and guns. About a mile west of Peña Pobre, and at about the middle of the day, Mexican pickets were met. The rifle regiment commanded by Major W. W. Loring—he would in time command a Confederate corps and would close his military career as chief of staff of the army of the Khedive of Egypt—was sent forward as skirmishers to clear the ground. Before one o'clock, the job of road building "came under fire of the enemy's batteries" and Captain Lee, who was in charge, reported that work would have to be suspended "until Valencia should be driven from his position." The working parties returned to their regiments and the tools were repacked. The business of the day, after all, was to be fighting.[5]

Guns were called up, and under the direction of Captain Lee, the light batteries of Captain John Bankhead Magruder and Lieutenant Franklin D. Callender, and the rocket outfit of Lieutenant Jesse Reno moved to positions near the western edge of the lava field, where they were emplaced behind a slight rise in the rocks within less than 1,000 yards of Valencia's heavier and more numerous guns. Beyond this point there was no advancing, but there the batteries stayed, from two in the afternoon until ten at night.

It soon became apparent that the light batteries could do nothing effective against the guns on the opposite ridge; but, as the afternoon wore on, they were found useful for another purpose—to hold the attention of the Mexicans while the infantry moved off to the right in the developing plan of battle. It was, on a small scale, much the sort of role which Captain Magruder would play fifteen years later when he was left in the lightly held Confederate lines east of Richmond to make a demonstration while Captain Lee swung out to the flank to open the battles of the Seven Days. Lieutenant McClellan, moreover, against whom the demonstration before Richmond would be made, not only helped to get the guns in place above Padierna but, when Lieutenant Callender was wounded, took charge of the mountain howitzers of that battery. And handling the guns of a section of Magruder's battery at Padierna that day was another lieutenant, Thomas Jonathan Jackson, who with his new name of "Stonewall," would come marching down from the Valley of Virginia to strike McClellan in flank.[6]

"Early in the afternoon" of the nineteenth, Colonel Riley received from Twiggs an order to move his brigade to the right, or northward, across the lava field and to occupy the village of San Gerónimo, "for the purpose of cutting off the retreat of the enemy when driven from his works at Contreras . . . soon to be stormed by our troops." The order, it appears from the findings of the court of inquiry which afterward investigated the claims of some of the generals to credit for the victories in the Valley of Mexico, originated with General Pillow, the ranking officer present on the Pedregal at the time. From Pillow's report, it appears that the plan was for Persifor Smith's brigade to assail the enemy in front, while Riley turned his left and assailed him in the rear. Cadwalader, of Pillow's division, was to follow and support Riley, and Pierce to support Smith.[7]

Cadwalader was soon started after Riley, when General Pillow, observing from the hill of Zacatepec the approach of heavy Mexican reinforcements from the direction of the city, ordered Colonel George W. Morgan's Fifteenth Infantry regiment (detached from Pierce) to follow and join Cadwalader. About this time, between three and four o'clock in the afternoon, General Scott arrived at the command post on the hill, studied the situation, received reports of what had been done, and gave it his approval.

Meanwhile, Persifor Smith, being on the ground directly in front of Valencia's position and seeing the utter impracticability of attempting an advance across ravines and slopes swept by the fire of twenty-two guns, determined to move likewise to the right and seek a way to the enemy's left and rear. He sent back word that he would do so unless he received orders to the contrary. No such orders coming, he left the artillery and a few supporting infantry to keep up the demonstration in front of Padierna, while his infantry filed off to the right, made its way for a mile across the lava and then descended to the "village of Encelda [Ansaldo] whose church was visible among the trees." There Smith found Cadwalader. Riley was in San Gerónimo, which lay a quarter of a mile farther on, up another ravine cut by a mountain torrent which ran from the southwest into the Magdalena brook.[8]

When the cannonading began at Padierna, in the early afternoon, Valencia had sent word to Santa Anna that the Americans were approaching in the place he had prepared for them and that battle was joined. Santa Anna at once started to the support of Valencia the brigade of Francisco Pérez, 3,000 strong, moving from Coyoacan, and hastened himself from San Antonio, taking two more regiments and five pieces of artillery—the reinforcements whose approach had been observed from Zacatepec. By five o'clock in the afternoon of the nineteenth, the reinforcements were drawn up on the heights in front of San Angel—and the Americans, having started out to get on Valencia's flank or rear and to cut his line of retreat to Mexico, were isolated from any prompt support. Totaling fewer than 3,500 men, the three American brigades plus one regiment, without a gun or a horse, found themselves squarely between two forces, either of which exceeded them in number and both of which were well furnished with cavalry and artillery. "The enemy," wrote Riley, indulged the hope that he had the Americans "cornered . . . ready for his next morning's capture." The situation was one which a bold and enterprising Mexican commander, with unity in command and the confidence of his troops, might well have turned into a major American disaster—and Scott's army could not afford disasters.[9]

But the boldness and enterprise, the unity and confidence, that evening were in the American camp. The late afternoon was spent by the Mexicans in fruitless reconnoiterings of the American brigades, at that time partly in Ansaldo and partly in San Gerónimo. The last hour of daylight was spent by Persifor Smith, who had taken command of the detached American forces in the ravines, in preparing for an attack against the reinforcements which were to be seen massing on the heights toward San Angel. But darkness intervened, and with the darkness came a cold, heavy rain which, throughout the night, poured upon American and Mexican alike.

Santa Anna withdrew his infantry to the shelter of the houses of San Angel and dispatched a messenger to pass around the American position, on the heights to the west, with orders to Valencia to spike his guns, abandon his camp, and make his way in the darkness back to San Angel, lest in the morning he be cut off and defeated in detail. But Valencia, intoxicated by the events of the afternoon of August 19, had no remotest idea of defeat. "After a desperate combat with all the Anglo-American forces," he wrote, he had "put them to shameful flight" and only required the help of the troops with Santa Anna at San Angel to "destroy the miserable remains of the Anglo-Americans, who are shut up in Ansaldo. . . ." At the same time, through general orders issued, he awarded to "all the generals, chiefs and officers who participated in this glorious battle, the promotions to which they are entitled." The order to withdraw, Santa Anna wrote, he "scorned and disobeyed."[10]

But while Valencia was inditing his announcement of victory, Lieutenant Z. B. Tower reported to General Smith at the village church of San Gerónimo, that he had been scouting up the ravine which led toward the southwest, and that "though very difficult," it offered a way practicable for infantry that led to the rear of Valencia's entrenched camp!

"We were, at most," General Smith wrote, "three thousand, three hundred strong, and without artillery or cavalry; and it was evident that we could only maintain our position . . . by the most prompt and energetic action. I therefore directed an attack on the works at the entrenched camp, by turning their rear before day."

Captain Lee, who was present at the conference of brigade commanders to whom this "prompt and energetic action" was outlined,

volunteered to return in the darkness across the Pedregal to inform
General Scott that Smith would march to the attack at 3:00 A.M., so
that any "diversion that could be made . . . from that side might be
prepared accordingly." The captain set out, to pick his way among
the boulders and across the fissures and chasms, without landmark to
guide him and with no light other than the fitful flashes of the light-
ning of the storm, all the while running the added risks of falling in
with a Mexican picket, or of being shot by mistake upon his approach
to an American sentry. It was, altogether, a journey which General
Scott was afterward to describe as "the greatest feat of physical and
moral courage performed by any individual, to my knowledge," during the campaign. General Scott spoke with the more emphasis because of seven staff officers sent out that night to cross the Pedregal,
not one got through.

About eight o'clock Lee, in the valley at the foot of the lava field,
met General Shields and the brigade which Scott had sent from Quitman's division to reinforce the Americans west of the Pedregal. Making arrangements for Shields to put himself in touch with Smith, Lee
kept on his hazardous journey, first to the command post at Zacatepec,
which he found deserted, and then to Scott's headquarters at San
Agustin. There, toward midnight, he reported that Smith, who would
move to the attack at 3:00 A.M., asked that "a powerful diversion be
made against the centre of the entrenched camp towards morning,"
but would make the attack in the rear "at all hazards," whether or
not a diversion was made in front.

Shortly after Captain Lee's report was received, Generals Pillow
and Twiggs, who had sought without success to go to the forces across
the lava, came into headquarters. To Twiggs, General Scott gave orders to return to the lava, collect what forces he could find, and make
the diversion about five o'clock in the morning—an enterprise in
which Twiggs was to have the indispensable help of Lee, who once
more, and for the third time in that day's work, was to cross the
Pedregal.[11]

Meanwhile, back at San Gerónimo, the troops stoods to their arms,
huddled in the rain in the lanes and corn and maguey fields of the
village, while the young engineer officers made a more careful reconnaissance, so that they might be able better to lead the heads of the
attacking columns to their positions in the darkness before dawn. At
midnight, General Shields and his brigade made their way into the
village—to bring the American total force to about 4,000. Shields

ranked Persifor Smith, who was a brigadier by brevet only, but Smith knew the situation and had made the plans and Shields, with rare generosity and good sense, refused to complicate things by claiming his rank. Instead, he furnished the answer to one of Smith's major problems by supplying a force which would remain in San Gerónimo and protect the rear.

At half past two in the morning, the columns of assault began to form. Riley was to go first, with Lieutenant Tower showing the way, to be followed by Cadwalader, guided by Lieutenants Beauregard and Brooks. Smith himself would march with Cadwalader's brigade, while his own brigade, under Major Justin Dimick, and guided by Lieutenant G. W. Smith, would close the column. So dark was the night that the men were ordered to touch one another from rear to front, in order that they might not lose the way as they stumbled and slid over the rough and slippery track up which they were to advance. The march started at 3:00 A.M., as ordered, but the difficulties of the way slowed down the movement and strung out the column, so that day broke long before the position for attack could be reached.

Meanwhile, General Twiggs and Captain Lee had found the batteries and supporting troops which had been withdrawn from the position opposite Padierna about 10:00 P.M. to bivouac on the lava near Zacatepec. From this bivouac they started, about one in the morning, to the positions from which they were to create the daybreak diversion. General Pierce, having been severely injured when his horse fell, could not accompany the troops, and the command devolved upon Colonel Trueman B. Ransom, of the Ninth Infantry—the "New England" regiment.[12]

By reason of the difficulties experienced by Smith's men, the daybreak battle was actually begun by Ransom's command, which opened fire and attracted the attention of Valencia while Smith was quickly and quietly making his dispositions for attack from the rear. Then, with Riley on the right, supported by Cadwalader, and Dimick on the left, Smith's men fired and, with bayonets fixed, charged headlong into Valencia's position. The Mexican infantry turned and the gunners worked frantically to reverse their pieces and open fire where no enemy had been anticipated. But the apparition of the Americans from the rear, combined with fire from in front, was too much—and in seventeen minutes by the watch the fighting was over and the flight had begun.

"His excellency, the general-in-chief, Don Gabriel Valencia, disappeared from among us, at the commencement of the battle," reported the second-in-command, General Salas, former President of the Republic. The cavalry, which General Salas tried to rally, he reported as "trampling under foot the infantry" in its retreat, as the fugitives streamed down the road toward San Angel. To make the route more stunning and complete, Shields's brigade—which earlier presented a bold front to reinforcements hovering on the heights to the northward—opened fire from the roadside near San Gerónimo.

Before the sun was well above the horizon, the Army of the North had ceased to exist as a military unit. Seven hundred of its men were killed, more than 800 captured, the rest scattered in flight. Seven hundred pack mules, great stores of small arms and ammunition, and twenty-two guns, were taken. The capture which gave greatest delight to the victors was made when Captain Simon Drum of the Fourth Artillery, closely followed by Lieutenant Calvin Benjamin bearing the color of the regiment, retook the two identical field pieces which another company of the same regiment had lost, though without loss of honor, on the field of Buena Vista.[13]

So ended, with a loss by the Americans of only sixty, killed and wounded, the first battle of August 20.

As General Smith was forming his column for the organized pursuit, General Twiggs, his division commander, arrived and took command. At San Angel, where a few more prisoners were made, General Pillow came up and took over, directing the advance to Coyoacan, with intent to move from there upon the rear of the Mexican entrenched position at San Antonio, on the main Acapulco road. The general in chief, having passed to the front by way of San Angel, overtook the column of pursuit and took command at Coyoacan.

At this juncture, the main intent of the Mexican commander seems to have been to withdraw his troops from advanced positions and concentrate on the inner line of the *garitas,* or gates, at the heads of the several causeways which reach the city across the marshy ground that, in the time of Cortes, had been the bed of the great lake in which the Aztec city of Tenochtitlán stood. From San Angel, Santa Anna dispatched aides with his orders—to Gaona and Bravo, holding Mexicalcingo and San Antonio, to fall back on the causeways to the Candelaria and San Antonio Abad gates; to Rangel, whose brigade had marched out to San Angel only the day before, to return to the Citadel by way of the bridge of Panzacola and the Niño Perdido gate; to Rincon, whose Independencia and Bravo battalions of the National Guard were stationed at the old Franciscan convent of San Mateo at Churubusco, to hold his position; to Pérez, to post his brigade along the Rio Churubusco at, and on both side of, the works at the bridge where the Acapulco road crossed. Santa Anna himself hastened to the bridge, crossed it, and thereafter took little more personal part in the battle which the impetuosity of the American pursuit soon precipitated.[14]

Had the Americans known the southwestern approaches to the city as they were afterward to learn them, or had they even paused for reconnaissance upon reaching Coyoacan, the chances are that the bloody battle of Churubusco might not have been fought as it was. Apparently the forces at Churubusco were intended to do no more than fend off the American onslaught for a season. There were practicable roads from Coyoacan and San Angel to Mexico which, in fact, the Americans used in their subsequent movements and which would have avoided the Churubusco position. But these were afterthoughts. In the ardor of pursuit, time was taken for no more than the sketchiest and most limited of reconnaissance. There was no opportunity for concealment of intentions, no chance for wide strategic turning movements—just headlong, impetuous and persistent attack against works which were bravely and stoutly held.

Taking over the command at Coyoacan, Scott sent Pillow with Cadwalader's brigade on the road toward San Antonio, two miles to the southeast, to carry out the purpose for which the whole turning movement had been undertaken, of taking that fortified post in the rear. Smith's brigade, soon to be followed by Twiggs with the other brigade of his division, under Riley, was sent against the fortified convent which the Americans persisted in calling San Pablo, less than a mile distant to the northeast. "Next (but all in ten minutes)," General Scott reported, he sent Pierce, "just able to keep the saddle" after his injury of the day before, under the guidance of Captain Lee, to move northward from Coyoacan, cross the river west of the Mexican position, and advance across fields and ditches to strike the main highway leading from Churubusco to the city on the enemy's right and rear. This movement was soon reinforced, upon the arrival of Shields's brigade, by sending it on the same mission.

But before even these hasty arrangements could be completed things began to happen at San Antonio. The first move, about 11.00 A.M., was made by Worth, who sent Clarke's brigade to the left, into the northern part of the Pedregal, to find passage around the works of San

Antonio and take them from the rear, without waiting for the arrival of the troops who were coming the long way around from Padierna. As Clarke's brigade emerged from the Pedregal, Garland's brigade and the artillery were to advance from the front. Under orders from Santa Anna, General Bravo's men did not await an attack from either front or flank, but commenced the evacuation of San Antonio to retreat along the highroad to Churubusco, two miles away.

Coming out of the Pedregal, Clarke's flanking column discovered the Mexican movement and by a rapid charge cut the column nearly in center, just about the time that Garland's brigade, which had been awaiting the signal for action, came through the undefended works with a rush, fell upon the Mexican rear, and drove its way forward to join Clarke's men, some 600 yards beyond the works. The reunited division hastened on against the works at Churubusco—Clarke's men in front advancing on the road; Garland's, coming on a little later, inclining to the right to make their way forward through the muddy fields of corn, more than head-high.[15]

Almost at the same time—maybe a little sooner, maybe a little later—Twiggs's men began to come into action against the convent, and Pillow and Cadwalader, seeing the retreat of the San Antonio garrison, left the road on which they were marching toward that point, and pushed their way eastward across marshes and ditches, and through the corn, to join in the attack.

The Rio Churubusco was a canalized stream, rising in the mountains southwest of the city and flowing almost straight east between mounded banks planted with maguey, to fall into the outlet of Lake Xochimilco. Where the Acapulco highroad crossed the stream there was a bridge, the southern end of which had been fortified with embankments, rising fifteen feet from the bottom of the wet ditch to the top of the parapet, and with emplacements for half a dozen guns— the *tête de pont* which looms so large in the American reports. South of the bridge, a quarter of a mile, were the houses of a village. About the same distance southwest of the bridge was the old convent church of San Mateo, surrounded by its enclosure of massive adobe walls a dozen feet high, behind which scaffolding had been placed with firing platforms for infantry. The position was further strengthened by entrenchments outside the walls and by emplacements for seven guns. The two main positions of defense, the convent and the church, were so situated as to offer mutual support, while both of them supported, and were supported by, the lines of infantry which took position under the protection of the raised banks of the canalized river.

The fight which came on a little after noon lasted about three hours. It was, in fact, not one fight but at least three, going on simultaneously and in large part without reference one to the other. On the right there was Garland's brigade of Worth's division, making its way through the corn, with the heavy slugs from the Mexican *escopetas* noisily ripping through blade and ear and stalk, perhaps to find a mark in the body of some American soldier. Driving up the road, partially blocked with broken-down Mexican ammunition wagons, was Clarke's brigade of Worth's division, to be forced off the road by the fire of the *tête de pont* and to seek the illusory safety of the cornfield, but always—like Garland's men—to return to the attack. On the left of the road was Cadwalader's brigade of Pillow's division, trying to fight its way into the fire-swept space between bridgehead and convent, and finally, crossing the road to join the advance in the cornfield.

Farther to the left, Smith's brigade of Twiggs's division went against the southern face of the convent, to find that it was a considerable work and strongly held—much more so than anyone had realized when the attack was launched. Riley, still farther to the left, attacked the convent position in flank and completed the assaulting line of the United States forces on the south side of the stream.

Across the stream, facing east and moving against the Mexican line of retreat was, first, Pierce's brigade, soon to be reinforced by Shields, who took command; and finally, when Captain Lee reported that Shields was hard pressed and having difficulty in making good his attack, reinforced by detachments of the rifles and the dragoons, under Major E. V. Sumner.

Thus the Americans were attacking, stubbornly, all across the front of the Mexican position and also on its right, in the direction of the ranch Portales, three quarters of a mile in rear of the bridge, and the village of San Andres Landrillera, still farther back, where, Santa Anna reports, he was in personal charge of the defense. The defense, on the entire front, was steady, answering fire with fire, and breaking up and driving back with heavy loss every attempt to rush the works.[16]

On the American left, the Palmetto regiment of Shields's brigade lost its colonel, Pierce Butler, who, already wounded, remained in the advance until he was shot in the head; lost its lieutenant colonel, John P. Dickinson, mortally wounded; and finished the battle under Major Adley H. Gladden, who, fifteen years later, would yield his life on the field of Shiloh, leading other troops from South Carolina. In the other regiment of the same brigade, from New York, Colonel Ward Burnett was wounded, and the command passed to Lieutenant Colonel Charles Baxter. Sergeant Major James L. O'Reilly, advancing with the national colors, was three times wounded. As he fell from his third, and fatal, wound, the flag was seized by Corporal Lake, who was immediately shot down. The flag was again saved, as he fell, by Orderly Sergeant Doremus. Disabled that day by wounds were two of Pierce's colonels—George W. Morgan, subsequently a brigadier general of the Union Army, and M. L. Bonham, to become Brigadier General Bonham, C. S. A.[17]

At length, however, the time came when the Mexican resistance could no longer be sustained. Ammunition supplies had begun to fail; the attackers had worked their way up to positions for the final assault. Almost simultaneously, the final drives came on the three main fronts of action. The bridgehead, which had repulsed earlier charges, was charged again by the Fifth and Eighth infantry regiments pelting up the causeway, with the support of other regiments on either side. Among the first to enter the bridgehead was Captain Larkin Smith, who promptly seized one of the Mexican guns, brought it to bear on the still-resisting convent and opened fire. On the other side of the convent, at almost the same time, another Captain Smith— James Madison, of the Third Artillery serving as infantry—led the party which first stormed into the work, and received its surrender. Some of the defenders escaped but the capture of the convent netted 1,200 prisoners, among them the interim President Anaya.

With his troops "disheartened," and with Shields's, Pierce's and Sumner's men pressing against his line of retreat, it seemed to Santa Anna that it was necessary "to fall back without loss of time," which he did, arriving at the Candelaria gate between five and six o'clock.

The battle was over except for dashing pursuit up the causeway to the gate of San Antonio Abad, led by Captain Philip Kearny of the dragoons. In the ardor of the pursuit, the leading horsemen did not hear, or did not heed, the recall sounded by Colonel Harney from the rear. When they ran into a storm of musketry and artillery fire, Kearny ordered his men to dismount and carry the works. "But when I looked around," wrote Lieutenant Richard Stoddert Ewell, "to my horror, I found the Dragoons retiring some distance in the rear . . . Colonel Harney had ordered the recall to be sounded . . . we were engaged while the rear was retreating." Kearny himself, fighting his way into and back out of the works, lost an arm but remained in the service to lose his life in fending off Confederate forces in the retirement from Second Bull Run. Major F. D. Mills of the infantry, who had accompanied the pursuit as a volunteer, was shot down and killed within the gate—the first of the United States soldiers who would meet such a death. The heavily punished troop was brought back from the *garita* by Lieutenant Ewell, who had two horses shot under him on the way but lived to spend years at frontier posts learning all there was to know about commanding fifty United States dragoons and forgetting all about everything else, as he was to put it, and cap his military career by commanding a corps of the Army of Northern Virginia.[18]

The cost to the United States Army of the battles of August 20 totaled 137 killed, 879 wounded, forty missing—or about one man in seven of those commands engaged. More than nine tenths of the loss was at Churubusco, which on that August afternoon was truly what it had been called by the Aztecs—*Huitzilipochco,* the place of the war god Huitzilopochtli, a name Hispanicized into Churubusco. The heaviest regimental loss was that of the Palmetto regiment from South Carolina, which suffered more than one tenth of all the casualties in the army. The Sixth Infantry of the regulars, which first went against the bridgehead, suffered almost as severely.

Much of the loss was attributed by the Americans to the skill and desperation with which Mexican guns were served by the San Patricio battalion, made up of deserters from the United States forces—sixtynine of whom were captured when the bridgehead and convent fell.

The fruits of the victory, as outlined by General Scott in his report, were "about 3,000 prisoners, including eight generals (two of them ex-presidents), and 205 other officers; killed or wounded 4,000 of all ranks—besides entire corps dispersed and dissolved; captured 37 pieces of ordnance—more than trebling our siege train and field batteries—with a large number of small arms, a full supply of ammunition of every kind, &c, &c." The last was a point of particular importance to an army which had no other source of replenishment for its magazines and ammunition wagons.

"These great results," the general concluded, "have overwhelmed the enemy."[19]

"After so many victories, we might, with but little additional loss, have occupied the capital the same evening," General Scott reported.

"But Mr. Trist, commissioner, &c., as well as myself, had been admonished by the best friends of peace—intelligent neutrals and some American residents—against precipitation; lest, by wantonly driving away the government and others—dishonored—we might scatter the elements of peace, excite a spirit of national desperation, and thus indefinitely postpone the hope of accommodation. Deeply impressed with this danger; and remembering our mission—to conquer a peace . . . I halted our victorious corps at the gates of the city. . . ."

On the same evening, having reached the city between five and six o'clock, General Santa Anna "retired to the [National] Palace, possessed of a black despair," and there assembled "the ministers and other persons of distinction" to whom he reviewed the events of the day, and explained that it was imperative to secure a truce for breathing time. J. R. Pacheco, foreign minister, was authorized to seek the assistance of the British Consul General Mackintosh and the Spanish Minister to bring about such a result. The Spanish Minister took no part in the proceedings but Consul General Mackintosh and Mr. Thornton, of the British Legation, drove out in the early evening to see General Scott, who had returned to his headquarters at San Agustin. Their visit was "ostensibly to ask for a safeguard for the English Minister and British subjects," noted Colonel Hitchcock, "but really to prepare the way for peace."

What passed between General Scott and his British visitors is not otherwise recorded but the actions of the following day indicate that the conversation further inclined Scott to listen to overtures for an armistice. He had, indeed, done what he said he would do in defeating the Mexican army in the very sight of its capital, and he had grounds for believing that the Mexican Government would now not only be willing, but politically able, to negotiate a peace. He determined, therefore, to advance on the morning of August 21, and "take up battering or assaulting positions" which would authorize him "to summon the city to surrender." Accordingly, headquarters was put in motion early on the twenty-first, to move from San Agustin to Tacubaya, a residential suburb only two and one half miles southwest of the city, and less than a mile due south of the fortified hill of Chapultepec.[20]

As Scott reached Coyoacan, toward noon of the twenty-first, he was met by General Mora y Villamil, chief of engineers in the Mexican service and a man of substantial character, bearing notes to Mr. Trist from Charles Bankhead, the British Minister, with which was transmitted a note from Señor Pacheco addressed to Secretary Buchánan.

Having still in mind the decree of April 20 imputing treason to one who might initiate peace negotiations, Señor Pacheco's letter was, in form, a reply to the letter from Secretary Buchanan which Mr. Trist had found so hard to deliver. The outcome of battles, Señor Pacheco noted, did not always accord with the justice of the causes for which they were fought; the President of the Mexican States had fought until the troops of the United States were at the very gates of the capital; and now, under his constitutional powers to receive ministers and negotiate treaties, he would hear what sort of proposals for peace Don Nicolas Trist had to offer, provided they were such as would accord with the honor of the Mexican republic. For the immediate present, he proposed that there be a truce of a year, while the Mexican Government would undertake to discuss "preliminaries of peace" which would have to be submitted "according to the constitution of the country, for the approval of the authority to which such matters appertain."[21]

Scott, after halting at Coyoacan long enough to read, with Trist, such a proposal to gain a year's time with no assurance of peace, promptly rejected such terms and sent in to Mexico his own "contemplated note to President Santa Anna, omitting the summons" to surrender.

The note opened with one of those peculiarly infelicitous phrases which made letter writing so dangerous a pursuit for General Scott. "Too much blood has already been shed in this unnatural war between two great republics of this continent," wrote the general, as an introduction to saying that he was "willing to sign, on reasonable terms, a short armistice," although he would, in the meantime, "occupy such positions as he deemed necessary to the shelter and comfort of his army."

The reply of Santa Anna, which Scott had said he would await "with impatience," came in the shape of a letter from Minister of War Alcorta, and took the attitude that Scott had asked for an armistice, which Santa Anna would grant. While doing so, the letter lectured Scott on the disregard of the rights of the Mexican people which had led inevitably to the "lamentable . . . shedding of blood by the two first Republics of the American continent," which, with "great exactness," he had "characterized as unnatural." As to the quarters which the American army would take up, the Mexican President was willing that they should be commodious and comfortable, but hoped they would be found "beyond the range of shot from the Mexican fortifications." Generals Mora y Villamil and Quijano were named to conclude the discussion of an armistice.

Such a letter gained time for Santa Anna, committed him to nothing, and sounded well in the newspapers. But Scott was sincerely anxious for peace, and trusted that Santa Anna entertained like sentiments, so to meet the Mexican generals he named—on August 22—Generals Quitman, Smith and Pierce. The commissioners, Mexican and American, met that afternoon at the house of Consul General Mackintosh in Tacubaya, where they sat up all night arguing about the exact phraseology of some of the points, but finally arrived at an agreement which was submitted on the twenty-third to the two commanding generals.

The terms arrived at were that "for the purpose of enabling the government of Mexico to take under consideration the propositions which the commissioner for the President of the United States has to make," hostilities would cease immediately and absolutely within thirty leagues of the capital. The armistice was to continue while negotiations were going on, or might be terminated on forty-eight hours' notice by either party. No fortifications were to be begun or enlarged, neither army was to be reinforced, nor to advance its positions. Supplies, translated *recursos* and interpreted to exclude arms and munitions, were to be allowed to pass into the city, and to be secured by the Americans from city or country. There was no definite undertaking that the armistice was the first step in the making of peace. There was no guarantee, and no requirement that the American army be permitted to occupy the commanding position of Chapultepec, as some of Scott's officers urged.

Both commanding generals accepted the terms, with minor modifications which were mutually acceptable, and on August 24 the military armistice went into effect, within thirty leagues of Mexico, while the diplomatic representatives sought a basis for a broader and more enduring peace.[22]

---

[1] Ex. Doc. 1, Sen., 30th Cong., 1st sess., p. 349; Ex. Doc. 65, Sen., 30th Cong., 1st sess., p. 462.

[2] Ex. Doc. 1, Sen., 30th Cong., 1st sess., p. 304; Ex. Doc. 65, 30th Cong., 1st sess., pp. 536, 541; Ramsey (ed.), *The Other Side*, pp. 268-274; Rives, *U. S. and Mexico*, II, 462-465.

[3] Ex. Doc. 1, Sen., 30th Cong., 1st sess., pp. 322, 340-342; Ex. Doc. 65, Sen., 30th Cong,. 1st sess., pp. 470-471.

[4] Ex. Doc. 1, Sen., 30th Cong., 1st sess., p. 306; Appendix, pp. 83, 126.

[5] Ex. Doc. 1, Sen., 30th Cong., 1st sess., pp. 322, 326, 333; Ex. Doc. 65, 30th Cong., 1st sess., pp. 79, 463.

[6] Ex. Doc. 1, 30th Cong., 1st sess., pp. 323, 324, 326; Appendix, pp. 66-69, 101-103.

[7] Ex. Doc. 1, Sen., 30th Cong., 1st sess., p. 332; Appendix, p. 84; Ex. Doc. 65, Sen., 30th Cong., 1st sess., pp. 332, 333.

[8] Ex. Doc. 1, Sen., 30th Cong., 1st sess., pp. 326, 334; Appendix, pp. 19, 20; Ex. Doc. 65, Sen., 30th Cong., 1st sess., pp. 147, 332, 333.

[9] Ex. Doc. 1, Sen., 30th Cong., 1st sess.; Appendix, p. 92; Ex. Doc. 65, Sen., 30th Cong., 1st sess., pp. 536-537, 541.

[10] Ex. Doc. 65, Sen., 30th Cong., 1st sess., pp. 537-541; Rives, U. S. and Mexico, II, 473, 474, quoting correspondence between Valencia and the Minister of War as published in Santa Anna's Apelacion al buen Criterio; Ripley, War with Mexico, II, 212, 213, 239, quoting correspondence as published in the Diario del Gobierno, August 21 and 22, 1847.

[11] Ex. Doc. 1, Sen., 30th Cong., 1st sess., pp. 306, 327; Appendix, pp. 79, 92; Ex. Doc. 65, Sen., 30th Cong., 1st sess., p. 73 (General Scott's statement). An outstanding feature of the first battles in the Valley of Mexico is found in the extraordinary exertions of Captain Lee, and the unusual recognition of his services, not only in the official reports of every general officer whom he assisted, which is virtually all of them, but also in the private diaries and letters of the time—all written, of course, without benefit of the reflected light of his career in the Confederate Army. To Inspector General Hitchcock, he was "'the' engineer." (Croffut [ed.], Fifty Years, p. 277). To Lieutenant Ewell, who was to become one of his lieutenants, he was one "whose daring reconnaissances pushed up to the cannon's mouth have enabled General Scott to fight his battles almost without leaving his tent." (Hamlin, Percy G. [ed.], The Making of a Soldier [Richmond, 1935], pp. 68-69). Raphael Semmes, future rear admiral of the Confederate States Navy, published in 1851 an unusually accurate and comprehensive estimate of the captain: "a mind which has no superior in its corps . . . great energy of character . . . judgment, tact, and discretion worthy of all praise. His talent for topography was peculiar, and he seemed to receive impressions intuitively, which it cost other men much labor to acquire." (Semmes, Service Afloat and Ashore, p. 379.)

[12] Ex. Doc. 1, Sen., 30th Cong., 1st sess., pp. 327, 328, 342; Appendix, pp. 88-92, 105-107. For Pierce's injury, see Nichols, Pierce, p. 161.

[13] Ex. Doc. 1, Sen., 30th Cong., 1st sess., pp. 307, 308, 328, 329, 331; Appendix, pp. 89, 93, 112-115; Semmes, Service Afloat and Ashore, p. 389. Scott promised that the "Buena Vista guns," appropriately inscribed, should be given to the Fourth Artillery "in perpetual token of its achievement." The Fourth was left at Contreras to provide for the wounded, bury the dead and secure the prisoners and captured guns, equipment and supplies.

[14] Ex. Doc. 1, Sen., 30th Cong., 1st sess., p. 308; Ex. Doc. 65, Sen., 30th Cong., 1st sess., p. 538.

[15] Ex. Doc. 1, 30th Cong., 1st sess., pp. 309, 310, 316, 338; Appendix, pp. 41, 42.

[16] Ex. Doc. 1, Sen., 30th Cong., 1st sess., pp. 310-313, 317, 318, 324, 330, 331, 338, 339; Appendix, pp. 47-52, 105-107, 117, 118.

[17] Ex. Doc. 1, Sen., 30th Cong., 1st sess.; Appendix, pp. 128-134.

[18] Same, pp. 313, 330, 331; Appendix, pp. 64-66; Ex. Doc. 65, Sen., 30th Cong., 1st sess., p. 539; Hamlin, Making of a Soldier, p. 72.

[19] Ex. Doc. 1, Sen., 30th Cong., 1st sess., pp. 313, 314, 348, 431-446. Colonel Hitchcock's report of prisoners taken on the twenty-ninth totaled 2,637. An account of the fighting from the Mexican side is given in Ramsey (ed.), The Other Side, pp. 282-299. Just as the Mexican army had its "San Patricios" the Americans had

Dominguez' "Spy Company" of Mexicans, recruited at Puebla from among the professional highwaymen on the road between Mexico and Vera Cruz, whose peacetime occupation had been disturbed by guerrilla warfare. The "Spy Company" was said to have fought with exceptional ferocity in opposition to the "San Patricios." There was difference of opinion among the Americans as to the value of their services.

[20] Ex. Doc. 1, 30th Cong., 1st sess., p. 314; Ramsey (ed.), *The Other Side*, p. 301; Rives, *U. S. and Mexico*, II, 494-496; Croffut (ed.), *Fifty Years*, p. 280.

[21] Ex. Doc. 52, Sen., 30th Cong., 1st sess., pp. 189-190; Rives, *U. S. and Mexico*, II, 496-499.

[22] Ex. Doc. 1, Sen., 30th Cong., 1st sess., pp. 308, 314, 356-359; Ex. Doc. 52, Sen., 30th Cong., 1st sess., pp. 192-193, 310-313, 350-354; Ramsey (ed.), *The Other Side*, pp. 300-306. The negotiations are discussed at length in Rives, *U. S. and Mexico*, II, 500-508.

The Storming of Churubusco.

CHAPTER 21

"A Few More Such Victories——"

ON AUGUST 25, 1847, Mr. Trist notified Señor Pacheco that he was ready to take up the negotiation for peace contemplated in the armistice approved the day before. Señor Pacheco suggested, on the next day, a meeting on the afternoon of the twenty-seventh. The slight delay was due to difficulty in securing commissioners willing to accept the task of treating for peace. First choice for the head of the commission was ex-President Herrera, but General Herrera, mindful of what had made him an ex-President, declined to serve for the reason that any terms which he might arrange would "be badly received" by a public which had driven him from office for even thinking of talking peace with the United States. To this, however, Santa Anna answered that one of the strongest reasons for desiring the ex-President's presence on the commission was that it would demonstrate that "two distinct administrations . . . have agreed on the essential point that it is proper for us to hear" propositions for peace. Thus persuaded, the patriotic ex-President consented to serve.

Other commissioners were secured and, on August 27, one week after the day of Churubusco, the commission met with Mr. Trist. Waiving the point that the Mexican commissioners presented powers authorizing them merely to hear what the United States wished to propose, and to "do nothing else," the American commissioner delivered, at the first meeting, the draft of a treaty which had been entrusted to him by Secretary Buchanan nearly five months before—thereby opening negotiations by "giving away" his position and his bargaining power.

Seeking once more to secure Congressional sanction for negotiation with the Americans, on the day after Churubusco Santa Anna requested President Salonio of the Mexican Congress to call that body

348

into session. Only twenty-six members appeared—a quorum being seventy-one. With Congress thus avoiding any share of the odium of talking peace, the President and his Cabinet felt their way forward, most gingerly, toward some goal of opportunity which probably was undefined even in the mind of Santa Anna himself.[1]

The rugged and tortuous pathway to peace was made no smoother by a riot in the city the morning of the day the commissioners were to have their first meeting. In accordance with the provisions of the armistice, a train of United States Army wagons went into the city that day to purchase supplies. By the time they had penetrated to the central plaza, opposite the National Palace, they were surrounded by a shouting mob, which soon became a stone-throwing mob, demanding "death to the Yankees!" Several teamsters were injured, one killed. After some delay, Mexican lancers dispersed the crowd, and the wagon train was drawn off to safety, but without the supplies for which it had come. The government made suitable explanations, which Scott accepted, and it was arranged that in future supplies would be drawn from the city at night, more or less clandestinely. But the affair was a discouraging beginning for a peace negotiation.

On the third day after receiving Secretary Buchanan's proposals for peace, the Mexican Cabinet issued instructions to its peace commissioners. These instructions were so wholly impractical as a basis for negotiation and so completely tied the hands of the negotiators that the commissioners promptly and unanimously resigned. But that was not the intended effect of instructions which seem to have been designed for "home consumption," partly to appeal to national pride and partly to relieve the government of the odious responsibility of authorizing concessions. Consequently, on the next day the instructions were modified, and the commissioners, in whose "hands the nation placed its honor and liberty," returned to their work. On September 1, and succeeding days, at the "House of Alfaro, on the Chapultepec Causeway," they discussed with Mr. Trist, earnestly and unreservedly, the differences between the nations.[2]

"In New Mexico," said Foreign Minister Pacheco after the negotiations were over, "and in the few leagues which divide the right bank of the Nueces from the left bank of the Bravo," the question of peace or war was contained. The statement is more rhetorical than exact. On the question of cession of territory—for a consideration to be agreed upon—Trist departed from the original draft proposed to the extent of eliminating the peninsula of Lower California, and also enough of Upper California to provide a connection by land with Sonora. He was willing, too, to exceed his authority by submitting to Washington a proposal that the Nueces should be the boundary of Texas, with the zone between that stream and the Rio Grande—including the present Valley region of Texas—to be kept vacant and unsettled as a buffer between the two nations.

As to questions other than the cession of territory, the Mexican commissioners withdrew the original demand that slavery must be prohibited in any territory acquired by the United States from Mexico—a demand which reflected the policy of the Wilmot Proviso. But it was insisted that, in addition to whatever was paid for the cession of territory, the United States should make compensation to Mexico and Mexicans for war costs and damages—in effect, indemnity from the winner to the loser.

But Mr. Trist did not have to take up with Washington the Texas boundary proposals, for on September 6, after consultation with their own government and in accordance with its determination, the Mexican commissioners presented as their final word a counterproject for a treaty which not only was inadmissible in its terms but was accompanied by a note suggesting that Great Britain be asked "to grant its guarantee for the faithful performance of the treaty which may be concluded." For an answer to this astonishing proposition three days were allowed, but Mr. Trist's answer was given orally and immediately. The negotiations were at an end.[3]

By its own terms, failure of the peace negotiations was to bring the armistice to an end. General Scott, however, put the termination upon the ground of violations of the armistice terms in the matter of provisioning of the American army and the matter of military preparations within thirty leagues of Mexico. On the day negotiations ended, therefore, he called for "explanation, ratification, and if possible, reparation" for the violations alleged, failing which he would consider the armistice terminated at noon of the seventh.

Once more General Scott had exposed his flank to dialectic attack. President Santa Anna indignantly repelled the charge of armistice violation. With "pain and indignation," moreover, he told of what he had heard of cities sacked, sacred vessels robbed and churches profaned by the American soldiery. With "profound affliction" he described "the complaints of fathers and husbands upon the violation of their wives and daughters." He had kept silence, he said, lest he hinder the negotiations to end a war which Scott himself had "justly characterized as unnatural," but he knew, and the world soon would know, that the real cause for the renewal of hostilities was refusal to sign a treaty which would diminish and dishonor the republic. To save the "first city on this continent . . . from the horrors of war," there would be left no recourse other than "to repel force by force."[4]

"And now, alas," wrote Captain Ephraim Kirby Smith, "we have all our fighting to do over again."[5]

It was to be done, moreover, with an army which, what with death, wounds and disease, was nearly 2,000 weaker than it had been on the morning of Contreras seventeen days before. During those days, the several commands had remained in the same positions in which the suspension of hostilities found them—army headquarters and Worth's division at Tacubaya; Pillow's division at Mixcoac, two miles to the south; Twiggs's at San Angel, another three miles southward; and Quitman at San Agustin, six miles more to the southeast. In strict compliance with the armistice, no arrangements had been made, and no plans laid, for the resumption of hostilities.

On the evening of the day on which he gave notice of the termination of the armistice, General Scott called together some of his officers, most informally, "to consider the best mode of threatening and attacking the city." It was agreed that plans would await a full reconnaissance which, it was hoped, would show that the approach to the city through the southern gateways was "more eligible than this southwestern approach" from Tacubaya, barred as it was, or at least flanked, by the "formidable castle on the heights of Chapultepec."[6]

On the next morning, after receiving Santa Anna's answer for war, Scott connected the observed movement of Mexican troops from the city with information which had come to him the night before that church bells were being cast into cannon at what he was told was a foundry in certain massive old stone buildings west of Chapultepec. From this, he conceived the unfortunate idea of sending a small force to seize the foundry, destroy its machinery and material and retire—an operation strictly limited in scope and value, and expressly no part of any plan for general attack upon the city or even upon Chapultepec.

The Molino del Rey, the supposed cannon foundry, formed the western end of the walled enclosure of the park of Chapultepec. The buildings extended 500 yards in a north-and-south direction, about three quarters of a mile west of the palace but within range of its

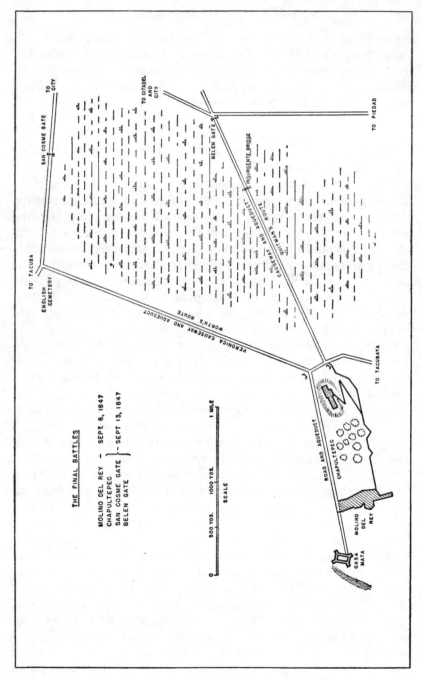

THE FINAL BATTLES

MOLINO DEL REY — SEPT. 8, 1847

CHAPULTEPEC
SAN COSME GATE } SEPT. 13, 1847
BELEN GATE

SCALE

0   500 YDS.   1000 YDS.   1 MILE

TO CITY

SAN COSME GATE

TO CITADEL
AND
CITY

TO PIEDAD

TO TACUBA

BELEN GATE

INSURGENTE BRIDGE

CAUSEWAY AND AQUEDUCT

QUITMAN'S ROUTE

ENGLISH CEMETERY

VERONICA CAUSEWAY AND AQUEDUCT

WORTH'S ROUTE

TO TACUBAYA

ROAD AND AQUEDUCT

CHAPULTEPEC

MOLINO DEL REY

CASA MATA

352

guns. Five hundred yards west of the northern end of the King's Mill was another massive stone building, squarish, surrounded by regular bastioned entrenchments—the Casa Mata. The space between the two was occupied by a battery with infantry support. Beyond the Casa Mata was a ravine, difficult of passage, and beyond that, a mile away, the hacienda Morales, held by a strong cavalry force. The number of Mexican troops who moved into the position on September 7 was large, though exactly how large was not discovered then and is not known now. Subsequent American estimates of 12,000 to 14,000 are undoubtedly greatly exaggerated.

But regardless of the exact number of defenders, the position was strong—very strong. The flanks were in solid buildings which could defy any ordinary bombardment by field guns and were at such an angle to one another that either could deliver a flanking fire against those attacking the other, or attacking the center between them. And, too, there was a gentle slope of the ground downward from Tacubaya toward the Mexican position which almost automatically corrected the common fault of firing too high.

Against such a position Worth was to go, at dawn on September 8, 1847, with a force of 3,250 men and nine guns, leaving not so much as a garrison in Tacubaya. Writing to his wife the night before what would prove to be his last letter, Captain Kirby Smith—who, because of the illness of C. F. Smith was to command the light battalion in the assault—observed with foreboding that "tomorrow will be a day of slaughter."[7]

And such, indeed, it was. At three o'clock in the morning the assaulting columns began to move. "When the gray of the morning enabled them to be seen, they were as accurately in position as if posted in midday for review," wrote General Worth, who was in entire command of the operation. On the right were two 24-pounder siege guns handled by Captain Benjamin Huger of the ordnance, and the two "Buena Vista" 6-pounders of Captain Drum, to batter the Mill itself, with Colonel John Garland's brigade to storm and take possession of the place. In the center was an assaulting party of 500 picked men, chosen from different regiments, under Major George Wright. To the left, directed toward the Casa Mata, was Duncan's battery, with Clarke's brigade, commanded for the day by Colonel McIntosh. In reserve, behind the center, was Cadwalader's brigade of 784 voltigeurs and infantry. Covering the left flank was Major Sumner, with 270 cavalry.

After the briefest of bombardments, the attacking columns were launched, to be driven back by terrific converging fire. In the picked party under Major Wright, eleven out of fourteen officers fell, killed or wounded, with a nearly proportionate loss in the ranks. As the first assaulting column staggered back, the light battalion went in, with one of Cadwalader's regiments, to retrieve the fight in the center. On the left, McIntosh's men moved forward with Duncan's battery firing over their heads. In their advance the infantry masked the fire of the supporting battery and arrived within thirty yards of the Casa Mata—to find the work surrounded by impassable ditches and themselves with no means of crossing. McIntosh was struck down, his second-in-command, Martin Scott, was killed, the third in rank, Major Waite, was desperately wounded, men of all ranks were falling "almost by platoons and companies" from the deadly musketry. The brigade broke back, rallied, and, with the help of one of the regiments from Cadwalader's reserve, was returning to the attack when the line of the enemy began to fail.

Farther to the left, across the ravine, hovered a cloud of Mexican horse. Their orders from Santa Anna, given the day before, were to cross the ravine at a place under protection of the Casa Mata and fall upon the flank of any American attack. Major Sumner, however, with his 270 men, boldly crossed first, within pistol shot range of the Casa Mata, and for the remainder of the engagement maneuvered and bluffed back the overwhelming mounted force opposed to him. The "numerous cavalry" of the Mexicans, as one of their writers put it, remained "cold spectators of the conflict."[8]

On the right, there was no well-defined pattern of attack, repulse, and rally, but rather a confused advance by small parties and even individuals, some exchanging musketry fire with the Mexicans on the parapeted roof of the Molino del Rey, others trying to find, or break, a way through some one of the few openings into that forbidding range of buildings. Finally, a gate at the southern end of the building was battered in, and, almost at the same moment, another at the northwestern corner, where Captain Robert Anderson—to be remembered as "Anderson of Fort Sumter"—was wounded as, "with great heroism," he led the way in. Assaulting parties began to fight their way through the gloom of the interior. Many of the Mexicans, after obstinate resistance, made their way out of the building into the grove of

Chapultepec. Others, on the roofs and cut off from retreat, surrendered.

Meanwhile, to the north of the buildings, Lieutenant Colonel William Montrose Graham, four times wounded, kept on with the fight until he fell with a fifth, and fatal, wound, as his men carried the position. A portion of the Mexican battery had imprudently been left outside the position. As the Americans advanced against it, the Mexican General Leon, commanding the National Guard, led a brave sortie from the works to save the guns. The sortie came too late and General Leon fell, as the Americans seized the guns and turned them against the Mexican lines. Persistent attack in the face of all losses and continued fire from the American guns caused even the determined defense of the Mexicans to waver. With the capture of the Molino del Rey and the loss of the battery, General Pérez, in the Casa Mata, cut off from direct contact with Chapultepec, began a retreat to his right and rear.

But these several retreats were to be no such routs as those in the earlier battles. General Peña y Barragan rallied the forces retreating along the north face of the Chapultepec hill and returned to the attack, not once but twice. When these counterattacks were broken up, the battle—after two hours of fighting—was over and the entire position was in American hands. Eager search failed to disclose any cannon foundry or any evidence of recent activity in casting cannon. A store of powder was found in the Casa Mata, which was overhastily blown up, adding to the death toll of the day another dozen men.

General Worth, now holding the western way into the Chapultepec enclosure, sought permission to follow up his advantage by an assault upon that position. Scott, not believing himself to be ready for such a venture and still hoping that he would be able to capture the city without the necessity for it, reiterated his orders to return to Tacubaya. The position won at such cost, and to so little purpose, was sullenly abandoned, and the "sad mistake" of Molino del Rey was over.

The fruits of the victory were the capture of 680 prisoners and three guns, and the infliction upon the enemy of a loss in killed and wounded which was not known but which Worth estimated, in his report, at above 2,000. The cost to the Americans was 117 killed, 653 wounded, eighteen missing—total casualties of almost one fourth of the command engaged—in less than two hours of fighting.[9]

Colonel Hitchcock, writing by the light of a midnight candle, spoke truth when he observed, "We were like Pyrrhus after the fight with Fabricius—a few more such victories and this army would be destroyed."[10]

---

[1] Ex. Doc. 52, Sen., 30th Cong., 1st sess., pp. 193, 309, 310, 313-326, 351, 352, 355-365; Ramsey (ed.), *The Other Side,* pp. 309-313, 315.

[2] Ex. Doc. 52, Sen., 30th Cong., 1st sess., pp. 330-335, 369-373; Ramsey (ed.), *The Other Side,* pp. 313-315, 318, 319.

[3] Ex. Doc. 52, Sen., 30th Cong., 1st sess., pp. 195-202, 335-346, 373-380; Ramsey (ed.), *The Other Side,* pp. 321-328; Rives, *U. S. and Mexico,* II, 508-515.

[4] Ex. Doc. 52, Sen., 30th Cong., 1st sess., pp. 346-348, 381, 382; Ex. Doc. 1, Sen., 30th Cong., 1st sess., pp. 359-361; Ramsey (ed.), *The Other Side,* pp. 329, 330.

[5] Kirby Smith, *To Mexico,* p. 216.

[6] Ex. Doc. 1, Sen., 30th Cong., 1st sess., p. 355; Croffut (ed.), *Fifty Years,* pp. 293, 395.

[7] Kirby Smith, *To Mexico,* p. 217.

[8] Ramsey (ed.), *The Other Side,* p. 339. American artillery fire from across the ravine, and the advance of a party of voltigeurs aided in keeping the Mexican cavalry out of action.

[9] Reports of General Worth and subordinate commanders are in Ex. Doc. 1, Sen., 30th Cong., 1st sess., pp. 354-356, 361-375; Appendix, pp. 134-166. Major Borland and Major Gaines, of the Encarnación prisoners, who had escaped from the Mexicans, acted as volunteer aides at Molino del Rey.

[10] Croffut (ed.), *Fifty Years,* p. 298.

Molino del Rey—Chapultepec in the distance.

CHAPTER 22

"The Halls of the Montezumas"

B UT other victories there had to be, and speedily, for attrition
was taking its steady toll of an army which could expect neither
reinforcement nor replacement.

On the day before the battle of Molino del Rey, on that day, and
on the days which followed, the engineers were at their reconnaissances of the approaches to Mexico, particularly the gates across the
southern face of the city from the outlet of Lake Xochimilco on the
east to the Belén gate at the city's southwestern corner. On the day
after Molino del Rey, Pillow moved forward from his post at Mixcoac to occupy the village of Piedad, half a mile south of the Belén
gate, where an east-west road crossed the causeway leading to that
entrance to the city. As reconnaissances continued during the next
three days, the fortifications at, and between, the southern gates were
extended, more guns were emplaced and an inundation spread over
the fields between the causeways.

General Scott accompanied the engineer officers on September 9
and again on the eleventh. That afternoon an informal council was
held in the church at Piedad. Most of the engineers who expressed
themselves agreed with Captain Lee in favoring the attack from the
south, although, as Lee afterward testified, such an attack would have
been easier on the ninth or tenth than at any time afterward. Most
of the general officers, too, looked with favor upon the attack from
this direction. One engineer, Lieutenant Beauregard, "expressed
himself strongly" in support of the idea of coming in from the west.
The general in chief announced that "to avoid the net-work of obstacles" on the south, he would "seek by a sudden inversion to the
southwest and west, less unfavorable approaches" to the city.[1]

To cover the real movement, however, the apparent threat against

357

the southern front must be kept up. Scott therefore ordered Quitman to march conspicuously by daylight to join Pillow at Piedad, after which the combined commands would countermarch by night to join Worth at Tacubaya. Pillow's place at Piedad would be taken by Twiggs, who was to maneuver actively and keep up the threat of attack from that direction.

"The first step in the new movement," Scott wrote, "was to carry Chapultepec," a position which, by reason of its historical associations and its formidable appearance, exercised upon the imaginations of both sides an influence out of proportion to its considerable military importance. It was not a fortress or a castle, as the Americans usually called it. In the time of the viceroys it had been a summer palace and, since 1833, had been the home of the Mexican Military College. The buildings crowned a narrow ridge of rock, rising to a height of nearly 200 feet above the plain, with its highest point and steepest slopes toward the city. The hill and surrounding gardens and groves were enclosed within walls, twelve or fifteen feet high, which extended east and west nearly a mile. The western end of the enclosure was the Molino del Rey. On the south side there was one narrow gateway, protected by an outwork. On the southeast, there was another gate, also fortified. The armament consisted of thirteen guns. The garrison within the work numbered fewer than one thousand soldiers and the corps of cadets of the military college, all under command of Nicolás Bravo, one of the old revolutionaries who had fought the Spanish, and former President of the republic. Outside the works and approaching on the causeways from the city there were considerable reinforcements—perhaps 4,000 men; but they came too late to affect materially the outcome of the struggle for the Hill of the Grasshoppers itself.

On the night of the decision to attack this hill—Saturday, the eleventh—batteries were laid out on the southern and southwestern fronts, under the supervision of Captain Lee, and guns were emplaced under the direction of Captain Benjamin Huger, of the ordnance. On the morning of the twelfth the bombardment began, directed by Huger, who as a Confederate division commander would never produce quite so decisive an effect as resulted from that day's bombardment. Mexican accounts relate that for fourteen hours the American guns kept projectiles in the air, with "the greater part of their discharges taking effect." Much of the victory of the thirteenth was achieved by the guns of the twelfth.

Under bombardment, General Bravo called for reinforcements, again and again, but Santa Anna was of no mind to expose more troops to the shaking effect of the sustained fire. Twiggs, moreover, was carrying out his assignment of demonstrating against the southern gates so well that it was not until too late that the Mexican commander was persuaded that Chapultepec and the western gates were to be the real object of the attack.[2]

During the day of the twelfth preparations went forward for the assault of the morrow. This was to be no hasty affair such as Molino del Rey; for this, as everyone knew, was to be the decisive affair of the war.

At three o'clock on Sunday morning, the twelfth, Pillow's men seized again the unoccupied buildings of the Molino del Rey and also the Casa Mata. During the day an additional battery was emplaced at the Molino, bearing on the palace. Early in the night Quitman moved his troops into position opposite the southeastern corner of the palace grounds. Pillow, at the same time, put the remainder of his command in position on the southwest and west. The assault was to be made by these divisions, reinforced with storming parties of 250 men from each of the veteran regular divisions, Twiggs to furnish the party for Quitman; Worth, for Pillow. Scaling ladders, pickaxes and crowbars were to be issued to assaulting parties.

Final instructions, given Sunday night, brought Worth's division forward in reserve near the Molino del Rey, as a support for Pillow, and P. F. Smith's brigade, of Twiggs's division, to support Quitman. The bombardment was to be resumed at daylight of Monday, the thirteenth, until the signal for the concerted advance of the assaulting divisions should be given by the momentary cessation of fire from the heavy batteries. That moment came at a little after eight o'clock, when the heavy guns fell silent and the assaults were launched.[3]

Pillow's division advanced from the west in three groups. On the right, outside the south wall of the park, were Lieutenant Colonel Joseph E. Johnston with a voltigeur battalion and Worth's storming party under the veteran Captain Samuel MacKenzie, ordered to make their way to, and through, a gate in the wall about half a mile to the eastward.

On the left, outside the northern side of the enclosure, were Colonel William B. Trousdale with two of the new regular regiments and a section of guns under Lieutenant Thomas J. Jackson. In the center, issuing from the buildings of the Molino del Rey, on a front of about

500 yards between the two walls, were three of the new regular regiments, the other battalion of the voltigeur regiment, the voltigeurs' mountain howitzer battery of Jesse Reno and a section of John Magruder's guns, all under Cadwalader. Pillow himself advanced with the force inside the enclosure.

There the advance was slowed by marshy footing and made uneven by the boulders and the giant cypress trees, within the shelter of whose trunks there was some lingering, followed by forward rushes from tree to tree. Even so, the advance was soon through the ancient grove and at the edge of an open space. Ahead was the fortified acclivity leading up to the massive retaining walls of the platform on which the castle stood.

MacKenzie's storming party had been delayed in making its way through the gate on the south wall and getting into position, but the lower works immediately ahead were carried without waiting for them. They were carried so rapidly, in fact, that advancing Americans and retreating Mexicans became so intermingled that the lieutenant who was to have fired the land mines on which the defense relied hesitated to touch his match to the powder trains. As he hesitated, the Americans cut and stamped out the trains, and no mine was exploded.

Halfway up the slope, however, the advance was stopped by a wide, deep ditch at the base of the retaining wall which supported the terraces of the palace above. There the advancing infantry and voltigeurs and the mountain howitzers which had kept up with them took such shelter as they could find and kept up a searching fire against windows and walls, while waiting for the men with the scaling ladders to come up.

While the troops were making their way thus far from the western end, Quitman was encountering greater difficulties on the east. His advance was to have been up the Tacubaya-Mexico road, which passed by the eastern end of the hill. But the road was cut before him, batteries were emplaced and long lines of infantry reinforcements had come out from the city. As the advance was held up, P. F. Smith undertook to move off into the marshy ground on the right of the road and work his rifle regiment into position to take the Mexican batteries and infantry entrenchments in reverse. At the same time Shields, with his own brigade and the Second Pennsylvania out of Watson's brigade, inclined to the west toward the south wall of the park. Fire from the batteries caused heavy loss. Shields himself received his third wound in as many battles during the war; Lieutenant Colonel

Baxter, commanding the New Yorkers, was mortally wounded; Lieutenant Colonel Geary, commanding the Pennsylvanians, was struck. The South Carolina regiment reached the wall, and went to work to breach it with picks and crowbars. The other two regiments passed farther along the wall; found the same gateway through which Joe Johnston's voltigeurs and MacKenzie's storming party had passed earlier; went through the gate into the park and, for the remainder of the action, were part of the movement of Pillow's forces.

When MacKenzie's storming party arrived at the ditch below the castle it was found that the men detailed to carry the scaling ladders had put them down to use their arms as they passed through the grove and had failed to pick them up again when they came on. Pillow, wounded, sent word to Worth "to bring up his whole division, and make great haste, or he feared it would be too late." Worth promptly dispatched Colonel Clarke's brigade; but, before it could get into position to affect the course of events, the scaling ladders had arrived and the final asault had begun.[4]

Men of all commands, intermingled, leaped into the ditch and fought to get the ladders up, so they could mount them. First into the ditch was Lieutenant Lewis A. Armistead, of the Sixth Infantry. Almost immediately he was wounded. He was to be wounded again on the field of battle sixteen years later as, with hat on the point of his sword, he waved to his brigade to follow him over the stone wall of the cemetery at Gettysburg—and to die that night in the hospital of the corps commanded by Major General Winfield Scott Hancock, his fellow lieutenant in the Sixth at the storming of Chapultepec. Not far behind Armistead was Lieutenant James Longstreet who, "advancing, color in hand," was shot down. The flag he carried was caught up and carried on by a very young lieutenant, George E. Pickett, barely more than a year out of the Academy—the same Pickett who, at a nod from this big, bearded Longstreet, would launch his division on the charge in which Armistead, and many another, would lay down their lives.

Mayne Reid, young English-born lieutenant of the New York regiment, who had obtained permission to leave the battery to whose working he was assigned and go forward into the assault with a party made up of New York volunteers and marines, was wounded. He survived his wound, to return in time to England and, through his fifty or so books for boys, to delight a whole generation of lovers of adventure.

The first man to succeed in placing a regimental color on the palace wall, Captain Moses Barnard of the voltigeurs, was twice wounded. The commanding officer of the Ninth, or New England, regiment, Colonel Trueman B. Ransom, was shot dead. Major Thomas H. Seymour, his successor in command, pressed on to cut down the Mexican flag from its staff above the palace.[5]

Meanwhile, at the eastern end of the Chapultepec enclosure, Quitman was delivering his attack. There, the Mexicans stood firm. "For a short time the contest was hand-to-hand; swords and bayonets were crossed, and rifles clubbed." Major Levi Twiggs, of the marines, was killed. Captain Silas Casey, who that day commanded the storming party from the Second Division and one day would command a division of the Army of the Potomac before Richmond, was severely wounded. The command of the stormers fell upon Captain Gabriel Paul, who would command Union brigades at Fredericksburg, at Chancellorsville and at Gettysburg, where a Confederate rifle ball would shoot out both his eyes. His storming party included, on the day of Chapultepec, Lieutenant Frederick Steele, who would lead one of Grant's divisions at Vicksburg; Lieutenant Daniel Harvey Hill, a studious young artilleryman who would lead a Confederate corps; and Lieutenant Barnard Bee, who would die in the first great battle of the next war, after bestowing upon Jackson his name of "Stonewall."[6]

Even determined resistance failed against the drive of the assaulting parties, and as the cessation of fire from the garrison's guns above showed that the palace itself had fallen, the defenders about the eastern end of the enclosure gave way—and Chapultepec was taken, entire.

The storming of Chapultepec had taken just an hour. In that hour the Mexicans lost brave officers and men killed, including General Francisco Pérez, who had led the final charge at the Angostura and had defended the bridge at Churubusco. They lost distinguished prisoners, including General Bravo and General Mariano Monterde, Superintendent of the Military College. They lost a fortress of interesting historical associations but of no very formidable military strength. But with all their losses, the Mexican army and the Mexican nation gained from Chapultepec an imperishable tradition in the story of "Los Ninos"—the boy cadets of the Military College—defending the flag, keeping up the fight to the last, even in some cases yielding their lives rather than to surrender.[7]

The fall of Chapultepec did not end the day's fighting. Just outside the walls of the park, on the northern side, Colonel William Trousdale's two regiments still were engaged with the heavy reinforcements under General Peña y Barragan which had marched out from the city. Trousdale himself was wounded and the advance of his troops—led by Lieutenant Colonel Paul O. Hébert, future leader of Louisiana troops in the armies of the Confederacy—was held up. Out in front of the infantry was that stern and stubborn Lieutenant Jackson, his horses and many of his men shot down and one gun of his section disabled; but with his remaining gun, which he had advanced across a ditch by hand, he was still blazing away at the enemy. And there he stayed until support and reinforcements came—Garland's brigade of infantry and Magruder with more guns. Lieutenant Jackson that day, his commanding officer said, displayed the "highest qualities of a soldier—devotion, industry, talent and gallantry."[8]

From Chapultepec, the Americans passed immediately to the offensive against the city. Two ways were before them. One, the causeway Verónica, with an aqueduct carried on masonry arches along its center, ran northeast two miles to the English cemetery. There it reached the Tacuba causeway—the same on which Cortes had retreated on the *noche triste*—and turned at a right angle to enter the city by the northwestern gate of San Cosmé. The other causeway, also carrying an arched aqueduct along its center with a roadway on either side, ran almost due east, directly to the southwestern gate of Belén. Both causeways were crowded with troops, interrupted with barricades and covered by the fire of artillery. An advance on either, in the face of opposition, was not to be lightly undertaken.

With Garland's brigade leading, Worth took the causeway leading to the San Cosmé gate. Quitman, with his own division and numerous others who in the confusion and commingling of commands had attached themselves to his advance, took the shorter and more direct road to the city. Scott sent two brigades to support Worth's move and one to support Quitman, and he himself followed Worth, whose column had the longer way to go but the lesser defenses to carry and so was intended to make the main attack. With Scott rode Captain Lee, but for one time in the campaign the commanding general would not have the services of his indefatigable engineer; for Lee, after almost three days of ceaseless activity without sleep or rest, fell from his horse in a faint.[9]

While the intention was that Worth should make the main attack, this did not prevent Quitman and his men from pressing forward, sometimes on the road, sometimes in the ditches alongside, most of the time advancing in small squads from the shelter of one narrow archway of the aqueduct to the next. The defenders made a stand at the Insurgente bridge but were pushed back to the southwestern gate. There Santa Anna himself was organizing the defense, bringing up men and guns that had been held at the southern *garitas* to meet the threat from Twiggs's troops.

At twenty minutes past one o'clock, as noted in the reports of the several commanders, Quitman's men were inside the gateway. Ahead of them was the open space of the Paseo and, 300 yards away, the massive stone building of the Citadel and the buildings of the Belén prison, with men and guns enough in them so that there would be no more advancing that afternoon. Instead, it was with some difficulty that the attackers held what they had gained. It was here that Simon Drum and Calvin Benjamin, who had been compelled to leave their beloved "Buena Vista" guns behind but were serving pieces captured from the Mexicans, were killed. Their battery-mate, Fitz John Porter, future major general who would suffer injustice for his part in the Union defeat of Second Bull Run, was wounded. John Brannan and Z. B. Tower, likewise to become general officers of the Union Army, were wounded. Loring lost an arm, and four other future Confederate generals—Beauregard, Earl Van Dorn, Mansfield Lovell, Gladden—suffered wounds.[10]

While Quitman doggedly held on to his position within the Belén gate, Worth was working away at the entrance to the city on the northwest. The first barrier, halfway to the English cemetery, was carried in a "handsome movement" led by Captain Horace Brooks of the Second Artillery and Lieutenant U. S. Grant of the Fourth Infantry. Other barriers were carried in like fashion until the angle where the way turned sharp to the right was reached and carried. From this point on, the way entered a section solidly built up with houses. From this point, also, the Mexicans made determined resistance throughout the late afternoon and early evening.

The expedient of Monterey was once more adopted. The American infantry began burrowing its way, with picks and crowbars, through the walls of house after house on both sides of the road. Meanwhile, Captain Oscar Edwards of the voltigeurs—who had succeeded to the command of the mountain howitzers of that conglomerate body when Lieutenant Reno was wounded at the foot of Chapultepec—brought up his little guns. Eager soldiers assisted in hoisting them to the roofs of houses on both sides of the road—Lieutenant U. S. Grant and the future Confederate naval commander Raphael Semmes among them. So successfully did young Grant handle the gun which he emplaced that his brigade commander reported that he "acquitted himself most nobly," and his division commander sent an aide, Lieutenant John C. Pemberton, to bring Grant to him. It was the first recorded meeting of men who, on July 3, 1863, at a critical time for the Union, would meet between the lines at Vicksburg to discuss terms for the surrender of that embattled fortress.

But while infantry was boring its way through the walls and the mountain howitzers were spitting fire from the roofs on either side, the road between was swept by fire from Mexican guns at the embrasured barricade. Into the fire-swept street advanced Lieutenant Henry Hunt with one gun and eight men—five of whom were to be struck. The time was to come when Major General Henry J. Hunt, Chief of Artillery of the Army of the Potomac would become the master organizer of artillery for massed fire; but on this day, as he and his men advanced their piece in what General Worth was to call a "brilliant exhibition of courage and conduct," he was simply a *gunner,* pushing his weapon up to the enemy's breastwork "muzzle to muzzle."[11]

Late in the afternoon, as the pressure against Rangel's defenders at San Cosmé persisted, an urgent call was sent for the presence of Santa Anna himself. By the time he reached there, however, Worth's men had forced their way past the barrier—although fighting would go on into the night.

Rightly realizing that the entrances to the city were breached, Santa Anna hastened back to the Citadel, where he assembled a council of war. There still were—or were supposed to be—some 5,000 Mexican infantry and 4,000 cavalry in and about the city, but to Santa Anna and his junta the situation seemed hopeless. It was accordingly determined to abandon the city at once, collect what troops remained— many had deserted—and move out of the city to the northern suburb of Guadalupe Hidalgo. By one o'clock on the morning of Tuesday, September 14, 1847, the evacuation, carried out in the utmost confusion, was complete. All that remained was the surrender and occupation of the city.[12]

The municipal government took over when the national government, in the person of General Santa Anna, departed. A deputation of the *ayuntamiento* showed up at Worth's headquarters at one o'clock in the morning, seeking terms of capitulation. The deputation was sent on to Scott, who had retired to Tacubaya after the fighting died down for the night. To the request of the deputation for terms, conditions and guarantees, Scott replied that he had had enough of such negotiations, and that the American army would enter the city "under no terms, not *self*-imposed." The deputation was sent back to the city about four in the morning, and at daylight orders were sent to Worth and Quitman to advance, with caution, from their out-lying positions to the center of the city.

But before word from the commanding general was brought to Quitman by Captain Lee, he had already had direct communication from the Mexicans in his front. As he was preparing to open fire from batteries at which his men had labored all night, a flag of truce came from the Citadel, to tell him that the Mexican army had marched out and to request that he march in. Lieutenants Lovell and Beaure-gard—both wounded the evening before—volunteered to go forward as scouts to "ascertain the truth of this information." When they waved from the ramparts of the Citadel, the whole command moved forward, finding the place and its fifteen guns abandoned, except for a Mexican officer left behind to take a receipt for the post and its war matériel—which no one was interested in signing.

Hearing that depredations were being committed in the National Palace, Quitman left garrisons at the gate and in the Citadel and ad-vanced to the Grand Plaza, which he reached at seven in the morn-ing. There, disposing his troops along the west and south sides of that great square, he entered the National Palace; ordered Captain Benjamin Roberts of the rifles—a soldier who in the coming war would command Union troops in combat in New Mexico and Vir-ginia and half the states between—to raise the American flag; directed that the plunderers be driven out; and installed as garrison and guard Watson's battalion of United States Marines—the veritable marines whose presence and police power in the "halls of Montezuma" is commemorated in the song of their corps.[13]

Worth, meanwhile, had sent Lieutenant McClellan and a party to scout as far as the Alameda and the streets between that pleasant park and the central plaza, and had followed with his column, marching along the northern side of the Alameda to turn along the east side to the site of the present National Theatre. There, before seven o'clock, the head of the column was halted, to await the coming of the general in chief.

About eight, General Scott arrived, with staff and escort all in full dress, to lead the march through the Street of the Silversmiths and of Saint Francis (the present Avenida Francisco I. Madero) to the central square. With the dragoon band playing "Yankee Doodle" and all the drums beating, the column turned right, then left, to form lines facing the Cathedral. General Scott dismounted, passed along the front of the troops, uncovered, and passed into the portals of the National Palace. There, after warning his entourage that they "must not be too elated at success," he presented to them the new "civil and military Governor of the City of Mexico, Major General John A. Quitman."[14]

Hardly had General Scott occupied the Great Plaza and the National Palace when firing broke out from "the flat roofs of the houses, from windows and corners of the streets, by some two thousand convicts liberated the night before by the flying government—joined by, perhaps, as many Mexican soldiers who had disbanded themselves and thrown off their uniforms."

"This unlawful war," General Scott continued in his report, "lasted more than twenty-four hours, in spite of the exertions of the municipal authorities, and was not put down until we had lost many men." Scott was in no position to be losing men. In the fighting of the thirteenth he had lost 130 killed and 704 wounded. In all the fighting in the valley his army had lost, in killed and wounded, more than 2,500, with a sick list of another 2,000. The army of more than 10,000 which had left Puebla less than six weeks before had lost forty per cent of its effective strength, and now was reduced to about 6,000 men.

Street firing was an accepted feature of political and military disturbance in Mexico; but with only 6,000 Americans, isolated and alone in a hostile city of nearly 200,000 people, it was not to be tolerated. Stern measures of repression were taken, including artillery fire upon houses from which shooting came. The major disturbance was over by the sixteenth, but for several nights thereafter nocturnal assassinations, and reprisals, were painfully common. The bodies of as many as nine Americans, most of them knifed, were found on one morning.[15]

On the sixteenth General Scott issued general orders calling upon every man to observe "compactness, vigilance and discipline" as "our only securities." On the following day he republished—this time as G. O. 287—his "martial law order." To help maintain peace and order in the city, Lieutenant Colonel C. F. Smith was put in command of a body of 500 special American military police, co-operating with the regular Mexican police.

In connection with the restoration of order, General Scott levied upon the city, through the *ayuntamiento,* a contribution of $150,000, payable in four weekly installments. The proceeds of this, the only military contribution levied, were to be used for the purchase of extra comforts for the sick and wounded in hospital and of blankets and shoes for the rank and file of the army.[16]

Three days after the martial-law order was reissued its text appeared, in English and Spanish, in the pages of Vol. I, No. I, of the bilingual *American Star,* the Spanish side of which bore at its masthead the name of *Estrella Americana.* Even this early, on September 20, confidence had begun to be restored to the point that Messrs. John H. Peoples and James R. Barnard, publishers, were able to carry advertisements of the theatrical company of Messrs. Hart and Wells, the professional cards of an American dentist and a "doctor of physic and surgery," and the announcement of a "private boarding house for officers only," conducted by Mrs. A. Tobler.

The major story in the issue, however, was the account of the punishment of the San Patricio deserters, after trial and sentence by court-martial. A dozen men whose desertion had taken place before the outbreak of hostilities, the story related, had been flogged and branded on the cheek with a "D." Sixteen had been hanged at San Angel on the ninth, four more at Mixcoac the next day. Thirty others had been hanged on the thirteenth, at the very day and hour of the storming of Chapultepec, having been "let live long enough to see the flag raised on the castle." The punishment seemed savage, particularly in view of the fact that so many of the deserters were not natives or citizens of the United States, and that some of them, no doubt, had had provocation for their desertion in what an intelligent Scottish soldier in the ranks described as the "various degrading modes of punishment, often inflicted by young, headstrong and inconsiderate officers, in their zeal for the discipline of the service, for the most trivial offenses. . . ."[17] But regardless of provocation the crime of desertion in time of war, compounded by taking service with the enemy and against their comrades, was great. The situation of the American army, moreover, was one in which the luxury of leniency such as might have been extended in later and safer times could not be afforded.

The issue of the *Star* published a week later was less forbidding and depressing in content. Two executions for mutiny and drunkenness on guard, set for September 22, had been suspended. A thousand Mexican women were at work for the quartermaster in the Custom House making clothing for the ragged and in many cases nearly naked soldiers, and others wanted similar jobs. The Grand Teatro Santa Anna, with its named changed to the National Theatre—described as "the most magnificent in the world"—would open on the following Sunday with a troupe of Italian opera singers. On the same day Mr. Bensley of the American Circus would stage a grand Bull Fight, with 14,000 seats available. The Eagle Coffee House was offering, in addition to food and drink, such other drugstore items as patent medicines, soap, toothwash and an oil which would make hair grow. But more significant than these and other signs of American business activity was the statement that "nearly all the stores and *tiendas* of the city are 'Open for Business.' "

---

[1] Ex. Doc. 1, Sen., 30th Cong., 1st sess., pp. 426-428; Ex. Doc. 65, Sen., 30th Cong., 1st sess., pp. 77, 80, 313; Basso, Hamilton, *Beauregard* (New York, 1933), p. 44.

[2] Ex. Doc. 1, Sen., 30th Cong., 1st sess., pp. 376, 377; Ramsey (ed.), *The Other Side,* pp. 353-360.

[3] Ex. Doc. 1, Sen., 30th Cong., 1st sess., pp. 378, 400, 401.

[4] Ex. Doc. 1, Sen., 30th Cong., 1st sess., pp. 378, 379, 391, 401, 402; Appendix, p. 203; Semmes, *Service Afloat and Ashore,* p. 454.

[5] Ex. Doc. 1, Sen., 30th Cong., 1st sess., pp. 378, 379, 403, 410-413, 417; Appendix, pp. 183, 198, 203.

[6] Same, pp. 378, 379, 410, 413.

[7] Elliott, *Winfield Scott,* p. 546; Ripley, *War with Mexico,* p. 423; Ramsey (ed.), *The Other Side,* p. 363.

[8] Ex. Doc. 1, Sen., 30th Cong., 1st sess., pp. 380, 391, 403; Appendix, p. 196.

[9] Ex. Doc. 1, Sen., 30th Cong., 1st sess., pp. 381, 382, 385, 392; Ramsey (ed.), *The Other Side,* pp. 366, 368.

[10] Ex. Doc. 1, Sen., 30th Cong., 1st sess., pp. 382, 383, 414-416, 418; Appendix, pp. 184, 185; Ramsey (ed.), *The Other Side,* p. 370.

[11] Ex. Doc. 1, Sen., 30th Cong., 1st sess., pp. 392; Appendix, pp. 167, 170, 172, 175; Semmes, *Service Afloat and Ashore,* pp. 459, 460.

[12] Ramsey (ed.), *The Other Side,* pp. 371-373, 383, 384.

[13] Ex. Doc. 1, Sen., 30th Cong., 1st sess., pp. 383, 416, 417; Appendix, p. 191; Wilcox, *Mexican War,* p. 482; Ramsey (ed.), *The Other Side,* p. 375.

[14] Same, p. 375; Appendix, pp. 168-169; Wilcox, *Mexican War,* pp. 482, 483; Semmes, *Service Afloat and Ashore,* pp. 461-464.

[15] Ex. Doc. 1, Sen., 30th Cong., 1st sess., p. 384; Ramsey (ed.), *The Other Side,* pp. 377, 378; Wilcox, *Mexican War,* pp. 483, 484, 490.

[16] Ex. Doc. 1, Sen., 30th Cong., 1st sess., pp. 387-390.

[17] *English Soldier in U. S. Army,* pp. 281, 282.

CHAPTER 23

Peace Unauthorized but Accepted

WITH the Mexican capital firmly occupied, the principal business before the Americans became that of making peace with a nation which wanted peace, which desperately needed peace but which had no government able to make peace.

The troubles of the would-be peacemakers were not due to continued military opposition—although that was attempted—but to governmental collapse. Before there could be negotiations, months were required to organize and establish a government in Mexico. Weeks were required for negotiation of a treaty, other weeks for ratification; so the yellow-fever season had come again at Vera Cruz before the occupying army was able even to start for home.

But, even without organized armed opposition on any large scale, the small American forces isolated in the interior of Mexico had sufficient military difficulties with which to deal. The most immediate, and the most serious, was the siege of the garrison which Scott had left in Puebla when he marched for the Valley of Mexico. The siege began on the very day on which the capital fell. Two days later, in connection with the celebration of the Mexican "Fourth of July" on the sixteenth of September, the American commander was formally summoned to surrender. Colonel Thomas Childs, in command, refused, and gathered his garrison of some 400 able-bodied soldiers and perhaps half as many convalescents and about 1,500 sick in buildings in and around the Plaza and Cuartel of San José, in the massive church of Guadalupe and the fort of Loreto on the heights just outside the city.

On the same sixteenth of September, in the suburb of Guadalupe Hidalgo outside Mexico, Santa Anna called a junta of officers to decide upon a course of action. It was apparent by then that the effort

370

at a popular uprising in the city had failed. To free himself for military operations, Santa Anna resigned the Presidency and marched with the cavalry and light guns to take part in the siege of Puebla. General Herrera, second-in-command of the army, had already started toward Querétaro, 150 miles north of the capital, with the infantry and heavy artillery. The marches of both wings of the army, according to Mexican chroniclers, were marked by "the outrages of stragglers and deserters" who "left behind them, by their unbridled license, an imprint of horror on the towns through which they passed."[1]

At Puebla on September 25, claiming to have a force of 8,000 men at hand, Santa Anna summoned Colonel Childs to surrender. To the summons the colonel returned a polite but positive refusal, and the ten-day-old siege went on. In its whole course there was nothing like an all-out attack on the American positions but rather a process of wearing out the defenders through "harassing, never-ending skirmishes both day and night," combined with efforts to starve them out through cutting off food, wood and water.

A few days of this sort of warfare was all the impatient Santa Anna could stand. And besides, word had come to the besiegers—and to the besieged as well—that a strong column was on its way up from Vera Cruz. To meet, or waylay, this column, the general marched away from Puebla on October 1, taking with him some 2,500 men and six guns.

Part of the column which Santa Anna set out to intercept—more than 1,000 recruits for the regular regiments, under command of Major F. T. Lally—started from Vera Cruz on August 6, the day before Scott left Puebla for Mexico. By the time this detachment reached Jalapa after two weeks of marching and fighting with guerrilla bands, it had lost one tenth of its strength in killed and wounded, the men remaining were broken down, the animals worn out. At Jalapa, it halted.

Early in September the new regiment raised "for the war" in Baltimore and Washington took to the road and marched as far as the National Bridge. It was followed in a few days by a battalion of recruits for the regulars, under Captain Samuel P. Heintzleman, future commander of a division in the Army of the Potomac. On the nineteenth, Brigadier General Joseph Lane left Vera Cruz with the First brigade to arrive from Taylor's army in Northern Mexico, consisting of Gorman's Indiana and Brough's Ohio regiments.

On September 27 while at the National Bridge, Lane received word of the siege of Puebla. Leaving the Maryland-District of Columbia troops as a garrison at the bridge, he set out to raise the siege, gathering up the detachments ahead of him as he went. At the Castle of Perote, he added Wynkoop's Pennsylvanians and a company of the mounted rifles, commanded by the same Captain Samuel H. Walker who, at the very beginning of the war, had carried word between General Taylor at Point Isabel and the besieged Major Brown. With the combined force of some 4,000 men, General Lane marched on toward Puebla.

On the way it was reported to him, on October 9, that Santa Anna was at Huamantla, a town some miles to the right of the line of march. Leaving his trains under guard, Lane set out to find and fight him. As he approached Huamantla, Mexican horsemen were seen moving toward the town. To head them off, Captain Walker with the mounted men pushed ahead at top speed and entered the town with the Mexicans in a running fight. It was fully three quarters of an hour before the American infantry could arrive, by which time the mounted men had taken the town, driven out the Mexicans and captured two guns; but in the fight Walker himself and a dozen of his men were killed.

Leaving Huamantla to be reoccupied by Santa Anna, Lane marched on to Puebla. The beleaguered garrison there had not suffered severely in killed and wounded, with total casualties of seventy-two, but after twenty-eight days of unbroken vigilance and ceaseless strain it was wearing out. It had no more wood for cooking, other than the little which could be torn from the doors and windows of the stone houses. The last ration of beef had been issued. For days they had received half rations of bread. The water supply was under threat of interruption. Colonel Childs was confident of victory in case of assault, but it was with the utmost relief and rejoicing that Lane's force was welcomed as it marched in to raise the siege.[2]

The besieging forces, under General Joaquin Rea, fell back to Atlixco, twenty-five miles southwest of Puebla at the foot of Popocatepetl, where the government of the state had taken up its temporary quarters. Thither the zealous and active Lane pursued, by forced marches. Arriving late in the afternoon, he had a brush outside the town; but, darkness falling, he was unwilling to risk his men in street fighting in an unknown place. A few shells from his light artillery, however, brought out the municipal authorities to surrender the city and to assure him that the Mexican forces had withdrawn down the valley in which Atlixco lay.

Further military operations in the region between the capital and the seacoast were to be, almost altogether, of the sort which General Scott described as "disinfesting" the road of guerrillas and robbers. The extent to which the road was infested is indicated by the extreme difficulty with which even limited communication was maintained between Mexico and Vera Cruz. Such messages as were transmitted were reduced to the smallest possible compass for concealment—in one case, at least, a letter was baked in a loaf of bread—and secreted about the persons of daring couriers who often traveled in disguise.

Best known of the guerrilla leaders was the Spanish-born priest, Padre Cenobio Jarauta, whose operations were so active and so widespread that he appears in most of the contemporary American accounts as two persons—"Cenobio" or sometimes "Colonel Zenobia," and "Jarauta." Great hopes were entertained among the Mexicans as to the results of such activity; but it was opposed by equal activity and by greater and growing strength, and so failed to accomplish an effective and sustained interruption of the American line of supply and communications.[3]

While active garrisons were being established at all commanding places along the line of communications with Vera Cruz, the American command was observing with the greatest interest the steps taken to establish a government in Mexico with which a treaty of peace might be negotiated. Santa Anna, perhaps without intending to do so, took the first step to this end on September 16 when, in renouncing the Presidency, he undertook to designate triumvirs to carry on the government, with Manuel de la Peña y Peña as President *ad interim*. Señor Peña, however, had no intention of accepting such a designation at the hands of Santa Anna and was most understandably reluctant to assume the office under any conditions. Finally, upon the insistence of many, he did so on September 26, not by reason of Santa Anna's designation but by virtue of the newly restored Constitution of 1824 which provided for the succession to the Presidency, when there was no Vice-President, of the President of the Supreme Court of Justice, the office which Señor Peña occupied.

It was fortunate for the cause of peace that there came to the Presidency at such a time, and in his own right, a man who was patient, wise and firm. Peña y Peña had become a member of the Supreme Court in the early days of the republic, almost a quarter of a century before, had served in the Cabinet of President Bustamante and had been Minister of Relations in the Cabinet of President Herrera. As such, it was he who had reluctantly refused to receive John Slidell in 1845. Now, the war which he had tried to avert having been fought and lost, it became his duty once more to seek peace.

The first test of the authority of the new provisional government came when, on October 7, it ordered General Santa Anna to turn over command of his troops to others and to hold himself at the disposal of a council of war which would investigate his conduct of affairs. The deposed general declared in a proclamation that he was being sacrificed by those who would make "an inglorious peace"; but he turned over the command, nevertheless, and retired to the watering place of Tehuacan, eighty miles southeast of Puebla.[4]

According to the instrument of government under which Peña y Peña assumed the Presidency, he was to hold it only until Congress could convene and elect a new President *ad interim* who, in turn, would hold office only until January 8, 1848, by which time it was anticipated that a new Congress would have been elected and a new President chosen for a full term. A month after the provisional government assumed authority the American commissioner notified Luis de la Rosa, Minister of Relations, that he was ready to resume peace discussions. No formal response was made by the Mexican Government, while it waited for a quorum of the old Congress to assemble at Querétaro, the temporary capital. It was not until early November that this was accomplished, and not until November 11, after an intense factional struggle between the peace party and the several parties for war, that Pedro María Anaya, former President *ad interim,* was once more elected to that post.

The new President promptly showed himself favorably disposed to the peace negotiations by naming Peña y Peña as Minister of Relations and, on November 22—one month after Mr. Trist had signified his readiness to resume negotiations—naming commissioners to meet with the American commissioner.[5]

But here the slowly developing peace movement struck another snag; for a week before the Mexican President got around to naming commissioners to treat with Mr. Trist, the American commissioner had received from Washington letters which terminated his authority to treat and recalled him from Mexico. The letters—one of October 6 and another of October 25—were based partly on disapproval of Mr. Trist's handling of the negotiations at the time of the Tacubaya armistice after the battle of Churubusco and partly on the conviction of

President Polk and Secretary of State Buchanan that the Mexican authorities had demonstrated in that negotiation that they merely sought to gain time and not to make peace. The United States, Mr. Trist was informed, would not again offer to treat for peace but would hold itself ready to receive any proposals which might be made. In such circumstances, it was felt that the presence of a United States commissioner in Mexico could do no good, and might do harm. Trist, therefore, was instructed to tell the Mexicans that future proposals could be forwarded through General Scott, and to pack up and come home.

The commissioner's first thought was to notify the Mexican Government of his recall. He deferred the official announcement, however, until he could send word privately, through the British Legation, to the government at Querétaro. The Mexican Minister of Relations, Peña y Peña, most earnestly insisted that the United States Government had made an offer to negotiate, that despite the opposition of the war party this offer had been accepted and commissioners named, though not yet announced, and that the United States, if it wished peace, could not refuse to go ahead with the negotiations as offered and accepted.

Even so, Mr. Trist at first persisted in his plan of obeying instructions and leaving the country. But transportation and escort shortages made this difficult to do, at the moment; and by the time opportunity to leave offered, Mr. Trist had become more and more convinced that the time for peace was "now or never." He determined, therefore, to take the boldly insubordinate but, as the event proved, the wise and fortunate course of remaining to negotiate and, if a treaty resulted, to submit it to his government.

On December 6, in a letter to Secretary Buchanan which was extraordinary both for its length of more than sixty pages and its tone of studied disrespect, he gave his reasoning. Stripped of a vast verbiage, the reason expressed was his conviction that his government wanted peace; that if the present opportunity were not seized at once, all chance for making a treaty would be lost for an indefinite period, and probably forever; that no Mexican government could by any possibility go beyond the boundary which he had proposed in September; and that the United States Government's action in withdrawing its offer to negotiate was "taken with reference to a supposed state of things in this country entirely the reverse of that which actually exists." To these expressed reasons, Mr. Trist no doubt added others not expressed—the knowledge that by negotiating he would please his friend Scott, and perhaps even the feeling that he would at the same time displease the administration at Washington.[6]

While peace between the two governments was thus deferred, there were such spectacular discords among the highest ranking officers of the occupying forces as might well have misled the Mexicans into the error of believing that the fighting machine which had occupied their capital was about to break up into warring factions. The start of the controversy was over the content of official reports on the battles in the Valley of Mexico. In the opinion of General Scott, Pillow's report of Contreras unduly minimized the part played by the commanding general, and as to Chapultepec, "General S. was sorry to perceive, in General P.'s report . . . a seeming effort, no doubt unintentional, to leave General S. entirely out of the operations." A short correspondence followed early in October, replete with expressions of mutual admiration and esteem, which resulted in "General P." making the corrections suggested by "General S.," with one exception. But Scott, feeling that this was done "more to oblige me than from any conviction . . . of error," curtly replied that he was submitting the entire correspondence to the War Department, "and here," he concluded, "I suppose all further correspondence between us on the subject ought to cease."[7]

Two weeks later, hearing that the commanding general had accused him of taking two small howitzers from Chapultepec as trophies, Pillow demanded a court of inquiry. The court found that Pillow had not himself taken the howitzers and had ordered those who did to restore them, but that he had not followed up to see that his instructions were obeyed until after army headquarters had issued a general order on the subject. Pillow objected to the findings as not in accord with material fact. Scott sustained the findings, and Pillow notified him that he would appeal to the War Department.[8]

With affairs in this state of strain, there showed up in the first mail which reached Mexico from the United States a copy of the New Orleans *Picayune* of September 16 in which there appeared a letter signed "Leonidas," which represented Pillow as "in command of all the forces engaged" at Contreras, and limited Scott's participation to "giving but one order." General Pillow, it was said, "evinced on this, as he has done on other occasions, that masterly military genius and profound knowledge of the science of war, which has astonished so much the mere martinets of the profession." This particular passage, and some of the others, were shown by subsequent investigation to have been inserted as a hoax by the editors of the *Picayune,* which had reprinted the "Leonidas" letter from the New Orleans *Delta,* in which it originally appeared. But even without the *Picayune's* additions, the letter in its original form was sufficiently ridiculous in its pretensions to excite mingled amusement and indignation in the army. It did not at first, however, arouse official action.[9]

That was to come two weeks later, when the next mail brought a newspaper from Tampico, in which there was republished from the Washington *Union* a letter which had originally appeared in the Pittsburgh *Post,* in which credit for the decision to march around Lake Chalco was ascribed to General Worth. On November 12, the storm broke, with the issuance by General Scott of General Orders No. 349, calling attention to the army regulation which prohibited letter writing for publication. That would seem to have been sufficient to meet the situation, but the general, by now thoroughly angry, went on to say:

As yet, but two echoes from home, of the brilliant operations of our arms in this basin, have reached us—the first in a New Orleans paper, and the second through a Tampico newspaper. It requires not a little charity to believe that the principal heroes of the scandalous letters alluded to, did not write them, or especially procure them to be written; and the intelligent can be at no loss in conjecturing the authors—chiefs, partisans, and pet-familiars. . . . False credit may, no doubt, be obtained at home by such despicable self-puffings, and malignant exclusion of others; but at the expense of the just esteem and consideration of all honorable officers who love their country, their profession, and the truth of history.[10]

General Worth, one of those at whom the language was obviously aimed, at once wrote asking whether the order did, in fact, refer to him. The reply was that it referred to "the authors, aiders and abettors of those letters—be they who they may." Worth demanded a more explicit answer. Scott said he "could not be more explicit" for he had "no positive information as to the authorship of the letters," but that if he did have, he would prosecute the authors before a court-martial. Worth, all still on the same day, closed the correspondence with Scott, declaring that since he could get no "satisfactory answer to just and rightful inquiries" he was exercising his right to "appeal . . .

through the prescribed channels to the constitutional commander-in-chief."

Before Worth handed in his appeal for forwarding through channels, Lieutenant Colonel James Duncan, his artillery chief and the officer who conducted the Lake Chalco reconnaissance, publicly avowed himself the sole author of the "Tampico" letter, assuming full responsibility and standing on the truth of what he had written.[11] Duncan was promptly ordered in arrest.

Worth filed his appeal against what he termed the "malice and injustice" of general orders issued without "information as to the authorship of the letter." Scott, treating Worth's appeal as in itself as an act of "contempt and disrespect," relieved him of command and put him in arrest. When, on November 22, Pillow filed his appeal against the findings of the court of inquiry in the matter of the Chapultepec howitzers, he too was relieved of command and put in arrest on the grounds that the filing of the appeal was insubordinate toward the commanding officer, that the offense was compounded by his forwarding a copy of the appeal direct to the Secretary of War, as well as through channels, "to guard against the hazard of miscarriage," and that he had some connection with the "Leonidas" letter.[12]

So it was that within two months of the occupation of the capital, two of Scott's four division commanders were in arrest. A third, Quitman, had gone back to the United States, though without rancor, because there were not enough troops at Mexico to provide a command commensurate with his rank. The fourth, Twiggs, went down to Vera Cruz early in December, to take command in that department.[13]

But more generals, and more troops, were on the way up from Vera Cruz. On December 7, the first replacements for the regular regiments came in. A day later Major General Robert Patterson arrived with 3,400 men. Before the end of the month, Major General William O. Butler, who like Patterson had been with Taylor earlier in the war, was up with another 3,600 men and Lieutenant Colonel Joseph E. Johnston, who had taken the first train down to Vera Cruz, was back with 1,300 recruits. Still other reinforcements under Brigadier General Thomas Marshall were halted at Jalapa, because of an epidemic of mumps and measles, and Lieutenant Colonel D. H. Miles was preparing to leave Vera Cruz on a march on which, as it turned out, he was to lose to guerrillas 400 mules and several wagonloads of money.[14]

Before the stream of reinforcements began to arrive, General Scott received a letter from Commodore W. B. Shubrick, commanding the Pacific squadron, asking that troops be pushed through to take over the occupation of Mazatlán, the principal west coast seaport, which the navy had taken on November 11. With the defensive works which had been thrown up under the direction of Lieutenant Henry W. Halleck of the engineers—future chief of staff to President Lincoln—it was estimated that 500 regulars could hold the port, and free the ships of the squadron to strengthen the American hold on the port of Guaymas, in Sonora, which had been briefly occupied on October 20 and then given up, and to insure that the American flag be "kept flying in Lower California," where the little army garrison at La Paz and the navy landing party at San José were seriously threatened. Even as Commodore Shubrick wrote, the detachment at San José, commanded by Lieutenant Charles Heywood, was under close and prolonged siege, which was to be raised only by the fortunate arrival in the port of two whaling vessels which were mistaken by the besiegers for American ships of war. Regardless of the obvious desirability of freeing the ships for such work, Scott was compelled to decline the undertaking of pushing a small column all the way to the west coast.[15]

After the arrival of reinforcements, Scott occupied outlying positions such as Pachuca, Toluca, and Cuernavaca, and even gave consideration to an expedition to San Luis Potosí. But, he wrote the Secretary of War on December 25, any "distant expedition" would have to be postponed, perhaps for many weeks, for the new troops were coming in without the clothing and equipment on which he had counted. And then, as he sat writing on Christmas Day, all his accumulated disappointments and grievances came flooding in on him. By "excessive labor," he said, he had brought the old regiments to "respectable degrees of discipline, instruction, conduct and economy" but now "the same intolerable work, at general headquarters, is to be perpetually renewed" if the army and the country were not to be disgraced by the indiscipline of "a few miscreants in every hundred" of the new arrivals. "My daily distresses under this head," the general cried, "weigh me to the earth."[16]

Subsequently, in the last general orders of the year 1847, the commanding general admonished his troops that the honor of the country, and the particular honor of the army, "must and shall be maintained against the few miscreants in our ranks." Scott's standard of conduct was high, and he sought to encourage and enforce like conduct among his men—and, to an astonishing extent, succeeded. There were, as the British Chargé d'Affaires put it, "some outrages naturally," but it is to be doubted that there were many more than would ordinarily be experienced in a city such as Mexico. The most serious criminal affair was an attempted robbery of a Mexican business house in which an employee was killed. The crime, credited in most accounts to "volunteer officers," is described in Colonel Hitchcock's journal as the work of a regular officer who was a graduate of the Military Academy and of two volunteer officers. All three were tried by court-martial and sentenced to be hanged, but in the latter days of the occupation the sentence was commuted and the prisoners allowed to leave the country, a degree of leniency not extended to those convicted of more numerous and less serious offenses.[17]

In the main, however, the American soldiers, quartered in the barracks and monasteries in the city itself and in the outlying villages of Tacubaya and San Angel, behaved with what the correspondent of the London *Daily News* described as "unexpected moderation." The occupying troops brought with them "Yankee ice, Yankee drinks, signs, manners, habits and customs." There was the anticipated reveling in the "halls," or, as the soldier wags soon put it, the "hells of Montezuma," but there was likewise a tremendous interest taken in seeing the strange and fascinating sights of what one young Tennessee soldier called, in a letter to his parents, "cirtenly the finest city I ever saw." The soldiers enjoyed the afternoon promenades on the Alameda and the *paseos,* where all Mexico gathered to see and be seen. They enjoyed the sight of the Indian girls bringing in canoes full of flowers on the canals. They could hardly be said to have enjoyed, but they certainly were interested in, the several earthquake shocks during the occupation, and they found a minor eruption of Popocatepetl better than the biggest fireworks show they ever saw. They went to the theaters, and to the American circus, until it left the capital in January and went on the road, putting on performances at the garrisoned towns on the way to Vera Cruz. And, of course, they went to the bull fights, where most of them sided with, or even applauded, the bulls. The more studious among them delighted in the exhibits to be seen at the National Museum, and were fascinated by the mysterious calendar stone of the Aztecs, while even those who were not studiously inclined appreciated the architectural character of the churches and other principal buildings of the ancient city. "I have been in the Halls of the Montezuma," the same young Tennessee soldier wrote—presumably referring to the National Palace—"and it cirtenly is the finest building in the world."[18]

Peace, which seemed so far from either the army command at Mexico or the provisional government at Querétaro, seemed no nearer to the Thirtieth Congress of the United States, elected in 1846, when it convened in December 1847 for its first session.

With an eye to 1848, the opposition adopted an aggressively critical attitude toward "Mr. Polk's war" and everything about it except the gallantry of the soldiers and the glory of the commanders in Mexico. The war was variously characterized as an "Executive war" in its origin, "unprovoked" by Mexico, "mercenary and base" in its purposes, "iniquitous" in its intent. None of the anti-war oratory rose to the impassioned pitch of Senator Corwin's "bloody hands and hospitable graves" speech of the previous session, but there was enough of endless debating about the origin, course, purpose and consequences of the war to delay the passage of necessary measures of finance and supply. The divisions in Congress were partisan, rather than sectional. Thus, the Whigs Abraham Lincoln of Illinois and Alexander H. Stephens of Georgia—one to become the war President of the United States, the other Vice-President of the Confederate States—were in thorough agreement in their speeches that by his insistence upon the Rio Grande as the boundary of the United States, the President had begun the war "unnecessarily and unconstitutionally."

It was in his speech on this subject that the future war President declared the right of revolution in words which afterward, when he was engaged in putting down what he called a rebellion, were to be quoted against him. "Any people anywhere," he said, "being inclined and having the power have the right to rise up and shake off the existing government, and form a new one that suits them better. . . . Nor is this right confined to cases in which the whole people of an existing government may choose to exercise it. Any portion of such people that can may revolutionize and make their own of so much of the territory as they inhabit."[19]

Much time was spent on demands that President Polk identify the precise spot on the left bank of the Rio Grande which was claimed as the American soil on which American blood was shed, but the more significant discussions looked to the future. As to the nature and extent of territorial cessions as a result of the war, Congressional views ranged all the way from no annexation to the taking of the whole of Mexico. And always, implicit in most discussions and explicit in many, was the insistent question raised by the proviso called by the name of David Wilmot, whether slavery should exist in any territory which might be added to the United States as a result of the war.

Three weeks after the session of Congress began, there arrived in Washington a new source of strife—General Scott's charges against Pillow, Worth and Duncan. The President noted in his diary on December 30 his feeling that the "unfortunate collisions" were due, more than to any other cause, to "the vanity and tyrannical temper of Gen'l Scott," and that "there seems to have been no necessity to make so serious an affair of them [the objectionable letters] as to break up the harmony and efficiency of the army while in the enemy's country."

No action was taken, however, for two weeks, and then only after much consultation with Cabinet and other advisers. On January 13, 1848, at the President's direction, the Secretary of War wrote Scott that his charges against his subordinates would not be tried by court-martial until a court of inquiry had first determined whether they were justified in making the complaints against him in the appeals which were the basis of his charges. In effect, the President refused to accept the filing of an appeal from a decision of the commanding general as in itself a punishable military offense, unless it was first found that the right of appeal had been abused. The entire affair, therefore—Scott's charges and the appeals of the subordinates—were to be made the subject of inquiry by a court.

Taking note further "of the present state of things in the army," and of the general's previously expressed wish to be relieved of command, the President ordered Scott to turn over his command to General Butler, and hold himself at the disposal of the court.[20]

Reports that this order was coming reached Mexico on February 7, and became the subject of an extra edition of the *American Star* newspaper. General Scott took notice of the "unofficial announcements" that "the President has determined to place me before a court, for daring to enforce necessary discipline in this army against certain of its high officers," expressing to the Secretary of War his pleasure that the officer who would supersede him was to be Butler, and his feeling that "my poor services with this most gallant army are at length to be requited as I have long been led to expect they would be."[21]

The actual order relieving Scott of command did not reach Mexico until February 18, when it was complied with promptly and handsomely. A week later Scott completed and dispatched to the Secretary a voluminous recital of the "neglects, disappointments, injuries and rebukes" which he had received from the War Department, culminating in the act of placing the "three arrested officers, and he who had endeavored to enforce a necessary discipline against them" all before the same court.[22]

The court before which they were placed began its session in mid-March in the hall of the Supreme Court of Justice in the National Palace. The sessions were widely attended and closely followed, not only by the American army but by the Mexicans. To some among the latter, the trial was a profound demonstration of the "moral force of the American government, which, by a single slip of paper, written at the distance of two thousand leagues, could humble a proud and victorious soldier and make him descend from his exalted position."[23]

To most, though not all, of the American army the removal of Scott and the proceedings of the court of inquiry were an intensely resented outrage, the result of a cabal against the commander who had led them to victory. There was, however, another side to the story in the dualism of the character of General Scott. Simon Bolivar Buckner, who served under him and was his great admirer and loyal supporter, said of him long afterward that "he was one of the biggest men in great things and one of the smallest men in little things I ever saw"[24]—and in the embittered controversies in Mexico after the fighting was over and the claims for credit and glory began, he was dealing with things which were irritatingly small.

Toward the end of April, the proceedings of the court which had been begun at Mexico were transferred to the United States, principally at New Orleans and Frederick, Maryland. Meanwhile the quarrel with Worth and Duncan had been dropped, but the inquiry as to Pillow's claims and his connection with the "Leonidas" letter continued until July. After accumulating a record of 635 large printed pages of testimony and documents, the court of inquiry came to the conclusion that Pillow had laid claim to "a larger degree of participation in the merit of the movements" at Contreras than the facts warranted, but that since his actual conduct had been approved by Scott at the time, and had been commended subsequently in official reports, "no further proceedings against General Pillow in the case are called for by the interest of the public service."[25]

Personal, factional, and partisan differences among the Americans had their counterparts, at the very least, among the Mexicans. Throughout the months of procedural delay, a struggle went on between the peace party and the several parties which, for widely different reasons, wanted the war to continue. There were those who believed that guerrilla warfare, carried on for years, would ultimately wear out the Americans and cause them to give up and leave Mexico. There were others who frankly wished to see the whole of Mexico absorbed into the United States, and wanted the war to go on to that end. There were those, represented by ex-President Paredes, who saw in the situation a chance for the establishment in Mexico of a European monarchy; others who entertained the delusive idea that, in extremity, Great Britain would intervene on behalf of Mexico; and still others who expected that Great Britain would guarantee the terms and observance of a treaty.

Amid all these, and a variety of other currents and crosscurrents, Señor Peña y Peña came to the conclusion that it was not necessary, after all, for the Senate to confirm the commissioners named by President Anaya. On December 30, 1847, therefore, instructions were issued to proceed with the negotiation.

For Mexico, the commissioners were Bernardo Couto and Miguel Atristain, who had been members of the negotiating commission at the time of the Tacubaya armistice, and Luis Gonzago Cuevas, former foreign minister of the republic. For the United States there was no commissioner with power to act, but Mr. Trist was ready to meet and treat. Formal meetings began on January 2, in the city of Mexico. While the meetings went on, the interim term of President Anaya came to an end, without a successsor having been elected and with Congress still lacking a quorum. Peña y Peña, still presiding judge of the Supreme Court, once more stepped into the breach by virtue of that fact, and again appointed de la Rosa as Minister of Relations. Negotiations went on without a break.

Wide differences in matters of boundary and compensation were gradually narrowed until finally, toward the end of January, Mr. Trist and the Mexican commissioners came to an understanding, and the draft of a treaty was sent to the temporary capital at Querétaro for final approval. Trist, anticipating that at any moment more positive orders for his return might come from Washington, knew that he and those with whom he conferred were working against time. The Querétaro government, having difficulties of its own, was more concerned with some of the details of the treaty, particularly the evacuation of the capital and the payment of some part of the proposed compensation immediately upon signing of the treaty. Trist, finally, found

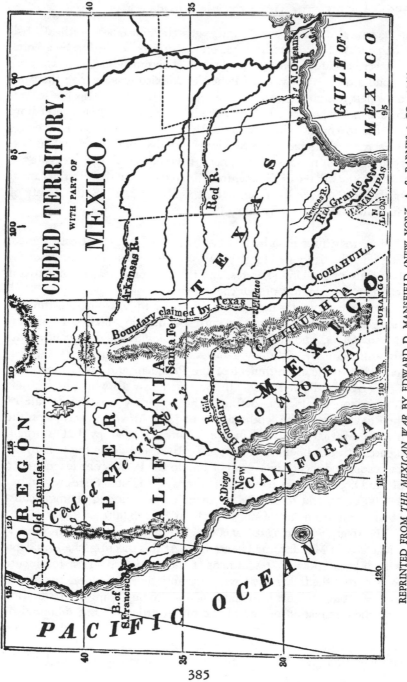

CEDED TERRITORY,
WITH PART OF
MEXICO.

REPRINTED FROM *THE MEXICAN WAR* BY EDWARD D. MANSFIELD (NEW YORK, A. S. BARNES & CO., 1848)

it necessary to take a stand, and, with the assistance of the British Chargé d'Affaires, to adopt what on the surface seemed to be a "now or never" attitude. On January 31, the government at Querétaro gave in, and a messenger was dispatched to Mexico to authorize the commissioners to sign the treaty as insisted upon by Trist. This messenger, the one man who seems to have been in haste in the whole proceeding, rode the 150 miles to Mexico in less than two days, and on the evening of February 1 handed to the Mexican commissioners their final authority to sign. For reasons of sentiment, it was determined to execute the treaty in the village of Guadalupe Hidalgo, rather than in the capital itself; and there, on the afternoon of February 2, 1848, the Treaty of Guadalupe Hidalgo was signed.[26]

More than four months had been required to get a treaty signed. And now the treaty had to go to Washington, there to be acted on by the Senate of the United States, and then to come back to Mexico for action by the Congress of that country.

Mr. Trist promptly dispatched the treaty to Washington, through the agency of James L. Freaner, correspondent in Mexico of the New Orleans *Delta*, who arrived in Washington with the document on the night of Saturday, February 19. Examination of the treaty showed, somewhat to the astonishment of the President and his Cabinet, that Trist's treaty followed closely the instructions with which he had left Washington ten months before. The boundary was the middle of the Rio Grande to the southern line of New Mexico as shown on the map of Mexico published in New York in 1847 by J. Disturnell, thence with that boundary to the Gila River and down the Gila to the Colorado, and thence in a straight line to the Pacific, one league south of San Diego. For the territorial cessions, the United States was to pay $15,000,000, and to assume payment of adjudicated claims against Mexico in the amount of not more than $3,250,000.

The treaty was discussed at a special Cabinet meeting on Sunday, and again on Monday, the twenty-first. At this meeting, the President, who did not allow his resentment at the conduct of Trist to obscure the fact that the treaty itself was substantially satisfactory, announced that he would submit it to the Senate, recommending its ratification with the elimination of one of the minor articles.[27] But submittal of the treaty to the Senate was delayed by the stroke suffered that day on the floor of the House of Representatives by John Quincy Adams, and consideration was delayed further by the death and funeral of the former President. It was not until February 28, therefore, that the treaty was taken up in the Senate.

The Committee on Foreign Relations first decided to report the treaty adversely on account of the irregularity of its negotiation, and to recommend that "an imposing commission" be sent to Mexico to negotiate. When Ambrose H. Sevier of Arkansas, chairman of the committee, told the President of this intention, Mr. Polk earnestly advised "that if the provisions of the Treaty were such as could be accepted, it would be worse than an idle ceremony to send out a grand commission to re-negotiate the same Treaty." The question, as the President said to Senator Sevier, was the treaty itself and not Mr. Trist's conduct. The committee, in that view of the case, simply reported the treaty without recommendation.[28']

Debate went on in the Senate, in executive session, for eleven days, during which there were thirty-eight roll calls on various amendments proposed. The major issue was on the extent and status of the territory to be received from Mexico by way of indemnity. But before the Senate could get down to discussion of such issues it first had to dispose of motions that the treaty be rejected because of the irregularity of its negotiation, offered by men of such diverse viewpoints as Sam Houston, who felt that not enough territory had been annexed, and Daniel Webster, who was against "this Trist paper," as he called it, because he was "against all accessions of territory to form new states."

When the Senate reached the main question of territorial cessions, views ranged wide. Jefferson Davis, who upon the termination of his army service had become a senator from Mississippi, proposed to re-draw the boundary farther south so as to include in the United States all or parts of the Mexican states of Tamaulipas, Nuevo León, Coahuila, and Chihuahua. The proposal was defeated, forty-four to eleven votes.

Senator Crittenden of Kentucky proposed, on the other hand, that territorial cession be limited to "a satisfactory establishment of the boundary of Texas and the acquisition of the bay and harbor of San Francisco." This may be regarded as the official Whig position, since it was supported unanimously by eighteen Whigs, and opposed with like unanimity by thirty Democrats. This proposition having been lost, Senator Badger of North Carolina offered a motion which would have had the effect of excluding from the territory to be ceded all of New Mexico and California. This received an almost unanimous Whig vote but likewise failed of adoption.

Having thus failed to avoid the issue of the extension of slavery in newly acquired territory by the expedient of acquiring none, there followed the inevitable motion, offered by Senator Baldwin of Connecticut, to add to the treaty the language of the Wilmot Proviso, prohibiting slavery in any territory acquired. This motion likewise was lost, thirty-eight to fifteen.

The Senate agreed upon a number of minor modifications, and added a preamble reciting at length the irregularities of Nicholas P. Trist. Finally, on March 10, 1848, the treaty in its modified form was ratified, thirty-eight votes for, fourteen against—more than the two-thirds majority required by the Constitution. The final vote was more on territorial than on party lines. Voting for the treaty were twenty-six Democrats and twelve Whigs; against it, seven of each party.[29]

There still remained, in the steps toward peace, acceptance by the Mexican Congress of the treaty as modified, and its final ratification by that body. It was decided, therefore, to send the modified treaty to Mexico by the hands of commissioners who could explain to the Mexican authorities the changes made, and the more certainly secure their consent to them. For that purpose, the President nominated, and the Senate confirmed, Senator Sevier and Nathan Clifford, Attorney General of the United States, who, within a few days, departed for the city of Mexico.[30]

During all the long period of negotiation prior to the signing of the treaty, General Scott had declined to enter into an armistice for the formal cessation of hostilities. The treaty itself, however, stipulated that upon its signing there should be such an armistice and Generals Mora y Villamil and Quijano were sent from Querétaro to negotiate its terms.

They arrived at the capital on February 17, prepared to negotiate with General Scott. On the next day, however, there arrived in Mexico the official orders from Washington relieving Scott of his command and naming General Butler in his stead. Butler, at first in something of a quandary as to whether he should act under a treaty so irregularly entered into by Trist, sensibly resolved his doubts in favor of peace, and named commissioners to deal with the Mexicans. Negotiations for an armistice dragged, and it was not until March 5 that one had been agreed upon and ratified both by the American commander and the government at Querétaro. Technically hostilities were at an end.[31]

But in the far north hostilities had broken out again. On February 23, Colonel Sterling Price, acting on his own responsibility, arrived at El Paso with a column for a second invasion and occupation of Chihuahua. Leaving El Paso on March 1, he made a rapid march to the vicinity of the capital of the state, where he was met with word from Mexican sources that a treaty of peace had been signed. Mistrusting the information, Price continued to advance, occupied the city of Chihuahua from which Governor Trias and his forces had retired, and made a dash for Santa Cruz de Rosales, sixty miles to the south. Arriving there at sunrise of March 9, he was met by Governor Trias with word, still unofficial, that the war was over. Price suspended operations for a week. At the end of that time, reinforcements having reached him from the north and no further word of the end of the war having come from the south, he resumed hostilities. Early on the morning of March 16, he opened fire on the town, skirmished with the enemy, and kept up an active day's fighting, with a loss of twenty-three killed and wounded on the American side, and an unknown but much larger loss to the Mexicans. At sunset the Mexicans surrendered, and this time hostilities were truly at an end in the north.[32]

In the remote region of Lower California, however, fighting was to go on for still another two weeks until, on March 30, 1848, in a skirmish of United States naval forces and New York volunteers with the forces of Manuel Piñeda, the last shots of the war were fired at Todos Santos, near the territorial capital of La Paz.[33]

The last shots had been fired, but still there was not peace. The American commissioners bearing the treaty, Sevier and Clifford, reached Mexico in mid-April, but it was not until May 3 that a quorum of the new Mexican Congress could be assembled at Querétaro to pass on the treaty. Those opposed to the treaty insisted that no Mexican government had a right to sign away Mexican territory. To this, the commissioners who had signed the treaty made answer that the territory was lost "in the war, and not in the treaty." Indeed, they pointed out, the treaty had the effect of recovering to Mexico much territory occupied by the American forces, which would be returned to Mexico, so that "the present treaty . . . is rather an agreement of recovery than it is an agreement of cession."

After lengthy debate of such points and detailed consideration of the modifications made by the United States Senate, the Chamber of

Deputies, on May 19, ratified the instrument by a vote of fifty-one to thirty-five. There still remained ratification by the Mexican Senate but, this being well assured, the American commissioners were invited to proceed from Mexico, where they had been awaiting the outcome of the debates, to Querétaro. Arriving there in the late afternoon of May 25, they found that an hour before the Senate, by a vote of thirty-four to four, had ratified the treaty. "The city appears to be in a great state of exaltation"; the commissioners reported "fire works going off, and bands of music parading in every direction."

On May 30, 1848, ratifications were formally exchanged, and the treaty of Guadalupe Hidalgo, signed four months before, was, and has since remained, in full force and effect.[34]

In anticipation, General Butler issued on May 29 his orders for the evacuation, and troops started to move on the following day. Early in the morning of June 12, the last of the American troops remaining—Worth's division—formed in the Great Plaza. At nine o'clock, to the salutes of batteries of both nations, the flag which had floated from the staff above the National Palace for nine months, lacking two days, came fluttering down; and to the salutes of both batteries, the tricolor of Mexico went up, as the last of the American military forces marched away. Mr. Clifford, of the Peace Commission, was left behind while the Mexican authorities laboriously counted the $3,000,000 in coin, which they insisted on doing before delivering to him a receipt for the first payment under the treaty.[35]

From Mixcoac, where he and his Cabinet had awaited the event, the newly elected President José Joaquin Herrera entered the capital from which he had been driven thirty months before by the revolution of the pro-war Paredes. The war which had been the political stock in trade of the Paredes party had been fought and lost. Mexico, as a result, had given up its claim to Texas, had relinquished its tenuous hold on California, and had lost its northern outpost of New Mexico. It had gained a common tradition of brave, even heroic, resistance to invasion and a new sense of nationality. It had taken a step toward stability of government, for the new President Herrera was to serve out his term and to be succeeded, without revolution or *pronunciamento,* by a constitutionally elected president, General Mariano Arista—the Arista of Palo Alto and Resaca de la Palma.[36]

For the United States, the war meant new territory and new problems. The controversy over the anticipated extension of slavery into territory acquired from Mexico soon ceased because—as President

Polk had predicted[37]—slavery did not extend into the areas annexed. But the discords which were introduced, or at least intensified, by the agitation of the subject persisted, in spite of all efforts at compromise, to culminate a dozen years later in the secession of the Southern states and the war for the Union.

But the relation between the war of the forties and that of the sixties is not one of cause and effect. The tensions which led to secession, and the sentiments which supported the Union, were rooted deeper than the agitation and the partisanship which, embalmed in the writings of a brilliantly vocal generation, have ever since warped the story of the War with Mexico.

---

1 Ramsey (ed.), *The Other Side*, pp. 385-393.

2 Same, pp. 394, 402; Ex. Doc. 1, Sen., 30th Cong., 1st sess., pp. 471-479; Ex. Doc. 60, H. R., 30th Cong., 1st sess., pp. 1029, 1030; Oswandel, *Notes*, pp. 288-346; Kenly, *Maryland Volunteer*, pp. 300-308, 318-325. Captain Walker, then commanding the Texas Rangers, had made the perilous journey from Point Isabel to Fort Brown and returned through the Mexican lines at the beginning of the war.

3 Ex. Doc. 1, Sen., 30th Cong., 1st sess., pp. 494, 495; Ramsey (ed.), *The Other Side*, pp. 439-442; Oswandel, *Notes*, pp. 257, 318; Kenly, *Maryland Volunteer*, p. 312; Jenkins, *War with Mexico*, pp. 472, 473; Wilcox, *Mexican War*, p. 525. Padre Jarauta, in association with former President Paredes, continued fighting against the Mexican Government after the Americans left the country, without success, and was executed near Guanajuato in July 1848. *Cyclopedia of American Biography* (New York, 1888): "Jarauta."

4 Ex. Doc. 52, Sen., 30th Cong., 1st sess., pp. 204, 210; Ramsey (ed.), *The Other Side*, pp. 403, 404; Rives, *U. S. and Mexico*, II, 574, 575, 586. Late in January, while still at Tehuacan, Santa Anna narrowly escaped capture by General Lane. After subsequent wanderings, he was permitted by the American authorities to leave the country and go once more into exile, from which, within five years, he was to return and once more become President of Mexico. It was during this last of his Presidencies that he sold to the United States, peaceably and without objection, and for a consideration of $10,000,000, the southern half of the Gila Valley, commonly known in the United States as the Gadsden Purchase.

5 Ex. Doc. 52, Sen., 30th Cong., 1st sess., pp. 99, 212, 217.

6 Ex. Doc. 52, Sen., 30th Cong., 1st sess., pp. 94, 95, 101, 102, 230-266; Rives, *U. S. and Mexico*, II, 595, 596; Reeves, *American Diplomacy*, pp. 322-323.

7 Ex. Doc. 60, H. R., 30th Cong., 1st sess., pp. 1015-1020.

8 Proceedings of the court of inquiry on the matter of the Chapultepec howitzers are published in Ex. Doc. 65, Sen., 30th Cong., 1st sess., pp. 338-373.

9 Ex. Doc. 65, Sen., 30th Cong., 1st sess., pp. 13, 384-406.

10 Ex. Doc. 65, Sen., 30th Cong., 1st sess., p. 454.

11 Text of the correspondence appears in Semmes, *Service Afloat and Ashore*, pp. 360-363. Duncan's letters appeared in the *North American*, the "anti-Scott" paper. The "Scott" paper was the *American Star* (Spell, "The Anglo-Saxon Press in Mexico").

12 Ex. Doc. 65, Sen., 30th Cong., 1st sess., pp. 604-612. Paymaster A. W. Burns testified that he wrote the "Leonidas" letter to the editor of the New Orleans *Delta*.

He explained its remarkable similarity to a highly laudatory account of his operations on August 19 and 20 which General Pillow had furnished to the regular correspondent of the *Delta,* but which had not been published, by saying that he (Burns) had found a paper on the general's desk from which he had copied the "Leonidas" letter, without the general's knowledge or consent. It was explained further that the paper from which he had copied was a rough, or partial, report from which the general had drafted the document furnished to the *Delta* correspondent. Paymaster Burns's testimony appears at pp. 32-42 and the several documents at pp. 384-406.

13 Ex. Doc. 60, H. R., 30th Cong., 1st sess., pp. 1021-1027.

14 Same, pp. 1033-1035, 1039, 1047, 1068, 1069; Frost, *Pictorial History,* pp. 617, 618.

15 Ex. Doc. 1, H. R., 30th Cong., 2nd sess., pp. 1083-1096, 1104-1117, 1122-1126; Ex. Doc. 60, H. R., 30th Cong., 1st sess., pp. 1083-1085; Jenkins, *War with Mexico,* pp. 484-486; Ripley, *War with Mexico,* II, 601-610; Frost, *Pictorial History,* p. 625; Du Pont, *Dispatches,* pp. 12-17; Wise, Lieutenant Henry A., *Los Gringos* (New York, 1849), pp. 136, 141, 146.

16 Ex. Doc. 60, H. R., 30th Cong., 1st sess., p. 1048.

17 Ex. Doc. 60, H. R., 30th Cong., 1st sess., pp. 1065, 1066; Ramsey (ed.), *The Other Side,* p. 422; Croffut (ed.), *Fifty Years,* p. 329; Ripley, *War with Mexico,* II, 571; Smith, *War with Mexico,* II, 226-228, 459-461.

18 Kenly, *Maryland Volunteer,* pp. 381, 383, 415, 416, 423; Croffut (ed.), *Fifty Years,* p. 307; Anderson, *Artillery Officer,* pp. 318, 321, 324; Oswandel, *Notes,* pp. 444, 446, 447, 455, 460, 463, 474, 475, 521; Wise, *Los Gringos,* pp. 256, 257; letter of Private Marley Young, Pekin Postoffice, Jackson County, Tennessee, dated City of Mexico, January 13, 1848, furnished through the courtesy of Mrs. J. K. Blackstone, San Antonio, Texas. By coincidence, the letter was received by the present writer on the 100th anniversary to the day of the date on which it was written in Mexico.

Most notable of the organizations resulting from the occupation of the Mexican capital was the Aztec Club, organized among the American officers with Brigadier General Franklin Pierce as its first president. Its roster contains the names of leaders on both sides in the war of the sixties—Grant, McClellan, Hooker, Philip Kearny, Fitz John Porter, Reno, C. F. Smith, Tower, Brannan, among the Union leaders; Lee, Joseph Johnston, Beauregard, Ewell, Hardee, Magruder, Pemberton, Lovell, Van Dorn, G. W. Smith, Mackall among the Confederates.

19 Beveridge, *Lincoln,* I, 424-429.

20 Quaife (ed.), *Polk's Diary,* III, 266, 267; Nevins (ed.), *Polk,* pp. 288, 289; Ex. Doc. 60, H. R., 30th Cong., 1st sess., pp. 1040-1045.

21 Same, p. 1087; Oswandel, *Notes,* p. 481.

22 Ex. Doc. 60, H. R., 30th Cong., 1st sess., pp. 1218-1227. Secretary Marcy's reply follows in the same volume, pp. 1227-1251.

23 Ramsey (ed.), *The Other Side,* pp. 421, 422.

24 Stickles, Arndt M., *Simon Bolivar Buckner* (Chapel Hill, 1940), p. 18. After the war, while residing in Tennessee, Buckner warmly defended Scott against aspersions by Pillow, in a series of newspaper letters. Four years later, Pillow and Buckner were to be associated in the command of Confederate defenses at Fort Donelson, where Pillow yielded the command to Buckner who, in turn, surrendered the post and garrison to his friend and fellow lieutenant of the Mexican War, U. S. Grant (pp. 40, 41).

25 Ex. Doc. 65, Sen., 30th Cong., 1st sess., pp. 334, 335.

26 Croffut (ed.), *Fifty Years,* p. 309; Rives, *U. S. and Mexico,* II, 590-592, 599-613; Ex. Doc. 52, Sen., 30th Cong., 1st sess., pp. 274, 275, 280-282, 286-293.

27 Quaife (ed.), *Polk's Diary,* III, 345-350; Nevins (ed.), *Polk,* pp. 304-308.

[28] Quaife (ed.), *Polk's Diary*, p. 365; Nevins (ed), *Polk*, pp. 312-313.

[29] Ex. Doc. 52, Sen., 30th Cong., 1st sess., pp. 3-66; *Mr. Webster's Speech in the U. S. Senate, March 23, 1848* . . . (Boston, 1848), p. 9. Like Clay, Webster lost a son in the war—Major Edward Webster of Cushing's regiment of Massachusetts volunteers, who died at San Angel on January 23, 1848.

[30] Quaife (ed.), *Polk's Diary*, III, 372-375, 378-383, 386-390.

[31] Ex. Doc. 60, H. R., 30th Cong., 1st sess., p. 1218; Ripley, *War with Mexico*, II, 597-600.

[32] Ex. Doc. 1, H. R., 30th Cong., 2nd sess., pp. 113-136; Ramsey (ed.), *The Other Side*, pp. 451-455; Ripley, *War with Mexico*, II, 611-613.

[33] Ex. Doc. 1, H. R., 30th Cong., 2nd sess., pp. 1138-1156; Ripley, *War with Mexico*, II, 608-610; Wise, *Los Gringos*, pp. 214-215; Du Pont, *Dispatches*, pp. 23-30, 33-37. Lieutenant Henry W. Halleck was with the New York volunteers in this final fight of the war.

[34] Ex. Doc. 69, H. R., 30th Cong., 1st sess., pp. 71-73; Rives, *U. S. and Mexico*, II, 647-655.

[35] Ex. Doc. 69, 30th Cong., 1st sess., p. 74; Wilcox, *Mexican War*, pp. 550-554. The last troops sailed from Vera Cruz, under General P. F. Smith, on August 1, 1848.

[36] General Arista succeeded President Herrera in January 1851. A revolution, starting eighteen months later, caused him to resign and leave the country, and, in April 1853, brought Santa Anna back into power for an administration which lasted a little more than two years.

[37] Quaife (ed.), *Polk's Diary*, II, 289, 350; Nevins (ed.), *Polk*, pp. 189-190.

Presidio of San Francisco.   Encampment of the New York Volunteers.

SYNOPTIC TABLE AND INDEX

A SYNOPTIC TABLE OF EVENTS OF THE MEXICAN WAR

PRELIMINARY EVENTS

1836. De facto independence of Texas established by decisive victory of San Jacinto; recognized in treaty made by Santa Anna, President of Mexico captured at San Jacinto, but not recognized by Mexican Government.

Mexican population of California revolted against central government.

Spain, after fifteen years' refusal, recognized independence of Mexico.

1837. United States recognized independence of Texas, followed by Great Britain, France and other European nations.

1838. New government in California recognized by President Bustamante of Mexico.

1839. Claims convention between U. S. and Mexico. Board of arbitration with King of Prussia as neutral organized April 25, 1840.

1841. Arbitration board awarded $2,000,000 in damages to United States citizens. Mexico suggested plan for payment of award in twenty installments. U. S. accepted in 1843 and payments started. Lapsed after third installment.

Texan expedition against Santa Fe failed. Texans taken to Mexico as prisoners.

1842. December. Santa Anna became dictator in Mexico.

1843. June. Santa Anna decreed renewed warfare against Texas. Troops sent to restore Mexican national supremacy in California. All United States citizens ordered expelled from California and three northern departments of Mexico. Trade between St. Louis and Santa Fe ordered closed.

August 23, and subsequently. Mexican Government announced that annexation of Texas by United States would be considered "equivalent to a declaration of war against Mexico."

1844. April 12. Treaty for annexation of Republic of Texas to the United States as a territory signed in Washington.

June. United States Senate rejected annexation treaty. No formal action taken by Texan Congress.

Renewed declaration of war against Texas by Mexican Government.

November. James K. Polk elected President of the United States on a platform declaring for annexation of Texas.

1845. January. Santa Anna driven from office and expelled from Mexico. José Joaquin Herrera became President, with Mariano Paredes head of the army.

February. Mexican national troops driven out of California by native insurgents. Pío Pico recognized as governor, José Castro as *comandante general*.

March 1. President John Tyler signed joint resolution of United States Congress offering Texas annexation as a state of the Union. Offer transmitted to Texas, March 3.

March 4. Polk inaugurated.

March 31. Diplomatic relations with the United States broken by Mexico.

May 17. Upon recommendation of British and French diplomatic representatives, Mexican Congress authorized President Herrera and Cabinet to receive propositions "offered by Texas" looking toward Mexican recognition of Texan independence, provided there be no annexation to U. S.

June 16. Congress of Republic of Texas rejected proposed treaty with Mexico and called convention to consider annexation proffered by the United States.

June 24. Instructions sent by U. S. to Commodore Sloat, commanding squadron in Pacific, to avoid aggression but to occupy California ports if Mexico should declare war.

July 4. Texas convention, meeting at Austin, adopted ordinance of assent to U. S. annexation proposal.

U. S. troops under Zachary Taylor moved to Corpus Christi, Texas, to protect newly annexed territory and Commodore David Conner ordered to assemble U. S. Home Squadron off Gulf ports of Mexico, in readiness if Mexico should treat annexation as an act of war.

Political and Diplomatic Events	Military and Naval Events in Mexico and Texas	Military and Naval Events in Calif. and New Mexico
	OCTOBER 1845	
15th. Herrera government agreed to receive U. S. diplomatic representative upon condition fleet be withdrawn.	U. S. force under Taylor at Corpus Christi; Mexican force under Mejía at Matamoros.	U. S. squadron in Pacific under Sloat under orders to avoid aggression unless word received of war.
17th. Larkin, U. S. consul at Monterey, Calif., instructed to oppose attempt by any other power to acquire California.	U. S. fleet under Conner withdrawn from before Vera Cruz.	
	NOVEMBER 1845	
10th. John Slidell appointed U. S. Minister to Mexico. Arrived Vera Cruz, 30th.		
	DECEMBER 1845	
16th. Herrera government decided Slidell could not be received as a Minister but only as a Commission-		Capt. John C. Frémont's exploring expedition arrived at Sutter's Fort on the Sacramento.

Political and Diplomatic Events	*Military and Naval Events in Mexico and Texas*	*Military and Naval Events in Calif. and New Mexico*
er limited to dealing with Texas question.		
31st. Herrera deposed as new President of Mexico.		

January 1846

4th. Paredes took oath as new President of Mexico. Reasserted claim to all Texas to the Sabine and intention of defending it.		Frémont at Monterey, California.
12th. Dispatch from Slidell with news of rejection reached Washington.	13th. Order sent to Taylor to advance to Rio Grande; Conner ordered back to Vera Cruz.	

February 1846

4th. U. S. rejected proposed arbitration of dispute with Great Britain over Oregon question.	3d. Taylor received order to advance to Rio Grande.	

March 1846

21st. Slidell finally rejected and given passport for return to U. S.	8th. Taylor marched from Corpus Christi.	Affair of proclamations between Castro at Monterey and Frémont on Gavilan Peak. Frémont left for U. S. territory in Oregon.
	28th. Taylor arrived on Rio Grande. Started construction of fort opposite Matamoros; base of supplies, Point Isabel.	

April 1846

23d. U. S. Congress voted to notify Great Britain of termination of joint occupancy of Oregon country.	12th. Ampudia, new Mexican commander at Rio Grande, demanded withdrawal of Taylor's force behind Nueces. Taylor refused. Ampudia took position that state of war existed. Taylor asked U. S. naval forces to blockade mouth of Rio Grande.	17th. Lt. Gillespie, U.S.M.C., arrived at Monterey, Calif., after six months' journey with instructions for Consul Larkin. Followed Frémont to Oregon.
23d. Pres. Paredes proclaimed that "from this day defensive war begins."		
	24th. Torrejon's Mexican cavalry crossed Rio Grande above Matamoros.	

Political and Diplomatic Events	*Military and Naval Events in Mexico and Texas*	*Military and Naval Events in Calif. and New Mexico*
	25th. Clash between Mexican cavalry and U. S. reconnoitering force under Capt. Thornton. Sixty-three of U. S. force killed, wounded or captured.	

MAY 1846

9th. News of clash of Capt. Thornton's party with Mexicans received in Washington.	1st. Mexican force crossed Rio Grande below Matamoros. Taylor marched to secure his base at Point Isabel. Major Brown besieged in works opposite Matamoros.	9th. Lt. Gillespie overtook Frémont in Oregon; Frémont turned back to California.
11th. Polk's war message received by Congress. House passed war bill.	8th. Taylor, returning to relieve siege, met and defeated Mexicans under Arista at Palo Alto.	15th. Stephen W. Kearny ordered to form "Army of the West" for march to and occupation of New Mexico and California.
12th. Senate passed war bill.		
13th. War bill signed by President. Volunteers called for. Blockade of Mexican coast ordered.	9th. Battle of Resaca de la Palma. Arista again defeated.	
	17th-18th. Arista evacuated Matamoros; Taylor crossed Rio Grande and occupied town.	

JUNE 1846

5th. Mexican Congress met.	14th. Troops ordered to San Antonio for expedition to Chihuahua, under John E. Wool.	5th. Advance of Kearny's army started from Ft. Leavenworth for Santa Fe.
12th. Paredes formally elected President by Mexican Congress.	Three and six-months volunteers arriving at Rio Grande.	Frémont, back in California, co-operated with "Bear Flag" party in proclaiming Republic of California.
15th. New British proposal for settlement of Oregon boundary accepted by U. S. Possibility of war with Britain ended.	24th. First regiment of twelve-months volunteers arrived at the Brazos.	
	Shorter term volunteers began to be discharged and returned home.	

Political and Diplomatic Events	*Military and Naval Events in Mexico and Texas*	*Military and Naval Events in Calif. and New Mexico*

JULY 1846

1st. Formal declaration of war by Mexican Congress.	6th. Taylor started advance up Rio Grande from Matamoros.	7th. Sloat raised U. S. flag over customhouse at Monterey.
27th. U. S. repeated offer to send representative to Mexico to negotiate peace.	14th. Camargo occupied.	23d. Sloat turned over command of Pacific Squadron to Commodore Stockton.

AUGUST 1846

6th. Salas proclaimed Acting President of Mexico, succeeding Parades.	7th. Naval attempt on Alvarado unsuccessful.	12th. Los Angeles occupied by U. S. forces under Stockton.
4th-10th. Polk sought appropriation of $2,000,000 to help promote peace. Attempt to add Wilmot Proviso prohibiting slavery in territory to be annexed, defeated. Appropriation bill filibustered to death. First session, 29th Congress ended.	19th. Taylor started advance from Camargo to Monterey.	15th. Kearny, at Las Vegas, declared New Mexico annexed to U. S.
		18th. Santa Fe occupied.
16th. Santa Anna, under safe conduct from U. S., returned from exile in Cuba, landed at Vera Cruz.		
31st. Government of Mexico postponed action on U. S. peace proposal until next meeting of Congress.		

SEPTEMBER 1846

14th. Santa Anna entered Mexican capital to become commander in chief.	20th-24th. Monterey captured by U. S. forces under Taylor. Armistice for eight weeks agreed on.	22d-23d. Californians rose against U. S. forces.
28th. Santa Anna marched north to meet Taylor.	25th-28th. Wool marched from San Antonio for Chihuahua.	30th. U. S. force at Los Angeles capitulated. Californians formed government.
		25th. Kearny left New Mexico with detachment of dragoons for California.

Political and Diplomatic Events	*Military and Naval Events in Mexico and Texas*	*Military and Naval Events in Calif. and New Mexico*
		28th. U. S. reinforcements under Price reached Santa Fe.

OCTOBER 1846

Political and Diplomatic Events	*Military and Naval Events in Mexico and Texas*	*Military and Naval Events in Calif. and New Mexico*
13th. U.S. Government instructed Taylor to terminate armistice after Monterey.	8th. Santa Anna arrived at San Luis Potosí. 8th. Wool crossed Rio Grande at Presidio. 15th. Second naval attempt on Alvarado failed. 25th. Navy's first occupation of Tabasco. 29th. Wool occupied Monclova.	7th. Attempt of U. S. forces to retake Los Angeles repulsed.

NOVEMBER 1846

Political and Diplomatic Events	*Military and Naval Events in Mexico and Texas*	*Military and Naval Events in Calif. and New Mexico*
U. S. Congressional elections: Whigs won majority in House of Representatives. 18th. Scott named to command of U. S. expedition against Vera Cruz.	5th. Taylor notified Santa Anna of termination of armistice on 13th. 14th. U. S. squadron under Conner occupied Tampico. 16th. Taylor occupied Saltillo. 24th. Wool abandoned march to Chihuahua; turned toward Taylor.	20th. Doniphan made treaty with Navajos in New Mexico.

DECEMBER 1846

Political and Diplomatic Events	*Military and Naval Events in Mexico and Texas*	*Military and Naval Events in Calif. and New Mexico*
6th. Mexican Congress met. Santa Anna elected President; Farías, Vice-President. 7th. U. S. 29th Congress met for 2nd session. Whigs denounce war.	5th. Wool occupied Parras. 13th. U. S. troops march on Victoria from Monterey, Camargo and Matamoros. 21st. Wool reached Saltillo to reinforce Worth against threatened advance by Santa Anna.	6th. Kearney worsted in fight with Californians at San Pascual. 12th. Aided by Stockton, Kearny reached San Diego. 12th. Doniphan left Valverde, N. M., for Chihuahua. 25th. Doniphan defeated Mexicans at El Brazito.

Political and Diplomatic Events	*Military and Naval Events in Mexico and Texas*	*Military and Naval Events in Calif. and New Mexico*
	21st. First naval occupation of Laguna.	27th. Occupied El Paso.
	27th. Scott arrived at the Brazos and went on to Camargo, hoping to meet Taylor. Taylor on march to Victoria.	29th. U. S. forces under Stockton and Kearny march from San Diego for Los Angeles.

JANUARY 1847

Polk urged Congress to create office of lieutenant general, to be filled by Thomas H. Benton.	3d. Scott, from Camargo, ordered troops from Taylor's army for Vera Cruz expedition. Letter to Taylor captured by Mexican irregulars.	8th. Californians defeated by U. S. navy and army forces at San Gabriel River.
		10th. Los Angeles reoccupied by Stockton.
11th. Mexican Congress passed, and Acting President Farías approved, law for sale of Church properties for benefit of the government.	4th. Taylor entered Victoria.	13th. "Treaty of Cahuenga" between Frémont and Californians.
Taylor let friends know he would accept nomination for President.	14th. Victoria evacuated; most troops sent to Tampico; escort returned with Taylor to Monterey.	29th. Mormon Battalion arrived at San Diego.
	23d. U. S. troops arrive at Tampico from Victoria.	
	28th. Santa Anna advanced from San Luis Potosí.	

FEBRUARY 1847

19th. Scott issued "martial law order" at Tampico.	5th-14th. Taylor advanced beyond Saltillo to Agua Nueva.	5th. Uprising in New Mexico ended by surrender of Taos to Price.
27th. Outbreak of "Polka" rebellion against Farías at Mexico.	15th. Scott embarked at the Brazos for Vera Cruz expedition.	8th. Doniphan left El Paso for Chihuahua.
	17th-21st. Santa Anna's army concentrated at Encarnación for attack on Taylor.	28th. Battle of the Sacramento, near Chihuahua.
	21st. Taylor retired from Agua Nueva to Buena Vista.	
	22d-23d. Battle of Buena Vista.	

Political and Diplomatic Events	Military and Naval Events in Mexico and Texas	Military and Naval Events in Calif. and New Mexico

MARCH 1847

21st. Santa Anna took oath of office as President; Polka rebellion over.	5th. U. S. forces arrive at Anton Lizardo, off Vera Cruz.	1st. Chihuahua city occupied by Doniphan.
	9th. American landing on beach below Vera Cruz.	
	29th. Vera Cruz surrendered and occupied.	29th. San José and San Lucas, Lower California, occupied by U. S. Navy.

APRIL 1847

1st. Farías ousted as Vice-President; Anaya elected President *ad interim*.	8th. March up from Vera Cruz began.	13th. La Paz, Lower California, garrisoned by U. S. troops.
15th. Nicholas Trist appointed commissioner to negotiate with Mexico.	18th. Battle of Cerro Gordo.	
	18th. Perry occupied Tuxpan.	28th. Doniphan left Chihuahua for home.
20th. Mexican Congress granted government extraordinary powers but prohibited any negotiation for peace.	22d. Worth occupied Castle of Perote.	

Political and Diplomatic Events	Military and Naval Events

MAY 1847

7th. Beginning of controversial correspondence between Scott and Trist.	4th. Scott returned twelve-months volunteers to U. S.
22d. Santa Anna resumed office of President.	15th. Worth occupied Puebla.
	28th. Scott at Puebla.

JUNE 1847

25th. End of feud between Scott and Trist.	May-June-July, naval operations on southeastern coast of Mexico.

JULY 1847

13th. Quorum secured in Mexican Congress but no clear action taken to authorize public peace negotiations; private negotiations go on.	8th. Pillow arrived at Puebla with reinforcements.
	8th-17th. Col. De Russey expedition from Tampico to release "Encarnación prisoners" (held at Huejutla) repulsed at Rio Calaboso and returned to Tampico.

Political and Diplomatic Events   *Military and Naval Events*

August 1847

24th. Armistice of Tacubaya, to afford opportunity for peace negotiations.

6th. Franklin Pierce arrived at Puebla with reinforcements.

7th. March started from Puebla to Mexico.

19th-20th. Battles of Contreras, or Padierna, and Churubusco.

September 1847

6th. Peace negotiations end in failure; armistice terminated.

16th. Santa Anna renounced Presidency.

26th. Peña y Peña assumed Presidency.

8th. Battle of Molino del Rey.

13th. Storming of Chapultepec; battles of the causeways and *garitas* San Cosmé and Belén.

14th. Occupation of Mexican capital.

14th. Siege of Americans in Puebla began.

October 1847

7th. Santa Anna deposed as head of army; order received 16th.

Querétaro became temporary capital of Mexico.

9th. Affair at Huamantla.

12th. Siege of Puebla raised.

19th. Affair at Atlixco.

20th. Port of Guaymas occupied.

November 1847

2d. Mexican Congress assembled.

11th. Anaya elected President *ad interim.*

16th. Trist received order of recall.

22d. Anaya appointed commissioners to negotiate peace.

11th. Port of Mazatlán occupied.

16th-22d. Worth and Pillow relieved of commands by Scott.

25th. Wool succeeded Taylor in command in northern Mexico; Taylor started for the States.

December 1847

6th. Thirtieth U. S. Congress convened for first session.

4th. Trist decided to stay in Mexico and negotiate treaty.

Reinforcements and replacements arrived for U. S. forces at Mexico.

Political and Diplomatic Events   *Military and Naval Events*

JANUARY 1848

2d. Peace negotiations began.

14th. U. S. naval detachment at San José, Lower California, relieved from siege by arrival of reinforcements.

8th. Anaya's term as President ended; Peña y Peña again Acting President.

13th. Polk ordered Scott relieved of command, and Scott, Worth and Pillow charges and countercharges to be heard by court of inquiry.

FEBRUARY 1848

2d. Treaty of Guadalupe Hidalgo signed.

18th. Scott received order relieving him of command; turned over command to Butler.

23d. Treaty submitted by Polk to Senate for ratification.

29th. Military armistice suspending hostilities in Mexico agreed on.

MARCH 1848

10th. Treaty ratified by U. S. Senate; with modifications.

16th. Price, not officially notified of armistice, captured Santa Cruz de Rosales, in state of Chihuahua.

30th. Last shots fired at Todos Santos, Lower California.

MAY 1848

25th. Treaty ratified, with U. S. Senate modifications, by Mexican Congress.

Notice of end of war received by Wool in northern Mexico, June 5.

30th. Formal exchange of ratifications by both nations. Treaty of Guadalupe Hidalgo in effect.

INDEX

407